Of Irish Descent

Irish Studies

James MacKillop, *Series Editor*

Of Irish Descent

Origin Stories

Genealogy,

&

the Politics of Belonging

Catherine Nash

Syracuse University Press

The paper used in this publication meets the minimum requirements of
American National Standard for Information Sciences—Permanence of
Paper for Printed Library Materials, ANSI Z39.48–1984.∞™

For a listing of books published and distributed by Syracuse University Press,
visit our Web site at SyracuseUniversityPress.syr.edu.

ISBN-13: 978-0-8156-3159-0   ISBN-10: 0-8156-3159-6

LIBRARY OF CONGRESS CATALOGING-IN-PUBLICATION DATA

Nash, Catherine.

Of Irish descent : origin stories, genealogy, and the politics of belonging / Catherine Nash. — 1st ed.

p. cm. — (Irish studies)

Includes bibliographical references and index.

ISBN-13: 978-0-8156-3159-0 (cloth : alk. paper)

ISBN-10: 0-8156-3159-6 (cloth : alk. paper)

1. Ireland—Genealogy.   2. Northern Ireland—Genealogy.   3. Irish—Genealogy.   4. Irish—Migrations.
5. Irish—Ethnic identity.   6. Genealogy—Social aspects.   7. Genealogy—Political aspects.   8. Human
population genetics—Social aspects.   9. Ethnicity—Political aspects.   I. Title.

CS484.N37 2008

929'.3417—dc22   2008001468

Manufactured in the United States of America

Contents

Illustrations

Catherine Nash is professor of geography at Queen Mary, University of London. She is a feminist cultural geographer with interests in geographies of identity, belonging, and relatedness. Her work has appeared in journals that include *Cultural Studies, Society and Space, Antipode, History Workshop Journal,* and *Irish Studies Review.*

Preface

This is a book about ancestral origins, identity and belonging, questions of connections between people and to places, and their significance in national and other forms of identity and identification. It is about the personal and political significance of the figuring of Irish ancestry, origins, and relatedness within popular genealogy and in human population genetics. The cultural geographies of relatedness that it traces have Ireland at their center, but are extended networks of interest, affiliation, and imaginative connection, shaped by histories of migration to and from the island and expressed through modern journeys home. This book also has its own origins and has also been shaped by travels to and from Ireland and Northern Ireland. These origins lie in my entangled personal and academic explorations of questions of who belongs in a place and on what basis—birth, parentage, generational rootedness, or other criteria of need, care, or commitment—and to whom places belong, both imaginatively and within the formal politics of statehood and citizenship. My journeys back and forth between Ireland, Northern Ireland, and Britain in doing the research for this book parallel a longer family history of moving between these two islands, of leaving homes, making homes, coming home, that span several generations, work in both directions, and continue.

So although this personal dimension only remains implicit in the chapters that follow, the questions that prompt ancestral research in others are also ones that have never been simply conceptual puzzles explored through empirical materials detached from my own considerations of origins, identity, and belonging. Yet, in the process of research for this book, the question of "where am I from," of my own genealogy and ancestral origins, could not always remain implicit. Those who I talked to about the practice and significance of genealogy and family history frequently asked me about mine. My attempts to explain its complex and doubly English and Irishness—of at least three generations of "mixed marriages" and the religious conversions they entailed on both sides of my family, the patterns of migration that led to family members' births in England and lives in Ireland, and births in Ireland and lives in England—confounds any simple category of "second generation" Irish in England and elicited different responses: consternation that a childhood in Ireland and an Irish grandmother didn't mean a simple identification as Irish alone, or empathetic understanding of the complexities of family and identity. Occasional invitations in academic contexts to "situate" myself within the work seemed to want more fixity than the oscillations of home and identity I could offer. As I explore in the genealogical projects of others throughout this book, origins stories can be kept satisfyingly simple or can be never ending and never straightforward narratives of belonging. While I largely disappear as researcher in this book, it is the product of an interpretative strategy of exploring the compelling questions that prompt others to genealogy or to follow new genetic techniques for exploring origins and ancestry, not as a detached observer but as one open to their pull, potency, and appeal. This means, I hope at least, that my critical engagement with the wider implications of ideas of ancestral origins and identity is balanced by an appreciation of their intimate and deeply personal nature.

This book is similarly both about the formal configuration and practice of relationships between people based on shared descent and is a product of the relationships that have made it possible, professional and personal and often both. Most formally, the research for this book has been funded by research councils and facilitated by institutional support. A British Academy research grant funded the initial research for the book in Dublin and Belfast in 1998. The following year a small Royal Holloway, University of London research grant supported my participation in the Ulster Historical Foundation's annual genealogical conference and tour in Northern Ireland. The book has also benefited from support from the Leverhulme Trust whose research fellowship funding supported my work on local history in Northern Ireland in 2000 and 2001. It would also not have been possible without the support of an Economic and Social Research Council Research Fellowship that funded further research and time to write over three years ending in December 2006. I am very grateful for this external support and for that provided by my academic homes over the course of this extended project—the geography departments of the University of Wales, Lampeter; Royal Holloway, University of London; and Queen Mary, University of London—and the Department of Geography, Trinity College, Dublin, and the School of Geography,

Queen's University, Belfast, who welcomed me as a visiting academic in 1998 and 2005 respectively.

Many other institutions, organizations, and individuals helped enormously over the course of this research. I am very grateful to the staff of the Genealogy Centre of the National Library of Ireland, of the National Archives in Dublin, and of the Public Record Office of Northern Ireland for allowing me to observe the genealogical research process and talk to researchers, to members of the Association of Professional Genealogists in Ireland and Association of Ulster Genealogists and Record Agents who allowed me to interview them and introduced me to visiting genealogists, and to the staff of the Ulster Historical Foundation, especially Fintan Mullen, for allowing me to participate as both researcher and delegate in the conference and study tour in 1999. I am especially grateful to Paul Gorry for his generosity in discussing the project and inviting me to present the research at the International Genealogical Congress in Dublin in 2001. The organizing committee of the O'Neill Summer School of 2005 welcomed me to the event, and Francis Jones helped me hugely by enabling me to access television and radio materials at the BBC Northern Ireland Community Archive, Ulster Folk and Transport Museum. Some of the material and ideas here were first developed in *Environment and Planning D: Society and Space* (2002) and in *Uprootings/Regroundings* (2003). I am grateful for permission to publish a revised version of "Irish Origins, Celtic Origins: Population Genetics, Cultural Politics," *Irish Studies Review* 14, no. 1 (2006): 11–37, as chapter 6. (Visit http://www.informaworld.com.)

The research also could not have been conducted without the help of others who generously responded to my inquiries and requests. My work on family history in Northern Ireland was enabled by the considerable help of Georgie Siberry and Ann Robinson who allowed me to contact members of the North of Ireland Family History Society and recruit interviewees through a postal questionnaire, by branch members who helped distribute it, and by all those who responded. I am very grateful for this help. Many other people were part of this research as interviewees, some of whom can be named and most who remain anonymous. I am very grateful to those who agreed to be interviewed and generously gave of their time, including Barra McCain, Patrick Guinness, Fergus Gillespie, Richard Warner, Daniel Bradley, and all those unnamed interviewees who interrupted their own research to help mine by responding to my questions in research centers in Belfast and Dublin, in their homes, and online. I hope they will feel that they have been fairly represented even if my perspectives do not always match their own. I am especially grateful to Mary Treanor and to Brian Turner whose generosity in responding to my inquiries over several years has extended far beyond the bounds of the research relationship. Many thanks also to Geoffrey Beattie, Douglas Carson, and Martin Gale for permission to include their work in this book. I am very grateful to Louise Allen and family for permission to include an extract from the poem "Heritage" by the late Alfred Allen.

The process of research and writing has also been supported by the interest, influence, and practical help of many others including Aidan Arrowsmith, David Atkinson, Alison Blunt, Noel Castree, Claire Connolly, Ian Cook, Tim Cresswell, Felix Driver, Jeanette Edwards, David Emmons, David Forai, Anne-Marie Fortier, Sarah Franklin, David Gilbert, Breda Gray, Gareth Griffiths, Jeanne Kay Guelke, Jane Jacobs, Willie Jenkins, Desmond King, Brian Lambkin, Denis Linehan, Eric Laurier, Kay Muhr, Patrick O'Sullivan, Ed Oliver, Bronwyn Parry, Chris Philo, David Pinder, Kathy Prendergast, Shaun Richards, Mimi Sheller, Peter Shirlow, Susan Smith, Divya Tolia-Kelly, David Trigger, Katherine Tyler, Peter Wade, Bronwen Walter, and Clair Wills. Many people heard parts of this book as conference papers and departmental seminars and contributed with comments and suggestions. I am especially grateful to Jonathan Marks, Sallie Marston, and to Dydia DeLyser for their enthusiastic efforts in making my visits to their institutions to present some of this research so rewarding, to Brian Graham for years of support, to Valerie Graham for welcoming me so warmly on my frequent visits, and to Phil Crang and Sallie Marston for all their generous advice, encouragement, and interest. Very special thanks to Clare Fisher with her inspiring ways with words, to Hester Parr for all we have shared, to my brothers, Declan, Kieran, and Damian, to my dear sister Gráinne, and to my parents, Bridgit Nash and David Nash, for their limitless love and understanding.

Many thanks to Glenn Wright at Syracuse University Press for all his considerate as well as efficient work in bringing this book to fruition, to Ann Youmans for such careful and engaged copyediting, and to the series editor Jim MacKillop for his initial and continued enthusiasm.

Finally, thank you to Eve for bringing so much deep joy and to Miles Ogborn for endless enchantment and trickery.

Of Irish Descent

1

Introduction

Origin Stories

In 1892 the fifth edition of *Irish Pedigrees; or, The Origin and Stem of the Irish Nation* by John O'Hart of Ringsend, Dublin, was published in two volumes in Dublin, London, Glasgow, and New York.[1] First published in 1876, this book was a compendium of the genealogies of the ancient families of Ireland. These genealogies, O'Hart claimed, showed the direct descent of these families from three brothers—Heber, Ir, and Heremon—who were the sons of Milesius of Spain, whose own genealogy could be traced directly, via Scythia, to Noah and back to Adam. Another set of Gaelic families were grouped together as descendants of Milesius' uncle, Ith. These four Milesian men propagate the nation, but they were not Ireland's "first peoples." Drawing on early modern manuscript versions of medieval Gaelic mythologies and genealogies and contemporary late-nineteenth-century nationalist accounts of the ancient history of Ireland, O'Hart locates the "Milesians or Gaels" within a chronicle of colonizing settlers: they overcome the earlier Tuatha-de-Danaan, who had themselves conquered earlier inhabitants, and rule for 2,885 years until the arrival of the Anglo-Normans in the twelfth century. *Irish Pedigrees* thus clearly defined the "origin and stem of the Irish nation" as Milesian and Gaelic, but it also recorded the "Anglo-Norman" and "English and Scotch Families" that in later editions O'Hart categorized together as the "New Settlers" in contrast to the "ancient Irish Chiefs and Clans."

O'Hart's book of pedigrees thus explains the origin of the Irish nation through a history of ancient migrations; it sets out a regional geography of Irish chiefs and clans and their place within a national genealogy of ancient descent, and situates this national "stem" on humanity's family tree with Adam as its founding father. Readers were encouraged to explore the specific pedigrees of their family name and trace its lineage from the founding fathers of the Irish nation. Many still do. Though genealogical experts now caution readers about its reliability, *Irish Pedigrees* remains one of the most famous and most used sources among the many guides to researching Irish ancestors that have been published as genealogy has grown in popularity in the late twentieth century and as more and more people in Canada, Australia, New Zealand, Britain, and the United States are interested in tracing their "Irish roots." Well-worn copies of *Irish Pedigrees* are consulted in libraries and archives in Ireland and Northern Ireland and in these Irish emigrant destinations. *Irish Pedigrees* lives on too in the online culture of genealogical research; over one hundred thousand Web sites refer to *Irish Pedigrees* as a source for clan or family genealogies. Most of them have been set up by groups and individuals who identify with Ireland through Irish ancestry.[2] Many have been established by people in the United States who are the descendants of post-Famine migrants, or by those whose ancestors include earlier eighteenth-century migrants from Ulster and nineteenth-century migrants who left the midland, eastern, and southern counties of Ireland for the United States before the mass migration that followed the Famine. It was the prominent presence of these Irish settlers in the United States that made the reviewer of the third edition of *Irish Pedigrees* in 1881 comment in the *Philadelphia Inquirer* that the book "contains so many of the names which daily surround us and are before our eyes, that one might suppose this city and country to be a continuation of Ireland," and commend O'Hart for his work in "preserving from loss the records of so many years for the use of our New World."[3]

This book is also about origins and descent in Ireland and the "New World." In his preface to the 1879 edition of *Irish Pedigrees*, O'Hart argued that "at all times the subject of genealogies must command the respect and attention of rich and poor; on the account of the intimate bearing it has upon the individual, together with the tribes, people, nation and family to which he belongs. So it was in the past; and so ever it shall be."[4] *Of Irish Descent* traces the "intimate bearing" of ideas of shared ancestry and descent on personal, familial, national, and ethnic identities and senses of belonging. But it does so by considering genealogy as a particular, rather than, as Hart implied, a universal, cultural practice and form of knowledge, and by focusing on questions of ancestry, descent, and origins in relation to the politics of identity and difference in Ireland, Northern Ireland, and the United States. These are places connected by migration and specifically situated in the extended economic, cultural, and political relationships that both shape migration and follow from these migrant connections. They occupy different positions in the geography of contemporary Irish diasporic affiliations and desires.

They are also places where "being of Irish descent" means very different things. Its varied interpretations and enactments are shaped by the different dimensions of popular Irishness worldwide and framed by competing approaches to the authenticity, hybridity, commercialization, and creative remaking of new versions of a modern, globalized Ireland and its traditional renderings. The meanings of "being of Irish descent" are entangled too in debates about Irish history, the disputed sovereignty of a region riven by rival affiliations to a united Ireland or United Kingdom, and the multicultural character of the Irish or American nation-state.

Of Irish Descent explores the intimate and extended implications of personal and collective explorations of origins and ancestry in popular genealogy and human population genetics. Long-established techniques of recording pedigrees in lists of lineage and reconstructing family trees through archives and oral histories have recently been joined by newly developed genetic methods of reckoning relatedness and finding Irish origins, as new genetic techniques of reconstructing prehistoric migrations and estimating patterns of descent and degrees of relatedness have been adapted for and taken up in popular genealogy. Old techniques of doing a family tree continue to dominate the work of researching Irish ancestry from afar and the pursuit of family history in Ireland and Northern Ireland. Yet new genetic accounts of the prehistoric settlement of Ireland and of the island's contemporary population are also being used in new projects to explore Irish clan ancestries. This book explores the ways these familiar and novel practices of tracing ancestry and finding origins are shaped by and in turn reshape the imagination of the nation and diaspora as a community of shared descent; their relation to the place of ideas of "native" and "settler" ancestry and origins in debates about identity, history, and politics in Ireland and Northern Ireland; and how they intersect with and inform old and new ideas of who belongs in Ireland and to whom Ireland and Irish culture belongs. Doing so entails situating contemporary genealogy in the history of its use to naturalize political power, claim distinction, and define the national collective community; considering the place of ideas of ancestry and origins in conventional and alternative accounts of the relationships between geography, identity, and belonging; and foregrounding the social dimensions of genealogy as a form of knowledge and cultural practice.

Irish Origins

Irish Pedigrees is a classic example of the collective origin stories that were central to late-nineteenth-century European nationalist projects to establish the historical foundations, ethnic identity, and cultural character of the nation.[5] Irish cultural nationalists in the late nineteenth century drew on an earlier effort to figure the unity of the people through shared descent. As early as the seventh century, powerful dynastic groups extending their territories within Ireland constructed a myth of ancient arrival to justify their conquests. The tradition of genealogical knowledge, or *seanchas*, that was so important to the organization of landholding and succession within the kin group was joined to a narrative of descent that stretched back from Míl Espaine, or Milesius of Spain, to Noah and to Adam. As Fergus Gillespie, now chief herald of Ireland, explained in his address to the first Irish Genealogical Congress in Dublin in 1993, this myth of antiquity legitimated the position of the most powerful dynastic groups, but over time the "conquered peoples were also given Milesian genealogies, fitting them into a genealogical scheme which provided a cultural and racial unity to all the peoples of Ireland."[6] Genealogists both maintained knowledge of some of the oldest genealogies in Europe and massaged them when necessary to match this myth of Gaelic origin.

O'Hart's account of Gaelic Milesian origins derives from that contained in the *Lebor Gabála Érenn* (*Leabhar Gabhála* in modern Irish), the "Book of the Taking of Ireland," more widely known as "The Book of Invasions," compiled in the eleventh century from eight- and ninth-century sources and reinscribed and reinterpreted by Geoffrey Keating in the seventeenth century. In this origin story, the new arrivals do not just rule over but replace the existing people. The subsequent genealogical unity of the people is thus based, as historian Thomas F. O'Rahilly argued in 1946, on "obliterating the memory of the different ethnic origins of the people."[7] An account of shared origins was needed to match the island's linguistic unity. "The task which the authors of the L G [*Leabhar Gabhála*], set themselves," he argued, "was to endow all the septs which possessed any importance in their day with a common Goidelic [or Gaelic] origin." They did so by pushing the arrival of the Goidels back into the distant past and inventing Goidal genealogies for "tribes of pre-Goidelic descent."[8] This narrative of common origin was paralleled by the practical function of genealogy as a major field of study in early Christian Ireland to distinguish lines of descent between and within powerful ruling families. As Richard Comerford writes, these families "justified their status by reference to the branches of a numerously ramified genealogical tree. The standing of a king was inseparable from his place on a chain of paternity reaching upwards to Noah and Adam (the male line only was considered). If all lines led back to Adam they were not all equal: whether in terms of individuals or lineages, the family tree established a hierarchy of worth. And to have any kind of genealogical tree was to belong to the aristocracy and to be set apart from the common people."[9]

In the late eighteenth century, this account of ancient migrations was caught up in competing attempts to describe Irish origins that were similarly framed by questions of the legitimacy of the power and presence of different groups within the social and political structure that resulted from the early modern English colonization of Ireland. The sixteenth-century Plantation of Ireland—the confiscation of land from Gaelic and Anglo-Norman elites and their granting by the Crown to new British Protestant "Planters"—was followed by the final defeat of the Gaelic aristocracy in Ulster and the Plantation of Ulster in the seventeenth century. This extended process was profoundly shaped by the Reformation and British Protestant state formation that made religion central to the definition of British and Irish identity and difference.[10] The development of antiquarianism, and especially its focus on the theme of ancient origins, in late-eighteenth-century Ireland was part of a wider, new European fascination with the distant past. But it was also central to the political and literary culture of the period in Ireland in particular ways. As Clare O'Halloran has argued, for both Catholic and Protestant authors of historical and antiquarian works, questions of "arrival," "settlement," "invasion," or "conquest" were deeply shaped by their consciousness of the colonial dimensions of the Anglo-Norman "conquest" in the twelfth century and the relatively recent histories of sixteenth- and seventeenth-century Plantations.[11]

Despite their different social positions in late-eighteenth-century Ireland, interest in myths of origin were shared by both Catholic and Protestant antiquarians. Protestant ambivalence about the degree to which the recent or late medieval past could lend legitimacy to their place in Ireland and historically locate them in the country, O'Halloran argues, led to their equal obsession with Gaelic origins. Different perspectives on sectarianism and colonialism shaped antiquarians' attempts to "validate the rights of their respective communities, whether in terms of religious toleration for Catholics, or of a growing sense of identity with the land of their birth among Protestant descendants of earlier colonists," as well as attempts by both Catholic and Protestant writers to produce a shared identity through shared historical endeavor.[12] Questions of origins were deeply political.

While arguments about ancient origins lost their political significance in other contexts, the development of Irish cultural nationalism and political challenges to colonialism over the course of the nineteenth and early twentieth centuries meant that questions of ancient origins remained potent in Ireland. Theories of racial and linguistic difference between the Saxon and the Celtic, mobilized in mid-nineteenth-century accounts of Irish Celtic identity by colonial commentators, were drawn on by Irish cultural nationalists in the late nineteenth and early twentieth centuries who supported their calls for Irish political independence and national cultural regeneration with claims of the pure Gaelic ancestry and ancient origins of the nation. Despite centuries of intermarriage between what were themselves often heterogeneous and fluid groups, many late-nineteenth-century unionists and nationalists shared a mythology of different descent. "Native" and "Planter" came to stand for different blood stocks as well as differences in religious adherence and political persuasion.

O'Hart's work thus exemplifies the way in which medieval genealogies that ordered power and authority among regional ruling elites came to be seen in the late nineteenth century as *national* genealogies and the way in which genealogical knowledge itself came to be seen as a national cultural tradition. Accounts of the old bardic tradition of reciting noble genealogies and stories of the continued existence of this knowledge among the dispossessed rural poor were symbols of a refined and sophisticated ancient culture, subjugated but surviving as a resistant native tradition. Reviewers of *Irish Pedigrees* in Ireland were quick to read it as record of a suppressed but unbroken cultural inheritance of genealogical knowledge whose recovery was part of a project of national cultural revival. A reviewer of the third edition for the *Munster News*, for example, recommended that the book ought to be in every household in Ireland and used daily in "teaching the young, and the old, too that they have a history—a grand history . . . the history of the Irish race, what they were before the heel of a foreign toe was set upon them." The pedigrees listed in O'Hart's book confirmed an ancient relationship between land and lineage. But for this reviewer, *Irish Pedigrees* was not only an account of the nation's origins but of a shared national character passed on through descent: a "tenacious love of country—that stubborn resistance to the yoke of oppression, which no matter how often overcome, springs up anew, and stands unconquered and unconquerable"—that existed today as it was "manifested for so many hundreds of years by their ancestors, whose names and pedigrees are by Mr O'Hart traced down for ages, even to this day."[13]

Irish Pedigrees was, however, a hybrid product. O'Hart's dedication of the first edition to Sir Bernard Burke, who held the British royal appointment of Ulster king of arms, the head of the heraldic office in Ireland, and son of the founder of the famous compendia of British aristocratic pedigrees, links an old Gaelic tradition of dynastic genealogies as origin stories and guides to succession to a British tradition of hereditary titles bestowed by the Crown. The Irish genealogies that O'Hart recorded, like the lineages of the English aristocracy listed in *Burke's Peerage*, were guides to inherited position, privilege, and power. But as national ancestral origin stories, these genealogies were mobilized by Irish cultural nationalists in the late nineteenth century in anticolonial projects of cultural resistance. At the same time, as the position of the predominantly, but not exclusively, Protestant gentry and aristocracy declined in the late nineteenth century, and as Irish nationhood was becoming increasingly and more exclusively linked to ideas of race, many "Anglo-Irish" families turned to genealogy and its evidence of generations of residence to locate themselves in Ireland as Irish.[14] These families were recorded within O'Hart's genealogical compendia even if the increasing coupling of Catholicism and native descent as criteria for membership in the nation marked out their suspect "settler" status.

The double function of genealogy both to legitimate the power of selected social groups and to define the broader collective traveled with European emigration to those places where Irish immigrants were themselves "settlers." In Canada, New Zealand, Australia, and the United States, the genealogical discourse of descent was historically mobilized to construct narratives of nation building by founding families and pedigrees of distinction for their descendants, and to differentiate them from later immigrant groups. In the United States, these groups included Irish immigrants who over the history of Irish emigration and resettlement have both struggled to join the category of white Anglo-Saxon and asserted ethnic difference against that category. Late-twentieth-century popular interests in Irish ancestry in the United States are preceded by a complex history of the ways in which Irish-born immigrants and their descendants have positioned themselves and been positioned by others within shifting categories of race, nation, and ethnicity.[15] Contemporary efforts to recover knowledge of ancestral origins similarly both challenge the legacies of late-nineteenth-century nativist denigrations of Irish immigrants and their descendants and celebrate a complex and sometimes shifting alignment of American and Irish ethnic cultures. They also reflect the wider appropriation of genealogy as a means of challenging historical, social, and cultural marginalization, and the profound shift from ideas of cultural assimilation to cultural pluralism as models for the cultural character of the state.

Lineage and pedigree have historically distinguished between high and low born, naturalized inherited position and privilege, and guided the transfer of property. As Elizabeth Povenilli has argued, when the significance of genealogy as a guide to royal and noble succession and political authority waned with the development of modern democratic forms of governance, genealogy was simultaneously democractized and extended as the new middle class sought to support their status through bourgeois pedigrees.[16] If no longer a determinant of political power, genealogy continued to ensure the straightforward and managed transfer of property within families or, more particularly, along patrilineal pathways of descent from fathers to sons. Yet popular genealogy is also shaped by the rise of forms of historical activism that have asserted the significance and addressed the neglect of those "hidden from history" and challenged the conventional historical focus on "great men and great deeds." Genealogy or family history, especially when aligned with other forms of popular or public history—women's history, ethnic history, community history—can be a way of recovering conventionally insignificant "ordinary" histories and can call into question what is deemed historically significant. Genealogy can be a mechanism for registering inherited position *and* a means of resisting inherited traditions and hierarchies of national belonging and historical significance. Alex Haley's account of his quest to discover his ancestral origins in Africa, published and televised as *Roots* in 1976 and frequently cited as the foundational moment for popular genealogy in the United States, itself reflects the harnessing of genealogy in cultural and politics projects of demarginalization and cultural recovery.[17]

The redemptive recovery of a historical connection brutally broken through slavery in Haley's *Roots* was also part of a wider challenge to the model of cultural assimilation that both denied and denigrated difference from mainstream white American society. *Roots* was an exploration of a specifically African American experience and desire for reconnection with a largely obliterated past. Within the context of an emerging multiculturalism, it fostered a wider interest in genealogy as an engagement with ethnic ancestry and origins. The family trees that many children are invited to do in American schools reflect this multiculturalist celebration of diversity. Yet the practice of tracing Irish ancestral roots, as Matthew Frye Jacobson has argued, demonstrates the resilience of a diasporic imagination that is most usefully envisaged as one of the causes rather than effects of the ethnic revival of the late twentieth century. This is a diasporic imagination in which the fate and fortunes of the homeland continue to matter to ethnic communities as they did to emigrant ones, even if, as Jacobson shows, the senses of obligation and loyalty to the homeland within Irish diasporic nationalism have been mobilized for different purposes and have been differently situated in relation to American national political discourses of assimilation and American foreign policy.[18] The specificity of Irish-American enthusiasm for recovering Irish roots is thus entangled in the wider growth of genealogy as a popular practice and in the wider politics of nation, race, and ethnicity. For many identifying with Ireland as descendants of Irish immigrants, genealogy has shifted from being the taken-for-granted foundation for a range of cultural expressions of Irish ancestry through music, storytelling, reading, parading, dance, food, and other cultural practices and forms to being a cultural practice in itself through which senses of Irish diasporic identity are explored and enacted.[19] It is a practice that is simultaneously situated in a contemporary social context in which the positive associations of Irishness feature so heavily in popular culture and enframe a diverse range of commodities.[20]

At the same time, popular interests in ancestry have been shaped by increased recognition of indigenous peoples' presence and political claims and the cultural resonances of being indigenous. In nation-states founded on the dispossession and displacement of indigenous people, their particular equations of race, ethnicity, and national belonging are not only shaped by the political challenge of multiculturalism but by the potency of the alternative model of native belonging.[21] Pluralist celebrations of diversity might include the culture of the indigenous, but the ideal of indigeneity is of a relationship to a place that has not been broken by the migrations that have made the settler society ethnically diverse. In some respects at least, settler genealogies of Old World ancestry reflect a nostalgia for an imagined time when place, identity, culture, and ancestry coincided. Where you lived was where your ancestors had always lived, and there was no dissonance between cultural identity and location. This is the ideal of bounded places, deep roots, and shared culture. The place of origin is the place where subjectivity is untroubled by the reflexivity of modernity and where collective identity is unselfconsciously lived. Tracing a family history back to Irish ancestors can thus be motivated by the appeal of ethnic particularity in an avowedly plural society *and* by the appeal of being "native" and deeply rooted.

However, interests in reconstructing family trees back to Irish origins and ancestors are not only informed by the cultural currents of Irish diasporic locations. They have also been encouraged by and enlisted in efforts to construct an Irish global community in Irish public culture and political discourse. Over the last decade of the twentieth century especially, the idea of the Irish diaspora has been mobilized both to encourage increased genealogical tourism and to create an understanding of Irish identity in Ireland, Northern Ireland, and worldwide as a plural cultural collective that is characterized by shared affinities, ancestral ties, and diverse expressions and experiences of being Irish or of Irish descent. These interests in origins and ancestry are also being fed by more recent scientific accounts of the ancient peopling of Ireland based on genetic surveys of the island's present-day population, which suggest much less fluid versions of ancestry and belonging.

Genealogy in Theory

Ideas of ancestry and origins thus have a complex relationship to ideas of national identity, ethnic diversity, cultural purity, and indigeneity. They feature within the model of an organic national community, bound to the land and sharing origins, ancestry, blood, and culture, and within accounts of national ethnic pluralism. They can be enlisted in political claims for the recognition of native title, exclusionary discourses of national cultural purity, and expressions of diasporic identities. Genealogy can be used to define collective group membership and to rank individuals according to lineage as more or less "well-bred" and more or less pure in pedigree, to affirm connections, and to reckon different degrees of relatedness between individuals and between groups. However, ideas of origins and ancestry have tended to occupy a less complex place within late-twentieth-century cultural theory, in which genealogical imaginations have been mostly associated with the national valorizing of purity and the geographical fixing of culture, blood, and people that Liisa Malkki has called a "sedentarist metaphysics."[22] The frequently invoked distinction between grounded "roots" and "routes" of travel as metaphors for understanding culture and identity marks a profound turn over the last two decades toward ideas of mobility, cultural hybridity, and fluid identities as alternatives to those of cultural origins, cultural purity, and rootedness.[23]

This now well-established attentiveness to complex cultural flows, transnational networks, patterns of migration, experiences of displacement, diasporic identifications, and hybrid cultural forms both challenges the notions of fixity that underpin the model of the racially rooted nation and engages with the intensified mobilities of late-twentieth-century globalization and their differentiated effects. In much cultural theory, mobility now describes the condition of the world and destabilizes collective identities and subjectivities hitherto understood to be foundational and fixed. In contrast, the language of family trees, roots, branches, ancestral lines, and origins in genealogy are presented as deeply dependent on the conceptual structures of Western epistemology that Gilles Deleuze and Félix Guattari have called arborescent thinking—the Western tradition of rigid, binary logics and systematic and hierarchical branches of knowledge rooted in firm foundations—and their manifestation in the fixed and bounded geographies of ethnic fundamentalism. The rhizome, their alternative conceptual imaginary, emphasizes shifting interconnections, alliances, networks, fragmentation, combination, and plurality. For Deleuze and Guattari, "there is always something genealogical about a tree. It is not a method for the people"; "the rhizome is an anti-genealogy."[24] Roots have been out of favor within critical theory for some time.

Yet the association of home and rootedness with political conservativism and the equation of mobility with cultural dynamism, as well as progressive politics, that has accompanied this conceptual counterposing of stasis and movement are now being questioned. Feminist critics have pointed to the masculinist romance of movement as transcendence and escape from the feminized stasis of the home within celebrations of mobility and have highlighted the ways in which both mobility and home are experienced through the entangled inequalities of sex, race, and class.[25] Recent critics have challenged the presumption that contemporary experience is best characterized through rootless mobility in contrast to fixity and rooted belonging. By drawing attention to the complex interrelationships between permanence and change, fixity and fluidity in experiences, mobility and the making of home, these critics upset the contrast between the condition of being at home and being migrant.[26] Both the energy expended by nation-states and regional federations in facilitating the movement of some and prohibiting the migration of others and the making of home as mobile and multilocational through transnational connections suggest the inadequacy of a simple analytical contrast between rootedness and mobility and the definition of home as single place of origin.

This complex relationship between located attachments and mobility is central to Paul Gilroy's influential elaboration of a critical diasporic consciousness. Gilroy's conceptualization of the diaspora as a subnational and transnational, nonterritorial collective identity challenges what he describes as the "sedentary poetics of either soil or blood" in which land, soil, genes, blood, culture, residence, and political affiliation ideally coincide within the boundaries of the nation-state.[27] Yet Gilroy's critique of the idealization of origins—fixity and cultural purity and their place in racism, nationalism, and ethnic fundamentalism—does not entail disposing of ideas of shared points of departure and shared forms of experience in favor of absolutely indeterminate identities. Instead, diaspora consciousness manages the tension between the bonds of shared experience and cultural heterogeneity, between feelings of affinity and senses of difference. Diasporic identities challenge the codes of modern citizenship because they are based on multiple identifications and multiple belongings always in motion between the place of residence and other places. Diaspora, he suggests, offers a way to "comprehend the dynamics of identity and belonging constituted between the poles of geography and genealogy."[28] Diasporic subjects, for Gilroy, refuse to accept the choice between identity defined either by "geography" as place of residence (where you are now) or by "genealogy" as ancestral origins (where you are from). "Geography" here stands for a liberal model of citizenship that refuses difference; the cultural particularities of the immigrant must be left behind in the process of assimilation. "Genealogy" stands for a model of ethnic fundamentalism in which the migrant must stay true to the place of origin. Diasporic identifications, as they are conceptualized by Stuart Hall and Paul Gilroy, reject each model and are more mobile, hybridized, and multilocational.[29] This critical diasporic imaginary counters the "sedentarist metaphysics" of the nation and understandings of culture and identity as fixed, foundational, and determining.

The critique of ideas of rootedness in contrast to ideas of mobility, and attempts to reconsider their relation in cultural theory, is paralleled too by a critique of genealogy as the problematic counterpoint to ideas of complex and dynamic relationalities. Genealogy describes another limited and limiting conceptualization of identity in Tim Ingold's "genealogical model."[30] This is an understanding of culture, identity, and relatedness as the product of inheritance. Drawing too on the figure of the rhizome offered by Deleuze and Guattari and on anthropological accounts of non-Western understandings of ancestry, generation, substance, memory, and land, Ingold expounds an alternative "relational model." From a relational perspective, persons are not products of inheritance but are continuously in a process of change and development in an all-encompassing network of relationships and situated activities. Persons, he argues are not "preconstituted—or procreated—entities, but rather as loci of growth, of the progenerative unfolding of the entire field of relationships within which each comes into being. The source of their identification is to be found in this unfolding." Memory, knowledge, and tradition are not handed on unchanged from generation to generation but are generated in the course of lived experience. His relational model thus directly challenges an imagination of shared identity based on shared bodily and cultural inheritance. "Ethnic and racial classifications are as foreign to relational thinking" he argues. "There is no room, within such a view, for the kind of classificatory project that groups individuals on the basis of whatever intrinsic characteristics they might happen to possess, by virtue of their biogenetic inheritance or cultural heritage, irrespective of their life in the world."[31] For Gilroy, genealogy denotes an understanding of identity defined by ancestry and as the product of unbroken lines of cultural and biological inheritance. In his account of an alternative diasporic consciousness, this version of identity is deeply problematized by the multilocational attachments and cultural hybridizations that are the result of complex geographies of displacement and homemaking. For Ingold, genealogy names a similarly fundamentalist understanding of identity and culture as inherited that is in sharp contrast to their continuous relational practice.

Ingold's critique of the idea of culture as inherited also resonates with Walter Benn Michaels's argument that the language of cultural heritage and identity, which has replaced the overt language of race in the United States in the late twentieth century, remains wedded to a model of culture in which cultural identity and cultural heritage is the property of individuals or groups by virtue of

descent. For culture to be understood as an inherited corpus of beliefs and traditions rather than description of what people currently do or believe in depends,
Michaels argues, on the idea of cultures as separate bundles of inherited traditions and traits transmitted genealogically. Similarly, the idea that what people
did in the past matters to contemporary collective identity is commonly based on
having a shared genealogical relationship to them.[32] The idea of biological connection that is fundamental to genealogical descent, for Michaels, inescapably
entrains a racialized model of culture as the property of different communities
of descent. This is a challenging corrective to familiar ways of conceiving of
culture and identity. Yet his critique of the idea of collective identity based on
genealogically transmitted memory and tradition are also in tension with commemoration as a political strategy of those who bear witness to suffering and
subjugation.[33] For Paul Gilroy and Stuart Hall, the politics of commemoration is
one strand of a critical diasporic consciousness, but both stress the dynamics of
memory and "imaginative rediscovery"[34] rather than "naïve invocations of common memory."[35]

Genealogy in these accounts stands for a set of politically problematic perspectives on place, culture, identity, and belonging rather than as a popular social
and cultural practice. But this disjuncture poses the compelling interpretative
question: What are the relationships between these old and alternative concep-
tualizations of the geographies of culture and identity and the ordinary practice
of genealogy or family history? Bringing together these critical cultural theories
and this popular practice offers an analytical framework for considering geneal-
ogy-in-action in relation to accounts of alternative diasporic and relational geographies of identity; of engaging both with the implications of the figuring of
origin, ancestry, and identity in popular genealogy; and of reflecting back on
these models of identity, culture, and geography. One starting point for doing so
is by attending to popular genealogy's own geographies. These include its own
origins in a specifically European tradition of recording descent and reckoning
relatedness and its dispersal with European emigration, the imaginative geographies that motivate genealogical quests to find and pilgrimages to visit ancestral
homes and origins, and the networks shaped by the transnational practices of
ancestral identification. Though the family tree appears to be a straightforward
record of the "facts" of family history, as cultural anthropologists have argued,
it is a diagram of relatedness based on a particular Western European model of

kinship.[36] This historically and culturally located but apparently universal model of who is related to whom traveled with European emigrants. As Elizabeth Povinelli puts it, "From the perspective of their roots, genealogical trees have been moving with Europeans for a very long time."[37] The family trees of third, fourth, and sometimes later generation descendants of Irish migrants are stretched out diagrams that chart ancestry back in time, map the migrations of their ancestors from Ireland, their arrival and subsequent movements, and figure their own imaginative connections with "ancestral homes." But they also reflect the travel of this cultural form.

For those who can afford it, these family trees also shape genealogical research itineraries. The search for roots sets people off on trips to local, regional, and national archives and on transatlantic and long-haul journeys to find distant relatives and significant places. Traveling in search of roots suggests complicated relationships between rootedness and mobility across often intersecting local, national, and transnational forms of identification. Personal genealogical journeys also reflect wider perspectives on global cultural change. The search for ancestral origins and the appeal of culturally and ethnically distinct homelands may be a reaction to new senses of globalized complexity.[38] Yet searches for Irish origins are, at the same time, stimulated by global cultural processes that shape the appeal of Irish roots and made possible though new technologies of travel and communication. Family trees not only record ancestors' migration but are products of the technologies that make genealogical information mobile and genealogical travel easy. Like access to other forms of knowledge and forms of mobility, genealogy is also shaped by uneven global and local patterns of poverty and wealth.

But the meanings of European or, more specifically, Irish roots are also shaped by particular historical geographies of colonialism and nation building and contemporary configurations of race, ethnicity, and nation in different places. Contemporary patterns of interest in Irish roots have been shaped by different patterns of Irish emigration and by shifting relationships between Irish migrant groups and other ethnic and socioeconomic groups in different national contexts. Diasporic genealogy is about significant places—family homes and ethnic "origins"—and complex global networks of travel, desire, and imagination. It is not simply a reflection of existing cultural networks but is a practice that creates networks, that produces new relationships and mobilizes novel flows of people, objects, ideas, and information in old and newly digital forms. Exploring genealogy as an expression and exploration of identity and belonging means situating the practice in the specific local dynamics of culture and ethnicity and within these networks.

Geographies of mobility, imaginations of fixity, locally situated cultural formations, and extended imaginative and social networks all constitute the cultures of diasporic genealogy. Avtar Brah has argued that diaspora should be understood "in terms of historically contingent 'genealogies' in the Foucauldian sense" that resist ideas of single trajectories and fixed origins.[39] Here the genealogies in question are more ordinary than Foucauldian, but the search for ancestral origins may itself involve complex senses of home, hybridity, and mobility. This complexity is masked by simply contrasting what is sometimes taken to be the intrinsically politically progressive nature of rootlessness and the intrinsically regressive idea of roots. Rather than endorse this orthodox opposition, this book explores the politically potent cultural meanings of ancestry or origins that feature within and are affected by the practice of genealogy, population genetics, and geneticized genealogy. This means attending also to the social dimensions of genealogy as knowledge and as practice.

Genealogy in Practice

Genealogy is a particular sort of knowledge of relationships between people that are ordered according to parentage and birth, the conventions through which those relationships are represented in family trees or genealogical charts, and methods through which that empirical knowledge is gained. In a formal sense, genealogy is an empirical record of the facts of ancestry that eschews family stories and subjective memory in favor of these verifiable "facts" of the past, even if in practice, contemporary genealogy shades into family history, memory, and memoir. To describe someone's genealogy is to locate them in a written lineage or on the diagram of the family tree, whose vital statistics are the names of dead relatives and the dates of their births, marriages, and deaths.[40]

In one sense, a person's genealogy—that set of relationships stretching back from the individual into the past—is there to be uncovered. In another sense, a family tree has to be actively made through the work of searching for records in archives and online. The investigative impulse to recover genealogy's vital statistics—its empirical detective work—is entangled with the imaginative work of constructing always incomplete family histories from evocative names and dates, fragmentary memories, sketchy stories, and nameless figures in old family photographs, the affective artefacts of family history. This empirical and imaginative effort is also one that involves making choices about what line to follow, which clues to pursue. Family trees are never complete since they can, potentially at least, keep growing back in time, laterally along the branches and forward in time along ever branching lines of descent. Their shape and content reflect the kinship relations of those they include and the availability and cost of records. But they are also shaped by the active choices made by those doing their genealogy about which line to follow and thus who counts as more or less significant members of the (ancestral) family. Genealogy is thus a form of knowledge of relationships there to be uncovered and is a process through which certain relationships are defined as significant.

The self in popular genealogy is similarly both there to be "found" and forged through self-exploration. Genealogy reflects the familiar idea that "my ancestors made me who I am," physically and culturally. Exploring a genealogical past is thus often a way of knowing, understanding, or exploring the self. The genealogical quest to know with certainty "who you are" and "where you come from" by knowing your ancestors suggests a primordial and predetermined identity that can be simply uncovered, as in the "genealogical model" Ingold described. Yet genealogy is also often a practice of self-definition and self-making, of choosing which apparently determining ancestries matter most. Genealogy promises a neat and satisfying pre-given collective identity—"Irishness" for example—guaranteed by descent. At the same time, however, it offers the potential pleasures of perhaps unselfconsciously choosing an "authentic" identity, in identifying, for example, with one surname, clan, or ethnicity among the range in a family tree. Its discourses are often simultaneously of biological and cultural inheritance. Family trees schematically track the flows of blood or genes that according to Western understandings of reproduction and inheritance produce the individual in their material embodied form. But these understandings of the self as the product of the confluences and particular combinations of genes are, in different ways and to different degrees, combined with a sense of cultural influence or inheritance, of attitudes, inclinations, affinities that are passed on through what parents teach children.

For genealogy is never simply about knowing the self. By its nature, it is always about degrees of connection and collective relationships—familial, national, ethnic. Individuals have unique locations on family trees and thus personal ancestries, but these ancestries and family trees are always shared with the other people who are connected on its lines and branches through birth and parentage. Genealogy, as Marilyn Strathern has argued, combines discourses of individualism and maps of relationality. Acquiring genealogical knowledge is used to confirm personal identity, yet the family tree also locates the individual in complex networks of kinship and affiliation.[41] Genealogy is about degrees of connection and difference; the links that define familial relatedness through blood and marriage can be close or distant. Shared descent both defines groups and differentiates them from others. Genealogy is thus a practice that is both self-centered and collective, both individualized and relational. It is fueled by a desire to know oneself through a family past and the appeal of making connections—of finding relatives, joining up family trees. The well-developed commercial genealogical service sector capitalizes on this naturalized sense that knowing one's ancestral past is a way of knowing oneself, the satisfactions of solving genealogical puzzles and the pleasures of discovering genealogical connections, by selling access to data and software to organize and share standardized genealogical data files, hosting e-mail discussion lists, and providing ways of linking personal genealogies into larger ancestral archives.

But the social relations and connections between people within the practice of genealogy are not just there to be found. Genealogy can be understood as a systematic way of acquiring and ordering information about ancestors who, through blood and marriage, make up the family tree. It is also a practice of making relations. In this book, I take genealogy—its social practices, encounters, and exchanges in research centers, in meetings with relations, in family reunions and visits "home"—to be generative of social and familial relations rather than just descriptive of the "facts" of ancestry. Sometimes these are newly discovered or recovered relatives; sometimes they are family-like relationships with newly made friends. Genealogy is a means of making distinctions and making connections, a record of relatedness and an active practice of making relations. Rather than dismissing genealogy as an indulgent and insignificance hobby, defining it as necessarily reactionary because of its origins in claims of pedigree and privilege, or alternatively affirming it as a natural innocent impulse or stressing its radical potential, my approach is to explore genealogy's diverse uses and effects. This hugely popular practice is now being inflected by new genetic accounts of ancestry and origins and through the development of new genetic tests on sale for "deep ancestral knowledge." Exploring the implications of this intersection for the cultural politics of identity and descent is one task of this book. It is also a practice whose personal and familial dimensions are joined to wider models of collective identity via its discourses of possession, ownership, and belonging.

Belonging and Possession

The reasons why people develop an interest in their genealogy are deeply personal and familial. The illness, aging, or death of parents or the birth of children or grandchildren may prompt a desire to secure and pass on the family's history. Locating oneself along a continuum of birth and death and new birth may assuage a sense of mortality. Within avowedly pluralist societies like the United States, it is also often a means of locating oneself in terms of a distinctive named ethnic ancestry. Engaging with the culture and the cultural politics of genealogical imaginations of collective ancestry and origins means attending to genealogy's simultaneously intimate meanings and worldly implications. Themes of possession and belonging traverse genealogy's public and intimate domains. As a contemporary popular practice, genealogy is no longer motivated by the concern with the ordered transfer of property between generations and the legitimate inheritance of material wealth. However, the language of ownership, possession, and inheritance still features within the culture of genealogy. Now the properties involved are both more embodied and more symbolic. The connections between people that are central to genealogy are those defined by shared bodily substances of blood or genes. The idea that people "belong to each other" because they share what belongs to them individually in the form of blood or genes is central to ideas of genealogical relatedness.[42]

In popular genealogy what is inherited, owned, and shared also includes family stories, memories, cultural traditions, and genealogical information. Genealogical knowledge—a mixture of stories and names and dates—may be passed down through the generations, shared among family members or held in protective or possessive custody by particular figures in the family. The expanded family trees produced by the efforts of the "family genealogist" are also often imagined as gift for contemporary and future family. The death of parents can make their children the new custodians of family knowledge, just as the birth of grandchildren can prompt a desire to collate an archive of the family's past to bequeath to the new generation. At the same time, genealogy is often a matter of missing and lost knowledge—stories heard but never recorded, questions not asked of elderly and now deceased relatives—of the absence of the dates and stories that could match and give meaning to the blood and genes that have been inherited.

Often the historical or cultural substance that can give meaning to the biogenetic transfers of reproduction is not only knowledge of the lives of those whose experiences and actions led to an individual's birth and upbringing but found in ideas of wider collective ethnic or national inheritance. Ethnic groups can be imagined as extended families bound together through shared biogenetic substance, cultural traditions, and narratives. Personal projects to recover and preserve family histories are paralleled by collective projects to reclaim and protect the cultural inheritance of ethnic groups. National identities are similarly conventionally expressed in terms of the shared possession of a culture and heritage within a bounded territory. In both, culture and tradition are imagined as the possession of the individual by virtue of birth and parentage.[43] Having a genealogical connection to a place and the cultural forms associated with it is a routine guarantor of the right to say "that is my culture." This model of cultural ownership can be mobilized for very different political projects: to inscribe exclusive limits on who has imaginative access to a set of traditions and, by extension, a right to belong in a place on the one hand, or to resist the aggressive or insensitive appropriation of the cultures, as well as the places, of indigenous groups on the other. Anticolonial nationalisms that assert the value of and seek to recover denigrated national cultures can transmute into postindependence models of exclusive cultural possession.

This book explores the ways in which personal senses of loss and projects to recover genealogical knowledge as both a cultural inheritance in itself and access to a collective ethnic heritage intersect with a specific national story of possession, loss, and reclamation. This is an Irish national history structured through a narrative of a Gaelic golden age destroyed by English invasion, the colonial dispossession of the ancient Gaelic clans and repression of Gaelic culture, Famine and exile as the product of colonial policy, and a long and unfinished struggle to repossess the nation. This potent nineteenth-century nationalist narrative of the nation continues to dominate many popular accounts of Irish history in the United States, often in relative isolation from the heated debates about the accuracy and adequacy of this national history that have taken place in Ireland and Northern Ireland over the last thirty years. The drama and pathos of this narrative of oppression and heroic struggle can fuel genealogical interest in Irish ancestry in the United States. But this account of Irish history can also be revised in light of the results of genealogical research and through visitors' encounters with contemporary perspectives on the past in Ireland and Northern Ireland. The tensions that arise and the accommodations that occur as different versions of Irishness and different interpretations of Irish history meet through genealogy are delicate incidents in the field of Irish-American international cultural relations. The sense of collective ownership of a collective national past and national culture through Irish descent that can motivate and be expressed through the genealogical research of visitors from the United States can be interpreted in Ireland or Northern Ireland as aggressively appropriative. The image of the emigrant as culturally corrupted, no longer truly Irish, haunts the experience of homecoming for these now distant descendants of those who left. Claims that intensely commodified and intensely popularized Irish culture in the United States is debased, commercialized, contrived and degraded, or anachronistically attached to romanticized images that have been discarded in Ireland, and arguments that Irish-American Irishness is shallow and sentimentalized and even dangerous, are deeply felt by those whose cultural attachments and affiliations are the subject of these critiques.

These sensitivities about claiming and sharing a cultural inheritance called Irish through Irish ancestry abroad refract upon, and are themselves shaped by, the politics of belonging and cultural property in Ireland and Northern Ireland. In these contexts, questions of belonging, both in terms of the formal politics of sovereignty and citizenship and in terms of symbolic and imaginative possession and inclusion, are still overshadowed by the old distinction between "native" and "settler," and more recently framed by new distinctions between "native" and "immigrant." Contemporary sensitivities about the disputed authenticity of Irish-American Irishness, the sometimes reciprocated and sometimes resisted assertions of collective diasporic heritage, and old and new accounts of the "native" and "settler" in public culture and political discourse involve delicate questions of cultural ownership and cultural difference. What counts as "authentic" Irish culture? Who is really Irish? Who belongs in Ireland? Who does Irish culture belong to? Who decides?

Of Irish Descent explores the complex geographies and political implications of ideas of ancestry and origins in popular genealogical interests in Irish roots, in the postcolonial cultural politics of noble ancestry in the Republic, in the practice of family history in Northern Ireland, in new genetic accounts of Irish prehistory and contemporary demography, and new genetic versions of Irish clan ancestry. It does so through a combined focus on the politics and geographies of identity and belonging. This analytical lens underpins its attention to how accounts of ancestry, origins, and descent shape and are reshaped by local contingencies of culture and politics and the ways these accounts travel, meet, and are mutually refracted in Ireland, Northern Ireland, and the United States. This triangulated geography of proximate and distant, multidirectional and bilateral connections is tilted toward the intimate entanglements of Northern Ireland and the Republic and stretched, across the Atlantic, to the United States. My asymmetrical analytical triangle, rather than a neat dual focus on Ireland and the United States, is deliberate. It foregrounds the inescapably political dimensions of all accounts of ancestry and origins by demonstrating the continuing costs of the categories "native" and "settler" for the politics of identity and division in Northern Ireland, and it highlights the ways local versions of Irishness via descent are shaped by and refract back upon configurations of belonging and identity elsewhere. Accounts of national and diasporic ancestry and origins are entwined with arguments about the constitutive role of migration—immigration as well as emigration—in Irish history, culture, and politics.

Thus, chapter 2 explores the relationship between the articulation of a diasporic Irishness in Irish cultural discourses of the 1990s and the meanings of Irish descent in relation to categories of ethnicity in the United States. Chapter 3 extends this consideration of the entanglements of accounts of ancestral connection and global community in Ireland and the United States by considering how the celebration of an inclusive diversity within the Irish diaspora is experienced by those who travel to Ireland in search of Irish roots, relatives, and reciprocated senses of reunion. Chapter 4 and 5, in contrast, focus on the ways in which ideas of "native" and "settler" ancestry are being explored in Ireland and Northern Ireland. Chapter 4 considers recent arguments about the recognition and regulation of Gaelic noble titles and categories of belonging and distinction in the Republic. Chapter 5 returns to more ordinary genealogies but in its focus on the practice of family history in Northern Ireland is concerned too with addressing the ways in which categories of "native" and "settler," which are fundamental to the division between the "two communities," are being explored via family history.

Questions of personal and collective ancestral origins that are being addressed in ordinary genealogy are also the subject of new scientific research. Chapter 6 focuses on the ways in which recent work on the prehistoric patterns of migration and the genetic character of the present population of Ireland is framed by and interpreted through themes of nationality and ethnicity, difference and descent, migration and mixture, the "native" and the "foreign." The implications of recent research by human population geneticists in Ireland extend beyond the cultural politics of belonging in Ireland and Northern Ireland. For as I explore in chapter 7, these findings and methodologies are being taken up by diasporic Irish clan and surname groups, whose newly geneticized accounts of ancestry and relatedness are now refiguring the diaspora as genetically differentiated according to patterns of paternal descent, and reigniting older claims that histories of settlement in Ireland can be detected in the bodies of the island's inhabitants. The genetic research is itself pursued with the interests of a large potential overseas diasporic audience in mind. Questions of ancestry and origins thus circulate, colliding and cross-fertilizing with different implications and effects as they do so, between Ireland, Northern Ireland, and the United States.

Of Irish Descent explores the ways in which Irish descent is differently situated in relation to categories of national identity, citizenship, and belonging in each location. It traces how ideas of roots and origins, "native" and "settler," and locally distinctive versions of Irishness travel with different effects and implications as they are mobilized and as they meet in different places. It does so by following the ways in which questions of belonging and property, possession and dispossession feature within, and move between, the personal and intimate domain of family and the wider scale of collective ethnic or national heritage and inheritance.

Although the distinction between native and newcomer, or, as O'Hart put it, "ancient Irish Chiefs and Clans" and "New Settlers" was central to *Irish Pedigrees,* O'Hart hoped his book would be read as an account of national genealogies for "the Irish and Anglo-Irish race of every class and creed all over the world".[44]

As the Work unveils the ancestors of the present day Irish, Anglo-Irish, and Anglo-Norman families, of various shades of religious and political opinions, we have endeavoured in its papers to subserve no sect or party. We beg to say that, while our IRISH PEDIGREES AND OUR IRISH LANDED GENTRY are necessarily *national* in character there is nothing in them to wound the feelings of Celt or Saxon, Catholic or Protestant, Liberal or Conservative.[45]

O'Hart did not limit his account of Irish pedigrees to Gaelic families and even argued for the native descent of those who were usually viewed as foreign. In the 1892 edition, he replaced the term "English and Anglo-Norman" with the term "New Settlers" since, he argued, many families "so entered, are of *Irish* descent" and as some "New Settlers" were the descendants of earlier "native" emigrants. The second volume of this 1892 edition incorporated his earlier supplement to *Irish Pedigrees*, entitled *The Irish and Anglo-Irish Gentry When Cromwell Came to Ireland* and included the Anglo-Norman and English settlers since the twelfth century, the "Names of the Settlers in Ireland under the 'Plantation of Ulster,' the Names of the Adventurers who came into Ireland with the Cromwellian Settlement, or with the Revolution; the Names of the Huguenot and Palatine families that settled in Ireland."[46]

Yet this encyclopedic effort to include all settlers regardless of the circumstances of their arrival did not prevent O'Hart from deploring the injustice of colonization. O'Hart dedicated the fifth edition of *Irish Pedigrees* to the Right Honourable the Earl of Aberdeen, erstwhile viceroy of Ireland, but told the fate of his own Gaelic noble family since the twelfth century as a "sad instance" of "the ruin which the English connection has produced in Ireland."[47] At the same time, O'Hart hoped that "the publication of the facts we record in this work will conduce to the removal of the causes of *discontent* which have long distracted our afflicted country" and that the account of Queen Victoria's "*Irish lineal descent* would endear her more to Irish people, and conduce to a more kindly feeling between the English and Irish nations than has, unhappily, existed between them for the last seven hundred years."[48]

Irish Pedigrees was thus at once a national narrative of ancient origins, record of colonial dispossession, statement of anticolonial cultural resistance, diasporic resource, inclusive index of ancestral distinction, and conciliatory account of interconnection. Accounts of ancestry can serve all sorts of arguments. This book explores the similarly varied and often unexpected ways in which categories of "native" and "settler" and ideas of connection and difference are reproduced and reworked with different implications in genealogical and genetic explorations of Irish origins and the meaning of being of Irish descent.

2

Special Affinities

Ethnic Origins and Diasporic Irishness

In 1998 the Constitution of the Republic of Ireland was amended following a referendum in support of the changes proposed in the Good Friday/Belfast Agreement. After years of negotiation and weeks of intensive talks, the Good Friday/Belfast Agreement that established the basis for devolved government and power sharing in Northern Ireland was signed by all parties involved in the Northern Ireland peace process on 10 April 1998.[1] The referendum that followed endorsed the revision of the Republic's constitutional territorial claim on Northern Ireland. This was one significant dimension of the agreement.[2] The amendments to the Irish constitution also included new wording of Article 2, which in its new version stated, "It is the entitlement and birthright of every person born in the island of Ireland which includes its islands and seas, to be part of the Irish nation. That is also the entitlement of all persons otherwise qualified in accordance with law to be citizens of Ireland. Furthermore, the Irish nation cherishes its special affinity with people of Irish ancestry living abroad who share its cultural identity and heritage."[3] The right of people in Northern Ireland to identify themselves as Irish or British or both and to hold Irish citizenship was thus guaranteed. But the Constitution also now formally enshrines an imaginative collective cultural community of shared ancestry, identity, and heritage beyond the island of Ireland.

This statement of "special affinity" between the "Irish nation" and "people of Irish ancestry living abroad" by the legislature of a geographically delimited nation-state codified an image of a global Irish diaspora that had emerged most prominently in the early 1990s in the electoral campaign and presidential speeches of Mary Robinson, who held office between 1990 and 1997. In her election speech, Robinson reflected on the honor of her role as figurehead not only for people in Ireland but for the "70 million people of Irish descent worldwide."[4]

For Robinson and other prominent cultural commentators, this new emphasis on a global Irish community challenged the way in which the experiences of Irish emigrants and the attachments of their descendants have been neglected despite the scale and significance of Irish emigration and its political, economic, social, and cultural effects.

The diaspora was also used to suggest ways of reimagining Irish culture as diverse and Irish identities as variously expressed and performed in different locations worldwide. Though this turn to ideas of a global Irish community or extended national genealogy was novel, this effort to rethink Irish culture and identity through the image of a global family was part of a much longer critical reflection on the model of the nation upon which the state was founded. Critiques of the cultural and social conservativism of the state and its ethos of Gaelic cultural purity accompanied its foundation, but from the 1970s onwards, explorations of its adequacy and effects from a variety of perspectives have characterized much contemporary culture and criticism. An alternative language of cultural plurality, hybridity, dynamism, and openness now has a prominent, even if contested, place in Irish public culture.

Yet ideas of cultural plurality or hybridity and more conventional appeals to uncomplicated ethnic origins were often interwoven in the accounts of a global Irish diaspora that emerged in the 1990s. As Irish emigrant experiences and cultures were being addressed within public culture and symbolically enlisted in new political imaginaries of inclusive and plural Irishness, diasporic identifications with Irish ancestral origins were being fostered to encourage inward investment and tourist revenue. In 1996 the Irish government reviewed the Irish Genealogical Project to index local genealogical records and establish county-based Family History Research Centres, and recommended a range of initiatives to increase tourism by foregrounding "familial connections with Ireland."[5] This emphasis on genealogical "homecoming" in tourist promotions in the 1990s extended earlier governmental campaigns and commercial schemes to encourage tourism among descendants of Irish emigrants by explicitly appealing to potential visitors through the promise of return to ancestral origins. These schemes were enormously helped by highly publicized work of the Irish Genealogical Office to verify the Irish descent of John F. Kennedy, and by his "homecoming" visit to Ireland in 1963. This tradition of researching the Irish ancestry of the rich and famous continues, and is paralleled by the ordinary genealogical work of many to achieve an Irish passport on the basis of Irish ancestry for the sake of its practical and symbolic benefits.

These sometimes overlapping and sometimes diverging ideas of cultural hybridity and singular origins and commercial and political motivations are also entangled in the formal as well as imaginative politics of belonging in Ireland and Northern Ireland. The constitutional amendment that emphasized diasporic attachments reflected Mary Robinson's view of the potential of using ideas of diasporic plurality to foster more constructive and conciliatory understandings of identity and belonging in Northern Ireland. It also enshrined a contested shift in the southern state's cultural self-definition. This expansive version of ethnic affinities enshrined by the 1998 constitutional amendment, which affirmed the special affinities between those in Ireland and those of Irish descent worldwide, imaginatively extended collective belonging beyond the island and at the same time affirmed birthright citizenship for the entire island. However, six years later the rights of belonging were formally curtailed. In 2004 the Constitution was again amended in ways that suggested how the valorization of shared ancestry can have much more exclusive effects. From 1921, rights to citizenship in Ireland were based on birth. The 2004 amendment, proposed and endorsed by a referendum in the context of a moral panic about immigration, removed the right to Irish citizenship of those born in Ireland of noncitizen parents. The rights to citizenship via descent for overseas residents with the appropriate and documented genealogical connections now outweighs the rights to citizenship of those born in Ireland to non-Irish parents.

At the same time, tourist board invitations to visit Ireland to explore Irish ancestry and the new rhetoric of diasporic reunion are directed at those whose interests in doing so are also shaped by different national versions of ethnic particularity and multicultural diversity. The genealogical interest in Irish ancestors among Americans today thus needs to be considered in relation to the intersections of new versions of diasporic Irishness, the meaning of Irish ancestry within the ethnic and racial politics of the United States, and new arguments and anxieties about immigrant belonging in Ireland. These intersections cannot be reduced to simply unilinear flows of influence—tourism campaigns and political pronouncements encouraging interests in Irish ancestry overseas, or popular Irish-American Irishness suggesting diasporic collective community. Instead they involve complex entanglements of different versions of Irishness and different versions of the nation and the people, American and Irish. In genealogy, these public discourses of collective identity also always intersect with private and personal family histories. How do the people who are imagined as part of the global diaspora actually explore, express, and experience the significance of Irish ancestry and its relationship to familial, national, and ethnic identities? The next chapter travels to Ireland with genealogical visitors researching genealogical roots, locating emigrant ancestors' homes and meeting relatives. Here I begin to trace these distinctive as well as mutually informing geographies of identity and belonging by considering the models of collective diasporic and distinctive ethnic identities that feature in the discourse of the Irish diaspora within American multiculturalism and in the accounts of those exploring their Irish ancestral connections through popular genealogy.

Ireland, Postnational, Diasporic

The constitutional statement that the Irish nation "cherishes its special affinity with people of Irish ancestry living abroad" directly echoed Mary Robinson's speech "Cherishing the Irish Diaspora" to the Oireachtas, the Irish Parliament, in 1995 in which she argued that the

> men and women of our diaspora represent not simply a series of departures and losses. They remain, even while absent, a precious reflection of our own growth and change, a precious reminder of the many strands of identity which compose our story. . . . They know the names of our townlands and villages. They remember our landscape or have heard of it. They look to us anxiously to include them in our own sense of ourselves and not to forget their contribution while we make our own.[6]

This argument for including the descendants of Irish emigrants "in our own sense of ourselves" and for remembering "their contribution" challenged the ways in which Irish emigrants have been marginalized from understandings of Irish culture and nationhood, even if the image of emigration as forced exile has been central to Irish nationalism.

The term *diaspora* is now used widely to describe a range of migrant groups dispersed from original homelands but maintaining shared senses of connection to the place of origin. Yet, in many scholarly accounts as well as in popular understandings, the term as a description of Irish migration applies a narrower and earlier meaning of diaspora as the product of forced exile, as it has been used to describe Jewish, African, Armenian, and Palestinian diasporas. This is a legacy of nationalist interpretations of emigration as product of colonial injustice. According to nationalist histories produced within Ireland and within Irish diasporic nationalism in the United States, mass emigration from Ireland in the nineteenth century was the product of colonial misrule or deliberate malevolence. The accounts of emigration that dominate Irish diasporic nationalism of are families torn apart by the effects of colonial oppression. The emotional wrench of emigration memorialized in diasporic culture is the result of the cruel colonial disregard for the deep and natural bonds of kinship and to the land itself. Famine and post-Famine emigration was perceived then and since as banishment, exile, and symbol of the suffering inflicted by English colonialism.[7] The death of one million in the Famine, the suffering of those who survived, and the pain of leaving for the two million that emigrated during and after the Famine is interpreted as the product of callous, colonial disregard or, in some accounts, genocidal intent and is central to this understanding of the Irish diaspora in terms of trauma, injustice, and exile.[8] This interpretation is reflected in the inclusion of the Irish Famine alongside the Jewish Holocaust as an example of genocide in the curriculum of some American schools, the legal campaign of Irish Famine/Genocide Committee to bring the British government to court for its responsibility for this genocide, and the histories that appear on many Irish-American Web sites.[9] The scale and significance of mid-nineteenth-century mortality and migration is indisputable, yet the emphasis on the Famine in diasporic Irish nationalism neglects the longer histories and more complex regional historical geographies of emigration. Questioning the interpretation of the Famine as the product of English racism or as a project of colonial genocide, or pointing to the limits of an exclusive focus on the Famine in the history of Irish emigration, can be read as a monstrous desecration of the memory of the million that died from hunger and disease and the millions who emigrated.

In contrast, recent explorations of the Famine by historians and others in Ireland have produced more complex accounts of its social, political, and economic context and its different historical geographies without diminishing or eliding the suffering of the Famine nor the failure of British governmental policy to alleviate suffering.[10] Questions of class, which have often been neglected in strongly colonialist explanations, are central to recent reconsiderations of the Famine. The "English" landlords demonized for driving tenants off their rented small-holdings, for example, may have seen the Famine as an economic opportunity to rationalize their estates, but their actions were shaped more by the class-based disregard for laboring classes than by "anti-Irish racism." Even if the pattern of landownership in nineteenth-century Ireland was fundamentally shaped by co-lonialism, to call the majority of landlords "English" or even "Anglo-Irish" can only be valid if Irishness is defined as pure and undefiled descent from a pure precolonial Gaelic Irish population.

This narrative of colonial oppression is itself the legacy of a more compli-cated history of nation, class, and modernity. Kerby Miller has argued that those who benefited from mass lower-class post-Famine emigration between the mid 1850s and 1930, the new rural middle class, laid the blame for emigration on "the political and economic consequences of "British misgovernment," "Protestant ascendancy," and "landlord tyranny.""[11] They blamed colonialism for emigration rather than acknowledge the effects of their resistance to any economic redis-tribution or restructuring that would have alleviated the economic imperative to emigrate for those surplus to modernizing agrarian capitalism. For those more precariously positioned in the rural class structure of nineteenth-century Ireland, emigration was a pragmatic family strategy of survival, even if the costs were sometimes painfully born by those who left and those who felt their loss. In the context of capitalist agrarian modernization, emigration persisted because having more children than could be married into farms or find work in Ireland but who could emigrate and send home money became an economic strategy of household survival. As historian David Fitzpatrick writes, "Children, in short, were 'reared for emigration.'"[12] If only one son could inherit the farm and only one daughter marry with a dowry, the rest could either stay and suffer unmarried dependency or emigrate. Emigration was a family business within the shifting class structure of post-Famine Ireland and inseparable from the Catholic familial policing of sex and succession in postindependence Ireland.[13] Emigration may not have been any less painful for those leaving, but these accounts of pragmatic economic strate-gies within an inequitable class system disrupt the idea of Irish emigrants as pas-sive, fatalistic victims of external agents of change.[14]

The popularization of the language of the Irish diaspora by the state and within public culture in Ireland was closely associated with the commemorations of the 150th anniversary of the Famine in the mid-1990s. So in one sense the emphasis on the diaspora could be understood as a commemoration of a particular strand of Irish emigrant experience and an endorsement of a collective global identity forged through shared experience of colonial injustice, poor Catholic Famine migration, forced exile, and antipathy to British colonial power. The symbolic candle that Mary Robinson lit in the window of her presidential home, Áras an Uachtaráin, radiated a traditional domestic welcome to the diaspora and burned as a long overdue commemoration of emigrant experience. Yet the most complex elaborations of the diaspora not only sought to redress the place of Irish emigrants in the national imaginary but also challenged the customary understandings of Irish migration and the geographies of identity in both domestic and diasporic nationalism. In the political and cultural imaginaries of the new Catholic middle class of post-Famine Ireland, emigrants suffered the fate of exile forced upon them by the inequities of colonialism rather than class. But once removed from the homeland, they were deemed to be culturally corrupted and potentially corrupting on return. The location of true and authentic Irishness could only be in rural, agricultural Ireland even if this definition excluded not only Irish emigrants worldwide but urban life and industrial livelihoods within Ireland and, after 1920, Northern Ireland. The new attention to the diaspora in Irish public culture in the 1990s was, in part at least, a commemoration of emigrant experiences. But for Mary Robinson and philosopher and cultural commentator Richard Kearney, reconsidering the Irish diaspora also involved critical reappraisals of this imaginative geography of national belonging, cultural purity, and corruption; of the constitutive role of migration—immigration as well as emigration—in Irish history, culture, and politics; and of accounts of the diaspora as an undifferentiated transnational community. Commemorating the Irish diaspora meant challenging both diasporic and national imaginaries of collective identity.

Refiguring the relationships between geography and identity is central to Richard Kearney's postnationalist challenge to the nation-state model of cultural identity. Echoing Paul Gilroy's conceptualization of a diasporic consciousness, Kearney proposed an understanding of collective identity that is not confined to those who reside within a nation-state. Irishness can be extraterritorial; the nation can be thought of as an "extended family." If, he argues, "over seventy million people in the world today claim to be of Irish descent, it is evident that this definition of nationality, or at least of national genealogy, extends far beyond the borders of a state or territory."[15] This genealogy of an extended "national" family undermines an imaginative geography in which single ethnic groups occupy spatially discrete nations. But senses of identity and belonging can not only escape the confining boundaries of state borders; they can also be multiply scaled: "When one speaks of the 'Irish community' today," Kearney argued, "one refers not merely to the inhabitants of a state, but to an international group of expatriates and a sub-national network of regional communities. This triple-layered identity means that Irishness is no longer co-terminous with the geographical outlines of an island."[16] This is a version of identity that is attuned to the ways people combine different senses of location, home, and belonging that do not conform to the ideal of native belonging nor the teleology of original homeland and assimilation following migration.

The new discourse of an Irish diaspora thus not only challenged the ways that those who left Ireland had been deemed to be external to the Irish nation. In this argument, the varied expression of Irish ethnic identities worldwide upsets a nationalist imagination in which culture, ancestry, and residence must coincide. It undermines territorially defined notions of Irishness, which locate true Irishness in Ireland and so challenges the opposition between "authentic" Irishness in Ireland and the quaint but anachronistic versions of Irishness elsewhere.[17] As Ireland has been reframed by ideas of global mobility and modernity, this contrast between Irishness in Ireland and elsewhere now includes a contrast between its new, self-conscious and heavily ironized forms in Ireland and what it deemed to be the outdated traditionalism of diasporic versions. But if this discourse of the diaspora disrupted this counterposing of the authentic and inauthentic or, more recently, the modern and outmoded across the geography of home and emigrant locations, it did so by replacing the idea of a transhistorical essence of Irishness traveling globally with Irish migrants and passed on through generations, with an idea of plural versions of Irishness. The Irish diaspora for Robinson and for Kearney represented a global community sharing a sense of attachment to Ireland through ancestry, as Irish-American or Australian-Irish for example, but differing in the ways these attachments are expressed and configured in relation to other categories of identity.

Conceptualizing the diaspora through both collective connections and difference is central to this elaboration of its meaning. Yet the emphasis in many popular accounts of the Irish diaspora can fall much more heavily on unanimity rather than plurality. The image of a global extended family bound together by the bonds of ancestry can imply a single, timeless, and essentialized Irishness that is transmitted regardless of context down lines of Irish descent. In contrast, as Kevin Kenny has argued, the most productive approach to conceptualizing and researching the Irish diaspora is one that is equally attentive to the interconnections between Ireland and the places of Irish migration through which senses of collective identity and interest were practiced and the distinctive histories of Irish migrant communities across the geographies of settlement in Australia, New Zealand, Britain, Canada, and the United States.[18] Not only were the ethnic identities of Irish migrants shaped by the specific configurations of ethnicity, race, and nation in these different contexts, but the very idea of a distinctive Irish national identity was sometimes the product of emigration. In the United States, the development of an Irish ethnic identity that overrode the predominantly regional identities of nineteenth-century migrants was a product of the emigrant experience and sometimes an accommodation to, or condition of, assimilation in America as Irish American.[19] This focus on the interconnected and specific geographies of the diaspora challenges those approaches that, as Kenny argues, "sometimes appear to posit a 'transnational nation'—a single, globally dispersed culture exhibiting common features wherever it took root, by virtue of a presupposed common peoplehood."[20] Recent studies have explored the diverse historical geographies of Irish emigration, the cultural and social histories of Irish migrant groups where they settled, and the complex location of Irish emigrants as colonial subjects in Ireland and as participants in British colonial and wider European settlement in the New World.[21]

This attention to the diverse geographies of Irish migration and the experience of Irish emigrants and their descendants is ideally joined to attentiveness to the social differences of class and gender. The work of Breda Gray, Mary Hickman, and Bronwen Walter has been especially important in addressing the neglected social histories of Irish women's migration and the ways in they have been positioned and have positioned themselves in relation to the gendered associations of mobility, home, and the reproduction of Irishness.[22] While the idea of the Irish diaspora may prompt alternative understandings of identity and culture in Ireland as well as in the diverse contexts in which Irishness is practiced, Mary Hickman argues for combining this attention to questions of culture and identity with a thoroughly materialist analysis. This is an analytical framework that addresses the structural shaping of migration through state regulation and economic policy, institutional and legal frameworks, and processes of inclusion and exclusion in the contexts of migrant origin and places of destination.[23]

Rethinking the history of Irish migration and attending to the diversity of Irish diasporic identities is also a matter of addressing the question of religion. For the idea of a primordial Irishness gone global through forced migration is often also confessional. The diaspora as popularly perceived is often imagined as an exclusively Catholic diaspora that is solely the product of Catholic post-Famine migration. Histories of the Irish diaspora in Ireland and the United States are dominated by the popular image of a global Catholic community descended from poor Famine emigrants escaping hunger and colonial oppression. Collapsing longer histories of emigration, the regional differences in migration and the social as well as religious background of immigrants from Ireland into the classic image of poor hungry Catholic Famine migrants from the western seaboard neglects the complexity of Irish emigration.[24] As Donald Harman Akenson has forcefully argued, the failure to acknowledge the migration of significant numbers of Irish Protestants, both Presbyterians and those adhering to the Church of Ireland, to the United States and Canada before and after the Famine, that is reflected in the dominance of Protestant religious identification of most of those in the United States identifying as of Irish descent, is a form of historical denial.[25] It excludes non-Catholic Irish people from the history of Irish emigration and their descendants from the contemporary diaspora. The result is that Irishness, even refigured as diasporic and culturally plural, is implicitly coupled again with religious affiliation.

Until very recently this has been the case. As historian Alan O'Day argues, the experiences and identities of Protestants of various denominations "have largely been squeezed out of histories of the diaspora."[26] The ethnic designation "Scotch-Irish" was adopted by descendants of earlier Protestant migrants to differentiate themselves from the poor Catholic migrants of the later nineteenth century.[27] It was also a response to the increasing coupling of Catholicism with Irish nationalism in Ireland over the first half of that century.[28] In turn, the neglect or purposeful exclusion in accounts of Irish emigration of histories of eighteenth-century migration from Ulster, as well as Protestant migration from other parts of Ireland before and after the Famine, suggests that the experience and presence of Protestants in Ireland can only be understood in relation to the history of colonization and is of marginal significance in relation to the story of the national Catholic community. This image of a Catholic diaspora produces a mirror image of Irishness in Ireland as fundamentally Catholic, implying that Protestants today are, at best, a tolerated exception from the island's majority national community of descent. Defining the diaspora not only as Catholic in complexion but as the result of colonial injustice further alienates those—Protestants of all backgrounds, North and South—who are positioned by nationalist histories on the side of the colonial oppressors. Recent popular and academic accounts of the histories of emigration from Ireland and from Ulster that challenge this image of the Catholic diaspora are enmeshed in the politics of belonging, identity, and culture in Ireland and Northern Ireland. The Ulster American Folk Park, near Omagh in County Tyrone, for example, was established to represent the Ulster homes and migrant experience of Presbyterians who left Ulster for the United States. In doing so, it presents one overlooked strand of the complexity of Irish migration, but it has been criticized for producing a covertly confessional and progressive narrative of emigration that does a historical disservice to the suffering of Catholic Famine migrants.[29]

These efforts to reconsider the diverse historical and contemporary geographies of Irish diasporic experience, identity, and cultures were also attempts to reconsider definitions of Irishness at "home." In the most developed accounts of the diaspora, its cultural pluralism was presented as evidence for the diversity that can be encompassed within a cultural category like Irishness in Ireland and Northern Ireland. The recognition of the production and performance of different and hybrid versions of Irishness worldwide, Robinson argued, suggested that Irishness in Ireland could be understood as dynamic, plural, and hybrid. If Irishness can be differently performed in diverse diasporic locations, Irishness in Ireland too could be imagined as a more open and plural category. The diaspora, for Robinson and for Kearney, offered ways of seeing collective identities as plural as well as shared, for understanding overlapping scales of identification—local, regional, national, transnational—of exploring the complexities of attachments that adhere to places but never simply to a singular point of origin, and for understanding identities and cultures as dynamic and fluid rather than static and fixed. This diasporic version of Irishness could undo an exclusionary ideal of national cultural purity. It also had practical political potential. For Kearney, understanding identity in terms of regional identification, membership of a state, and sense of connection with an international Irish community offered possibilities for new political arrangements for Northern Ireland. The nation-state as conventionally conceived can only include cultural difference in minimalist terms. Alternative modes of governance based on decentralized power, shared sovereignty, and membership in a larger federal collective could, he argued, accommodate the positions of both nationalists and unionists, since both groups could feel included in their respective cultural communities, one spanning the border and one spanning the Irish Sea.

This emphasis on interconnections across the customary borders of the nation-state as ideally envisaged reflects Kearney's broader perspective on the complexities of Irish migration. The idea on a globally extended family was part of his wider emphasis on the cultural connections shaped by the long histories of migration to and from the island. For Kearney, migration is central to understanding Irish history and culture but not in the sense of traditional narratives of colonial invasion and national exile. Instead, Ireland can be imagined not as an ideally isolated island, violated by colonialism, but in terms of the continuous contacts and exchanges that characterize a dynamic maritime culture. Ireland, he argues, can be reimagined as a "migrant nation." These long historical geographies of interconnection between Ireland, Britain, continental Europe, North America, and further afield, shaped by the migration of people, ideas, and material cultures, exceed in their range and complexity the traditional historical narrative of island isolation and colonial incursions. Kearney's metaphor of the "migrant nation" foregrounds the cultural, social, familial, and commercial relationships between two adjacent islands that have both been shaped by colonialism but that go beyond the ability of a rigid model of colonizer-colonized to describe them. Irish culture, he suggests, has always been shaped through the specific nature and confluences of these flows. "What does it mean to be Irish?" he asks:

> Is it some unique "essence" inherited from our ancestors? Is it a characteristic of a specific language (eg, Gaelic) or religion (Catholic/Protestant) or ideology (nationalist/unionist)? Is it a matter of ethnic memory, genetic heritage or geographical residence? One thing is certain: the question of what it means to be Irish—who we are and where we are going to—cannot be limited to the frontiers of our island. The affirmation of a dynamic cultural identity invariably involved an exploratory dialogue with *other* cultures.[30]

Ireland is refigured here as a node in mobile cultural flows rather than site of cultural purity and authenticity threatened by external forces and in need of protection. This focus on long histories of cultural exchange works against a temporality that portrays Ireland as a place of untroubled, stable social and cultural unanimity before the advent of the global, diasporic (post)modernity. It counters accounts of Ireland's novel multiculturalism as the product of recent immigration, which seem to reinforce rather than problematize the idea of a prior cultural and social homogeneity.[31]

Yet while the turn to the idea of the diaspora reflected new approaches to questions of the nation's cultural composition, it was also a response to questions of Ireland's new place in the global economy. This mobilization of the idea of a global Irish diaspora was one reaction to the transformations in Irish society that resulted from the rapid economic growth of the 1990s. Breda Gray has explored the ways in which the cultural character of the nation was articulated through different versions of home and mobility, tradition and modernity, the local, national, and global, in critical as well as celebratory reactions to the new modern and affluent Ireland. The ideas of migrant mobility and global interconnection evoked by the media and politicians in some versions of the Irish diaspora, she argues, furnish an idiom of mobility and hybridity that help refigure Ireland as flexible space for neoliberal economics and global capital.[32] The orthodox narrative of Irish modernization is of a process of leaving behind an agricultural economy, protectionist and isolationist economic policies, and a reactionary, nationalist past, beginning in the late 1950s with new policies to attract inward investment and educate for a new electronic information economy, which, with help from European Union subsidy, bore fruit in the 1990s.[33] In their recent engagement with the origins and implications of this account of an Irish economic and cultural journey to modernity, Peader Kirby, Luke Gibbons, and Michael Cronin argue that this story of Ireland's transformation into a booming economy and liberal polity naturalizes a specific model of Ireland's modernization into a neoliberal economy situated within global capitalism. A new global Irishness, defined through its distance from old images of rurality and tradition, becomes the marker of a new confident, liberated, and progressive society, but this account of Ireland as globalized, dynamic, mobile, and modern elides its costs in increasing disparities of wealth, retrenchment of the welfare state, and the erosion of social solidarity and effective democracy by a new "individualist, competitive, acquisitive culture."[34] "A cultural discourse prioritising individualism, entrepreneurship, mobility, flexibility, innovation, competitiveness," they argue, "displace[s] earlier discourses prioritising national development, national identity, family, self-sufficiency and nationalism."[35]

Critics argue that this new discourse of globalized nationhood and national mobility naturalizes neoliberalism. It produces a new ideal of citizenship defined through "flexible relationships to the labour market, flows of capital and internal labour flows"[36] and new patterns of marginalization and disadvantage both for those unable or unwilling to participate in new forms of flexible labor or those whose mobilities do not match the image of a highly skilled and highly rewarded migration.[37] The recent interpretation of the migration patterns of well-qualified young Irish people as evidence of a new dynamic Irish modernity, Jim Mac Laughlin argues, replaces the earlier nationalist model of emigration as political exile and product of colonial injustice, but it similarly displaces questions of structural inequality.[38] Different versions of a diasporic, global Ireland shaped by immigration in the past and mobility in the present thus have different political implications both for the ways identity and difference are imagined within and between Northern Ireland and Ireland, and in relation to patterns of impoverishment and privilege under neoliberal economic development. So while the ideal of a single place of ancestral origin, and all the authenticity and security that implies, is promoted to increase revenue from genealogical tourism, ideas of dynamic mobility are used to encourage other sorts of inward investment and labor flexibility. The image of the global collective encourages identifications with the "old country." But the nature of "New Ireland"—urban, secular, high tech, globalized, and consumerist—tests the traditional image of Ireland as a refuge from the alienation of modernity that has made Irish ancestry so appealing.

The images of migrant mobility and diasporic cultural identities enlisted in these different, overlapping, and sometimes contradictory political and economic projects to redefine Ireland and Irishness in Ireland also have implications beyond Ireland. Those exploring their ancestral connections to the "old country" do so in relation to the particular configurations of race, ethnicity, nationhood, and multiculturalism in the countries that were the historical destinations for Irish emigrants, and they do so as the cultural, ethnic, and, implicitly, racial definitions of belonging in Ireland are the subject of heated debates in response to new patterns of immigration. It is to these genealogical definitions and reconsiderations of ethnicity and Irish origins in the United States, and the intersections of these private and public projects in both places, that I now turn.

Irish Origins and Ethnic Options

It is frequently stated that 40 million people in the United States are of Irish descent. The origins of this number lie not only in the history of Irish migration to the United States and the subsequent demographic histories of Irish migrants. This statistic is also a product of a particular way of thinking about and counting ethnicity. It reflects an ordinary, usually unremarkable and common understanding that ancestry matters as a meaningful, legitimate, valuable, natural source of personal and collective identity: "Without my ancestors I would not be here today. It makes me who I am." This idea of the fundamental significance of the patterns of sex and birth that led to the fact of personal existence, and of the cultural traditions, values, or attitudes passed on in families, is strongly linked to the similarly routine idea that everyone has an ethnicity and that this ethnic identity is derived from ancestral ethnic origins. This is central to American multiculturalism. As Reginald Byron has argued, the counting of ethnic identity in the United States census, from which that figure of 40 million American people of Irish ancestry is derived, reflects a profound shift over the twentieth century in the ways in which American society has come to understand itself and a particular model of ethnicity that is the product of this transformation.[39]

This shift from an ideal of assimilation, in which migrant groups discarded their attachments to their countries of origin and the traditions they brought with them in the process of becoming American, to the model of multicultural pluralism stems both from the challenge of the black civil rights movement and from reactions to African-American demands for political justice and cultural recognition. Persistent discrimination on ethnic and racial grounds highlighted by the civil rights movement severely undermined the ideal of the culturally neutral liberal nation-state and its assimilationist political philosophy.[40] The "ethnic revival" of the 1960s in the United States also exerted a profound challenge to the model of national assimilation, but it was at least in part a response to black political militancy. The reassertion of ethnic identities by working-class and lower-middle-class Americans whose families had migrated to the United States from southern and Central Europe earlier in the twentieth century, and whose sense of economic vulnerability and marginality informed their antagonism to affirmative action for African Americans, challenged what was seen as a selective cultural recognition.[41] Though the wide popularity of ethnic distinctiveness is now distant from the particular politics of race and class from which it arose, as Desmond King has argued, "Even if these revived ethnic loyalties are principally symbolic, this possibility does not necessarily render them politically trivial either for those holding them or for others in American society observing them from an excluded position."[42] While ethnic and racial categories continue to affect the treatment and experiences of many who fall outside white European America, the idea of ethnic distinctiveness has been taken up by middle-class Americans for whom ethnicity is personally meaningful but of little or no consequence in terms of their political rights or opportunities. Mary Waters has argued that for Americans with European ancestry, ethnicity is a significant but voluntary aspect of personal identity that provides a sense of distinctiveness and collective identity without compromising ideals of choice and freedom.[43]

The inclusion of questions on ethnicity in the U.S. census thus reflects both the multiculturalist strategy to record and address patterns of ethnic or racial disadvantage and the significance accorded to ethnic identities more widely. Yet the census only measures a particular model of ethnicity. The results of the 1990 census describe ancestry in terms of three categories: "single ancestry," "first mixed ancestry-component," and "second mixed ancestry-component." Thus, although it allows for a self-definition as of mixed ancestry, it can only record two dimensions of the mix and so is unable to record the complex ancestries of most people descended from mid-nineteenth-century migrants. As Reginald Byron has argued, the calculation from census returns that 40 million Americans descend from Irish immigrants is based on ignoring their other ethnic ancestries. As he points out, "A minimum of 74 per cent of those of Irish ancestry across the United States were of *mixed* Irish ancestry in 1989, at least 74 per cent of these same 40 million persons, were simultaneously something else: German-American, English-American, French-American, Italian-American, and so on, in addition to being Irish-American. Any such individual, depending on his or her ancestral mixture, could be a number of these things at the same time." Thus, he warns, 40 million Irish Americans should not "be confused with whole persons who form a neatly bounded group; rather they were, at least 74 per cent of the time, fractional identities of widely varying degree, components of the ancestries of persons having mixed, complex pedigrees of national origin."[44]

Furthermore, as Byron makes clear, those who identify themselves today as descended from mid-nineteenth-century post-Famine Irish immigrants are on average five generations removed from the ancestor or ancestors who came to America between 1847 and 1854. Despite common assumptions of the predominance of marriage between Irish migrants, intermarriage with other ethnic groups was common from the second generation onwards. Those with Irish ancestry are thus just as likely to also have English, Scottish, German, Italian, Polish, or French Canadian ancestors. This likelihood grows with each generation. According to a strictly arithmetic account of ancestry, Byron notes, "while the numbers of people descended from the Famine immigrants increase—in theory geometrically, one Famine immigrant giving rise to two children, each producing two grandchildren, these four producing eight great-grand-children, sixteen great-great-grandchildren, and so on—the proportion of their ancestral inheritance derived from this one original Famine immigrant decreases over the generations in inverse ratio, to a half, a quarter, an eight, a sixteenth, and a thirty-second by the sixth generation." Furthermore, "this is complicated by the random generational mixing as people have married the descendants of immigrants who arrived in America either before the Famine, or decades later." In purely numerical terms, "a member of the third generation who has one grandparent who emigrated between 1847 and 1854 is 25 per cent a child of the Famine; but a member of the sixth generation who has but one single great-great-great-grandparent who emigrated to the United States between 1847 and 1845 is 31/32—or 96.875 per cent—not a child of the Famine."[45] This reckoning of ethnic fractions corresponds to the common way in which people describe their ancestry—in halves, quarters, eighths, and smaller fractions—but at the same time it reveals the degree of selectiveness that this often entails both in the everyday accounts of ethnic origins and in official records of ethnic diversity. Since ethnic identities are themselves more complex than numerical calculations of ancestry suggest, this is not surprising. Yet its effects in producing a collective category of descent deserves consideration.

The masking of mixed ancestry and complex ethnic identifications that occurs in generating the figure of 40 million Americans of Irish descent applies also to that other oft-cited figure—the 70 million people of Irish descent worldwide. Thus while the idea of the Irish diaspora has been used in Ireland to emphasize cultural complexity and hybrid identities, it can also suggest a model of a single ethnic identification. The figure of 70 million people of Irish descent worldwide seems to conjure up an uncomplicated notion of pure descent in the generations that followed migration, or, alternatively, that all other ethnicities in a postmigration family tree are overridden, ignored, or subsumed within the Irish line. Identity, it seems, is a matter of naturally and simply being Irish and Irish alone if an ancestor came from Ireland. This question of the basis and persistence of Irishness as an ethnic category after emigration is central to historical research on the diaspora in all its geographical variety. It is fundamental to the whole concept of the Irish diaspora. In his primer on the Irish diaspora, Donald Harman Akenson admits that the hardest definitional task in discussing the Irish diaspora is pinning down the term "Irish." His solution is that a "person is part of the Irish ethnic group—whether he or she is of the first generation or the fifth or anything in between—as long as his or her primary sense of ethnic identity is Irish."[46] This practical definition avoids ideas of ethnic purity or degrees of Irishness according to descent, but at the same time, it does not allow for more complex senses of mixed ethnic origins. Identity is defined through giving primacy to one ethnicity. Irish ethnicity is thus simultaneously inclusive and limited. Allowing for multiple senses of identification or interethnic ancestry would clearly complicate the figures for the numbers of descendants of Irish emigrants in the United States and in the world.

Thus the easy invocation of the diaspora in terms of numbers of people of Irish descent can promote notions of a simple, single, and enduring ethnic identity that the concept of diaspora, at least in its most critically theorized versions, is meant to dispel. Though the model of the Irish diaspora has been used to emphasize a global community composed of different versions of Irishness, as identification with Ireland intersects with other identifications (as an American, as Australian, and so on), the emphasis on Irish roots can result in other sources of identity via ancestry being overlooked, ignored, or dismissed as insignificant. Having Irish ancestry, even in an ethnically mixed family tree, simply means being of Irish descent alone.

For some people, at least, this is the case. Reginald Byron's empirical study of the attitudes, knowledges, and practices of those who identify themselves as of Irish ancestry in the city of Albany, New Jersey, demonstrates that this identification with Ireland is seldom accompanied by much knowledge of who their Irish ancestors were, where in Ireland they came from, or of the circumstances of their departure. Many people in United States who identify with Ireland through descent from Irish immigrants, he shows, know very little and sometimes nothing about their genealogy. Therefore concentrating, as I do here, on those who have been moved to actively address this lack of knowledge or have redressed this lack of knowledge through years of genealogical research means considering a particular subset of those who are taken to constitute the "Irish-American community" as part of the Irish diaspora. They also constitute a particular strand of the wider growth of genealogy as a hobby. How then do their specific interests in Irish ancestry relate to the wider culture of popular genealogy and the valorization of ethnic particularity upon which it rests? What do their varied approaches to the nature and meaning of ancestry, ethnicity, and inheritance demonstrate about diasporic Irishness in practice? How does the particular empirical ethos of genealogy shape their decisions about ethnic options and identifications? What are the implications of their personal genealogical explorations of their location within the categories of race, nation, and ethnicity and in relation to ideas of "native" belonging and "settler" status in Ireland and in the United States?

Addressing these questions involves attending to the diverse nature of this group as well as the commonalities of attitudes and experiences. For those who are doing their family trees and tracing their genealogy back to Irish immigrant ancestors and back to Ireland do not constitute a homogenous collective. Most of those who take up the hobby of finding Irish roots do not do so as members of Irish neighborhoods in the classically Irish cities of Chicago, Boston, Philadelphia, and New York. The "Irish-American community" has a symbolic existence but is largely imagined rather than reflected in the inner-city ethnic enclaves that figure in popular and academic accounts of Irish America.[47] It stands for an ideal of a close-knit ethnic community within the broader society, but those who celebrate it are largely geographically dispersed in suburban homes across America. Many, but not all, are middle aged and older and therefore able to give time to visiting libraries and record offices and online research. But they differ in the length of time they have been interested in genealogy and actively pursuing their research and in the extent to which their genealogical interests extend to wider reading on the history of Ireland or the ethnic and social history of the United States. Undertaking genealogy is not necessarily a reliable index of investment in ethnicity since it can be both an intense expression and enactment of ethnicity and a pleasurable but emotionally detached numerical exercise. This range of approaches, from the concentration on names and vital genealogical statistics to advanced self-education in Irish and American history, is often cross-cut by different attitudes to those contentious questions of the authenticity and inauthenticity of different versions of Irishness and equally contentious issues of cause and culpability that surround the Famine.

The historical and genealogical place and number of Irish emigrant ancestors in the family histories of those tracing Irish ancestry obviously differ. However, most of those with interests in Irish ancestry are several generations removed from the ancestor or ancestors who left Ireland. Very few have family trees that only contain people who also descend from Irish emigrants. In family histories, which are seldom characterized by marriage within only one ethnic group, and in a genealogical tradition, which now includes maternal and paternal descent, doing genealogy involves choices about which line or lines to follow and which ancestors matter. In every step of the process, choices continually arise about whose line to research or at least to start on first—the mother's line or the father's, the maternal or paternal grandmother or maternal or paternal grandfather—and so on backwards in time. Family trees can endlessly bifurcate. As in genealogy in general, some concentrate on one line; some work simultaneously on several; many focus on one branch or another for a while and then shift focus as interests wax and wane, or with the discovery of new sources or new contacts. In diasporic genealogies that are shaped to varying degrees by identification with the places, culture, and people that count as ancestral homes, the questions of the value and significance of some lines over others that arise in the doing of genealogy involve ethnic choices, imaginative identifications, and cultural politics.

For some, the decision to concentrate on an Irish connection over others is made self-consciously. For others, the choice of identifying with Irish ancestry does not seem to be a choice but the dictate of their genes: the attributes and affinities that they recognize as Irish in themselves are a direct inheritance from their Irish ancestors. Irishness is in the blood, in the genes, is biological. This is a potent notion of embodied Irishness. Yet computing ethnicity via biology does not necessarily mean valuing all biological inheritance equally. Some of the strongest expressions of the profound personal significance of a genealogist's Irish roots might be followed immediately by a conventional description of ancestry via ethnic fractions and percentages that could, but often did not seem to, temper or qualify those statements of single ethnic affiliation. One respondent to my online invitation to describe the meaning and experience of researching Irish ancestry[48] described her identification with Ireland and Irish ancestry in this way: "We are talking about the blood and guts and the molecules that make up the human body. I feel and believe I am more Irish than anything. My father was ¾ Irish, ¼ Scotch/American Indian/German, I believe. My mother was 100% British (brother and sister born in UK the rest of the family in Canada)."[49] Another expressed the depth of identification with one side of the family: "My nationality is American . . . but my cultural identity is definitely Irish. . . . my father's family is 100% Irish, my mother's family is 100% Polish, but my identity is totally with Ireland. . . . [Ireland] is my true homeland. . . . Ireland is my heart, my hope, my heritage."[50]

Thus the meaning of Irish ancestry can sometimes be figured in terms of a biological inheritance—"Irishness is in my blood." Much of popular genealogy is shaped by the "genealogical model" in which individuals are the product of their ancestral inheritance.[51] At its most logical, this would imply that all sources of biological or genetic inheritance matter equally. But in practice, the choices of identification sometimes simply override this logic. A single strong and certain Irishness is an alternative to a convoluted mathematics of ethnic fractions. Accounts of the meaning of Irishness often combine descriptions of the cultural influences of particular family members or locality and the naturalness of why Irish ancestry matters—the choice that is not a choice. The social and the biological are often flexible criteria for defining who counts as a relative, and in diasporic genealogies, which ancestors matter.[52]

Foregrounding this issue of active identification with Irish ancestry in family trees, which in a country shaped by complex historical and contemporary geographies of immigration are very unlikely to be solely Irish, is not to suggest that those identifications are somehow inauthentic, invalid, or unsupportable. But it does convert forms of identification that are often deemed to be natural into social and cultural practices to be explored. Any attempt to explain why an Irish ethnic identity might be chosen from among a range, or over other possible choices, has to acknowledge the deeply intimate and personal nature of the attitudes and experiences that shape these choices: closeness to one parent or grandparent over another, the appeal of a family story, parents' own decisions—or indeed conflicts—over which part of the family history to downplay or emphasize, the familial, school, and community contexts that shape processes of identification, the significance of an Irish surname.

But these personal choices are also inescapably made within wider cultural, social, and political contexts and shaped by practical issues. The popularity of

Irishness as an ethnic identity partly lies in a set of positively valued cultural traits—warmth, energy, humor, gregariousness, generosity, independence, tenacity. Irish ancestry can have the value of working class, colonized, or more generally "underdog" associations, but it also suggests the credentials of connections via descent to the ancient noble families of precolonial Ireland. In late-twentieth-century popular and commodity cultures of the United States especially, Irishness has had a preeminent status as a marker of authenticity and of traditional social values "unsullied by consumerism and modernity."[53] The Celtic is shrouded in mysticism that for many is an otherworldly antidote to the alienation and rationality of modern life. This image of a people endowed with an ancient culture, descended from kings and noble clans, gifted with humor, warmth, and a talent for words in talk and writing, surviving oppression and making good through struggle and hard work in the land of the free is central to Irish-American diasporic imaginaries. But Irishness is also an accessible as well as an attractive cultural heritage. Genealogical records in English make tracing Irish ancestors so much easier than Polish or German. Since Ireland is an English-speaking country, genealogical visitors to Ireland can potentially enjoy all the interaction with "warm and welcoming" locals that is so much part of the mythology of the visit "home." Enthusiasts can enjoy the large and celebrated body of Irish writing in English. This attractiveness and accessibility undoubtedly shapes interests in Irish roots.

But the significance of being of Irish descent is not just a reflection of the relative ease of researching English-language records or its appealing associations; as some of those involved recognize, it also reflects both the cultural resonance of roots and origins and pride in a specifically American national origin story. The relatively recent recognition of the rights of indigenous groups, Native Americans in this case, are entangled in complex ways with a romantic imagination of a timeless relationship between place, nature, ancestry, identity, and culture unbroken by migration or modernity. This ideal of indigeneity is a largely implicit but significant influence on popular settler genealogies. Some of those exploring their Irish ancestral connections explained their interest in genealogy in terms of a model of belonging that locates "roots," and all that "roots" signify as formative and foundational, not in recent family history but in the distant past and distant places: "I think we as Americans want to feel a part of what was, before America was. We are a young country and our roots are elsewhere."[54] Others referred to the meaning of ethnic particularity in a "young" and culturally plural society: "It may be the fact that the United States is a relatively young country that makes us search for our past. We are so large and varied a country that there really is no National bond. Each of us has held on to the culture and heritage that our families passed down to us, be it Dutch, English, Swedish, German etc. There is a need to know that even though we are mortal our line will live on as it has in the past."[55]

Apprehensions of mortality and the desire to preserve a specific cultural inheritance are often joined to pride and respect for the struggle and achievements of immigrant ancestors. The sense of connection with ancestors that comes from researching their lives often also comes with a strong sense of the contrast between the conditions of their ancestors' lives and those of their descendants. For many, even the discovery of minimal information about the specific lives of these ancestors—hints of disease, infant mortality, poverty, and wider reading about the causes and conditions of Irish emigration—that accompanies their genealogical research leads to deep and profound respect for "the experiences they endured, the sacrifices they made and their determination and willingness to give up everything to start over to build a better life for themselves."[56] Immigrant ancestors personalize and embody wider histories of settlement, struggle, suffering, and survival in the New World. This pride in ancestors' achievements can also be pride in a history of American openness and opportunity. One respondent wrote that genealogy "gives me a new-found respect for America and the high regard the immigrants had for America as the 'land of opportunity.' I feel honored that my homeland afforded so many the opportunity to enjoy a better life and discover new opportunities and advantages they might not have the chance to discover in Ireland."[57] For many, the counterpoint to the United States as "land of opportunity" is Ireland as place of persecution and British colonial oppression. The struggles of Irish emigrant ancestors are often imagined in terms of the classical image of desperately poor migrants fleeing the Famine in the west of Ireland.

But the narrative of Irish historical experience as a onetime British colony also mirrors the founding story of the United States achieving independence from Britain, and accounts of Irish immigrant struggle and success stand too for wider family histories of immigrant hardship and hard work. The popularity of Irishness rests in part on the way the most positive associations of Irishness—religious commitment, family values, belief in hard work and education—coincide with wider mainstream American values. Reginald Byron suggests that the story of Irish immigration now stands for broader collective American identity. St Patrick's Day, he argues, celebrates a specific ethnic identity but in doing so commemorates a wider shared history of immigrant struggle, sacrifice, and success in climbing "the social and economic ladder out of the old urban immigrant neighborhoods to become part of the modern, suburban American Dream."[58] The parade thus stands for not just a "celebration of Irishness, but of Americanness." And the category "Irish American" thus stands for a broad collective-origins story of immigrant struggle and success.

A White Diaspora?

For some at least, Irishness is not simply a quintessentially American ethnicity but more specifically part of an emerging *white European* American identity. This emerging collective ethnic identity that encompasses diverse European ancestries is characterized, Richard Alba argues, by a shared sense of belonging to a history of European immigration, hard work, sacrifice, individual effort, upward social mobility, and nation building.[59] Despite the decline of social distinctions based upon origins in America's white ethnic hierarchy, the equalization of labor and educational opportunities for people of European ancestry, and their social integration, intermarriage, and detachment from conventional ethnic networks, neighborhoods, and organizations, ethnic identities continue to be significant among "European Americans." In one respect, this is a highly privatized ethnic identity, but it is also a socially useful one, as family histories serve as cultural capital among affluent and educated white Americans. Genealogy can be a way of tracing a personal family narrative within a dominant account of Euro-American history that can be mobilized in times of conflict over resources or in response to the political challenges of non-European groups to the distribution of wealth and recognition. The assertion of European ancestry as the basis for an American community of shared descent in turn shapes the ways recent immigrants from Asia, the Caribbean, and Central and South America to the United States "are being categorized, learning race and experiencing racism."[60] The contemporary celebration of ethnic distinctiveness among white Americans coincides with widespread hostility toward positive discrimination and alarm about immigration.

Respondents to my query about the reasons for a genealogical interest in Irish ancestry sometimes hinted at and sometimes made explicit their anxieties about the cultural composition of the United States or Canada. As one put it: "western European people are heading toward minority status in this country within the next couple decades. I'd like to leave a written record of my bit on western European ancestors."[61] One participant on a genealogical study tour explained that his genealogical work was a conscious form of resistance to the tenets of multiculturalism and linguistic diversity. Others saw their genealogy as a direct response to the unwelcome effects of immigration, voicing their hostility to the cultural strength of Spanish and to educational policies that stress diversity rather than assimilation into the Anglo-Celtic culture of the United States or, in this case, Canada: "The world is moving awfully fast. We are losing our identity. Canada is a melting pot of the peoples of the world. Because of our immigration laws we have huge numbers of new 'Canadians' every year. We learn about and celebrate one another's cultural heritage but it is not a part of who or what we are. . . . I want to know my own identity and that comes only from my forefathers."[62]

Irishness thus doubles as a marker of ethnic distinctiveness and as an emblem of a white European North American culture. The commemoration of Irish emigrant experience though genealogy can be part of a reactionary appeal to a white European heritage. For some people, at least, the value of their Irish roots is that they are white European roots; the turn to Irish roots is a reaction to fears of the erosion of a white European heritage. Thus when the economically pragmatic and politically well-intentioned invocation of the Irish diaspora and Irish roots travels from Ireland and meets discourses of race and ethnicity in the United States, for example, the focus on white ethnicities that can result is not always progressive.

Yet the now taken-for-granted and naturalized whiteness of Irishness follows a history of American immigration, class, and racial politics in which Irish emigrants to the United States struggled to achieve recognition as "white." The contemporary racial significance of Irish ancestry involves not only this particular history of race and class but a longer and tangled history of changing meanings of race itself and the changing ways in which Irish people have been located and have located themselves in categories of difference. The term "race" itself is not a static or straightforward in its meaning. The semantic slippages between "race," "culture," "language," "spirit," "ancestry," and "nation" in the history of the construction of ideas of difference between "the English" and "the Irish," or between "Irish" and "Anglo-Saxon" Americans still recur in scholarly as well as popular accounts of "the Irish."[63] Discussions of race and Irishness are frequently narrowly focused on nineteenth-century English representations of Irish people as simian and savage.[64] However, the construction of the categories of Celtic and Anglo-Saxon by nineteenth-century philologists and ethnologists also needs to be situated within wider nineteenth-century European efforts to scientifically establish racial groups and thus categorize human difference, and especially racial difference between European and non-European people.[65] Ideas of race, as both biological in their basis and cultural in their expression, served both colonial and Irish nationalist discourses of difference. Though some Irish nationalists of the late nineteenth and early twentieth centuries replaced the "effeminate" category of the Celtic with an overtly masculine version of a Gaelic "Irish race," they retained the notion of racial distinction.[66] Yet, as labor historians have argued, Irish immigrants to the United States in the mid–nineteenth century, whose whiteness was sharply in question, strove to join the English, and earlier "Scotch-Irish" migrants, as white.[67] In doing so, they both challenged anti-Celtic Anglo-Saxon supremacy and helped naturalize a model of white American citizenship. As historians Barrett and Roediger have shown, in competing for wage labor and seeking political citizenship, Irish-American men—for these were gendered arenas[68]—used their newly achieved whiteness to maintain a status above the "not-yet-white" southern and central European immigrants of the early twentieth century, and above Asian Americans, African Americans, and Native Americans, in the nation's racial hierarchy.[69] The contemporary associations of Irishness in the United States are similarly bound up with the politics of race, ethnicity, and immigration.

To some of those now tracing their Irish ancestors in late-twentieth-century North America, Ireland can appeal as a place far from the trouble of immigration and demanding "minorities." In response to my question about what social or cultural changes might shape interests in genealogy, one woman from Canada expressed her distress and annoyance at Canada's "such loose immigration laws" and immigrants "complaining about discrimination." She longed to go to Ireland and longed for "some of the old values to return to our society," for a time "when you could trust your neighbors and live in peace, and enjoy the simple things in life." Her comment that Irish and Scottish cultural traditions in North America "represent multiculturalism at its finest" suggest a pluralism within white limits.[70]

This is a multiculturalism confined to the old varieties of European settler ethnicity. One genealogical researcher from Boston visiting the National Library in Dublin talked to me at length about the significance of her Irish connections. She praised Native Americans for "holding on to their traditions" but was irritated by Spanish-speaking migrants for refusing to "assimilate" and speak English. She also adamantly refused to accept that school children who for her were simply black could describe their ethnic identities as Haitian or Jamaican. In this instance, arguments about the importance of indigenous people maintaining their cultural distinctiveness are appropriated to support the significance of Irish ancestry as a source of identity, but the celebration of ethnicity is limited to those with white European origins. Racist assumptions that blackness determines identity are used to suggest that specific black ethnic identifications are fanciful fictions. Thus some who enjoy the privileges of Irishness as whiteness and Irishness as cultural difference refuse to acknowledge the legitimacy of other self-definitions. The commemoration of the trauma of leaving Ireland and the celebration of ancestral emigrants as nation builders in the New World does not necessarily lead to an understanding of the experience of more recent migrants. Even when parallels are made between Irish migration to the United States in the past and contemporary immigration, the argument that recent immigrants are experiencing the same struggles as earlier waves of immigrants and, like them, will ultimately prosper can be used to suggest that support for contemporary minority groups is unnecessary.[71] Similarly, accounts of the racialization of Irish emigrants to the United States, and their ultimate success in resisting discrimination on racial grounds, can be interpreted as support for an argument that black and Asian Americans should also "get over" race.[72]

To what extent then is the Irish diaspora imagined as a white diaspora? Are there racialized limits to the hybridized identities that are encompassed with this global collective? This is in part a question of geography. The ancestral connections to Ireland being explored through genealogy in the United States link two places with particular histories and contemporary politics of race, ethnicity, and whiteness. It is a question that involves considering the relative newness of race as an explicit issue in Irish society in response to new patterns of immigration in contrast to a formerly unquestioned collective genealogy of Irish whiteness.[73] In the mid-1940s, a cartoon appeared in *Dublin Opinion*, a light, satirical monthly magazine, that demonstrated the implicit place of race in this national imagination of shared descent. This racial and national imaginary furnished the basis of a joke that poked fun at American enthusiasm for Irish roots in general but more specifically at what was presented as an implausible genealogical connection. The cartoon featured a black man in an American soldier's uniform sitting at the desk of an official in an office marked "Genealogical Research," who tells him, "I can't be sure about distant relatives, Mr. O'Malley, but I'm convinced that your branch of the family emigrated long ago—quite long ago.[74] The joke here is that the perplexed but polite official has to explain the obvious impossibility of relatedness across the bounded categories of race. But since the official admits the possibility of Irish ancestry "quite long ago," the joke is also that the combination of the soldier's skin and surname is the product of distant sexual miscegenation. This cartoon would not be published in late-twentieth- or early-twenty-first-century Ireland because of greater sensitivities about charges of racism and because recent migration to Ireland unsettles its racial logic of white Irishness, interracial sex and ancestry, and the assumed national community of readers equally sharing the joke. After centuries of emigration, Ireland became a country of net in-migration of both economic migrants and asylum seekers in the mid-1990s.

Yet the imagination of a collective national community defined by shared ancestry persists and has a complex relation to ideas of racial and cultural difference. As Ronit Lentin has argued, the reimagining of Irish society in response to modernization, recent economic prosperity, and the resulting new patterns of immigration needs to address questions of racism. But this means critically examining the idea of the national community as one of shared blood and belonging, the shared national genealogies that obliquely code for race, rather than view racism as the product of immigration.[75] The 2004 constitutional amendment that removed the citizenship right of children born in Ireland to noncitizen parents was passed in the context of a moral panic about immigration and, more particularly, about asylum-seeking women achieving rights to remain by supposedly deliberately arriving pregnant and giving birth in Ireland. As Eithne Luibhéid argues, just as some women are charged with the reproduction of the national population, other women's childbearing is figured as a threat to, or violation, of the nation.[76] New difficulties in recognizing the Irishness of black and "mixed race" people in Ireland make the taken-for-granted whiteness of Irishness explicit.[77] At the same time, the logic of figuring the Irish diaspora as white because of its European

The Genealogical Office

an amusing cartoon which depicted a negro in American uniform consulting an official of the Genealogical Office, the latter remarking that it must have been a considerable time since the client's ancestors emigrated from Ireland (see illustration). I am not sure that some of the family have ever quite satisfied themselves that the fortuitous choice of the name O'Malley by *Dublin Opinion* in this connexion was not inspired by me.

One of the cases we had to investigate was that of Col. O'Callaghan-Westropp (to whom I gave some prominence in Chapter V). A near neighbour of my own in Co. Clare, I had known him from my youth – it was at his place, Coolreagh, that I went to my first shooting party – and I was very reluctant to strike him off the roll. Actually it transpired that the O'Callaghan Chief was a man whose family was long settled in Spain and

98   *Dublin Opinion*

" I can't be sure about distant relatives, Mr. O'Malley, but I'm convinced that your branch of the family emigrated long ago—quite long ago."

193

1. Cartoon from *Dublin Opinion*, c. 1946. Reproduced from Edward MacLysaght, *Changing Times: Ireland since 1898* (Gerrards Cross: Colin Smythe, 1978), 193. Courtesy of the National Library of Ireland.

origins has the effect of making Irishness an identity that is unnaturally stretched across boundaries of race and racialized descent. Definitions of Irishness are always both geographically specific and constituted through the ways the cultural and constitutional renderings of Irishness circulate across the genealogies of homeland and diaspora.

As Mairtin Mac An Ghaill has argued, engaging with new patterns of racism and hostility toward new immigrants, asylum seekers, and refugees in the Republic of Ireland entails addressing the complex historical and contemporary geographies of Irish racialization and Irish racism.[78] This is not narrowly based on an analogy between the experience of Irish emigrants in their destinations and the experience of contemporary immigrants in Ireland. Instead, he argues that contemporary anxieties about and hostility toward immigrants need to be addressed in an analytical framework that is attentive to the particular configurations of race, ethnicity, and difference that cannot be encompassed within the model of white power and black oppression as it has developed with American antiracism. Reducing the semantic slippages between race, culture, nation, ethnicity, and ancestry to a model of black-white relations of power and subordination, he argues, fails to capture the ways ideas of difference have been differently mobilized in different historical and geographical contexts: in early modern and modern British colonial accounts of "native" Irish inferiority; in anti-Irish attitudes in nineteenth-century Britain and America; the ambivalent position of Irish emigrants in the racialized categories of citizenship and belonging in the New World; the histories of racism, anti-Semitism, and discrimination toward Travellers in Ireland; and the anti-Irish racism experienced by Irish people in Britain.[79] Recent research also points to the ways in which Irish emigrants and their children in Britain negotiate their location in relation to categories of race, nationality, and ethnicity and articulate alternative models of identity and belonging.[80] The focus on the making of difference in Ireland and across the diaspora and greater attentiveness to new alternatives to old categories of identity among second-generation emigrants could, Mac an Ghaill argues, inform a multiethnic vision of the Irish state and nation.

The conventional marking of Irishness as white in the United States, however, means that the presence of African ancestry in predominantly European genealogies is often overlooked by those who identify as being of Irish descent. At the same time, the identification with Irish heritage by African Americans with Irish ancestors has to be asserted against the assumptions that blackness determines identity and that Irishness is fundamentally and naturally white. So while the figure of 40 million Americans of Irish descent seems to rest on an Irish "one drop rule"—that having an Irish ancestor makes you primarily of Irish descent—it seems to be overruled by an older one that makes blackness override ethnic identity as Irish. In opening up the question of how recent Irish immigrants are located and locate themselves in the racial hierarchies of American society, Eithne Luibhéid reflects on the ways in which most Irish immigrants in interracial relationships "quietly drop out of Irish institutions, activities and political group-ings" because of the implicit equation of whiteness and Irishness. "What place," she asks, "do mixed marriages, and racially-mixed children, have in the Irish di-aspora so eloquently evoked by President Mary Robinson in her February 1995 address to the Oireachtas"?[81]

Ancestral Complexity and Alternative Histories

Interests in Irish ancestry in the United States are not necessarily tied to asser-tions of white Euro-Americanism or informed by antagonism to new immigrant groups, however. Nor does genealogical research on Irish ancestors always foster ideas of simple ancestral roots or pure cultural categories. As a practice of ac-tively researching and often actively reflecting on ancestry, genealogy can cross-cut dominant ways of locating oneself according to ethnic categories of descent. Though genealogy's traditional emphasis on lineage can lend support to an idea of an uncomplicated ethnic pedigree, the empirical and encyclopedic impulses of genealogy as a research practice—the desire to get another generation complete and another generation back—push in other directions. In genealogical research, the emotions of hope, loss, nostalgia, and desire meet the ethos of rigorous and painstaking empiricism. Over the twentieth century, genealogy has become in-creasingly professionalized through accredited organizations and societies with codes of good practice and models of thorough genealogical research that combat the legacy of spurious and status-hungry genealogies of the past. As professional genealogists explained to me, the key to good genealogy is primary documenta-tion. Each link in the family tree, starting with the self and working systematically backwards from the present generation, must be meticulously researched and fully documented. The knowledge provided by older family members should be the first resource in beginning research rather than general maps or guides to sur-name origins. Visitors arriving in Ireland in search of genealogical details about a great-grandmother or great-great-grandfather are encouraged to start with the most recent generations to make sure that the links to the great- or great-great-grandparent are accurate and supported by evidence. This emphasis on properly establishing the connections to Irish ancestors means that visitors are encouraged to research the more recent generations that are often overlooked. This professional advice—that researchers work backwards from the present—can produce family trees that reflect family connections across ethnic groups and challenge some of the neatness of an idealized Irish identity, in which a single Irish line is the only one that matters. The work of tracing ancestry back from the present can direct attention to varied ethnic origins of those who feature in the close and distant generations of a family tree or, as one Canadian visitor to the genealogical advice center at the National Library in Dublin put it to me, "the Italian and Mexican and Chinese and East Indian and all sorts of colourful mixtures."[82] The Irish line may still be the one that matters most, but the factual presence of ancestors with diverse ethnic origins within the family tree can make the process of choosing Irishness more overt and more self-conscious.

Like other forms of data collection, genealogy is often driven by a desire for comprehensiveness that can stretch the family tree laterally in every generation to include other offspring, each potentially with their own descendant chart. Amateur genealogists often described genealogy pathologically, as an infection, an obsession, a bug you catch and cannot shake off. This means that even those who begin with a straightforward sense of their Irish roots are taken in new directions through the desire to know more. Having exhausted her research on her Catholic ancestors, an American woman told me that she then turned to her Protestant side and realized their formerly overlooked significance in her family. Genealogical results do not always confirm an identity that had previously been assumed, and the connection with Ireland can become more distant and less stable than imagined. The ideal of a fixed point of origin is frustrated by the potentially infinite nature of the family tree. The "Irish" connection can become one element of a longer history of migration: as a Canadian woman wrote, "First and foremost, I thought I was 'Irish.' I had grown up thinking my grandfather was from Ireland. . . . I found out he was born in Manitoba, Canada. Then I thought his father (my g-grandfather) was born in Ireland. . . . he was born in Brampton, Ontario. His father was born in Ireland, but it seems the family was previously from Scotland. . . . and prior to this, probably Normandy . . . now what am I??"[83]

Though genealogy may appeal as way of recovering that original place, as family trees grow backwards in time they can fail to supply a neat answer to that question "where I am from?" In reflecting on the ways even comprehensive family trees are always partial (since they can always be infinitely extended along lines of relatedness along generations and backwards in time), Rebecca Solnit argues that "you can find yourself in origins, though you may have to choose an arbitrary point—a great-grandmother, ancestral home, the Irish Cliffs of Moher—and beyond that you can lose yourself in origins."[84]

Sometimes genealogical research leads to a personal multiculturalism based not on a single neat ethnic ancestry within a culturally plural society but on ethnically hybrid family trees.[85] Those whose genealogical work has lead to realization of the variety of ancestral origins evident from the places of birth of emigrant ancestors and in the varied surnames in their family trees sometimes interpret the personalities or aptitudes of contemporary family members in terms of a range of possible ethnic inheritances. Individual family members are thought to have particular biologically inherited cultural traits. Sometimes these cultural traits are manifested in their pure form in one person who is "typically German," for example; sometimes these ethnically marked characteristics are combined in one individual. One respondent rejected the idea of pure Irish descent in favor of a personal ethnic hybridity from a diversity of distinctive "ethnic ancestries" that mirrored that of the nation:

> My research also lets me have an appreciation for all people. We are so many nationalities here, that it should be hard to be a racist. I see through my research that all people have something to share, a "piece of the puzzle" to give. . . . It makes me appreciate the diversity of our nation. My father is Irish, small, laughing, quick-tempered. My mother's brother is German, tall big-boned, brilliant. . . . Doing family history work has helped me to understand the many facets of myself and from where they probably came. . . . I am proud to have gleaned so much richness from my diverse ancestors.[86]

Even if this implies a fixed bundle of ethnic traits that can characterize one individual or be combined with other ethnic traits within another, this reflection on ancestry and ethnicity though family history is clearly strongly tied to self-identified antiracist politics. Others come to realize that their Irish ancestors share a place in the family tree with so many others from so many other places that even a language of ethnic fractions could not adequately describe their ancestry. To them, shorthand descriptions of descent always seem an oversimplification. Pure categories are a fiction. Genealogy, I was told by a man from the United States, can dispel ideas of cultural purity: "One thing that I have learned is that we are all one people, a distinct pure line is not a reality. There was such migration, cross-breeding, raiding, plundering, such purity is impossible."[87]

In contrast to the dominant language of culture or ethnicity fixed in the blood and in the genes, inherited rather than practiced, some argue that it is through doing genealogical research that they come to an understanding of culture as dynamic and fluid: "I think that one of the ideas I have received from my research is that culture is not as fixed or stable as most of us believe. I think that this is an important idea because it means that we don't have to be so protective of our culture if we see it as evolving. I would hope that this idea gives groups who hate permission to see things differently."[88] Genealogy can also be deployed within a discourse of shared humanity and nonhierarchical difference. One woman reflected on what doing genealogy has meant to her: "I feel a connection to all people of the world now. We are mostly all immigrants in one way or another and we need to celebrate our differences and encourage our sameness (decency, mercy, understanding)."[89] Even if the idea of shared connections with "all people of the world" rests on an assumed system of equivalence, where there is no dominant group and no differentiation between the different conditions of migration, here genealogy has informed an approach that is clearly distanced from ideas of racial hierarchies and antagonistic difference. So while some family histories of emigrant struggle and survival are used to argue that contemporary immigrants to the United States will ultimately prosper too and so should not be supported, others researching their genealogy find senses of connection in a diverse human story of migration.

Yet ideas of commonality can elide past and continued structures of power and privilege. Though the whiteness of Irishness may be enlisted by some in reaction to what are perceived as the cultural and social threats of multicultural policies and immigrant incursions, Irishness can also serve to distance others from the tainted associations of whiteness with domination. An Irish heritage figured in terms of forced exile under the cruel conditions of British colonialism offers a guilt-free ethnicity dissociated from the power of whiteness. As Catherine Eagan has argued, aligning histories of Irish colonization and anti-Irish discrimination with African-American histories of enslavement and racial oppression serves to deny or underemphasize the historical and contemporary benefits of whiteness enjoyed by Irish Americans. Many, she argues, are increasingly interested in connecting the histories of discrimination and hardship of Irish and Irish-American ancestors to those of other ethnic and racial groups, drawing on the now relatively well-known story of the making of Irish whiteness in America and accounts of British anti-Irish racism to dissociate themselves from mainstream white culture. This reassertion of "lost innocence," through assertions of solidarity in shared victimhood and common oppression, is largely achieved by eliding the history of Irish-American racism, the different subject positions occupied by Irish, other European immigrants, African Americans, and Latinos in hierarchies of race, and the past and continued privileges of whiteness. Irishness offers both "racial innocence and multicultural belonging."[90]

This issue of the limits and implications of empathetic engagement based the identification of shared experience is central to Breda Gray's insightful exploration of pro-immigration discourses in Ireland. Challenging anti-immigration attitudes, these commentaries repeatedly invoke the history of emigration from Ireland as the basis of a moral obligation to support immigrants in Ireland. Though supportive of the intention to articulate counterdiscourses to anti-immigration rhetoric, the idea of a shared but repressed national memory of the trauma of emigration, she argues, is problematic, for it constructs an idea of a collective national (sub)conscious passed on unchanged, assumes a shared relationship to that history of emigration, elides the complexity and diversity of the reasons for and experiences of emigration, and makes recognition of similarity a precondition or basis of political solidarity. Instead she argues for the need to develop a feminist politics of solidarity with new immigrants in Ireland through forms of identification that both recognize the specificity of the other and acknowledge the complex relationships between power, domination, and exclusion in the historical geographies of Irish emigration and of Irish settlement. This is a solidarity across difference rather than an empathy that elides difference.[91]

Interests in Irish ancestry may reflect both reactionary strategies and limited liberal empathies of shared suffering. Yet complex senses of identity and the complex locations of Irish emigrants in histories of settlement, displacement, and domination can also characterize some diasporic genealogies. While the whiteness of Irishness is reinscribed by some diasporic imaginaries and deemphasized by other versions, genealogy can also lead to critical historical perspectives on the dynamics of racialized power, ethnicity, and class, on family histories as histories of European settlement, and on senses of interconnected histories that trouble straightforward categories of colonizer and colonized. These understandings of family histories differently shaped by the ways ancestors have been positioned within and responded to the configurations of race, class, and ethnicity could furnish the basis for forms of political solidarity that do not collapse those differences.

One respondent's research has lead her to a much deeper knowledge of the different ways in which her ancestors were part of American history: "We have learned that they were among the very early pioneers. They fought Indians, carved homes and farms out of the wilderness, and served in every war from the late 1600s to the present. Some were deeply religious Quakers who opposed slavery, and ran stations on the Underground Railroad, others were southern farmers who owned slaves." Though she doesn't feel she has to be personally responsible for her ancestors' treatment of Native Americans or involvement in slavery, she does "feel that I must do everything I can during my lifetime to prevent such injustices."[92] In her reflections on family history, Katherine Brown writes of the importance of critical and contextual family histories. In her case, this means bearing the burden of one ancestor's role in fixing slavery in the economic system of the early colonies of Virginia. Brown uses family history with students in her community college who are African Americans whose families came from the cotton fields of the Deep South or white working-class students with Central or Southern European backgrounds to locate themselves within an official history of "American Civilization" that largely excludes them.[93] Another visitor to the National Library in Dublin who had come to work on her family tree explained that she was concerned with what she called "social" rather than "biological" heritage, and she told me how she uses genealogy to teach middle-class children in Minnesota a socialist, anti-imperialist, and feminist history as part of what she described as her "little subversive agenda."[94] One woman born in Northern Ireland of Protestant and Catholic parents, now living in England and linked through shared stories, letters, and genealogical connections to families in Ireland and Australia, spoke to me of how genealogy keeps stimulating her to read and reflect on the impacts of capitalism and colonialism as the history of her own family intersects both with the history of the Highland Clearances and white settler treatment of Aboriginal people in Australia. Genealogy can locate the individual in complex and overlapping historical geographies of displacement and settlement.

The interests of those tracing family histories back to Ireland can also challenge understandings of Irish history. In her opening address at the first Irish Genealogical Congress held in Dublin in 1991, Mary Robinson suggested that overseas interests in ancestors in Ireland could begin to redraw a picture of social and cultural diversity in Ireland to replace the image of division between a homogenous Catholic society and a Protestant minority. Robinson praised the conference organizers for embracing in their program "Irish people from every era who left these shores, whatever their class, creed or reason for leaving" and for emphasizing the diversity of migrant experience and its cultural expression worldwide. But for Robinson, the exploration of family history and genealogy in Ireland and among descendants of Irish migrants could also be a way of recovering the histories of all those who settled in Ireland as well as those who left who do not fit the category of poor, rural, Catholic post-Famine migrants:

> The conference programme helps bring to light the various cultural and religious threads which together make up the tapestry of what we call "Irishness." Often when "Irishness" is discussed only the island's two or three major traditions receive consideration. For this reason it is good to be reminded by a conference such as this that the history of the Irish people includes the stories of the country's minorities: the Huguenots, Quakers, Palatines and the Jewish community.[95]

By drawing attention to these overlooked histories of settlement, genealogy, she suggested, undoes the exclusive coupling of Irishness with Catholicism and the crude polarization between "native" and "settler." But it also replaces the image of the "two or three traditions"—Catholic, Church of Ireland, and Presbyterian, or Irish, English, and Scottish—with the image of a complex cultural "tapestry." The implicit suggestion is that this could help shape new constructive understandings of collective identity and diversity in Ireland and Northern Ireland. So while the idea of forced and painful exile has been part of Irish nationalist discourses of colonial injustice, for Robinson, diasporic genealogical interests can be a means of rethinking Irish national identity. Though romantic views of Ireland as a culturally homogenous, Catholic, rural society have been, at least in part, a product of diasporic imaginations (which in the United States have fueled financial and political support for republican violence in Northern Ireland), here genealogy is being used to question the simplicities and exclusions of this version of Ireland.

Genealogical interest in roots is not counterposed to diasporic hybridity but is seen as a means of exploring and expressing cultural diversity.

Genealogical research can also work to uncover those who have been marginalized in or excluded from the conventional narratives of the Irish nation on other grounds. Though diasporic genealogy is strongly framed by diasporic Irish nationalism and its account of colonial oppression and nationalist struggle, tracing Irish ancestors can involve searching for those whose lives have been shaped not by the effects of colonialism but by the strictures of Irish nationalism. Visitors can find their perspectives on Irish history challenged by their own genealogies and by the attitudes they encounter in Ireland. But their genealogical research can also direct new public attention to those who have been overlooked in the conventional narratives of Irish nationhood. Even if many with interests in Irish roots hold onto the story of pure republican struggle, the work of genealogical visitors also points to absences in the conventional narratives of the Irish nation as they trace ancestors whose lives and experiences have been edited out of traditional accounts of Irish history. Visitors to the Genealogical Advisory Service in the National Library of Ireland while I was there included an elderly nun trying to discover something about her grandfather who was awarded a Victoria Cross in the Crimean War but who could never be spoken of in the family because of shame and embarrassment about this history of service in the British army after the rise of Irish nationalism and Irish independence. Another visitor was there to find out more about her great-grandfather, an English solider stationed in Ireland in the 1880s who married an Irish woman. One man was following the painful story of his grandfather who had joined up and fought in World War I but who left Ireland after being ostracized on his return in the 1920s. These family histories of Irish service in the British army and of Irish and English intermarriage present a more complex picture of the complexities of loyalty, affiliation, and interconnection that characterize Irish history.

These personal genealogical projects of recovery and reclamation redress the effect of a nationalism that led to the ostracism and exclusion of those who upset its model of absolute loyalty, cultural purity, and sexual morality. Though some strands of late-nineteenth- and early-twentieth-century Irish nationalism entwined the cause of women's rights and national liberation, the version that became the foundation of the state joined a rigid code of sexual morality and conservative familism to the code of purity of allegiance and culture.[96] Those whose stories are being recovered by their descendants include the thousands of women who left or were forced to leave Ireland pregnant and unmarried because of the shame of violating this moral code, and the thousands of babies taken for adoption from other unmarried mothers who stayed. Here genealogy works in its radical mode, uncovering hidden histories that challenge socially conservative and culturally absolutist nationalist narratives. So while American genealogy in general may be prompted by ideas of ethnic particularity and popular Irishness that reduce the complexity of postmigration family trees to one or a few determining Irish lines of descent, in practice genealogical projects that have their origins in one national context can have quite different effects in another. The popular genealogy of Irish ancestry and origins can both feed and be informed by the most conventional renderings of national history, character, and culture and provide evidence for costs of those national narratives and the complexities of identity, belonging, and experience that they eclipse.

Conclusion

The identifications with Ireland through migrant ancestry that are used to demonstrate the existence of a global Irish community are themselves expressions of the complex interconnections between the ways in which Irishness is presented in official and popular cultural forms within and beyond Ireland, and the ways in which Irish ancestry is situated within configurations of race, ethnicity, and nationhood in different diasporic locations. These interconnections between expressions of global Irishness in Irish political rhetoric and public culture and the overseas ancestral affiliations—the welcome projected to a global community from Ireland and the ancestral identifications reaching back to Ireland—are entangled in complex political geographies of identity and belonging, race and ethnicity, nation and diaspora. Different versions of identity with different implications for the politics of belonging traverse these political discourses and personal genealogical projects. A diasporic consciousness of plural attachments, hybrid cultural forms, and multilocational senses of belonging stands as an alternative to ideas of cultural purity and singular and simple ethnic origins. Yet different deployments of the idea of the Irish diaspora sometimes emphasize and sometimes combine ideas of global interconnection, multilocational attachments, plurality, and mobility and the appeal of a pure point of ancestral origin and an essential, often Catholic, Irishness transmitted via descent. Different versions of the diaspora can have different effects, encouraging an unreflective celebration of ethnic distinctiveness that is both essentializing and conservative, or enlisting overt demonstrations of Irish-American culture as examples of plural and performative Irishness. Irish diasporic identities can be mobilized both in reaction to anxieties about new patterns of immigration in the United States and to reimagine the Irish nation as a plural "diaspora space." But as the 2004 constitutional amendment to the rights of citizenship of the Irish-born suggests, the invocation of a plural community sharing ancestral affinities can support not only a model of modern mobility that elides the social costs of new economic progress but also a racialized version of belonging via descent.

As ideas of the diaspora have been developed and debated in Ireland, those who identify themselves as part of this global Irish community have been engaging these questions of cultural connection, ethnicity, and the meaning of Irish ancestry through their own genealogical research, sometimes espousing ideas of direct and undiluted descent and sometimes embracing ideas of mixed roots. The practice of researching Irish ancestral connections is shaped by the meaning of ethnicity and, more specifically, the cultural associations that Irish ancestry and Irishness carry in the United States. But it is also often an active exploration of a personal location within the categories of race, nation, and ethnicity. Searching for Irish roots can be one of several ways of identifying strongly and often exclusively with Ireland and Irish cultural traditions and asserting an Irish ethnicity. Alternatively, Irish descent can be valued as one strand within entangled ancestral charts of diverse origins and intersecting ethnicities. What genealogy means and does for the politics of race, immigration, and ethnicity depends on the ways in which individuals locate themselves in relation to the positive associations of ethnic distinctiveness, the specific characteristics attributed to particular ethnicities, and, for the majority of Americans, their own mixed ancestries. Extended from one place and taken up in another, the idea of diasporic Irishness is mobilized and remade for different sorts of projects. The intended inflections can slip as the meanings of Irish descent are mobilized across the geographies of homeland and diaspora.

This suggests that David Lloyd's criticism of the effects of a celebratory turn to the idea of the Irish diaspora on the politics of race, ethnicity, and immigration in the United States points to these interconnected political geographies but is less sensitive to what may emerge through an active genealogical engagement with "Irish roots." For Lloyd, an apparently benign but depoliticized version of cultural difference informs what he critically describes as the "sentimentalising and fetishising desire" of Irish Americans "to establish their genealogy in the old country." This, he argues, "has been augmented recently by the successes of liberal multiculturalism that has left many white Americans, whose roots are by now twisted and entangled in the soil of several European lands, seeking the cultural distinctiveness that they have learned to see as the 'privilege' of ethnic minorities."[97] However, the political implications of genealogical imaginations of ancestry and ethnicity are more complex and often contradictory. Culture can appear to be a set of characteristics that are transmitted unchanged through generations along with bodily substance. Its language is one of transmission and inheritance rather than process and production. At the same time, culture, in the sense of collective heritage, can be figured as vulnerable to cultural dilution or corruption, hence the defensive turn to genealogy. However, genealogical research can be a practice that points to culture as a fluid and continuous making of meaning that challenges fixed, essentialized, exclusive, and proprietorial versions of culture and that disrupts ideas of pure family lineages and national cultural purity. Critical genealogies that explore the relationships between family history and wider structures of power and patterns of inequality stand out because of their significance in contrast to more conservative versions. But they suggest ways of harnessing the appeal of roots for politically progressive approaches to migration, nationhood, and culture. In the next chapter, I extend this discussion of the meanings and implications of genealogical explorations of Irish ancestry and origins by considering the ways in which senses of ancestral affinity and diasporic Irishness are expressed and tested through the experience of being in Ireland and of meeting and making relations.

3

Irish Roots and Relatives

Return, Reciprocity, and Relatedness

In his 2005 memoir *Booking Passage: We Irish and Americans*, Thomas Lynch, a poet and funeral director of a northwestern suburb of Detroit, Michigan, describes three decades of a deep connection to Moveen West, near Kilkee in County Clare on the far west coast of Ireland. Moveen is the townland his great-grand-father emigrated from at the end of the nineteenth century. As a young man in 1970, Thomas Lynch visited the farm his great-grandfather left in 1890, and was welcomed by his second cousins Tommy and Nora Lynch, who still worked the farm, and he visited them again almost every year after. Twenty years of letters, phone calls, and visits later, he inherited the farmhouse as Nora Lynch's next of kin. In many ways, this is an ideal Irish-American connection. He is the first of Nora Lynch's family to come back from America, so his return is especially charged with significance. His discovery of Moveen happens when he is young enough for it to shape the rest of his life, and it happens with visceral intensity "as a whole body, blood-born, core experience; an echo thumping in the car-diovascular pulse of things, in every vessel of the being and the being's parts."[1] It is a discovery not just of the ancestral home but one that has remained in the family left behind and will now stay in the family, a farm of "stone walls, stone floors, thatched roof and open hearth"[2] and pastoral simplicity on the beautiful coast of west Clare. All that he was shown in his "first days in West Clare years ago, the house and haggard, hay barn and turf shed, cow-cabins and out-offices, gateposts, stone walls, fields and wells and ditches, forts and gaps, church and grave vault, names and dates in stone—all the works and days of hands that be-longed to the people that belonged to me, all dead now, dead and gone back to the ground out of which arose these emblems of humic density" connect him and his own family to the sacred family cycle of birth and death, to his ancestors and to their place.[3] In *Booking Passage* this ancestral, lifelong, and afterlife connection with Moveen is at the center of his poetic reflections on the "press of family history," on being in Ireland and being Irish American.

In Irish diasporic genealogy, this single, known, and acknowledged place of origin is a longed for anchor of belonging. Researching Irish ancestry is often a search backwards to the ancestor or ancestors that left Ireland, a search not only for who they were but where they lived and where they were born—where in Ireland they were from. These places are sometimes found and visited and sometimes never found, or never found in this singular and richly simple sense. The length of time since the ancestor or ancestors left Ireland profoundly shapes the nature of people's genealogical projects and the experience of being in Ireland. Sometimes the connections in time and generations are close, and continuities of residence link American families to the relatives in Ireland who still live in the places that emigrant parents, grandparents, or great-grandparents left behind. But they are often distant or just unknown. If the departure of their ancestor from Ireland was relatively recent, then genealogical research can involve reconstructing the generations of the family in Ireland that preceded the emigrant ancestor. But all that some may know is the name of a great-great-grandparent and the rough date they departed from Ireland. If the ancestor from Ireland is known by name alone and came to the United States long ago, then finding their place of origin—county, town, village, parish, townland, or even ideally a farm or cottage—is the goal of genealogy. For many pursuing their family trees to Ireland from afar, finding that place of origin in a cottage or farm that matches a model of Irish rurality and finding warm and welcoming Irish relations is the dream of diasporic return. Yet while traveling to Ireland to find the ancestral point of origin and, if possible, to meet relatives in Ireland is central to Irish diasporic genealogy, visitors differently experience the intersections between grounds of connection and senses of difference that these returns and reunions entail.

The nature of the trip to Ireland also depends on when the visit occurs in new or established genealogical projects. It is reported that thousands of tourists come to Ireland every year because of interests in their Irish ancestry, but this number counts together those with a range of approaches to their genealogical investigation. Time for a little family history research in the National Library in Dublin and a visit to the Heraldic Museum nearby may be scheduled for American tourists on organized tours who may have done a little research already or none. Parking the coach on Kildare Street and allocating time for visiting these sites and the nearby shops selling Irish music, heraldic gifts, and handicrafts is a standard feature of guided tourist itineraries. Some visitors attend clan gatherings that combine field trips and talks with celebrations of shared ties of descent that correspond to shared surnames. Some come on specialized genealogical study tours. Many also travel independently, hiring cars and dividing their time between research in archives in Dublin or Belfast and local libraries and genealogical centers, visiting the standard tourist sites and searching for places and people that they are connected to through ancestral family ties. Some visitors will only make the trip after years of advance research that has enabled them to locate their ancestors' places of origin, or after commissioning professional researchers in Ireland or Northern Ireland to so do. Many come with some research done and more to do and the hope of finding that place of origin and finding and meeting relatives in Ireland.

Professional genealogists who help visitors to the National Library's genealogical research center offer guidance to those who have done some or considerable amounts of research already or who have so far only consulted popular guides to the historical and geographical origins and heraldic insignia of their own surname or a particular Irish ancestor's surname. In genealogical research centers, those who sit leafing through guides to doing genealogy in Ireland can include people whose returns reflect the diverse historical geographies of Irish emigration and the cultures of being of Irish descent in different places. A late-middle-aged man returning to Dublin after decades of working on English building sites and bringing up a family in Birmingham, with never enough time or money until now to come back, can sit alongside a visitor from America claiming descent from the high kings of Ireland, or another moved to tears by the sorrow of ancestral impoverishment and emigrant exile and the intensity of diasporic return, or another interested in the practical and economic advantages of an Irish passport.[4] Research centers and study tours bring together a diversity of attitudes, experiences, and investments in Irish ancestry that are encompassed within the collective category of Irish diasporic descent.

This chapter explores the senses of difference, connection, and relatedness that emerge through the practices of searching for and discovering ancestors' places of origin, meeting relatives in Ireland and online, and through the emotional economies and new technologies of exchanging genealogical knowledge.

Return is frequently framed as a homecoming that is affirmed if visitors' senses of its significance is reciprocated by those they encounter. Yet reciprocity is not guaranteed; assumptions of affinity can be tested and resisted. Questions of difference run through the culture of Irish diasporic genealogy.

Homecoming: Being in the Places That They Left Behind

Many genealogical projects being undertaken by the descendants of Irish migrants to the United States, Canada, New Zealand, and Australia begin because of a desire not only to reconstruct the family tree back to the ancestor or ancestors who left Ireland but also to discover where in Ireland they were born and where in Ireland was their home. Having an Irish ancestor is meaningful, but that knowledge alone is not enough for those who are moved by the mystery of an unknown point of ancestral origin in Ireland to take up genealogy. Having a full and informed answer to that question of "where in Ireland did your ancestor come from?" authenticates and verifies what was previously a general but unspecific ancestral connection. Locating and visiting that place of origin is often a private and personal experience that is deeply meaningful and intensely moving. For many it is understood and experienced in terms of the religious intensity of a pilgrimage, a way of honoring ancestors' place within a "communion of the saints." The significance of this journey back to the point of ancestral origin is sometimes marked by ceremonies that symbolically and materially link the places of dispersal to the places of origin. These are often mortuary rituals that mark a parent's or grandparent's emigrant life and memories, rituals of reconnection: people bring soil from a grandfather's grave in the United States to scatter in the fields they knew in Ireland, a grandmother's prayer book is buried in an Irish graveyard; Irish soil is smuggled back to America to be added to a emigrant ancestor's grave. The visit to Ireland is a pilgrimage in honor of ancestors who could never go back.

In this ritual of return, connections between people and between people and the place are imaginatively reconstructed, materialized, embodied, and performed. For many, having an ancestor for whom the place was home means that their descendant is linked to that land via the genealogical tie. This can be imagined as an embodied inheritance: the descendant inherits the blood or genes that were shaped in the ancestor by generations of life and work on that particular land and landscape. Ancestors' bones are in the land and their genes are in their returning descendant, so the act of return reunifies a bodily inheritance carried down the generations and the formative familial landscape. This understanding of ancestral connection as a link between body and soil means that being in these places is often experienced in intensely affective and embodied ways, with "goosebumps" and "shivers down the spine." The sense of a place as site of ancestral burial, evinced by names on headstones or imaginatively reconstructed, locates the individual life in a longer organic cycle of return to the land.

But if the ancestral connection links the returnee to the land, the land also deepens the visitor's connection to the ancestors for whom the place was home. When the emigrant ancestor was a close relation—a parent or grandparent—traveling to the places they left as children or adults is a way of knowing them differently, adding the knowledge of the places they lived in Ireland to the ways they are known by their children or grandchildren. James Murphy writes of "finding home" when he traveled with his father back to the farm in Leitrim that his father had left forty-five years earlier and of coming to realize that this earlier life—"a whitewashed cottage in Leitrim, no running water, three rooms, a central fire—in this place, my Dad and the aunts and uncles of my growing up were all born"—was so much a part of his father's and his own life in Irish-American Brooklyn.[5] But in many cases, the emigrant ancestor can only be sketchily known through the genealogical information that can be built up around them—names and dates of birth and marriage and death, their place in family trees, and perhaps occupation—and if fortunate, through fragments of family stories. Being in the places that they left is thus a way of knowing something of them. Seeing their former homes, if they still exist and can be found, is part of this. But it is also a matter of seeing what their ancestors would have seen, the view from the windows, the shape of the land, the pattern of light across a garden, field, or valley though a day, walking the land, experiencing the contours of the topography, the rise of a hill, the turns of a lane, of hearing the sea or a stream. Professional genealogists in Ireland encourage visitors who cannot trace an exact location to visit the likely area anyway and "get a feel of the place." An American woman visiting the National Library talked to me of her experience of visiting the place she knew her ancestors has come from:

> It is interesting to see where they lived. The land does not really change very much. You can build over it and put paved roads over the top of it.

But the land itself does not really change much. We just went to Tara the other day and you could see that people had been there. They had gone but the land was still there. And so to go back to the place that they lived you see the land they lived on, that shaped the kind of people that they were. . . . What I am most interested in are the stories, what they did, what were their experiences, and part of going to a place is imagining what they did there and how they did it and what it was like when they were there if it was very different. You imagine that they must have walked this hill because who could resist in any age. The hill was always there and who could have resisted it. So you imagine that they climbed the hill and stood on the very spot that you are standing and they saw the things that you are seeing and it makes them be real to you and then you have that connection.[6]

For Thomas Lynch, the continuity of his connection to Clare is matched by his sense of what remains the same despite what has changed: "the same fields, the same families, the same weather and worries, the same cliffs and ditches define Moveen as defined Moveen a hundred years ago and a hundred years before a hundred years ago."[7] Despite what may have changed, the experience of the topography, the shape of a valley, the sight of the horizon is often imagined as a physical embodied experience that their ancestor would have known and that links ancestors to their descendants across time and difference.

Finding an ancestral home produces a regional or local geography of genealogical origin that promises a deeper knowledge of the particular places that were the homes of emigrant ancestors and a greater sense of historical connection to the unknown but imagined generations of ancestors that preceded them in Ireland. The named place of origin has a potent particularity that authenticates an ancestral connection. It may be the place that was spoken of in family histories, or talked of by grandparents as home, or passed down as the place a grand- or great-grandparent came from long ago. Or it may be a place that is discovered through genealogical research despite the reluctances of older or dead generations to talk about their life before America. While genealogy is often conceived of as a practice that honors family memories of emigration, it can also often entail overriding the desires of some family members to forget. Diasporic genealogy can be a way of making intergenerational connections between younger generations and older ones who experienced emigration or knew the generation that did. But it can also be marked by generational differences between those for whom emigration was a lived experience, whose practical and emotional demands were sometimes coped with by not talking about Ireland to their children, and the generation now wanting to recover, remember, and honor their Irish origins.

This dialectic between connection and difference within families is also a dimension of the wider domain of collective descent. For some who identify with Ireland though ancestry, this named place of origin can also be a means of differentiating their relationship with Ireland from the millions of others who claim Irish descent. Having Irish emigrant ancestry matters because of its meaning as a measure of collective belonging within an ethnic or national community of descent that extends from Ireland with all its celebrated cultural associations. However, being of Irish descent often also involves efforts to distinguish between those it encompasses on the basis of the strength of their connection, the depth of their attachment, and the authenticity of their Irishness. In *Booking Passage*, Thomas Lynch contrasts the transformative effects and intensity of his and his brother's attachment to their Irish heritage with the temporary and superficial character of the "annual mid-March Oirish" of St. Patrick's Day. These lines of distinction run through the culture of diasporic Irishness; expressions of the depth of attachment to Ireland are often made by contrasting the closeness of the relationship or degree of connection to the superficially of those of other people. In the United States, Irishness is a mark of cultural distinctiveness in a culture that, within limits, celebrates ethnic diversity, but the popularity of Irishness means that those who want to assert the strength of their connection often do so by differentiating themselves from others who also claim membership in the ethnic collective.

The diaspora sometimes seems less characterized by an ideal balance between plurality and communion, as it was conceptualized by Mary Robinson and Richard Kearney, and more by culture of competitive authenticity. This competition over authenticity is not only between the "rooted" and resident in Ireland and the diasporic but *within* the overseas "extended family." Making the trip to Ireland marks a deeper commitment and deeper connection. Finding the place of origin not only commemorates an ancestral connection to Ireland but is the basis of a personalized sense of difference from the mass of "Irishry," including others making the trip. For Lynch, the family farm and family in Moveen mark the difference between his relationship to Ireland and those who "take the standard ten-day tour bouncing in the bus from the Lakes of Killarney to the Blarney stone."[8] His brother Pat's encounter with Ireland on arriving to attend the funeral of Nora Lynch, like his, was not the same as others: "While most Americans spend their first fortnight tour rollicking through bars and countryside, searching none too intently for ruins or lost relations, Pat was driven straight away to the home that our great-grandfather had come out of a century before, and taken into the room in which that ancient had been born. For Pat it was no banquet at Bunratty, no bus ride to the cliffs of Moher, no golf at the famous links at Lahinch, no saints or scholars or leprechauns."[9] For Lynch, the search for "ruins or lost relations" parodied here is simply unnecessary. The ancestral home is not a mystery. Deep connections are lived, not just longed for or imagined.

But for many, the search that he contrasts with his sense of secure and certain ancestral rootedness is a search for what he seems to have found—a single known place that is ancestral home. This dream of a place of origin is based on an imagination of ancestral connection that tracks back through the geography of family migration within the United States, or other emigrant destinations, and back along the lines of direct or step migration to a single and settled place of belonging. For many, this is where sense of self and sense of place coincide, where there is no dissonance between culture and geography, a place of settled, pure, and primordial location rather than the unsettled belonging of European settler identities and the confusions of cultural pluralism. Yet, unless emigrant ancestors were very recent and all come from the same place in Ireland, finding a single place of ancestral origin is always finding the single point of origin for only one ancestral line. For some, that place is the only place. The reduction of ancestry to singular ethnicity from entangled lines of origins—which identification with Irish roots often entails—can be reduced further to a single line and single place of origin in Ireland, too. In theory at least, even thoroughly Irish-American family trees that reflect intermarriage within Irish-American communities would have several points of origin in Ireland. However, the conventions of reckoning ancestry directly, and, for some at least, paternally, mean that the geography of origins can be imagined in terms of a single place. In *Booking Passage*, no other line of connection through the marriages of the Lynches within their Irish-American community is afforded enough significance to merit mention alongside the patrilineage—"my name and the names of my kinsmen repeating themselves down generations"—that binds him to Nora and Tommy Lynch and to Moveen.[10] For others, an ancestral place of origin in Ireland is knowingly a place of particular rather than sole ancestral connection.

Yet it is because the return to roots and origins is so heavily charged with the commitment to commemoration, the promise of reconnection, the resolution of longing, and the reconciliation of location, identity, and belonging that visiting Ireland and a specific place of origin in Ireland is not always experienced as an unambiguous or unreflective reunion. Most experiences of visiting Ireland involve resolving the disjunctures between Ireland as imagined from afar and known though its most conventional and even most complex cultural rendering in print and images. In the past, unexpected poverty could jar with stories of blessed greenery. More recently, prosperity can be a shock. Yet this contrast between the expected and found can be incorporated into an understanding of travel as more an exploration of the meaning of home and ancestral connections than a simple journey of discovery and source of fulfilment.

While the idea of a single and ultimate place of origin is a potent attraction, more qualified interpretations of the nature of connection can frame the meaning of return. A women from New Zealand expressed her sense that "We cannot turn the clock back and have the connection to those places that our ancestors did who grew up there" but that "out of curiosity and also a sense of homage to the ancestors I would like to see, visit, experience and try to comprehend something about those places."[11] For others, the place ancestors came from matters, but rather than being imagined as a single site of origins and ultimate home, it is incorporated into a more complicated sense of identity, ancestry belonging, and location. A Canadian man visiting the National Library's genealogical center talked to me of combining a sense of geographic roots in Canada and genealogical roots elsewhere.[12] One woman from New Zealand was adamant that doing family history in no way "downgrades" how she feels about her own country and used both her Irish ancestry and Maori expressions of family, home, and belonging to locate herself firmly in New Zealand and in opposition to "clichés" of a white settler crisis of identity and cultural location. Both consciously rejected the model of a singular place of origins and the absolutism of the ideal of being indigenous. Liisa Malkki has argued that "to plot only 'places of birth' and degrees of nativeness is to blind oneself to the multiplicity of attachments that people form to places through living in, remembering, and imagining them."[13] Nevertheless, for some people, their genealogical research—that plotting of places as well as dates of birth and lines of migration—can be an expression and exploration of those complex multilocational attachments.

Rebecca Solnit's book of essays published in 1997 and structured around her travel in Ireland does not fall neatly within the emerging genre of genealogical travel writing and memoir.[14] She was not traveling to undertake genealogy, nor to find the homes of her four Irish emigrant great-grandparents, nor to reactivate relationships with Irish relatives, but to explore the meaning of being of Irish extraction and wider questions of belonging. Her book begins with her sense of bemusement that her uncle's genealogical research has allowed her to become an Irish citizen. Her "purple passport with its golden harp seems" for her "less like a birthright than a slim book on the mythologies of blood, heritage and emigration."[15] She goes to Ireland to reflect on ideas of mobility and memory, geography and identity, and the conventional ways of understanding culture and location. Her visit to Ireland is framed by her awareness of the political challenges and appeals of being "native": "for those Americans who descend from historical emigrations: questions about what it means to be and whether it is possible to become native; about what kind of a relationship to a landscape and what kind of rootedness it might entail; and about what we can lay claim to at all as the ground of our identity if we are only visitors, travellers, invaders in someone else's homeland."[16] Her travel around Ireland is a journey of reflection on two responses to these questions about belonging: the celebration of universal spirituality through the cultures of the indigenous or the search for an alternative sense of being native.

Solnit is critical of the appropriative nature of New Age models of universal spirituality accessed through the cultures of the ancient and indigenous that have developed in response to the cultural potency of being native and its associations of holistic harmony of people and place and uncomplicated symmetries of culture and location. But she is critical too of the reification of ethnic or cultural difference that has solidified out of the dynamics of identity politics. The search for alterative origins in Europe in response to the politics of indigeneity may be a way of avoiding the cultural appropriation of indigenous forms of belonging. But it suggests a model of cultural ownership based on clearly delineated groups possessing pure and unchanging cultures, a "this is yours, and this is mine" model of cultural difference. A multiculturalism imagined in terms of bounded ethnic groups tied to the culture of original homelands, Solnit argues, fails to accommodate the routine hybridities of identity in the United States. It does not offer a model for engaging with the place of residence as well as remembering the place of origin. For while the old model of cultural assimilation demanded a forgetting of the past, the contemporary model of ethnic particularity depends on an insistence on a remembering of the Old World that leaves little room for engaging with the past and the present of those places where people live now:

> There are fashions to remembering and forgetting; the melting pot assimilationist ideal of much of this century celebrated jettisoning the past to reach more quickly a utopian future like a shimmering white city; while recent reaction against this restless forward lurch has stressed roots, blood, ethnicity, difference, remembering, a past as dark as dirt. The place of the tangled present, and of place itself, seems never to have surfaced in these schemes built on hope or on history.[17]

So although Solnit's visit to Ireland repeats a journey that others also take in response to these questions, she rejects the model of origins, culture, and identity in Ireland that many bring with them. "According to the way people tend to talk about blood and roots and other charged images now," she writes, "this unknown country is what's mine. It isn't, but I thought that Ireland was a good place to think about it all."[18] For Solnit, the bloody history of the American West and the formative landscape of her Californian childhood seems more hers than that of "a faraway continent" that is the source of her Irish and Jewish ancestry. Her argument is for a more complex historical engagement with the places of domicile and descent than suggested by the tenets of ethnic absolutism. Identity, she argues, is a "geographical science," a chemistry of "ethnicity and geography," not an immutable quality that travels down ancestral lines that stretch to the descendants of immigrants and back to a single and pure place of origin. This alternative model of belonging is forged out of her sense of the ways the historical geographies of Irish colonization, migration and settlement confounds simple categories of "native" and "settler" in Ireland and in the New World.[19] By the end of her Irish journey, she gives up explaining her part-Jewish and part-Irish background, tired of defending her hybridity, and finds no firm foundation for her identity in Ireland. Instead, her visit confirms her sense that being of Irish extraction is not the same as being an inhabitant of Ireland. Ireland complicates the meanings of "native" and "home."

Unlike her mother and her uncle who have "visited several times each, sometimes to track down umpteenth cousins and see homesteads of ancestors,"[20] Rebecca Solnit "never did track down any of the cousins I had scattered over the island, people with whom I shared nothing more than a sixteenth or thirty-second of a gene pool and a common past beyond our recollection."[21] Her sense of the limits of connection, implied in this admittance, also suggests her reluctance to be implicated in a model of belonging that overprivileges ancestry and elides the complexities of identity and geography that she has been exploring. But many do track down Irish relations, and their experiences testify not only to the appeal and promise of making connections but also demonstrate that genealogy can be a social practice that itself reveals the complexities of diasporic relatedness.

Irish Relations: Connections, Difference, and Reciprocity

The belief that family matters, or, more particularly, that shared ancestry is the basis of the bonds of affinity and affection that those who share ancestors also share, runs deeply through the culture of popular genealogy. This powerful pull of genealogical connection is especially potent in Irish diasporic genealogies when those connections are with relatives in Ireland. The reciprocal recognition of genealogical connections by relatives in Ireland is not only rewarding to visitors because it affirms a family tie. It also testifies to the visitor's connection to a place and to an ethnic ancestry and all that entails in terms of cultural heritage and inheritance. Their warmth and welcome as relatives can symbolize a whole country's and culture's embrace. Irish relatives' responses when contacted by distant but known or newly established relations from abroad can be read as measures of inclusion within an entire ethnic imagined community. Meeting distant relatives in Ireland is thus often as significant to the genealogical experience as finding the location and being in the place ancestors left behind. These two dimensions of the genealogical trip are often entwined. For many visitors, meeting newly rediscovered relatives, or reactivating known connections that have hitherto not been or have only just been maintained, or searching for possible relatives is an important part of their genealogical trip to Ireland. As the numbers of people traveling to Ireland from the United States and other places because of their interests in Irish ancestry has increased over the last twenty years, it has become very common, during the summer especially, for people to arrive in towns and villages asking around for anybody who may be connected or know someone who is related to the family their immigrant ancestor left behind. Telephone directories are often used by visitors in the hope that cold calling those sharing the surname of interest may lead to the discovery of a relation.

The experiences of discovery vary greatly. Meeting new or rediscovered relatives can be a hugely confirming experience when the visitor is welcomed as part of a family and when the visitor's feeling of the special significance of being linked together by a shared ancestor is fully reciprocated. One American woman's experience of unexpectedly "coming across living relatives," Irish-speaking relatives "still living on the land that my ancestors left in 1847" in the beautiful countryside of west Kerry, presents an ideal of reunion. One member of the family in Kerry helped her document their connection until the family could tell her "We are sure now, you are ours." For her, this "overwhelming" welcome extends backwards in time to earlier generations of her family in America: "I felt I was being welcomed home along with my grandfather, and his grandfather." Other visitors also report "the very best experience" of genealogy being "connecting with Irish relatives (a first cousin once removed, and many second cousins), and finding them absolutely accepting and interested in me and my life." The feeling that the welcome they receive encompasses not just them but those before who never returned is often expressed by those pursuing Irish genealogical connections:

> The visits to Ireland have been wonderful—and both exceeded my expectations. I felt as though I was fulfilling a family mission. Each of my parental grandparents left Ireland near the turn of the century. Neither returned. None of their four children were able to visit Ireland. I was therefore the first to return in a century. It felt as though I was completing the circle. . . . Meeting the relatives in Ireland has been an absolute highlight. [They] do seem to share my interest and appreciation in family history and are intrigued by what happened when family left Ireland for the US.[22]

This reciprocal interest confirms the family bonds that are understood as fundamental. But anxiety about how these reunions may go and suggestions of relief that these interests have turned out to be shared, and connections have been appropriately acknowledged, also suggest people's awareness that the existence of a genealogical connection is an unreliable guide to the nature of these new relationships.

Years of research and the significance of genealogical relatedness make the occasion of meeting Irish relatives for the first time highly charged. While meeting are loaded with the particular personal and wider resonances of return for genealogical visitors, those being visited can have concerns too about having visitors, what they might expect, and how to fulfil or manage those expectations. The ordinary self-consciousness of meeting strangers who are simultaneously deemed to be significant can make these encounters laced with anxiety on all sides. Sometimes the genealogical connection may be quite close; sometimes it can be very distant or only guessed at. But even when the genealogical connections are relatively close, these meetings always involve the search for points of connection across cultural difference, for, as one visitor put it to me, someone may be "on paper a relative but in person a stranger." When commonalities are found, they are invested with meaning because they are established across transatlantic differences in experiences, ways of life, and location that are signaled in what may seem superficial but inescapable symbolic alterities of accent and attire—how people talk and what people wear. Martin Gale's painting *Family History* (2002), of two men in an overgrown graveyard, poignantly pictures these relationships between connection and difference within diasporic genealogical return (figure 2).

Sometimes these differences are most evident in relation to the meaning of Irishness itself. For some visitors, their interest in Irish ancestry is expressed not only through genealogy but also through involvement in or enthusiasm for cultural practices that are central to the performance of Irishness in the United States: the cooking of "Irish foods," step dancing, Irish traditional music, and even Irish language learning. Visitors' interests in Celtic mythology, folklore, or the Irish language may not seem unsurprising to the families they meet in Ireland but can be far removed or only marginally connected to residents' everyday interests and concerns. American children schooled in step dancing can meet Irish teenagers more interested in the products of the global music industry. Accounts of Irish history as a straightforward narrative of colonial oppression and national struggle, or more particularly accounts of the Famine as genocide, and general anti-Englishness expressed by some visitors can jar awkwardly with the perspectives on the past held by their hosts and genealogical guides. Professional genealogists talked of being polite but noncommittal in response, feeling that they weren't there to "give a history lesson" but would say that Irish history is "more complicated." However,

2. Martin Gale, *Family History*, 2002, oil on canvas, 40 x 66 in. Private collection. © Martin Gale. Reproduced with permission of artist.

more explicit expressions of dissatisfaction with the persistence of historical over-simplifications and misrepresentations can appear in print, such as professional genealogist Paul Gorry's review in the magazine *Irish Roots* of the documentary *Out of Ireland* screened on PBS in 1995, which frames its history of Irish emigration to America with an introduction to Irish history as "all downtrodden natives and baddie, land-grabbing English."[23]

Meetings between Irish and Irish-American relatives are often negotiated accommodations to different attitudes and expectations. If some visitors become more sensitive to this in the process, others who visit or consider contacting relatives are acutely aware of the potential for visitors to be seen in terms of a stereotype of American Irishness. A woman whose parents decided to emigrate to the United States with their children in the 1950s rather than watch them leave as young adults expressed her concern about how she would appear to her relatives in Ireland. She was keenly aware in advance of the question of cultural difference. She would like to visit but hasn't, as she explained: "I would love to see them. I worry about being considered a 'Yank' since I know how my parents felt about such people."[24] Distant and more immediate family ties can be the basis of hoped for and fulfilled relationships that bind the children, grandchildren, grand- or great-grandchildren of descendants back into a geography of Irish relatedness. But as some visitors are aware, categorizations of difference are also easily made across those lines of genealogical connection. American visitors may be accepted as family, but they can still be considered really American "deep down," whatever their claims to shared Irish heritage.

There are apocryphal stories of the accommodation of visitors' desires—a village priest who shows all visitors the same ruined ancestral cottage, and families warmly receiving visitors they know aren't related—that play on the comic edge of diasporic attachment. This caricature of needy gullibility would be read by visitors as insults to the seriousness and significance of their ancestral research. Their comedy implies an effective cultural boundary between being Irish in Ireland and being of Irish extraction, and between being host population and being visitors in the dynamics of diasporic relatedness. Genealogical return creates two communities of the visited and visitors as well as cross-community connections. Sensitivities about what counts as Irish, who is really Irish, and who decides run through Irish diasporic genealogy. Thomas Lynch includes an extract from Flann O'Brien at the beginning of *Booking Passage,* which describes O'Brien's nightmarish vision of going to the Patents Office in Dublin Castle to try to patent being Irish: "You see, I want this unique affectation protected by world right. I am afraid of my life that other people will find out that being Irish pays and start invading our monopoly. I am not sure that certain sections of the population in America have not already infringed our immemorial rights in this regard. I did not get very far with the stupid officials I saw. They held that it was open to any man to be Irish if he chose, and to behave in an Irish way."[25] Lynch leaves it to the reader to reflect on the tensions between protective possessiveness, the policing of authenticity, and the free-for-all of choice and performance. The geographies of being born and bred in Ireland or elsewhere matter in the definition of who is Irish and to what degree, even as degrees of connection among those of Irish diasporic descent are also used differentiate the depth of each claim to diasporic Irishness. Meetings between relatives can be subtle or raw experiences of the wider dynamics of diasporic cultural relations.

The different attitudes to Irish heritage—history, music, dancing, language, mythology—that can surface in encounters between genealogical visitors and Irish relations also intersect with the ordinary awkwardness of the different priorities and amounts of time and money of hosts and guests. As one professional genealogist in Dublin explained to me, "You can have a visitor going down to a farm. They are on holidays but the people on the farm aren't on holidays so you can have that kind of tension you know. . . . You see it depends on what kind of situation you are coming to, what is the relationship first of all, in the house or the cottage or whatever, questions of money. Do they come back to see their cousins but stay in hotels?"[26] Choosing not to stay with the family, for whatever reason—because of a desire not to impose or due to a preference for en-suite autonomy—can be read as rejections of hospitality. But the threat of having visitors can also cause cautious reunions. Until recently, disparities of wealth between American relations and Irish relatives were a familiar aspect of these meetings. Those who grew up being dressed in the castoffs of American cousins sent over for the family in Ireland would finally meet their American relations. Smart hire cars would turn up outside small farms or modest rural or suburban homes making reunions sometimes occasions of embarrassment or self-consciousness on all sides.

These sensitive asymmetries of culture and class can also involve more immediate concerns about material ownership and inheritance. Two sisters from Boston visiting the Genealogical Centre in the National Library talked to me of meeting their relatives on the Aran Islands in County Galway:

> Oh they were very, very nice. You know, we were kind of nervous because we had never met them before and first they were kind of hesitant. They thought we were coming to take over the family home, which we weren't at all. And then once they realized that we weren't . . . we were living in an eight-room house in Galway Bay that my cousin has just built brand new. His was so small you couldn't get your foot in it. He was the only one who could get inside the house . . . so no, we weren't interested at all. But once they cleared that they were very, very nice.[27]

As it became more possible for emigrants or emigrants' descendants to return in the decades after their departure in the late nineteenth and early twentieth centuries, their return often prompted concern about their potential claims to the land or property that was left behind. Although a few long-distant emigrants did return and often faced "an uneasy blend of resentment arising from their assets or accents, and contempt for their evident inability to 'make it' overseas," as David Fitzpatrick notes, "the 'Yank' nevertheless became a familiar figure in rural folklore, a symbol of loneliness: the woman bringing home a fat fortune with which to find a husband and 'redeem' his farm; the man flourishing ready cash to secure land or pub; the lost offspring summoned home to take over from faltering parents."[28] But, as Aidan Arrowsmith has argued, in twentieth-century Irish culture the figure of the wealthy returnee coming back to claim inheritance or to buy land in Ireland was also framed by ideas of the emigrant's cultural inauthenticity and cultural corruption. Their earlier departure from Ireland makes them ineligible owners of the land that symbolizes rootedness and confers authenticity. As famously dramatized in John B. Keane's play *The Field* (1965), their attempt to buy or reclaim land is read as a new form of colonialism, one that exposes the economic inequalities in the new state that make emigration necessary and make the returnee a threat to those vulnerable small-tenant-farming families who survived through the emigration of sons and daughters.[29] By the mid–twentieth century, the emotional complexities of return were also registered in images of the emigrant returnee. While the relative success and cultural difference of the returnee is judged by the family and community they left, visits home could also involve the returned emigrant finding only traces of a former life. In the 1940 edition of the *Capuchin Annual*, the figure of the well-dressed returnee stands in somber reflection gazing at the ruined gable ends of what the caption suggests is his former home (figure 3).[30]

While their return has been associated with the threat of a new form of colonial appropriation, visitors' genealogical trips to Ireland are themselves framed by narratives of Irish dispossession under English colonization and ideas of the act of return as imaginative repossession. For those who identify themselves as the descendants of Famine and post-Famine migrants, this return is frequently made meaningful through accounts of the colonial dispossession, forced exile, and the trauma of displacement of their ancestors and the Irish in general. The return journey commemorates national dispossession and imaginatively enacts a diasporic nationalist repossession. But desires for imaginative repossession of Ireland can create anxieties about claims to material repossession of property. Reflecting on her experience of doing genealogical research for overseas customers, one professional genealogist in Dublin explained how diasporic return can reignite old disputes or disrupt fragile peace within families about land, property, and money: "You don't have to go back very far and in families who have something to leave or something to inherit . . . you have major rows going on for years because

3. *Home* (Dublin: Capuchin Annual, 1940), 84. Courtesy of the National Library of Ireland.

so and so got something who shouldn't have got it. And then you have farms that have been inherited and someone comes back and upsets the whole system. It is a recurring theme."[31]

The passage of generations makes it less likely that genealogical visitors in the late twentieth and early twenty-first centuries are looking for the land that was passed on or sold in their ancestor's absence. The economic prosperity since the 1990s that has brought wealth to many but not all in Ireland shifts the former relationship between the emigrant returnee who comes back better off than their poor Irish relatives. The Irish relatives may now be the ones better off. This creates other configurations of class and culture in diasporic family reunions. The new consumerism of Irish relatives can clash with the Celtic mysticism of Irish-American relations. Visitors can find that the cottage or farmhouse that is deeply significant as the home their emigrant ancestors left behind has been left to fall down nearby the Irish relatives' large and luxurious new home. These ruins are still deeply evocative for visitors, but their attachment to them is not necessarily shared by the family enjoying the comforts and space of the newly built house. Or the ancestral home may simply no longer exist, cleared away in the process of modernization, replaced by a single new home or the houses of a new estate. Late-twentieth-century economic prosperity intensifies the sense that the return to the place of ancestral origins can very rarely be to the same place the ancestors left.

Contacts with Irish relations who have been discovered or rediscovered as part of the genealogical projects of visitors to Ireland are thus often meetings of different understandings and performances of Irishness and different intersections of culture and class. They can foreground different attitudes about the value of genealogy, the significance of ancestry, and the importance of the genealogical connection itself. This can also be a matter of property and possession, not the distribution of family money but of the sharing, exchange, or withholding of genealogical knowledge itself. At one level, genealogical knowledge, with its mix of names and dates and stories, is the family's common inheritance, but the hard work of gathering it together means that it can become invested with more particular property rights. Genealogy is often a memorial to past relatives, sometimes distant ones whose move from Ireland is a "pivotal event" in the family history, sometimes more close—a parent or grandparent—whose aging or death prompts an interest in finding out about the family's past. It also often understood as a bequest to future generations as the birth of children or grandchildren prompt a desire that the new generations should know the family's past and questions about the extent and content of the family history to be passed on. An Irish heritage can be valued as a gift from parents, grandparents, or more distant ancestors. James Murphy writes that "Ireland had been one of my parents' gifts to me; perhaps without their even intending it as a gift."[32] Thomas Lynch writes of conceiving of his book as a "gift in thanksgiving for the gift that had been given to me, of Ireland and the Irish, the sense of connection, and the family I found there and the house they all came from that was left to me."[33]

At the same time, for those who trace family trees back to Ireland, the labor of this research, with its demands of time, money, and emotion, is often figured as a way of making sense of family traditions and individual experiences and as a more or less appreciated gift to immediate and future family. But even the gifting of genealogical knowledge implies a prior personal or more exclusively shared ownership that is the product of that work. The value of the gift is that it gives up the ownership that the labor to produce it ascribes. As one woman explained, "I think I am doing my family and relatives a favor to dedicate my life to find where they came from and what our predecessors had to go through for them."[34] Genealogical data can be mobilized as a gift, shared inheritance, or personal possession that creates new sorts of relationships within immediate and diasporic extended families.

The work of constructing family trees and collecting family stories can reflect belief in the deep significance of the biological connections shaped though familial reproduction, that "family is everything." But it can also be a response to its apparent insignificance to others. Although family trees record the facts of familial relationships, the construction of family trees can be used in attempts to reanimate their existence in practice. Genealogy can be a way of forging family bonds between generations in the face of concerns about the fragility of close family networks and the decline of "family values." It is often framed by the significance of family relations, but many people explained their work as a response to the apparent insignificance of blood and family among their own relatives and in Western society more generally:

> People today, relatives whom I have written to do not seem to care about genealogy at all . . . unfortunately for we who are interested in finding out more of who we are . . . and where we have come from. It bothers me that they are not very helpful . . . and also because family is important to me and hope often that it is to others as well. . . . No one else does. My Aunt M— did but she passed away about 12 years ago. I get the impression from people that I am bothersome with my queries etc.[35]

Genealogical research can be a response to the absence of family closeness, both geographical and emotional: "I also feel that I was seeking more family connection as my own family began to spread themselves across this country and we began to be both separated by miles and/or busy schedules, with less emphasis being put on 'our own family.' . . . Times in this country (and perhaps others as well) are different and the structure of the family has changed. Families do not seem as 'connected' as they once did."[36] For some, genealogy can provide a compensatory sense of family or mark a resistance to the erosion of a culture of familial care by materialism and consumerism:

> I come from a family where the word "family" has very little meaning—some Aunts and Uncles, I've not seen for 20 years. This hobby has given me the sense of having a family.[37]

> Today's society is so caught up in so many im-material [sic] "things" of life. Back in the days of my ancestors, people were more important and the family unit was just that . . . a family . . . not 5 or however many people going in 45 different directions all the time. We have lost the perspective in our society today of what it means to "be" family and to live as a family unit. . . . We have lost the perspective of family living in our society today. We need to slow down and live life at a much slower pace and re-learn what it means to be "present" to one another as family for more than 5 minutes at a time.[38]

The giving of genealogical knowledge to the family is often a mechanism for reestablishing connections.

Interest in the family history within families can be a source of shared pleasure. Yet what is figured as a gift by some can also be the object of more proprietary control by others. Tensions over ownership emerge if genealogical information—stories, documents, dates, letters, photographs—is not adequately reciprocated, is monopolized by one person, or when one member's role as custodian of family history is challenged by another's genealogical research. If family trees and family stories theoretically belong to the family however tightly or widely it is defined, rights to shared possession can be structured by claims to authority and by who counts as close and distant family. The response of family members to the genealogical work of some are not guaranteed, as one woman recounted:

> As I have got on with my research in New Zealand I have made contact with relatives previously unknown to me. In most cases they have been pleased to have copies of what I have put together and to share

information that they have on their particular lines. The most hostile reactions have been from my mother's sisters as they feel I am digging too deeply into things that are not nice to know about, and one of my father's brothers has written to me telling me that I am no longer welcome at his home. He was the alleged expert on that family's history but was not willing to share any information with me, and has made it clear that I have no right to speak to any living relation and his view is that I should not be doing any family history research until everyone of his and my parents generation has died. He states that the right to research the family history belongs only to that generation—not to the generation of his children!!![39]

Though shared ancestry can be the basis of new relationships, proprietorial attitudes to genealogical knowledge can effectively "cut the network" that the family tree represents and that genealogy celebrates.[40]

The relationships forged by or infused with the pleasures of sharing connections, or stalled or strained by resistance to requests for information, or being figured within other people's particular versions of the family history are especially significant when they also involve family histories of emigration and the return of the descendants of emigrants. Visitors' interests in genealogy are sometimes naturalized by a notion that knowledge of ancestors is a universal human attribute and that this form of self-knowledge is a cultural right, as if "everyone has a genealogy" and ancestry is of universal significance. In this view, genealogy itself charts preexisting bonds of bodily and affective connection, and the extension and deepening of these connections by the ready exchange of information follows naturally from their prior existence. When this is deliberately or unknowingly thwarted by official or family record keepers, these assumptions of ethnic and family affinity and reciprocity are painfully revealed and put in question. Sometimes eager and hope-filled contact by overseas genealogical researchers can meet the apparent disinterest of possible distant relations in Ireland in "sharing their family ancestry." One Canadian woman reported on her experience of trying to make contact with people in Ireland. They do not, she realized

have any interest in sharing their family ancestry, and were actually rude about the interest in their family and country. I know this is an isolated case, but for those of us thirsting to know more about our Irish heritage, every bit of information is like a new gold nugget. I would think that it would be in the best interest of all Irish people to share their beautiful history and ancestry. We are not trying to take over their country, or to Americanize it in any way. We only have a right to find out where we came from, and finding information easily available would do much to increase the tourism and good will of Ireland.[41]

Even in happier contacts, many visitors are surprised that their deep interest in genealogy and family history is not shared by the relatives they meet. Popular genealogy is grounded in a sense that relationships between people based on blood and marriage matter within reciprocal familial systems of affinities, rights, and duties and that these connections should naturally matter as much to all those who are related. The lack of interest in genealogical connections or genealogy itself among newly discovered family in Ireland confounds these expectations and reveals genealogy to be a personal practice with no guarantee of reciprocation. The resistance of some families to genealogical inquiries can make some visitors feel that their interests appear acquisitive rather than natural. In other cases, the lack of interest among relatives in Ireland suggests to visitors that genealogy is an unnecessary project for those already rooted by residence and unbroken ancestry. This difference is the subject of thoughtful reflections on the difference between the meaning of ancestry, roots, and being of Irish descent by those tracing their family ties back to Ireland:

I suppose we spend time trying to assess who we are, and where we come from, in order to pass it on to the succeeding generations. . . . One of the things that amazed me was that so many of the Irishmen in Ireland don't seem to much care to learn about their "ancestry." Perhaps, it's because they know that their "kin" have lived in the surrounding countryside for centuries. They know their past stories through storytelling and music. We, here in the U.S. are newcomers to this land. Our ties are back in the old country, and we wish to find them.[42]

Another reflected on her experience of meeting her husband's cousins: "They were very generous and hospitable. It was rather curious that they weren't interested in their family history. My husband's cousin and I had shared our research and they were astonished at our findings. Something that they had never considered worthy of research. Perhaps since they hadn't left, they didn't feel the compulsion to research their family history."[43]

Tracing ancestors in Ireland is often an expression of a deep sense of Irish ethnicity or a less intense but nonetheless significant affinity with Ireland. But the devotion to genealogy can be a marker not so much of being Irish or of Irish extraction, but of being American. As some visitors realize, a fascination with Irish ancestors can be characterized by those they encounter as an American rather than Irish trait. As one women put it, "I have found most of the Irish think we Americans are weird to be searching and so aren't as interested as we are."[44] The Irish diaspora can thus be imagined as an extended family based on shared descent, but the cultural diversity it contains includes different approaches to Irish ancestry and different degrees of interest in shared Irish descent.

These different degrees of interest means that sometimes relationships between relations in Ireland and relations abroad are sustained—photographs, letters, and e-mails continue to travel back and forth—and sometimes they are not. The newly found family in Ireland may welcome visitors but not respond to subsequent letters or e-mails: "When I went back to Co. Waterford last Oct–Nov, I felt like I came 'home.' I became acquainted with a H— family (my paternal surname) who treated us like family, even though we could not find the connecting link. We're all convinced that we are related. One of my 'frustrations' has been that they do not respond to any contacts I've made since. This saddens me." For this American woman, the most difficult aspects of genealogy include "the discovery that in spite of apparent links and a great time together, my contacts in Co. Waterford have not responded to any of my contacts since I was with them. I can't imagine why."[45]

However, this sense of asymmetry of commitment to maintaining contact or deepening relationships established through diasporic genealogy can work both ways. If the giving of genealogical knowledge can be used to establish or reestablish relationships within families, requests for information that are made to previously neglected or ignored relatives, especially elderly relatives, can sometimes reduce these relatives to important but dangerously mortal sources of genealogical data, now only valued for what they can say about the family's past. This figuring of older family members as newly valued informants on the family's past can be mirrored in the ways in which Irish relatives are contacted. Irish relations matter not just as affirmation of ancestral and cultural connection but also as potential sources of information about the visitor's ancestor or ancestors. As well as archives and record offices, people in Ireland that share ancestral connections to the visitor's family tree are key sources of family history and genealogical information. But relatives that help are sometimes only temporarily valued as sources of information. Getting acquainted can be time-limited. One woman visiting the National Library in Dublin to do some genealogical research described meeting her second cousin during her trip to Ireland:

> He is a crusty old fellow just two years older than I am but—and just a year older than my husband—but being a farmer he is beaten and weathered. He looks a lot older but he has a twinkle in his eye. He has been a widower. He was only married six years when his wife died and he raised the children and he never did remarry or anything. The place, you know, looked old and being alone with so much work to do on a farm it is not kept up real well. When we took back the pictures my husband said "here we want to take yours" and he disappeared and he ran into the house. So we said "oh did we offend him?" And his farm worker was out there and we were chatting with him and he was a real friendly fellow. And then a few minutes later A— sticks his head out and says "well you can come in." And here he is. He's put on his shirt and tie and he has a cordless electric razor. And he says "Well I only do this on Sundays" but he is cleaning up his chin. It was delightful really. I'd liked to have had a chance to talk to him more but we had to get out here and do research.[46]

Extending the family tree can sometimes seem more important than the people and places that are connected through its ancestral lines. And while being in the ancestral place is often talked about as a sacred moment of return, this is not always matched by what professional genealogists in Ireland feel to be an appropriate and sustained engagement with that place. One professional genealogist in Dublin expressed her irritation with the apparently superficial and impatient approach to genealogy and the lack of sustained engagement with the places their ancestors may have come from shown by some visitors:

> I am a very placid person but when I find myself suddenly getting cross it is when you find people, they want the whole thing, like mathematic, there and there and they can't . . . when you really want them to walk

the land, you know, where they came from, get yourself into that. . . . But they are people in a hurry. You need to be open, be interested. Not on the highway all the time. Not the person who is going to do three hundred miles in one day and then more the following day. Stop and don't have a timetable. Be patient and interested.[47]

Establishing meaningful connections with the country through relationships with living distant relatives is central to many people's processes of genealogical identification with Ireland. But rushed trips around the country can mean that sustained encounters are sacrificed for the sake of getting back to the archives and doing more genealogical research. As in genealogy more generally, this research is prompted by the significance of family connections, but it can be pursued at the expense of the practice of kinship. Yet it is also a practice that can forge new forms of relatedness that tests the assumptions of diasporic family connections.

"They're Family!": New Geographies of Relatedness

In Irish diasporic genealogy, a family connection reconnects descendants of emigrants to a homeland and place of ancestral origin and binds them into shared ethnic community of Irish descent. This means that when that welcome is reserved, or when the deep significance of genealogy among descendants of the Irish emigrant is not shared by newly found relations, this is not just a matter of the quality of family relationships but a matter of the nature of being of Irish descent and the depth of ancestral connection. Bonds of shared ancestry are not always matched by shared interests in those genealogical connections. Nor do relationships that are established always have the intensity or depth of an imagined ancestral reunion. One visitor told me that her distant cousins in Ireland turned out to be like any family, "some great, and others are ok, just like any other group." But if these asymmetries of interests in ancestry among those who share blood can seem to undermine the significance of blood ties, shared interests in genealogy can foster relationships that feel like family with those who are unrelated in the conventional genealogical sense. These are often technologically enabled as well as unconventional forms of kinship.

Genealogy has been transformed by new communication technologies. Large amounts of genealogical data have been digitized and made accessible free or at cost through the Internet. But equally significantly, e-mail has extended the established practice of contacting other people who are potential relatives or those whose local knowledge can be drawn in the hunt for genealogical information. The use of e-mail and the Internet is now a routine part of genealogy. People post and respond to inquiries on personal or organizational Web sites and on a range of general and specialist e-mail discussion lists devoted to genealogy. Several genealogical e-mail lists exist for Ireland in general, for particular sorts of diasporic communities and for each county in Ireland. There are hundreds of surname groups with their own e-mail discussion list. Most are hosted by companies selling genealogical software, magazines, and access to genealogical data. Internet sites and e-mail discussion groups foster informal online networks that link individuals across the world who share interests in specific places in Ireland and in specific ancestries. This interest in linking family trees across the migrant geographies that have stretched them globally is also encouraged by commercial providers of genealogical software who sell packages, such as RootsWeb World-Connect, that make it possible to convert personal family trees to online electronic archives that can be searched for genealogical connections.

These Internet sites and networks create new opportunities for personal online relationships. The e-mails that travel back and forth between people in Ireland and other places, and between other places but about Ireland, in response to shared interest in a surname or a particular place—Ireland in general or a specific county, town, parish, village, or townland—sometimes lead to connected family trees or more often to a sense of commonality and affinity through shared interests in family history and the exchange of gifts of genealogical and geographical information. E-mail messages are followed by posted packages of photocopied documents or family trees and copies of photographs. Someone in Australia, for example, who learns of someone in Canada who is no relation but interested in the same place, sends them photographs they took on their trip to Ireland. Or, as one man helping with his wife's research explained:

> In an effort to start tracing her ancestors through this line, I subscribed to the Donegal message board at rootsweb and posted a brief message giving the birthdates of John and Jane and the name and birthdate of each child, all of whom were born in Donegal. Within 24 hours, I had a response from a gentleman in NZ who had marriage records for Donegal

going back to the 1600's. He identified that John and Jane were married in 1815 in a C of I church in the parish of Drumholm. And then, 24 hours later, another message arrived from a woman in Australia who was able to find the parents of both Jane and John from the birth dates of our John and Jane and each of their children. So in just 48 hours with the help of some dedicated volunteer searchers from halfway around the world, we were able to push that family back another generation. . . . There is even a woman in Donegal who contacted me over the internet who has offered to go to the 90 year old keeper of the Drumholm church parish records and to copy out all references to Crawfords and Dinsmores therein and to fax me her findings.[48]

These relationships can involve people in Ireland as well as places of Irish historic immigration. On county-based and general Irish genealogical e-mail lists, members living in Ireland frequently help solve mysteries about the microgeographies of place names and administrative boundaries that arise in diasporic genealogy. Other informal networks link people who live far apart though a shared interest in a specific place in Ireland. They can include distant relations in Ireland and other places, or simply be established by people willing to share knowledge about sources and exchange genealogical stories. In many cases, these networks of interest and exchange are focused on Ireland but link people in other places together in what are extraterritorial relationships founded on shared interests in ancestral ties to Ireland. Thus Ireland is imaginatively and empirically central to these relationships based on shared appreciation of the pleasure and meaning of personal genealogical projects, but it is at the same time rendered secondary to them.

Sometimes these transnational enthusiasms among members of these temporary or sustained relationships contrast with the response of individuals or institutions in Ireland and Northern Ireland to genealogical inquiries from overseas. For those researching Irish ancestry from afar, Ireland can be imagined as a place of rolling green fields and cottages and, more prosaically, as a site of genealogical data. The country is a place of authenticity and ancestral origins but also of more or less accessible and intensely desired genealogical sources. Although many researching their ancestry want to know much more than names and dates of births, baptisms, marriages, and deaths, these are the "gems" of genealogical information that allow family trees to grow, help locate key places, and structure the narratives of family life and migration. Despite the amount of material available online and in national archives overseas, the Genealogical Office, National Archives, and National Library in Dublin, the Public Record Office of Northern Ireland in Belfast, and county-based genealogical and heritage centers are key sites in this imaginative geography of Ireland. These places are both sources of genealogical information and points of mediated or restricted access to original documents and their promise of verifiable genealogical information. The dissatisfaction of some with the quality and cost of information from heritage centers and the frustration of restricted access to diocesan and parish records—certain Catholic bishops in particular refuse to grant access to them—mean that the intense desire for genealogical connection and the imaginative investment in Ireland has to be reconciled with difficulties of getting data. Love of Ireland has to withstand bureaucratic or ecclesiastical blocks to information.

> If Ireland would combine the county records and allow people (charging an appropriate fee) to search for family groups (with approximate birth days known), we might have a chance. The archaic system that is currently in use is very territorial. In addition, the clergy in Limerick appear to have set up additional road blocks. We love Ireland and will continue to do our research, but we have more respect for the systems in Canada, Mecklenberg, France and Germany. If the records had not been destroyed in 1921, we might have had a chance. We do not blame the Irish for not wanting the English to have the records but we wish there had been another option than destroying them. Our ancestors came to the U.S. before 1860 so the national records are of little use. We wish our ancestors had waited to emigrate so that we could have used the Irish vital records and our emigration records. My discontent [is] with the lack of a central place for Irish records.[49]

For some, this problem of restricted access to knowledge seems to imply that their research, and by extension that their genealogical connection to Ireland, is insignificant.

> The most frustrating aspects have been from the Irish Cultural Centres. The raw data is there, but no one is looking at it through my eyes.

How devastating it is to find a clue, and then to be told that that area of County Cork has not been put on computer, and that it will be another 10 years before the data is online. Also, while I have had some very good experiences with people helping me from Mallow Heritage Centre, the small parishes that I have contacted do not have any one there to look things up and copy them and send them off to you. And in some instances, don't see what the big deal is, and don't do a thorough search. This is my own family they are looking for, and it is like a religious experience for me—I would expect them to take the time to look thoroughly for me.[50]

The practical process of researching Irish ancestry within genealogical archives again involves these questions of imaginative possession, cultural ownership, and claims to membership in the collective heritage called Irish. While many experiences of seeking information in Irish archives and through professional genealogists are undoubtedly rewarding, these concerns about mediated and sometimes blocked access to genealogical data reveal something of what is at stake when intense identifications with Ireland are tested in the process of genealogical research. In contrast, the exchange of information among those researching Irish genealogical connections outside Ireland or Northern Ireland can seem to be based on more mutual understanding of its significance. One woman from Canada explained that, in her experience, "It's the people who do not live in Northern Ireland who are willing to help! I've written upwards of 100 letters, to parish ministers, city councils, people of the same surname, the PRONI, Libraries, and I can say, I've received, maybe 6 letters back!"[51] This contrast runs counter to the expectations of genealogical connection.

However, shared interests in genealogy can also foster unexpected relationships among those who do not share ancestry. Genealogy clearly prioritizes relationships to relatives living and dead that are related through blood. Yet doing genealogy can also create forms of relatedness that do not depend on the closeness or even the existence of biological connection. New forms of relatedness are forged, sometimes with very distant relations or with people of no blood relation but bonded through a shared interest in genealogy. These relationships may start from a shared interest in a shared surname and thus a possible genealogical connection, in Irish roots in general or in a specific place in Ireland, but they are shaped and sustained by shared beliefs in the significance of ancestry and shared experiences of doing genealogy. The experience of doing genealogy is the basis of these relationships rather than genealogical connection itself. This was frequently commented and reflected upon by those involved, as in this comment by an Australian woman tracing her Irish roots: "I believe genealogists are so helpful and supportive of each other because they have an understanding of the trials and frustrations involved and the possible importance of one little clue or piece of information. I have never come across anyone who was not positive, even if they couldn't help much. There is a real sense of community amongst amateur researchers who are selfless in their attitude to other researchers."[52]

The degree of cooperation and sense of community is sometimes emphasized by the fact that this culture of relatedness is not based on the "natural" bonds of blood: "We have never had a rebuff or unpleasant response from anyone, even those who turned out to be unrelated to us. . . . All have been unfailingly helpful and kind. I, in return, share information and give help whenever I can. None of these people shared my surname, but all were willing to help, and even though I will probably never see any of them in person, I feel their friendship is genuine."[53] The depth of these relationships is in fact often expressed by attributing to them the quality of family bonds. Family ties are figured as natural, but these naturalized bonds, which might be missing within families, are found between genealogical enthusiasts, as one American woman explained: "As I meet distant cousins over the internet from all over the world—we immediately bond, it seems—we really do begin to feel like 'real cousins.' I have become very close to some. We have even begun to arrange to meet. Always seems like we have known one another forever. It seems to be a very 'natural' kind of feeling."[54]

These expressions of "a very 'natural' kind of feeling" between conventionally unrelated people evoke the contrast between the biological and the social that is central to Western understandings of relatedness and in doing so both reproduce this contrast and challenge its prioritization of blood over other grounds of commonality or care.[55] Although fundamentally concerned with relationships structured through the biological fact of birth and parentage, genealogy as a practice can point to alternative models of relatedness.

Unexpected family-like relationships and unfulfilled senses of affinity with "real family" can complicate the meaning of being of Irish descent. One American woman's account of the significance of ancestry to her and of her experience of being in Ireland demonstrates the complex relationships between ethnic affiliation, family connections, and cultural difference:

> I feel very close to the Irish. I've read extensively on the famine years
> and all the hardships they went through . . . how they left their beloved
> country and immigrated . . . that took a lot of nerve and fortitude. My
> ancestors went to Canada, and I remember my father telling me about
> his pride in Canada. . . . They were very brave people and I'm so proud
> of them going to a new country to forge out a new life for their families.
> I'm proud of my Irish heritage. Each bit of information regarding their
> lives puts a piece of the puzzle together. I can almost picture what their
> lives were like and how they lived. This is a deep connection. I feel deep
> empathy towards the Irish.

Yet this sense of closeness and empathy was challenged by her experience of visiting Ireland:

> I was very surprised when I got to the county where my father's family
> came from. The people there didn't seem to understand WHY I wanted
> to know about my heritage. They know who they are . . . where they
> came from . . . I didn't. When I explained it to them, they then under-
> stood. I thought that a bit odd since so many Irish have researched their
> ancestors. . . . No it wasn't what I expected. 90% of the Irish I talked to
> seemed to have big chips on their shoulders . . . which surprised me. I
> found the land "unfinished" as well as the people. Which made me sad
> because I was so excited about going to Ireland . . . to walk the land my
> ancestors worked.

In contrast, she explains, "I have met many, many people over the internet in regards to the surnames I'm researching. There's a kinship with these people that no one else can experience. They're family!"[56]

These new maps of relatedness chart networks of connection that are shaped by shared interests in genealogical and geographical roots. But at the same time, they challenge the significance of consanguinity and conventional geographies of identity. They are about significant points of origin and stretched-out networks of relatedness in which blood both matters and doesn't matter. This is a complex geography of relatedness that at once prioritizes and overrides biological relatedness. Though genealogy privileges blood relations, genealogical networks constitute forms of kinship based on shared interests and mutual support. In these genealogical networks, Ireland is thus one node in a complex geography of genealogical connections that do not depend on conventional notions of consanguinity. Though reports on the experience of meeting relatives in Ireland can be close to an ideal of family reunion and ancestral return, many experiences are described as less straightforwardly rewarding. In contrast, many of the strongest expressions of the connection with people are made about the value and meaning of these online family-like relationships.

Yet even this online culture of mutual support and enthusiasm can be disrupted by tensions over ownership and exchange. As in conventional families, e-mail relationships are strained when the gifts of genealogical knowledge are not reciprocated or when trust is violated. Information may be freely given and exchanged, but this does not mean that the culture of genealogy is free from the tensions that arise when the labor of production of knowledge is not appropriately acknowledged. The relationships of mutual exchange and tacit rules of attribution are broken when family trees and written histories based on shared information are published or presented online as if they were produced by one individual genealogical progenitor of the family tree. Strong relationships with "online cousins" are thus often the result of careful screening for potentially exploitative or simply insensitive fellow genealogists: "I don't mind being contacted, but if I make a connection, and send information to someone, I expect that they will send some information back to me. Another unthinkable thing happens, as well. Some people take your genealogy and publish it on the Net, as if it was their own. That is disgusting, and we must do something about this. So, now I don't send a lot of info at once, until I have a trust for someone."[57]

The culture of collective interest and enthusiasm for genealogy and more specifically for Irish ancestral connections can also be riven by tensions over the accuracy and authority of historical and geographical knowledge that genealogists use and refer to in explaining their ancestors' lives. Sensitivities about different degrees of knowledge within these transnational networks are undoubtedly also about the authority that is attributed to or asserted by those involved who live in Ireland. The members of online Irish genealogical discussion lists are predominantly diasporic but often include people in Ireland, who may contribute their local knowledge of geography or historical knowledge in group e-mail exchanges. This help is often welcomed, but at the same time, overseas researchers can feel that the depth of their commitment, degree of knowledge, or validity of their identification with Ireland are challenged when list members from Ireland correct genealogical or historical misinformation online. E-mail discussions can often become contests of expertise in which residence in Ireland is asserted or resisted as a criterion of authority and guarantor of truth. Those who have spent years reading about Irish history as part of their interest in their Irish roots can feel affronted by the irritation expressed by members in Ireland at "being told about their country by foreigners."

The question of the degree of genealogical closeness to Ireland and the disputed significance of the difference between being born and living in Ireland rather than being of Irish diasporic descent can therefore disturb the harmony of these extended families of genealogical kin. These tensions over who can assert authority in disputes over historical or geographical knowledge are often experienced also as implicitly disputes about who can claim knowledge of Ireland as their own. But even if overseas genealogists resist this model of ownership and belonging, their genealogical commemorations of their Irish ancestors are also sometimes celebrations of a model of belonging that they can never achieve. Those who celebrate the significance of their ancestors being Irish born, bred, and thoroughly rooted inadvertently undermine their own qualifications as Irish since, being descendants of immigrants from Ireland (and often many other places), they fail to meet their own criteria of "true" belonging in Ireland. For those who look to the old world and idealize a relationship between identity, place, and culture based on long, undisturbed ancestral residence, ancestral connection alone becomes an unstable guarantee of the legitimacy of settler descendants' claims to cultural ownership of the "homeland."

Conclusion

The question of difference is thus central to the cultures of Irish diasporic genealogy. The constructive reimagining of the diaspora posited a harmonious alignment of cultural diversity and cultural communion. However, a visit to Ireland and the discovery of places of origin can be used to assert a deeper, more particularized and personalized relationship to Ireland against the superficiality or inauthenticity of other claims to Irishness. In practice, diasporic returns in search of ancestral roots and relatives can demonstrate the labor of its achievement across alterities of culture, asymmetries in attitudes to Irishness, and the shifting dynamics of class. Visiting Ireland ideally involves locating and visiting the local places that ancestors lived in and left behind and meeting Irish relatives who can confirm the veracity and the significance of the genealogical tie, and by extension authenticate the visitors' sense of Irish ethnic affiliation. In these emotionally charged meetings with newly found or rediscovered relatives, recognizing what is not shared despite shared ancestry can be a challenging part of the process of exploring the meanings of belonging, identity, and Irish ancestry. This is especially the case when visitors come to feel that their interest in Irish roots point more to their Americanness than their ancestral Irishness. For those researching what are now distant Irish roots, the sense of the difference between those whose ancestors left and those whose ancestors stayed creates a troubled sense of cultural loss, disconnection, and difference. Their identification with Ireland and Irishness is upset by any suggestions that their claims to Irishness and Irish culture are not equally valid. Unreciprocated interests in genealogy or different perspectives on Irish history or heritage temper the joys of being in Ireland. Visitors' intense investment in Irishness can meet casual disinterest as well as generous openness.

Irish ancestry can be imagined as a gift from ancestors to their descendants, and genealogy itself can be figured as a gift to other family members. But the emotional economies of exchange across diasporic distance can involve tensions of authorship and ownership. The possession of ancestral connections, ideally confirmed through genealogical research, are often mobilized to support and naturalize a desire to say "this is my culture" and "this is my home." Yet journeys to imaginatively repossess Ireland—which once created anxieties for the visited about material repossession—now often involve concerns about access to and possession of genealogical data. Thwarted access to genealogical information from relatives and institutions can be interpreted as intimating that visitors' cultural belonging in Ireland and the legitimacy of their claims to be Irish through Irish migrant ancestry are questionable. Though sharing ancestry implies that in some sense relatives discovered through genealogical research belong to each other, the meeting of distant relatives can undermine the significance of biological relatedness, especially when the most striking cultural difference is the value that is accorded to shared ancestry itself. In these encounters, the potentially limitless nature of the family tree meets the self-limiting practices of kinship, which determine who among an infinite number of possible relatives really are "family."[58] The character of these encounters is shaped by where families in Ireland draw lines of connection and lines of distinction across geographical and genealogical distance. For many traveling to Ireland to undertake genealogical research, the ancestral "return" can intentionally or unexpectedly be a process of exploring the meaning of connection, difference, and Irish descent.

At the same time, genealogical data can be mobilized as a gift or shared possession in ways that generate new forms of relatedness. Genealogy is thus not simply descriptive but generative of kinship connections. Using the idiom of kinship and the family to describe relationships to people who share an interest in ancestry but are not related in the conventional sense suggests that new forms of relatedness are realized through the practice of genealogy: the significance accorded to blood relations shapes relationships between people of no conventional genealogical connection. Genealogy can generate new and unexpected forms of relatedness and new geographies of genealogical kinship. Although the conventional reckoning of kinship in this form of genealogy privileges blood relations, as a practice genealogy can also generate these new and unexpected forms of relatedness and new geographies of genealogical kinship by fostering online "family-like" relationships between people who share interests in family history and exchange genealogical knowledge. These new modes of genealogical relatedness are often global networks of relationships that electronically crisscross the geographies of European settler societies. Like blood and biological relatedness in genealogy's new cultures of relatedness, Ireland is both central to this imaginative geography and decentered by transnational genealogical networks.

4

Postcolonial Nobility, Diasporic Distinction,
and the Politics of Recognition

The publications of Burke's Peerage Limited, the firm devoted to printing the complete genealogies and coats of arms of every British peer, baronet, and landed gentry family, since it was established in London in 1826, may seem an unlikely source for extending this study of the cultures and politics of "being of Irish descent." Nevertheless, two books published by Burke's Peerage Limited in 1976 are suggestive starting points for exploring the place of ideas of noble descent in Irish diasporic genealogies, in narratives of national history, and in contemporary categories of belonging in Ireland and Northern Ireland. One, *An Introduction to Irish Ancestry*, published in New York and London, contained a series of essays on the histories of Irish high kings and chiefs, Irish migration to the United States, genealogical and heraldic institutions in Ireland, and guidance on how to go about tracing Irish ancestors. The companion volume, *Burke's Irish Family Records*, detailed the "genealogical histories of 514 Irish families from their earliest recorded male ancestor down to the present day."[1] The first book thus marks an early stage in the development of Irish diasporic genealogy in which those involved in Ireland and Britain recognized the expanding interest in Irish ancestral connections in the United States and the utility of an introductory guide. The second suggests more directly the ways in which the nature and meaning of nobility in Ireland and its material culture of heraldry and genealogical lists, like Burke's, have been shaped by the political and cultural processes of both colonization and postcolonial state formation.

The adoption of the title *Burke's Irish Family Records* instead of *Burke's Landed Gentry of Ireland*, the serial title that had been used since the compendium was first published in 1899, was, as the editor explains, a belated response to the decoupling of landed gentry status from landownership in Ireland at the beginning of the twentieth century. After a series of land acts broke up the estates formerly owned by landed families and occupied by tenant farmers, gentry status was no longer securely linked to landownership. In a strict sense, those included in *Burke's Irish Family Records* of 1976 are not the noble families of the Irish peerage of dukes, marquises, earls, viscounts, and barons whose pedigrees continue to be recorded in Burke's Peerage publications. They were instead the old formerly landed families without hereditary title and new families "distinguished in Ireland for more than one generation."

The authority of Burke's to determine this list of distinction at all, and especially in a period of violent conflict over the British state's jurisdiction in Northern Ireland, did not go unquestioned. In his preface to the volume, Hugh Montgomery-Massingberd acknowledged that the decision to work on the new edition "provoked surprise and hostility in some quarters. One irate Irishman told us it was an outrage for an English firm to tackle such a project at such a time." In response, Montgomery-Massingberd pointed to the Irishness of the "remarkable Burke family of heralds and genealogists" and the Irish staff on the project. "As for the current situation in Ireland," he continued, "*Burke* is totally apolitical and possesses no racial, ethnological or religious bias."[2] However, the book did adopt a political position: one in which the varied distinguished genealogies included "reflect Irish Social History and the variegated constitution of Irish Society." For Montgomery-Massingberd, *Burke's Irish Family Records* challenges the "disgusting" "ignorance and apathy about Ireland which exists in Britain" and, prefiguring more recent pluralist arguments about Ireland and Northern Ireland, presents the volume as a record of social and cultural diversity:

> When all right-minded Irish men and women are trying, or should be trying, to do all in their power to bring all sections of the community peacefully together we, in our small way, offer this book of over one million words as a positive contribution. Between the covers of *Burke's Irish Family Records* there may well be Southern Catholics, Northern Protestants, Northern Catholics, Southern Protestants, Southern Republicans, Northern Unionists, Northern Republicans, Southern Unionists, and, at any rate, Celtic Irish, Anglo-Norman Irish, Anglo-Irish, "Scotch-Irish," Franco-Irish, Euro-Irish, Irish Americans, landed families, political families, artistic families, professional families, business families and many

other different categories, types and sorts of Irish families which are for once united.[3]

The publication was interpreted as an anomalous, and for some, insultingly inappropriate case of a London publishing house strongly associated with the British royal family, aristocracy, and gentry, and the cultures of rank, deference, privilege, and elitism they entail, continuing to compile genealogies of the "distinguished" Irish families of a postcolonial republic and of a province whose relationship to the British state has been violently disputed. At the same time, its compilation of "distinguished" family histories was presented as a resource for understanding historical complexity and appreciating the cultural diversity of Ireland. These two contrary perspectives presage the themes of contested authority, authenticity, distinction, belonging, and nobility that are the subject of this chapter.

They also suggest that a simple contrast between the traditional and conservative dimensions of genealogy as a means of legitimating power and position and its radical or progressive aspects as a tool of recovering the histories of the marginalized or oppressed is an inadequate model for tracking the role of ideas of noble or distinctive descent in diasporic identifications and accounts of the national past. In former settler colonies, genealogy can be a way of making distinctions between groups based on group origins and descent and thus marking a collective ethnic difference and identity, such as Irish-American. But it also often entails establishing special sorts of distinctive diasporic connections that differentiate *within* that community of shared descent. Diasporic genealogy is as much about enacting distinction as it is about making connections, differentiation as much as collective identification. A more exclusive ancestral link to a noble Gaelic heritage may be more appealing for some than just sharing Irish origins. While an Irish working-class emigrant background is a mark of authenticity within Irish diasporic writing in Britain, the public culture of Irish-American genealogy is dominated by references to ancient Gaelic kings and clans even if this is far removed from, or of marginal interest in, many personal genealogical projects.

This contrast between the conservative and progressive dimensions of genealogy also obscures the close, but often now forgotten, relationships between the traditions of titled genealogy and heraldry in Britain and Ireland and the popular versions that were emerging in Britain, Ireland, and North America in the 1970s, as the publication of *Burke's Introduction to Irish Ancestry* suggests. These relationships have historical foundations and contemporary continuities. Sir William Burke, son of John Burke the founder of the eponymous publishers, served as the Ulster king of arms—the head of the heraldic authority, the Office of Arms in Dublin—from 1853 to 1892. Now located close to the National Library of Ireland in central Dublin, the Office of the Chief Herald of Ireland (formerly known as the Genealogical Office after the Office of Arms was renamed in 1943) and its Heraldic Museum are key sites in organized and independent genealogical visits to Ireland. Those with the necessary connections and enough money can pay to have personalized coats of arms designed and registered in the Office of the Chief Herald. The desire to recover and commemorate the histories of the most poor and most powerless and the attraction of noble lineage and ethnic distinction are entangled strands of Irish diasporic genealogy. This means that the neatness of this contrast between the political implications of "elite" and "ordinary" ancestry fails to capture genealogy's ambiguous and often surprising effects.

However, this contrast between reactionary traditions of pedigree and progressive "ordinary" family history is complicated further by the different meanings that "noble descent" holds in Ireland and, indeed, the different categories of Irish nobility. Writing in the magazine *Irish Roots* in 1995, Chevalier William F. Marmion identified four categories of nobiliary titles more or less recognized in Ireland: "Peers of England/Great Britain who are *also* peers of Ireland," "Peers of Ireland," "Feudal Baronies/Manorial Lordships/ Miscellaneous," and "Gaelic Titles." Marmion divides these four categories into two groups: the first three "emanated from the British Crown in one of its personalities, and one is native Irish."[4] From a nationalist anticolonial perspective, the origins of noble title, stemming either from the British crown as colonial power or from the collective authority of the native Gaelic order, distinguish between illegitimate and legitimate nobility. In Irish national history, the high kings, kings, and noblemen of medieval Ireland and those in the early modern period such as the sixteenth-century Gaelic leaders Hugh O'Neill and Hugh O'Donnell, who resisted Elizabethan colonization in Ulster, are, like the warriors of Irish mythology, heroic figures of native culture and native resistance. Celebrating Gaelic noble lineage can thus serve an anticolonial reassertion of a natural and native nobility.

According to strictly nationalist criteria of belonging, the different origins of those recognized as noble—Gaelic, Anglo-Norman, Scottish, English—determine the legitimacy of their presence and title and differentiate between native Gaelic and intrusive settler nobility. The "Anglo-Irish" aristocracy have occupied the position of alien oppressors in Irish nationalist history. Yet distinctions between "native" and "foreign" do not neatly align with the categories of Crown or Gaelic nobility. Many Gaelic lords were granted English Crown titles in the colonial process of dismantling the old Gaelic order in early modern Ireland. Under the policy of "surrender and regrant," Gaelic chiefs threatened with confiscation could surrender their land to the Crown to have it returned to them with the bestowal of new earldoms in exchange for their loyalty and acceptance of English law. Those still holding British peerages in contemporary Ireland and Northern Ireland include "settler" families who have been in Ireland for centuries. Those claiming direct descent from the old Gaelic kings, princes, and lords as "Chiefs of the Name" or other noble Gaelic titles may descend from families who have lived in Spain or Portugal for over two hundred years.

Exploring the meanings of nobility and noble descent in relation to colonial history, Irish nationalism, diasporic identifications, and the entanglements of royalty, heraldry, and "native" heritage in a postcolonial republic involves attending to the double meaning of distinction. This term denotes the noble or distinguished and, through the work of Pierre Bourdieu, the cultural processes through which individuals differentiate themselves from others.[5] In the cultures of Irish noble and ordinary genealogy, ideas of taste and aesthetic judgement that Pierre Bourdieu famously identified as ways of asserting class difference intersect with the question of the appeal and disputed authenticity of different versions of Irishness, which produce a range of approaches to the heraldic crests, pottery cottages, shillelaghs, and shamrock-covered tea towels on sale to genealogical visitors. Contemporary interest in Gaelic noble descent, arguments about the appropriateness of a republican government formally recognizing Gaelic or Crown titles, and disputes about commodification and ownership that this chapter explores involve competing approaches to questions of historical justice, national history, the role of the state, cultural authenticity and cultural property, and what counts as "native" or "foreign." These perspectives are the bases of alliances and tensions between those located across the geography of Irish homeland and diaspora.

Summer School Lessons

On the evening of Wednesday, 15 June 2005, in the former railway station house by the ruins of Shane's Castle on the north coast of Lough Neagh in County Antrim, Northern Ireland, the first of five annual O'Neill Summer Schools was officially opened. The location was the estate of Raymond O'Neill, Lord O'Neill of Shane's Castle, fourth Baron O'Neill and current lord lieutenant of County Antrim, who welcomed the gathered group of speakers, local participants, a small group of visitors from England and the United States, and one distinguished guest. This special guest was Hugo O'Neill, Hugh Mac Ui Neill Buidhe, The O'Neill of Clanaboy of Lisbon who, as the mayor of Antrim acknowledged in his welcome, had traveled "from his home in Portugal to his ancestral home here."[6] This was not the first occasion that Lord O'Neill and Hugo O'Neill had both attended an O'Neill event. In 1982, the first International Gathering of the Clan O'Neill took place at Shane's Castle. This event featured the "first inauguration of an O'Neill Chieftain, that of Jorge O'Neill, (as the O'Neill Buidhe of Clanaboy), a Portuguese Noble, to take place for centuries" in the presence of "The Rt. Hon. The Lord O'Neill of Shane's Castle, The Rt. Hon. The Lord O'Neill of the Maine, Hugo O'Neill (Chieftain elect) and many other dignitaries."[7] Ten years later at the 1992 O'Neill gathering, "on the eve of the summer solstice at the historic hill fort of Grianan Aileach," Hugo O'Neill, Jorge O'Neill's son, was inaugurated as chief of the Clanaboy O'Neills.

These clan gatherings have become familiar occasions in the culture of Irish diasporic genealogy and regional cultural events calendars in Ireland and Northern Ireland. As with the first two O'Neill events, local enthusiasts organize a series of talks, tours, and entertainment, sometimes including ceremonial inaugurations of "Chiefs of the Name" for locals and international visitors who share the "clan" name. Though the first gatherings of this kind took place in the 1950s, encouraged by the Irish clan enthusiast Eoin O'Mahony, who hosted a series of "Clans of Ireland" radio progams on RTE, Irish clan gatherings drawing on the model of Scottish clan gatherings were popularized from the late 1980s as way of encouraging genealogical tourism. This popularization has been presented as contributing to "the national cultural revival" of the twentieth century.[8] In 1989 the Irish government instigated the establishment of the Clans of Ireland, Ltd., as a registered charity "to co-ordinate the activities of Irish clans," which, as the organization's Web site explains, "function as special interest groups which actively safeguard our cultural heritage and traditions" by their "research into the origins and early history of the surname, and . . . guidance to members who wish to trace their Irish ancestry." The conditions of clan and personal membership are broad but clearly defined: "An Irish Clan may be registered if the surname is either authoritatively documented as being of Irish origin, or has a documented presence in Ireland prior to the Great Famine." "Membership of any Irish clan is open to any and every individual with an ancestor having the family surname, with no restrictions as to race, religion or gender."[9] Clan gatherings such as those of the O'Driscoll, O'Malley, Kavanagh, and Gallagher clans are now familiar events.

The O'Neill Summer School, like other clan gatherings, focused on one notable Irish family. Yet its format also followed another well-established tradition of lively discussion between participants and specialist presenters in the many literary or historical summer schools that take place in Northern Ireland and Ireland. Christine Doherty, the principal organizer of the O'Neill Summer School, wanted this event to be different from the previous O'Neill clan gatherings—"to be more inclusive." Though the theme of the event was a history that surrounds one noble family, and though the significance of genealogical continuities of descent were clearly featured within the event, the history of the family was explored as a way of addressing a history of a locality and region that was not the exclusive possession of those with ancestral connection to that name.

An appreciation of the historical significance of lineage was evident in the enthusiastic response to the involvement of Lord O'Neill and his sister Fionn (O'Neill) Morgan, Hugo O'Neill, and Hector MacDonnell, uncle of Randal Mac-Donnell, The MacDonnell of the Glens, as well as in the focus of the summer school. But this was not an event in which direct connection via a surname among and between participants was celebrated. Only three people bearing the O'Neill surname were present: Peggy, Raymond, and Hugo. Peggy, originally from Boston and now living in Virginia, told me she wasn't sure where in Ireland her O'Neill ancestors—who had arrived in the United States via Manchester—came from. On this occasion, then, the shared O'Neill surname links not a single lineage or family history but three strands in the complex Irish history of settlement and migration: British colonial settlement in Ireland, the emigration of Gaelic nobility to continental Europe, and the familiar story of "ordinary" Irish emigration. The different relationships of these three "O'Neills" to noble O'Neill descent were not explicitly explored in the event. But the involvement of Lord O'Neill and The O'Neill posed a puzzle of relatedness. It set in train a process of trying to decipher the relationships between the branches of the O'Neills of Ulster, histories of succession, and the wider historical contexts that shaped the transfer of names, land, and power in early modern Ulster.

In Northern Ireland, the reading of surnames as clues to political and religious identity is a familiar practice, but events that center on patrilineal inheritance of noble names and titles can bring the known unreliability of this system to the surface in striking ways. At the O'Neill clan gathering of 1982, Lord O'Neill of the Maine, uncle of Raymond O'Neill and formerly Captain Terence O'Neill, Unionist prime minister of Northern Ireland from 1963 to 1969, congratulated the O'Neills gathered: "As an O'Neill you can be proud of your ancestry. It is not everyone who can claim to be a member of the oldest traceable family left in Europe." This celebration of pride in membership in an ancient Irish family by a former Unionist and Protestant prime minister may have been unexpected for overseas visitors and local participants for whom the O'Neill name is a particularly charged patronym that stands not only for one Gaelic royal family but is part of the origin story of the Irish nation.

The almost successful but failed resistance of Hugh O'Neill to Elizabethan ambitions in sixteenth-century Ulster has long been remembered as a heroic stand for the last of the old Gaelic order before its final collapse. But the heroic figure of "The Great O'Neill" is also situated in a lineage of collective national origins. Cultural nationalists in the early twentieth century took the medieval genealogies of noble Gaelic families as evidence of Gaelic national origins that stretched back to Milesian settlers. In Thomas Matthews's foldout chart of the genealogy of the O'Neills of Ulster that accompanied his history of the family published in 1907, the O'Neill pedigree begins with "Nail, or Niul, son of Fenius the Antiquary, King of Scythia (son of Boath, son of Magog, Son of Japhet, son of Noah)" who are the predecessors of Milesius, whose male descendants are the progenitors of the great families of the Irish provinces including Niall of the Nine Hostages, the founding father of the O'Neills of Ulster.[10] The traditional association of the O'Neills as one of the five ancient "royal bloods" of precolonial Gaelic society persists locally and travels with genealogical tourists to these Irish clan events.

Clan gatherings may thus bring together people who share an interest in one clan but who hold markedly different perspectives on the historical processes that are reflected in the presence of different forms of noble descent in Ireland. Though based on a celebration of shared ancestry, these events can point to differences that trouble the taken-for-granted meaning of being of Irish descent. As clan gatherings became increasingly popular in the early 1990s, they also became the focus of critical attention. Despite their presentation in terms of cultural revival, critics argued that they were contrived ventures that sacrificed authenticity and historical accuracy for commercial success.[11] Nevertheless, by the mid-1990s clan gatherings were being incorporated into Mary Robinson's argument about diasporic Irishness as opportunities for international dialogue and interconnections.[12] These gatherings may provide opportunities for "dialogue" as Robinson suggested, but, like family gatherings, they also present the demands of dealing with the juxtaposition of difference within an assumed collective identity.

Terence O'Neill's presence at the O'Neill clan gathering of 1982 may have jarred with a diasporic nationalist celebration of a Gaelic and Catholic Ireland. His appreciation of pride in ancient Gaelic ancestry may have been unexpected and unexpectedly challenging to assumptions that the O'Neill lineage is solely associated with heroic Catholic and Gaelic resistance. It would have seemed incongruous to those inclined to read this Lord O'Neill's name and title as products of an unjust and illegitimate English neocolonial state and to those who consider the history of Gaelic Ireland as the rightful property of only those with the appropriate qualifications of unqualified Gaelic descent. The involvement of both Terence O'Neill and his nephew, the current Lord O'Neill of Shane's Castle, in O'Neill events suggests more complex relationships between history, ancestry, attachment, and belonging. As this O'Neill gathering suggested, events like these, however staged and "inauthentic," can nevertheless be more challenging than Robinson's version of diaspora is often taken to imply.

At the O'Neill Summer School of 2005, the heroic and noble Gaelic associations of the O'Neills were both evoked and deflated. For Hugo O'Neill, as a descendant of the last early modern Clanaboy O'Neill chieftain and whose ancestor Shane O'Neill left Ireland for Lisbon in the early eighteenth century to escape the Penal Laws enacted against Catholics and Presbyterians, his direct lineage to a noble Gaelic family and its aristocratic native culture are profoundly significant. At the inauguration of Hugo O'Neill as chief of the name in 1992, Fergus

Gillespie, then deputy chief herald of Ireland, spent half an hour reciting Hugo's patronymy in Irish.[13] For Hugo O'Neill, this is a long lineage of men of honor. Launching the summer school program initiative in 2004, he described his ancestors' character: "The seventeen centuries of our family's recorded history, provide ample examples of extraordinary leaders, always chosen as a result of their courage, their warring ability, their cunning and competent bargaining power. They were invariably the paradigm of a great gentleman, physically fit, witty, generous, and, judging by the number of children left, many times by different wives, they were also competent lovers."[14] This is an exclusive heritage, but, for Hugo, it is also one that "moulded the character of all Irish people . . . each one is son of kings." In this way, having a direct O'Neill connection both matters deeply and, more democratically, doesn't matter.

But the persistence of an ideal of purity of descent and direct connection can trouble the senses of historical location and belonging that participation in the event suggests. Raymond O'Neill, whose commitment to supporting cultural and historical activities is evident in his work for all three events and role as patron of the 2005 summer school, explained at its opening that "his group are somewhat watered down"; he is, he admits, "not pure, but proud of the association" with the O'Neills. Raymond O'Neill inherited his title from his great-great-grandfather Rev. William Chichester, descendant of a earlier marriage to Mary O'Neill, who inherited the estates in 1855, took the name O'Neill, and was created first Baron O'Neill in 1868.[15] So in contrast to Hugo O'Neill's Gaelic title and patrilineage, his title derives from the Crown and his O'Neill name was inherited via "the female line." Raymond's acknowledgment echoes his uncle's. In his biography, Terence O'Neill, although proud to use the O'Neill surname, regretted that "according to Burke's *Peerage*, the O'Neill family is the oldest, tracable family left in Europe, but unfortunately and for the record, we are only descended from this ancient lineage, through the female line."[16] Peter Beresford Ellis, champion of early Gaelic Ireland and Gaelic noble lineage today, is blunt in his assessment that this O'Neill link "to the O'Neill royal house of Ulster by this family through one distaff connection, descended from the Clanaboy line in the nineteenth century, is very tenuous indeed."[17] This failed ideal of pure lineage and legitimacy via patrilineal descent was not addressed directly in the summer school because of the sensitivities of calling it forth even in order to dismiss its significance. These are sensitivities about the conventional contrast between Gaelic purity and resistance and the equivocal position of those whose status derives from fealty to the Crown. At an event like this, even questioning these distinctions of belonging could have divisive or at least discomforting effects.[18]

In contrast, the treatment of earlier claims to noble O'Neill lineage and heroic status was much more robustly demythologizing. The choice of speakers by the organizing committee of academics, local history activists, and heritage experts clearly reflected a policy of using the theme of a noble Gaelic family, whose genealogies traditionally stretch to antiquity, to explore the prehistories and histories that surround this long family history. The first full day began with Brian Warner, keeper of archaeology and ethnography at the Ulster Museum Belfast, challenging the mythology of the arrival of the Celts as the founding people of Gaelic Ireland to which the ancient genealogies of the O'Neills stretched. The arrival of people in the fifth century AD did not mean the replacement of a population but, he argues, the replacement of one dynastic nobility by another. Warner presented Ireland in the Iron Age not as a Celtic country but comprised of a small aristocracy of outside origin and a common population of Mesolithic origin. Rather than representing early Gaelic settlers, the original Uí Néills, antecedents to the O'Neills, were "warrior adventurers who had come into Ireland from Britain and the continent in the late first century AD" including Irish returnees who in Britain were "named Goidels, the Welsh word for Irishmen."[19] Warner's image of noble and mercenary traffic between Ireland and Romano-Britain disrupts an image of Gaelic isolation, broken only by Norse invaders until the arrival of the Anglo-Normans.

The archaeologist and historian Brian Lacey followed Warner's deconstruction of myths of Celtic invasion with an account of the mixture of fact and fiction that characterized medieval O'Neill genealogies of "alleged descent." The name O'Neill, deriving from "grandson or descendant of Niall," he explains, began to be used as a surname in the tenth century for descendants of the Uí Néill king, Niall Glundubh. Uí Néill is thus a dynastic name that includes other patronymically named lineages and does not correspond directly to O'Neill. Neither were all who held the O'Neill name directly related since the advantages of noble connection prompted the fabrication of genealogical connection. Genealogies themselves were representations of a more fluid range of relationships that could be based on blood or blood-like connections.[20] In answering a query from Hugo O'Neill, Brian Lacey likened early medieval O'Neill genealogies to "spin and PR."

This demythologizing also extended to an earlier attempt at undoing a previous mythology. The target of the historian Hiram Morgan's challenge was not the nationalist image of Hugh O'Neill, Great Earl of Tyrone, but a mid-twentieth-century biography that took the story of Hugh O'Neill as an exemplar of the complex interculturalism and complex affiliations that feature in Irish history. In 1942 Sean O'Faolain published an influential biography of the sixteenth-century Hugh O'Neill that was informed by O'Faolain's wider critical relationship to the new Free State's dominant ethos of narrow cultural and social conservatism.[21] For O'Faolain, Hugh O'Neill could not be reduced to "the Patriot myth" of "each new Hero rising against the old Tyrant," but was a figure conscious of the danger of a "suffocating" Gaelic Ireland heedless to modernity who tries to reconcile "two worlds—the Renaissance and the Medieval."[22] In Brian Friel's dramatization of Hugh O'Neill's life in his play *Making History*, which is strongly influenced by O'Faolain's biography, O'Neill struggles to manage his loyalties to Gaelic kin, the influences of his early years of life in noble homes of England, and his love for his English Protestant wife Mabel Bagnel, sister of his enemy, the queen's marshal in Ulster, Henry Bagnel.[23]

This hybrid, equivocating figure is based, Morgan argues, on "faulty historiography." There is no evidence for O'Neill being fostered in Kent. His marriages were based on their political usefulness. But Hiram Morgan also eschews the categorization of Hugh O'Neill as traitor or patriot and foregrounds instead O'Neill's pragmatic self-interest and family loyalties as well as his innovative articulation of an ideal of a united Catholic Irish nation led by Gaelic Irish and Old English dynasties.[24] Morgan challenges the replacement of one sort of romanticization of simple heroism with another of "troubled split-mindedness."[25] Rather than see O'Neill as a figure torn between irreconcilable cultures, he is better understood as making politically expedient decisions in the entangled world of Gaelic and Elizabethan Ireland. This summer school, focused on one especially symbolic noble family, thus finely balanced a mixture of celebration, commemoration, and challenging correctives to historical certainties of heroic ancestry, ancient origins, and unbroken patrilineage.

But it was not always a smooth or stable balance. Subtle eddies of dissension occasionally broke the surface and revealed the participants' different relationships to the nature and meaning of the past. The organizers were aware of the tension between the spectacle of clan gatherings—the sort of ceremony that Hugo

O'Neill said he missed and that may attract more overseas participants—and the serious scholarly historical engagement that they wanted to achieve. Other tensions remained implicit. The past is still potentially divisive and continues to be sensitive in Northern Ireland despite the efforts of the organizers to provide a "forum for open discussion and exchange of opinions." At an evening event, one organizer jokingly apologized to "Her Majesty's Lord Lieutenant of County Antrim" for the guest singer's ballad recounting the unwelcome presence of the Black and Tans. Another man tutted with obvious irritation at the joke. Other perspectives on what a focus on nobility may elide were less overt but still evident. After that evening of song and reminiscence, one participant told me that he felt that the nostalgic narration by a former servant of his relationship to the titled local landowner concealed the compulsory deference and class relations it entailed.

The question of patrilineal inheritance of title and the subordinate and subsidiary position of women in this tradition surfaced also. The privileging of male descent and the implied inferiority of "the female line" was alluded to briefly in Fionn Morgan's speech in which, reflecting on the inheritance of the O'Neill title via a female ancestor, she suggested that the work of the Oxford geneticist Bryan Sykes on mitochondrial DNA may show that female descent may matter more in inheritance than previously supposed. This awareness of the exclusivity of a model of nobility and local history dominated by O'Neill men in the past and the present may have shaped the summer school's program. Planning the 2005 event around the theme of the relationship between the O'Neills and the Mac-Donnells of the Glens of Antrim and the Western Isles of Scotland, through the seventeenth-century alliance of Protestant Lady Rose O'Neill and the Catholic Royalist Sir Randal MacDonnell, perhaps reflected a wish to simultaneously foreground the Scottish dimension of Ulster's history, explore a historic example of noble "mixed marriage," and balance the focus on O'Neill men.

The O'Neill Summer School thus suggests that exploring history through a noble lineage may not simply reinforce the traditional significance of pedigree nor the romance of Gaelic nobility. The history of the family, like the history of Ulster, turns out to be more complex. The histories explored in the event do not confirm certainties of national origins; the involvement of both Raymond O'Neill and Hugo O'Neill suggest historical and contemporary interconnections between nobility across any simple divides of place, affiliation, and religion. Though most strongly attached to the significance of a patrilineal pedigree to Gaelic Ireland,

Hugo O'Neill, the O'Neill of Clanaboy who returned home to Portugal, does not conform to a model of belonging where domicile and descent neatly coincide. Instead the summer school offered puzzles and lessons in the complexities of identification and belonging. The O'Neill Summer School subtly succeeded in making a noble lineage the starting point for exploring a complex history. Other approaches to nobility in relation to the nation, state, and diasporic Irishness suggest equally complex and often more conflictual perspectives in which distinctions between different forms of nobility figure much more overtly.

The Politics of Recognition

Another more exclusive event took place during the O'Neill Summer School in June 2005. Hugo O'Neill, as The O'Neill and "Chief of the Name" used the occasion of the summer school to call a meeting of the Standing Council of Irish Chiefs and Chieftains. The banquet, held in the Londonderry Arms Hotel in Carnlough on the Antrim coast road, was the first time that the chiefs had met in Northern Ireland. This organization was established in 1991 to represent the interests of the men who are recognized as the direct descendants of the men who held Gaelic noble titles as leaders of their extended kinship groups, and are commonly known as Chiefs of the Name. The current Chiefs of the Name and their places of residence are The O'Brien, Prince of Thomond (County Clare); The O'Conor Don, Prince of Connacht (East Sussex, England); and The O'Neill (Setubal, Portugal). As descendants of three high kingship dynasties, these three are also claimants to the position of Ard Rí, or High King of Ireland. Other Chiefs of the Name who descend from provincial kings are The MacDermot, Prince of Coolavin (Naas, County Kildare), The McGillicuddy of the Reeks (Mulligar, County Westmeath), The O'Callaghan (Barcelona, Spain), The O'Donaghue of the Glens (Tullamore, County Offaly), The O'Donovan (Skibbereen, County Cork), The O'Morchoe (or Murphy) of Oulartleigh (Gorey, County Wexford), The Fox (Mildura, Victoria, Australia), The O'Grady of Kilballyowen (Sussex, England), The O'Kelly of Gallagh and Tycooly (Dalkey, County Dublin), The O'Donnell of Tirconnell (Harare, Zimbabwe), The MacMorrough Kavanagh (Pembrokeshire, South Wales), The O'Long of Garranelongy (Faranes, County Cork), The O'Dogherty (Ó Dochartaigh) of Inishowen (Cadiz, Spain), The Maguire of Fermanagh (Dublin), The O'Carroll of Ely (Stockton, California), The

O'Ruairc (O'Rorke) of Breifne (London), MacDonnell of the Glens (Dublin), and Joyce of Joyce Country.[26] Most are members of the council.

With members in Ireland, England, Wales, Spain, Portugal, Australia, and the United States, the council is thus a transnational organization committed to the continuance of a precolonial nobility as a national cultural heritage. Nobility in the Standing Council refers strictly to Gaelic noble ancestry with the exception of The Joyce, who is included because of the early and thorough Gaelicization of this Norman family in medieval Ireland. Until 2003 the Chiefs of the Name were also recognized by the Irish government through the Genealogical Office and chief herald. The origins of this tradition of state recognition, different interpretations of the authority of the Genealogical Office, and the recent change in policy are part of continuing process of working through the legacies of a colonial administration and the relationship between the postcolonial republic and precolonial Gaelic royalty, practically and legally as well as symbolically.

One institution of the Crown and British civil service in Ireland inherited by the new Free State in 1922 was the Office of Arms. As Susan Hood explains in her history of its survival, the Office of Arms was founded in 1552 to cater for the design and registration of heraldic arms and titles of the English men granted land in the Tudor plantations and of those Gaelic Lords gaining English titles in exchange for acceptance of the new order and authority of the Crown. The Office of Arms derived its heraldic authority from the monarch and was charged with overseeing matters of ceremony and protocol for the British administration in Ireland, and by the mid–nineteenth century it was central to the organization of the elaborate ceremonial events of Dublin Castle. Despite its direct relationship with the British monarchy and its strong associations with the colonial order, the Office of Arms survived the foundation of the Free State in 1922 and continued to grant arms under the authority of the Crown until 1943, when its name was changed to the Genealogical Office and the title of the former royal appointment of Ulster king of arms was replaced the title of chief herald of Ireland. As Susan Hood notes, "It was the last Office of State to be transferred from British to Irish control."[27] The reasons for the continued existence of an office authorized by the British Crown and supported by the British treasury, she explains, reflected both British and Irish perspectives on its continued service to Northern Ireland as well as the Free State, which included the design of the arms of the new Northern Irish government. Though the office was commonly viewed as a "last relic of British rule in the twenty-six counties,"[28] the Taoiseach, Eamon De Valera, recognized the symbolic significance of a body whose jurisdiction defied the partition of Ireland. British authorities were correspondingly reluctant to sever the imperial connection and especially concerned that the heraldic needs of the new Northern Irish state be adequately catered for by the Office of Arms. Its eventual transfer created the unusual situation of a heraldic office within a constitutional republic, catering for the needs of residents and institutions of both Ireland and Northern Ireland and the heraldic and genealogical interests of those with emigrant ancestral connections to all parts of the island.

In the 1950s, the newly named Genealogical Office was recognized as a cultural asset in strategies to encourage tourism to Ireland. Though its heraldic function continued, its work in responding to genealogical queries that had begun to dominate in the 1920s expanded significantly in the 1950s. The National Library now offers the genealogical help once paid for by visitors to the Genealogical Office, but the Heraldic Museum remains an important site on the genealogical tourist itinerary. Shops nearby supply coats of arms that correspond to names in diasporic family trees and that, on plaques and mugs and Web sites, both materialize and mark distinctive Irish connections. For many visitors, these coats of arms are strongly associated with an old native Gaelic Ireland and ancient Gaelic noble families even if the material culture and aesthetics of heraldry derive from an Anglo-Norman heraldic tradition, and even though those arms were historically authorized by the herald as a formal member of the British royal household.

But arguments about the value of the Genealogical Office are not confined to its contribution to genealogical tourism. In 1995 plans to incorporate the Genealogical Office within the National Library, and the degraded autonomy of the office that this implied, prompted a series of responses that argued for the importance of its function and asserted its cultural significance. Implicitly challenging the view that the Genealogical Office represents a remnant of British imperialism, Susan Hood argued instead that it was an institution that had served the needs of Anglo-Norman, Gaelic, and English nobility in Ireland and continues to serve a diverse constituency in Ireland, Northern Ireland, and across the diaspora and thus should be recognized as a shared heritage. In her letter to the *Irish Times* in October 1995, she made the case that the "office should now be preserved and strengthened as a symbol of continuity and common heritage within the whole of Ireland. It should not be sacrificed for the sake of bureaucratic efficiency."[29] The office is significant because of its historical continuity and contemporary status as a unique "cross-border" institution. Its record of serving different constituencies—Anglo-Norman lords, Gaelic families from the early modern period, seventeenth- and eighteenth-century émigrés in continental Europe, nineteenth-century "Anglo-Irish" families, early-twentieth-century "Anglo-Irish" families leaving Ireland on the eve of and after independence, and, since the 1920s, the New World diaspora—reflects a long and complex history of emigration and immigration and claims to status and statements of identity within and beyond Ireland. The heraldic office is thus reinterpreted as an institution that reflects a complex colonial history and a postcolonial cultural politics of pluralism.

Less sympathetic interpretations of the role of the Genealogical Office focus on its disputed authority to recognize noble titles. But arguments about its legitimacy can be differently nuanced. Though the constitution of the Republic forbids the granting of titles, it is bound by international law to recognize those granted prior to independence, and it recognizes proprietary rights to titles as "incorporeal hereditaments." For some, the existence of an institution associated with claims to noble status is simply incompatible with the egalitarian ethos of a republic. Others argue not that noble titles are illegitimate in a republic but that the authority for recognizing them cannot lie with the Genealogical Office. Terence MacCarthy, whose title as MacCarthy Mór was recognized by the chief herald in 1990, argues that the Genealogical Office did not in fact inherit the authority to grant title from the former Office of Arms. This remained with the Crown and after independence was subsumed back into the London College of Arms. Thus for McCarthy, due to the Irish constitutional proscription against title, the Genealogical Office has neither Crown nor state authority to grant arms that confer nobility. He questions "whether applicants to the Office for grant of arms realize that under Irish law they, and their descendants remain ignoble and enjoy neither place, position, nor gentility in consequence of receiving arms from the Republic's Chief Herald."[30] Though MacCarthy would presumably reject the Crown's continued authority to confer nobility in Ireland, this does not dissuade him from pointing to the Genealogical Office's reduced role in relation to noble title: "Whereas the arms granted by Ulster Kings of Arms were patents of gentility, those issued by the Chief Herald of Ireland are mere devisals, neither conveying, nor recognizing, nor originating hereditary social status."[31] He doubts whether this is understood by American applicants for arms since he considers it "inconceivable that anyone would pay almost $1,500 to receive a certificate devising arms, but conveying no claim to gentility or nobility, when for a much smaller sum he could simply devise his own arms and copyright them in his country of origin or residence."[32] MacCarthy challenges the authority of the office to convey any title, Gaelic or otherwise. But further cases are made against the office's relationship to specifically Gaelic noble titles, such as those held by the Chiefs of the Name, that were formerly ignored by the Office of Arms as non-Crown titles.[33]

Soon after his appointment in 1943 as chief herald, Edward MacLysaght set about tackling what he described as "the vexed problem of the Irish 'Chiefs.'" In his memoirs, he explains,

> Ulster's Office has always ignored it with the result that anyone could call himself "The MacThis" or "The O'That," and without much difficulty such people could get themselves included in the list which appeared annually in *Thom's Directory*, *Whitaker's Almanac* and elsewhere under the heading "Ancient Irish Chieftains," and so acquire in the eyes of the world a certain *cachet* which simple assumption would not give. The situation verged on the ridiculous when a Mr Phelan become *motu proprio* "O'Phelan Prince of the Decies" and half a dozen other persons were quasi-officially designated by titles to which they had no right, as fine sounding as that of the genuine O Connor Don.[34]

Continuing to ignore the question of the popular or informal recognition and adoption of Gaelic noble titles, he felt, could lead to a proliferation of spurious and completing claims. Yet instituting a system of recognizing the noble titles of verified descendants of Irish chiefs by the state through the Genealogical Office could directly violate the state's constitutional proscription of title. Faced with this problem of the existence of Gaelic noble titles contravening the laws of a republic that was founded on Gaelic nationalism, MacLysaght consulted De Valera, who "agreed that the chieftainries were designations rather than titles and that consequently we (the Genealogical Office) should go ahead and, after thorough investigation, formally register any person claiming to be Chief of his name when the evidence was found acceptable."[35]

Thus began a policy of checking the descent of chiefly claimants "by primo-geniture from the last inaugurated or *de facto* chieftain"[36] that resulted in the first publication of the Genealogical Office's official list or register of chiefs—"Clár na dTaoiseach"—in 1944 and 1945, that was expanded to twenty by the early 1990s. The "semantic side-stepping" that the heraldic expert Gerald Crotty recognizes in attempting to differentiate "title" from "designation" reflects this effort to honor a Gaelic heritage without contravening the ethos of the Republic. This is also reflected in the different ways in which noble titles are expressed by the Genealogical Office and the Standing Council of Irish Chiefs and Chieftains, with the Genealogical Office avoiding including titles of "Prince," as in *The MacCarthy Mór, Prince of Desmond*, that the Standing Council has no inhibition about using.[37]

Nevertheless, for Crotty, "the situation whereby the government of a republic purports to authenticate successions to the headships of noble and indeed royal families whose titles derive from a long-extinct political system is a very extraordinary one indeed. . . . Perhaps Dr MacLysaght and Mr de Valera saw the chiefships as a link with the Gaelic past. By definition however, no republic can claim to represent the old Gaelic order, which was essentially monarchical."[38] However, Crotty appreciates the stimulating effect that the Genealogical Office's list had on the foundation of the Standing Council, which, he feels, is the most appropriate body for examining claims to chiefships. The most severe critics are less appreciative, arguing not that the recognition of Gaelic title is anomalous within a republic—although this is often acknowledged—but that more significantly, the recognition of Gaelic titles by the state is both illegitimate and detrimental to the Gaelic culture it purports to represent, especially when paralleled by the policy of encouraging clan tourism, and with it the creation of "honorary chiefs."

Writing in *Irish Roots* in 1993, Eoghan McNarey challenged the authority of the Genealogical Office to have any regulatory function over Gaelic chiefly titles. For him the Genealogical Office is "not only English in it origins but was established to undermine the Gaelic order."[39] The early modern promotion of heraldry in the Gaelic aristocracy, he argues, was part of a policy of Anglicization that set out to destroy that order. For McNarey, MacLysaght's creation of the list of surviving Gaelic chiefships was, like the adoption of the terms "Taoiseach" and "Tániste" for prime minister and deputy prime minister, a superficial gesture of respect for Gaelic heritage that "caused more damage to Gaelic chiefship than Oliver Cromwell! It discouraged valid claims from being made and caused genuine titles to be abandoned (such as MacSuibhne na Tuatha, held by the late Marquis MacSwiney of Mashanaglas in the Papal States). It inhibited the re-establishment of the Gaelic order, and by restricting the number of 'recognised chiefs' to a mere dozen, prevented any sensible development of a clan spirit in Ireland."[40] The list is considered to be an unwelcome interference in matters of nobility.

MacLysaght's decision to adopt the principal of primogeniture to determine chiefly status, and by implication subsequent succession, is also taken as another affront to Gaelic tradition. The Gaelic system of succession, known as tanistry, whereby a successor to the chief is elected by an extended kin group from among those eligible—the derbhfine composed of the sons, grandsons, and great-grandsons of an original chiefly ancestor—lasted up until the early modern period. As Crotty notes, "With the possible exception of the O'Neills, the chiefly families did not turn to primogeniture until the implementation of the Tudor policy of surrender and regrant" (although, as Crotty also notes, "those families who did maintain the continuity of their chiefly titles from Tudor times all followed primogeniture").[41] Viewing the implied enforcement of succession by primogeniture as a violation of Gaelic tradition in exchange for recognition of title, Terence Mac-Carthy argues that MacLysaght's system "operated as a sort of policy of 'Surrender and Regrant' by sleight of hand."[42] The work of the postcolonial state, via the Genealogical Office, is thus again likened to the cultural violence of the former colonial power. For McNarey, the existence of Gaelic chiefs not only rightfully contradicts the republican constitution, but it challenges the cultural authenticity and authority of the state:

> Like it or not, the Republic cannot so falsify history as to "deroyalise" the surviving Gaelic dynasties. Their status has been recognised by many sovereign states, including the Holy See which, in the 1890s, styled the then O'Neill as "Most Serene Prince of Clanaboy," and is perfectly agreeable to International Law. The fact that some people wish to deny this status, for political reasons is understandable. The continued existence of these royal, princely and aristocratic houses challenges the Republic's paint thin "Gaelicness" and its perception of itself as a resurrected Gaelic Ireland.[43]

As the reference to the title conferred on the O'Neill by the Holy See in Mc-Narey's argument illustrates, those arguing for the significance of the remaining

Gaelic nobles often support their cases by pointing to the recognition they receive within a network of noble and royal families exchanging honorary titles and belonging to international chivalric orders. Though critics reject the authority of the British Crown in Ireland and see restoring a system of formal terms of noble address for Gaelic chiefs and their nobility as a form of postcolonial cultural recovery,[44] arguments about their national significance are often made through a transnational noble network and their retinues of enthusiasts for the former noble and royal families of modern European democracies.

In other words, these anticolonialists celebrate precolonial culture and disparage the cultural ethos of the postcolonial republic through an international network of noble alliances and monarchist supporters. This approach parallels a similarly complicated, and in some ways contradictory, critique of the Genealogical Office. Some critics argue that it lacks the authority of the Crown that it once had and is not authorized by a constitutionally republican state; that its attempts to regulate Gaelic titles were unwarranted, intrusive, and culturally damaging; and that the origins of the office and heraldry itself are part of alien and aggressive colonial culture. Yet the Genealogical Office is also charged with a failure to uphold the "Law of Arms." According to the Law of Arms, coats of arms belong exclusively to the individual they have been granted to and those who subsequently inherit them directly. Arms thus belong as property to an individual rather than a "name" or "clan." For Terence MacCarthy, the sale of coats of arms outside the formal system of application and grant, including the sale of heraldic souvenirs, constitutes "tresspass on the rights of Irish armigers."[45]

Chief Herald MacLysaght is often blamed for promoting what MacCarthy describes as the "absurd concept of Sept Arms" in which the arms of a sept (or these days, clan) belong to all those bearing the sept (or clan) surname. Although he was critical of the commodification of heraldic arms for genealogical tourists in the 1950s,[46] in his *Irish Families* of 1957, MacLysaght argued for a generous interpretation of the shared symbolic ownership of the heraldic insignia of Gaelic noble families. For MacCarthy, this stance further eroded a privilege of noble descent:

> by publishing the totally erroneous opinion that if a person could establish the fact that his surname originated in a given area of Ireland, then he might bear the arms of the relevant "Sept," which is to say, the

undifferenced arms of the Chief of the Name! No one, MacLysaght confidently but naively, asserted, "can reasonably object to an O'Kelly taking a PROPRIETARY INTEREST in those arms, provided that he is unquestionably of a family originating in the O'Kelly country of Connacht." MacLysaght must have been as ignorant of the basic principles of law as he was of heraldry if he thought that anyone other than The O'Kelly himself could have a PROPRIETARY INTEREST in the undifferenced arms of his own chiefship![47]

Crotty is similarly critical. Even if the idea of sept arms were acceptable, he argues, those eligible to bear them would have to prove their connection to the chiefly house genealogically. In contrast to the popular material culture of clan insignia enjoyed by those bearing Irish names within Irish diasporic genealogy, for Crotty, "It certainly seems absurd to suppose that all O'Briens may use the arms which came into existence in 1543 at the creation of the earldom of Thomond. It is equally absurd to suppose that the arms granted to Donogh McGillicuddy in 1688 belong to all bearers of the name. Quite a few chiefs possess certificates from Ulster King of Arms which leave no doubt that the arms are personal in the same sense as those of any armiger."[48]

Thus a desire to identify oneself through a distinct lineage and to identify with those who share that ancestry, which prompts genealogical visitors to buy and display the crest of the name, conflicts with propriety claims to individualized hereditary insignia. A sense of belonging via ancestral connection is challenged by a protectionist argument about to whom these icons of ancestry rightfully belong. A broad and extended familial sense of collective inheritance is challenged by a strictly patrilineal mode of property transfer.

The critique of the concept of extended symbolic ownership is closely tied to the wider critique of the effects of "clan tourism" on the meaning and nature of noble chiefly status. For Crotty, the anomalous situation that results from a "benevolent" policy of offering "courtesy" recognition to those who descend from Gaelic royal and noble families, as a way of honoring the Gaelic culture they are taken to represent without departing from constitutional republicanism, is compounded by a further tension. Crotty points to the contradictions between the government policy that regulates claims to Gaelic nobility and the government policy that stretches the meaning of "clan" and the authenticity of chiefly descent in order to generate tourist revenue. Similarly, for McNarey the new role of Clans of Ireland, Ltd., in registering clan organizations and distributing grants to support those registered adds to the injustice of the Genealogical Office's adopted regulatory function by again infringing on the autonomy and authority of genuine chieftains and confusing the distinctions between "historically valid" and "invented and spurious" chiefs.[49] The target of Crotty's critique is both the "clans industry" and the apparent disregard at government level for veracity in honoring Gaelic heritage:

> In recent years we have seen a spate of pseudo-chiefs "elected" or acclaimed at clan rallies. This development is aimed at the tourist market, but things have gone so far that *Bord Failte* and the company called *Clans of Ireland* now speak of "bloodline chiefs" and "honorary chiefs," as though descent from the chiefly house were not the first requirement in the matter. I don't suppose that many people are fooled by this, especially where we see pseudo-chiefs appearing for non-chiefly surnames. The clans industry is one thing. It is quite another thing, however, to see a government minister allowing himself to be acclaimed an "honorary chief" in this way, as happened just over two years ago. One is bound to ask what value the recognition of real chiefs by the government can have if a member of that government participates in a semi-theatrical parody of chiefship.[50]

The creation of "honorary chiefs" defies the system of inherited chiefly status. Furthermore, for Crotty and for others, the promotion of the idea of the "clan" to describe distinct Gaelic lineages is a distortion of the kin-based political system they are meant to represent. The assumption that a specific family name defines a clan misrepresents the Gaelic system of septs, in which, unlike the Scottish system, distinct septs, each with their own chief, can share a surname. Crotty argues that "Chief of the Sept" would be more accurate than "Chief of the Name."[51] This troubles the assumption that a Gaelic surname in the present corresponds to descent from a specific clan in the past.

Clans of Ireland, Ltd., does not restrict membership to clan societies on the basis of accepted Gaelic names but allows any surname common in Ireland before the Famine. Therefore an honorary chief may in theory be elected to associations based on names of Anglo-Norman, Scottish, or English origin. For advocates of a

"genuine" Gaelic nobility, this is an insult to Gaelic culture. Those who are critical of the role of the Genealogical Office in regulating recognized chiefs may at
the same time be anxious about the possible proliferation of "honorary chiefs" or
"bloodline chiefs" for non-Gaelic lineages. Critics reject one form of regulation
by the Genealogical Office but are concerned about having none at all. A diffu-
sion of title threatens distinction since, as McNarey argues, "When everyone's
someone, no one's anybody."[52] For MacCarthy, the inclusion of Joyce of Joyces
Country among the additions to the chief herald's list in 1990 suggested a future
in which the status of Chief of the Name is no longer limited to those of Gaelic
descent: "This surname is Anglo-Norman in origin, and the family concerned
settled in Ireland fully a century after the Fitzgeralds. Possibly a future Chief
Herald will recognize the head of the latter eminent Anglo-Norman family, the
Duke of Leinster, as 'The Fitzgerald of Kildare.' Given time, present day immigrants from the subcontinent or from Taiwan might well be listed as 'The Patel' or
'The Wong.' We must simply wait and see."[53] Deploying old distinctions between
native and foreign, MacCarthy evokes more contemporary categories of belonging and recognition. Racialized difference is used here to challenge the extension
of noble title to a descendant of an Anglo-Norman family in Ireland for centuries.
Combining racism and ethnic fundamentalism, MacCarthy presumes the absurdity of non-white as well as nonnative men being granted Gaelic styles of address
to argue that a man of Anglo-Norman descent is ineligible for this form of native
nobility. The assertion of old categories of belonging is inseparable from new
racial categories of natural and unnatural presence.

But MacCarthy's concern about the elasticity of the list is now unnecessary.
In 2003 the chief herald, Brendan O'Donoghue, on advice from the Office of the
Attorney General, decided that the policy of recognizing Gaelic titles should be
discontinued. The flags of the then twenty recognized Chiefs of the Name were
removed from the walls of the Heraldic Museum. The official reason was a need
to rectify the position on granting recognition in light of the lack of its basis in
law. However, the decision was precipitated by the crisis that ensued when the
claim of Terence MacCarthy to the title of the MacCarthy Mór, Prince of Desmond, and thus claimant to high kingship of Ireland was exposed as fraudulent.
In 1999 it was discovered that MacCarthy, who was vehemently opposed to the
Genealogical Office but who sought its recognition, had falsified his claim to title.
In his account of the scandal, Peter Berresford Ellis, who had previously been

an enthusiastic supporter of Terence MacCarthy's promotion of Gaelic nobility traditions, explained the elaborate and clever ways in which MacCarthy, with a north Belfast working-class Catholic background, built up the credibility of his claim.[54] The exposure of this hoax deeply embarrassed the Genealogical Office (who had recognized his title), the Standing Council (in which he was heavily involved), members of the MacCarthy Clan Society worldwide but especially in the United States, those to whom he had bestowed noble titles in his role as Prince of Desmond, those involved in the the Royal Eoghanacht Society he founded, and those who paid to join the Niadh Nask (a "nobiliary fraternity" he established as a continuation of a "two thousand year old" Gaelic dynastic order of nobility).[55]

The episode remains an understandably sensitive subject for all involved, and the controversy is likely to continue since the validity of other claims to the title of "Chief of the Name" is being contested by the historian and genealogist Sean Murphy, whose research was instrumental in uncovering the McCarthy fraud.[56] But the decision to end state recognition of Gaelic titles through the Genealogical Office is regretted by those who argue that the lack of any formal system of verifying Gaelic chiefly pedigrees makes it even more likely that "bogus" chiefs will proliferate, and who interpret the annulment of courtesy recognition as breaking "the link between the modern Irish State and the old Gaelic nation."[57] Now courtesy recognition is withheld from Gaelic chiefs but may be afforded to those whose titles were created by foreign crowns and or by the British Crown in Ireland prior to independence. Ironically, this change of policy coincided with the new inclusion of Irish and Scottish chiefs in *Burke's Peerage* and its recognition that their titles are older than many of the hereditary crown titles that *Burke's Peerage* traditionally recorded.[58] This history of the institution and the discontinuation of the list of Gaelic Chiefs of the Name has been a significant part of the ongoing process of addressing the relationships between old forms of hereditary privilege and position and new postcolonial political configurations. This has also entailed alternative models of the role of the Gaelic chiefs in the state as well as alternative perspectives on the place of nobility in Ireland.

Aristocratic Ireland

The status and significance of the descendants of Gaelic nobility are now detached from the state. This presumably is the best outcome for those who maintained that the Genealogical Office had no constitutional mandate nor authority over the Gaelic customs adhered to by the chiefs. But others have argued not only for a more formal role in the Irish state for those holding hereditary Gaelic titles but for their potential political role in resolving the disputed political status of Northern Ireland. Hugo O'Neill feels that "all the dispossessed Irish aristocrats, like his own family—i.e. descendants of the Wild Geese—should be provided with Irish passports and that all officially recognized heads of the old yet enduring Gaelic aristocratic families should sit in the Irish Senate." During the Northern Irish peace negotiations, he wrote to U.S. senator George Mitchell suggesting that "a re-instated O'Neill dynasty should head an independent Ulster—re-structured as a constitutional monarchy."[59] This is not the only proposal based on the perceived political utility of a Gaelic restoration. Robert von Dassanowsky, Austrian-American filmmaker and royalist, has suggested,

> If the country were to return to the high kingship, it could operate on the alternative principal of the past—much as Malaysia operates today—so that each of the three dynasties in turn might provide a sovereign. Also, the fact that the Chiefs of these dynasties are not exclusively Roman Catholic and are genealogically linked to the early English kings might recommend itself to the Northern Ireland Protestants who still assert a monarchist preference in Ireland—albeit an English queen in London.[60]

This proposal, like Hugo O'Neill's, is for a solely Gaelic restoration. An earlier suggestion for a restored political role for those of noble descent in Ireland had a more expansive perspective on what constitutes Irish nobility. As Anne Chambers recounts, in 1983 an Canadian clergyman, the Rev. Dr. Tyrone O'Brien, in an open letter to the queen of England, the president of Ireland, the Taoiseach, and the British prime minister, proposed a scheme to unite Ireland under a rotating system of royal presidency that "would be agreeable to Monarchists and Republicans":

> The office of President of Ireland would be vested firstly in the person of The O'Neill of Clanaboy, a Roman Catholic heir and successor of the O'Neill high kings. Upon his demise, O'Neill would be succeeded by his Protestant kinsman Lord O'Neill of Shane's castle, who in turn was to be succeeded by the Catholic O'Connor Don and, on his demise, by

the Protestant O'Brien, Baron of Inchiquin, "the succession to be forever perpetuated in the persons of the heirs of the above chieftains."
The elected Catholic Chief would be inaugurated as both Monarch and
President-for-Life of all Ireland at Dublin Castle, the Protestant candidate at Stormont.[61]

This creation of a "royal republic," he suggested, might be acceptable not only to
Catholics and Protestants but also, echoing O'Hart's optimism regarding the Irish-
ness of the Crown pedigree, to the queen of England who "traces her descent from
Niall of the Nine Hostages, and is therefore a kinswoman of all four claimants."[62]

The negotiation of the relationship between the Chiefs of the Name and the
new state though the debate about recognition is paralleled by other attempts
to protect the old relationships between the Irish peerage and the British Crown
and government. With the Act of Union in 1800, Irish peers who had inherited
titles from those ennobled in Ireland by the British Crown since 1175, and who
formerly sat in the Irish Parliament in Dublin, were granted the right to elect
twenty-eight members of the Irish peerage to sit in the House of Lords in London
as "representative peers." Despite the creation of the Irish Free State in 1922, the
remaining hereditary representative peers continued to be summoned to sit in
the House of Lords until 1961, when the last survivor died. The Irish Peers Association was founded at this time to campaign for the recognition of the right
of Irish peers to elect representatives to sit in the House of Lords and to repeal
the Peerage Act of 1963, which for the first time explicitly excluded them.[63] Their
efforts included commissioning a history and register of the Irish peers.[64] This list
was ineffectual in repealing the act but is an index to a history of nobility that
includes those like The O'Brien, Baron of Inchiquin, whose doubly Gaelic and
Crown nobility is a reflection of the historical and contemporary complexities of
categories of (noble) belonging. By including O'Brien, Baron of Inchiquin, among
the rotating monarchs in his power-sharing scheme, Rev. Tyrone O'Brien not
only suggested an arrangement in which the religious affiliation of the monarch
and head of state rotated, but he included a Chief of the Name who at the same
time was a member of the Irish peerage as a baron. In 2004 O'Brien was also
chairman of the Standing Council of Irish Chiefs. Though the efforts of the Irish
Peers Association were unsuccessful, its campaign represents another strand in
the process in which different groups, differently "noble" and differently situated

in relation to the legacies of precolonial and colonial history—patterns of loyalty, affiliation, and inherited position—have been working out their relationships to new configurations of nation and state. These patterns of loyalty and cultural location continue to be understood in oppositional terms as national or colonial, but they are also being imagined in more complex ways.

Now that the embarrassment of the MacCarthy Mór case has faded and arguments about courtesy recognition have abated, the Office of the Chief Herald has been reorganized and reinvigorated through a new clarified role and incorporation into the National Library of Ireland. The office adheres to the tradition of heraldic arms following the patrilineal inheritance of surnames—women can apply for arms but their link to surnames is broken if arms are passed on via the maternal line—but it is inclusive in terms of who can have Irish arms. Paternal or maternal descent from a person living in Ireland in the past is still a requirement for those seeking Irish arms who are citizens of other places. But the right to bear Irish arms is not limited to those of Irish birth or ancestry. As the recently appointed chief herald Fergus Gillespie explained to me, the application for arms made by someone applying as a long-term resident of Ireland—"someone from Czechoslovakia living in Ireland for twenty years"—but not a citizen would be looked on favorably.[65] Bearing Irish arms is still a privilege but one based on wealth—the fee for a personal grant of arms is 3,300 euro—and not on pure Gaelic descent.

Meanwhile the Standing Council of Irish Chiefs and Chieftains continue to debate their criteria of inclusion and the mechanisms of succession of title. Debates about succession include not only the issues of tanistry and primogeniture but also patrilineage. Any imminent change to this tradition is unlikely, but the issue has at least been persistently raised by Nuala Ní Dhomhnaill, the sister of the current The O'Donnell, Father Hugo O'Donnell, a Franciscan missionary priest who has worked in Zimbabwe for over twenty-five years and is now a parish priest in Harare.[66] The official tanist is Don Leopold O'Donnell y Lara, Duke of Tetuan in Spain. Nuala Ní Dhomhnaill challenges her traditional ineligibility to hold the title, and thus take a title that is of no interest to her brother who will not, in any case, leave an heir. She has appeared on television in Ireland with The O'Neill of Clanaboy and The O'Conor Don arguing that "in this day and age when women are beginning to take their proper place in society, I cannot see any reason to shift the title three hundred years across the sea to Spain." To enthusiasts like Peter

Beresford Ellis, this "would be totally contrary to the Brehon law of succession as well as primogeniture inheritance."[67] An extended geography of Gaelic nobility is preferable to a regendering of noble descent. Despite the acceptance of equality as a fundamental social principle if not necessarily the aim of social policy in Ireland, the Council remains largely immune to any muted critique of its basis in inherited patrilineal distinction.

Debates about criteria for membership of the Council are also indicative of the continued exploration of ideas of noble descent in Ireland. Some members of the Council argue for broadening eligibility so that descendants of Anglo-Norman dynasties could be included such as the well known Fitzgerald knights—Desmond Fitzgerald the Knight of Glin and Lord Fitzgerald, Knight of Kerry and the "White Knight"; most share a "strong ethno-centric conviction," that "the first prerequisite for inclusion is a predominant and direct Gaelic lineage."[68] Yet these debates about distinctions between different forms of noble descent and the possibility of extending membership in this organization also coincide with an argument about the complex interconnections and shared cultural heritage of Irish aristocrats and their place in contemporary Irish society.

In 2004 two books were published about nobility in contemporary Ireland. The publication of *At Arm's Length: Aristocrats in the Republic of Ireland*, by the Dublin-based biographer and novelist Anne Chambers, coincided with an account of the old Gaelic chiefly dynasties entitled *Vanishing Kingdoms: The Irish Chiefs and Their Families*, by Walter Curley, former U.S. ambassador to Ireland. While Curley confines his account to the Chiefs of the Name as the survivors of the Gaelic dynasties of old Ireland, for Chambers the category "aristocracy" includes the "Gaelic, Anglo-Norman, Elizabethan, Jacobean, Cromwellian, Williamite, Victorian and Edwardian-created aristocracy."[69] As Chambers writes, these families can recount the particular origin of their noble titles in the different phases of British strategies to settle and secure the loyalty of those in old and new positions of wealth and power in Ireland (from ennobled Gaelic chiefs and Old English to New English settlers, soldiers, and statesmen). Yet their family histories are also accounts of intermarriage across the categories of "native" and "settler" and of a shared cultural world orientated to both Ireland and, through elite English education and British military service, to England, Britain, and Empire.

Chambers's exploration of the history, culture, and contemporary place of aristocrats in Irish society is thus an exploration of these categories of "native" and "foreign" and of the meaning of Irishness itself. In her account of this thoroughly entwined aristocracy, as in Curley's shorter family histories, the Chiefs of the Name occupy a much more complex position than their symbolic status as bearers of an ancient Gaelic civilization would imply. Though some Gaelic chiefs descended into impoverishment as a result of their resistance, many held on to land and position through accepting the terms of British power. Their family histories of intermarriage with the Old English, New English, and English nobility; of military careers in the British army; involvement in the British Empire; and tradition of education in England complicate that image of pure precolonial cultural inheritance. Many of the present-day chiefs—who for many in Ireland and especially in the diaspora represent continuity with an ancient pure Gaelic world suppressed by English colonialism—have been educated in elite English public schools and universities and have continued a family tradition of service in the British army. These are traditions shared with the rest of the Irish aristocracy, whose histories of intermarriage complicate the categories of "native" and "foreign" and suggest complex forms of cultural affiliation. These fuller accounts of the biographies and family histories of the chiefs do not undermine their commitment to their Irish heritage but point to the ways in which, for many, this commitment is in no way incompatible with their sense of the significance of the other strands of their cultural inheritance.

Chambers's argument is also about recognition: not the courtesy recognition of Gaelic chiefs but the cultural recognition of the place of the aristocracy in Irish history and in contemporary Ireland. As she notes, by the late nineteenth century those encompassed within the labels of "Anglo-Irish" or "Ascendancy" were collectively depicted in popular nationalism as "foreign, rapacious land-grabbers, tools of an evil empire, intent on keeping the majority of Irish people landless, ignorant and poor."[70] Many of the hated "Big Houses" of the landlord class were burned down in the Irish War of Independence and Civil War as symbols of a class system with origins in colonization. Chambers traces the ways in which the aristocracy's cultural inclinations toward Britain as well as, in many cases, their religious difference created a gulf between them and local people that compounded the detachment of class. Their contemporary marginalization from the public roles that the nobility are still accorded in other republics, she argues, reflects a residual antipathy or ambivalence towards them that stems from the nationalist construction of true Irishness as Catholic in religion and purely Gaelic

in ancestry and culture, tied to the land rather than "landed." In contrast, the aristocrats she interviewed largely reject the term "Anglo-Irish," with its connotations
of qualified Irishness, and insist on their identities as Irish. But this does not entail
denying their ties to England. As the position of the largely, but not entirely, Protestant gentry and aristocracy declined in the late nineteenth century and as Irish
national identity was being increasingly defined through ideas of native descent
and racial distinctiveness, many sought to demonstrate their ancestral roots in
Ireland and thus their Irishness through genealogy.[71] Today their family histories
of aristocratic intermarriage and location within the worlds of ascendancy Ireland
and Britain also locate them in Ireland as Irish but within a more complex understanding of that category. Noble pedigrees trace the lineal passage of title and
name through male lines of descent, but their wider family trees blur the purity of
"Gaelic," "Norse," "Anglo-Norman," "English," or "Scottish" ancestry.

For Chambers, the cultural identities and senses of belonging among Irish
aristocrats are instructive for Irish society more widely since they challenge a
model of Ireland as monocultural. Chambers argues that their acceptance of their
"Anglo" heritage could be extended to a more comfortable acknowledgment of
English cultural influence in Ireland. "From language to entertainment, from
commercial investment to blood relationship," she writes, "the Anglo side of the
Irish is an undeniable fact that we prefer to ignore, instead leaving one section
of our society to bear the tag."[72] Yet, conversely, the attachments to Ireland "of
those who once stood accused of being more Anglo than Irish," she suggests,
counter the effects of the contemporary obsession "with all things English" that
has accompanied Ireland's economic prosperity. For Chambers, "The attitudes
and opinions of the descendants of the old ascendancy express a concern and an
emotional attachment to Ireland considered outdated by modern Irish society in
its rush to become part of and make its mark on a wider international stage."[73]
Most of the current generation of aristocrats in Ireland do not send their children to English public schools, and they foster their children's sense of their Irish
nationality and culture. Many struggle to maintain the homes they inherited or
reestablished in Ireland and have worked to protect Ireland's architectural heritage more widely:

> Many of the descendants of Ireland's former ascendancy have abandoned
> lucrative and exciting careers to return to the mixed burden and blessing

of making their historic and anachronistic properties relevant and contributing to the local and national economy. Even among the aristocratic diaspora the hold of the old country is still strong. "My youngest son has just recently bought back the ruins of my old family home for sentimental reasons," Lord Carberry, one of the diaspora told this author. "Such is the pull of our roots."[74]

Thus both the English and Irish cultural heritages of the Irish aristocracy, including those of most of the Chiefs of the Name, and their commitment to historical continuities and protection of the built heritage suggest to Chambers values and senses of identity that may serve "the new emerging Irish nation." An old sense of nobility contrasts with a current culture of consumerism and the cult of celebrity. Thus those who have been traditionally seen as a culturally foreign and illegitimate colonial class, as the antithesis to the Irish nation, are not only reconsidered as part of a more complex and plural national collective but as models for a combined commitment to historical continuity and sense of hybrid heritage. This version of "the pull of our roots" suggests that the Irish diaspora can be reimagined to include not only those identifying with descent from Ireland's ancient Gaelic kings and chiefs, and those formally claiming Gaelic chiefly status from afar, but also those who at least some clan enthusiasts would categorize as the descendants of the "Anglo-Irish," or English enemy, and oppressors. If the term "Irish noble descent" remains strongly wedded to ideas of an ancient and pure Gaelic Irishness within the global culture of popular Irishness and Irish diasporic genealogy, Chambers's account of the Irish aristocracy suggests a much more complex understanding of Irish history, culture, and Irishness itself.

Conclusion

By its very nature, the idea of noble descent is about distinction from and superiority over those of ordinary ancestry. Its origins are in hierarchical social structures in which power, property, and privilege were inherited and naturalized through genealogies of aristocratic ancestry. The cultural currency of noble descent could easily be dismissed as romantic nostalgia for a world of splendor and status or individual illusions of genealogical grandeur, distant from and dissonant to the political work of recovering the histories of the hidden, marginal, ordinary, oppressed. In relation to the national and diasporic cultures of Irish genealogy, at least, this would overlook the entanglements of the appeal of noble descent and the potency of family histories of poverty, Famine, and exile. It would miss these complex relationships between the category of nobility, understandings of the colonized past, and approaches to the character and composition of contemporary Irish society. Anticolonial assertions of precolonial native nobility turn the politics of pedigree into a form of political resistance to the assumptions of colonial superiority. But the assertion of native nobility can also be directed against the authority of the postcolonial republic and against any move to define noble descent more inclusively. Yet, while old models of the "native" and "foreign" are asserted or maintained by some, the adequacy of these definitions are also being questioned by others attuned to multilayered, interwoven, and often transnational aristocratic family histories that upset those categories of belonging.

These continuing debates involve both tensions and coalitions between enthusiasts for Irish noble heritage in the diaspora and homeland. As the arguments about recognition of Chiefs of the Name have shown, the assertion of the significance of these representatives by descent of the old Gaelic order is often articulated through, and draws support from, an international network of enthusiasts for particular lines of noble descent or nobility more generally. But that international interest in chiefly clan connection is also a cause of concern. Complaints about the authority or ability of the state, through the Genealogical Office, to regulate claims to chiefship are paralleled by unease with the effects of diasporic interest in clan belonging and chiefly status. For some, "honorary chiefs" or "bloodline chiefs" of non-Gaelic surname groups stretch and diminish chiefly status. There are concerns about authenticity and concerns about property. Celebrations of a culturally enriching and commercially lucrative extended diasporic family encouraged and expressed through clan gatherings, and diasporic desire to identify with a family name and its history, collide with the defense of the ownership rights of the heraldic insignia that officially belong to individuals, not clans as often assumed. The tensions between the material culture of coats of arms as markers of collective and distinctive diasporic Irish ancestry and proprietary interests in them strains the ideal of the diaspora as a harmony of plurality and affinity. At the same time, arguments about the illogic of non-Gaelic lineages being afforded official or popular recognition in Ireland point to wider questions of cultural belonging, aristocratic status, and the nation and to the contemporary resilience and contemporary revision of the categories of "native" and "settler."

The politics of recognition that this chapter has explored evokes both the issue of the formal state recognition of title and the term's associations in contemporary cultural politics. This expression has come to describe demands for and debates about the cultural appreciation and cultural rights of groups who through the intersections or race, class, and ethnicity occupy economically disadvantaged and cultural disenfranchised positions as "minorities." Here the politics of recognition have a different inflection, since the descendants of noble dynasties are a special and often celebrated "minority" and are the descendants of the formerly powerful and privileged, whether in the precolonial or colonial past. The question of the relationship between a republican state and a national aristocratic heritage have shaped arguments about formal state recognition of Gaelic chiefs. But events like the O'Neill Summer School and accounts of aristocrats in Ireland such as Anne Chambers's book suggest a more complex politics of recognition. The O'Neill Summer School was a lesson in the complexities of identity, in the collisions and accommodations of different approaches to the past, and different investments in noble descent. Different interpretations of Irish noble descent can remain unspoken, subtly register and sometimes surface more directly in events of this kind. Chambers's account challenges the categories of pure Gaelic and "foreign" nobility and in doing so invites her readers to recognize the formerly vilified Irish ascendancy as Irish and to recognize the value of their commitment to Irish homes and history, symbolically and materially. She thus challenges both the conventional narrowness of this category—Irish—and its erosion through globalization.

Familiar arguments about recovering histories of the marginalized and producing more democratized accounts of the past that include the lives of the politically and economically marginal and conventionally forgotten are thus complicated in a context in which the dominant histories have been shaped by anticolonial nationalism. Rethinking history does not simply involve challenging the history of great men and great deeds, although socialist and feminist historians have significantly questioned the traditional focus on Irish political history.[75] Figuratively at least, the marginal and oppressed have already been central to Irish national history as the evicted, the starved, and the banished. In Ireland, rethinking history means not only complicating traditional national narratives through attending to questions of class and gender. It also means thinking differently about the ways in which the privileged—the traditionally maligned, largely Protestant, land-owning aristocracy as well the traditionally romanticized Gaelic nobility—have been positioned in relation to the category of Irishness and within Irish history.

The compendium of distinguished pedigrees in *Burke's Irish Family Records* of 1976 was prefaced by a poem, "Heritage" by Alfred Allen. While "this is an ancient land, and in it still is felt the pull of older generations," Allen advises:

> Now while we turn to the way ahead
> Let us remember those who went before
>
> For all our antecedents press us on,
> This land of ours was moulded by their being,
> All those who came to steal it one by one
> Are mingled in it. We are all one thing,
>
> And all the ghosts of all the years gone by
> Are all our ghosts. For are there many now
> Can say, "my blood is pure," our ancestry
> is bastardised in race. Not any bough
>
> Of all our tree can say "I am pure"
> Irish or English man, Norman or Dane,
> In our dissentions we can now be sure,
> The victor's throat shouts forth the victim's pain.[76]

The "Allen" entry in the volume explains his descent from Abraham Allen, an army officer who settled in Ireland during the reign of Elizabeth I. But for Allen, ancestry joins rather than divides "victor" from "victim." Recognizing the deeply entwined histories of Irish noble families and the complexity of their ties of loyalty and identification is not to endorse the structures of power and privilege that their titles reflected in past, nor the inheritance of advantage or status in the present, but to radically undo those categories of "native" and "settler" belonging.

5

Of Ulster Stock

Native, Settler, and Entangled Roots in Northern Ireland

The Public Record Office of Northern Ireland in Belfast is an important site for family history research. Its genealogical users are local people who travel across the city and within the region to access its records. Others using its archives for genealogical research include those visiting from Britain having left Northern Ireland as children or adults and those who come from Britain and further away—Australia, Canada, New Zealand, and the United States—as descendants of earlier emigrants. The Public Record Office of Northern Ireland is thus a site for both diasporic and local family history research where local researchers share knowledge, sources, and facilities with visitors from overseas. It is also a place in which local researchers and visitors often share a sense of the significance of discovering the names and details of ancestors in records but do not necessarily share perspectives on the meaning of being of Irish descent or of having roots in Northern Ireland. These dissimilarities are not just between visitors and locals but also among local users, since descent is one significant dimension of categories of identity in Northern Ireland.

The appeal of finding the place of origin or ancestral home, which may be prompted by the cultural associations of indigenous rootedness in Canada, New Zealand, Australia, or the United States, leads visitors to a region that is itself riven by the categories of "native" and "settler," which are named in Northern Ireland "Gael" and "Planter." The diasporic explorations of ancestry and identity through family history that are shaped by the particular configurations of ethnicity, race, and nationhood in the countries that visitors come from are paralleled by, and sometimes prompt, the genealogical explorations of personal and collective relationships to those categories of settler/Planter and native/Gael being undertaken by people in Northern Ireland. Described in the crudest terms, Northern Ireland is divided between those who identify themselves with a native Gaelic and often Catholic nation that was severed by the partition of Ireland and who support nationalist or republican politicians, and those who maintain loyalty to the United Kingdom as Protestant descendants of seventeenth-century settlers and support political parties committed to maintaining the Union. These "two communities" are conventionally defined through differences of descent as well as denomination—Catholic, Gaelic, and native or Protestant, British, and Planter.

The themes of ancestral origins, migration, and settlement that run through diasporic genealogy have particular cultural and political connotations in this context. For many contemporary descendants of emigrants from what is now Northern Ireland, this region is a place of origin, the original place where their ancestors had lived for centuries and that they left behind. It is the place in which a quest for a sense of belonging and roots may rest. Yet this is also a place in which the claim to original presence and natural native ownership are fundamental to its violently disputed political status, current "culture wars," and deep divisions.[1] For most descendants of those who left Ulster, this place, like the island entirely, is imagined as a place of emigration. Yet it is also a place deeply divided by conflicting interpretations of its histories of settlement and immigration. Diasporic family histories of arrival, survival, struggle, and success are understood as part of the history of New World nation building. However, in Northern Ireland, Scottish and English settlement on the early modern "frontier" of Ulster is both fundamental to its history and the subject of fundamental and deeply political differences of historical interpretation between the "two communities." Familiar genealogical themes of migration and settlement are thus highly charged. The legitimacy or the illegitimacy of settlement—that is, early modern Plantation—and the legitimate or illegitimate presence and power of the descendants of that settlement are central to bitter political division.

But the origins of these "two communities," Protestant-British and Catholic-Irish each with "different ancestors, different anniversaries, different wars,"[2] lie not simply in the seventeenth-century Plantation of Ulster. Immigration is not the natural cause of division. Rather, the origins of these "two communities" are found in the interconnected effects of the centrality of Protestantism and anti-Catholicism to British state formation, cultural identity, and colonial ideology; the construction of Irish nationhood in the later nineteenth and early twentieth centuries as Catholic and Gaelic; and the corresponding making of Ulster unionism through a Protestant settler identity. In the late nineteenth century, the alignments of religious and political allegiance were also increasingly imagined in terms of pure and particular ancestry.[3] Terms like the "two communities" or "two traditions" now name what came to be imagined as two distinctive communities that differed in descent as well as denomination. This model of distinctive and separate ancestry, religion, political loyalties, and cultural identity masks the diversity of class and culture within the categories, their entanglements and commonalities, and forms of identity and culture that these ethnonationalist categories cannot encompass. Yet the categories continue to shape political conflict, personal identities, and understandings of society in Northern Ireland. These shorthand categories also underemphasize the degree to which they are being variously explored, revised, reconstructed, and deconstructed through the collective work of cultural groups of all kinds and by individuals exploring their relationships to these models of identity and descent: settler and native, Planter and Gael.

The encounters between local and diasporic researchers in the research rooms of the Public Record Office where local and diasporic meanings of ancestry meet are thus characterized by different degrees of enthusiasm, empathy, and estrangement. Experienced local genealogy enthusiasts who help visitors may share their excitement about finding ancestors in archival records, but may not necessarily share versions of Irishness or identification with an Irish ethnic identity. Local responses to visitors' "wearing of the green" through harps and shamrocks on sweatshirts, baseball caps, and windcheaters and their voluble fervor may be rueful, understanding, or wryly amused. But visitors' accounts of their quests to recover the history of their Irish ancestors "driven from the land" jar more awkwardly with those who feel alienated by narratives of native Irish dispossession that characterize them and their ancestors as illegitimate settlers. They jar too with those in Northern Ireland who could claim descent from the native dispossessed but choose not to define themselves through this version of the past. Visitors may be more or less self-conscious about expressing their enthusiasm for their "Irish roots" in a context in which the category "Irish" is deeply politicized, espoused as a national or cultural identity by some, rejected by others, and reworked by others still in relation to the conventional criteria of descent, domicile, political affiliation, cultural affinities, and religious denomination. Some visitors are perplexed about "why people can't just get on together." For others, an

English or American accent can uncomfortably belie their sense of recent or close connection and sensitivity to the logics of identity and belonging in Northern Ireland. But the range of perspectives on the meaning of ancestral roots in Northern Ireland among visitors is found among residents too. This chapter considers the practice of family history and genealogy by "locals" in Northern Ireland in relation to questions of belonging, identity, and difference. It explores the enduring potency and continued costs of the ideas of "native" and "settler" identity and descent, but also the ways they are being reworked within the practice of family history through ideas of genealogical interconnection and previously unrealized shared patterns of experience across familiar divisions.

Family History in a Divided Society

Since genealogy is an exploration of the ancestral lines that extend from an individual in the present back into the past and, at the same time, is necessarily about relationships between people defined through birth and parentage, it is always both personal and collective. But family history is also often a social practice that involves enjoying mutual interests with fellow enthusiasts who are not necessarily genealogically connected. This social dimension is reflected in electronically assisted family-like relationships online and in the clubs and societies that have long been part of the culture of genealogy. The North of Ireland Family History Society was established in 1979 and has grown from its original branch in Bangor in County Down to eleven regional branches. With the exception of the branch in Omagh, most branches are in the east of the province. Most of the members live in Northern Ireland and attend monthly meetings, but the society also has associate members in over fourteen countries worldwide.[4] It maintains a small society library in east Belfast, which a rota of volunteers opens twice a week, and publishes a biannual journal *North Irish Roots*. Many of its members are active in collating genealogical sources for members' use, transcribing gravestone inscriptions or parish registers, for example, as well as exploring their own family pasts.

So in many respects the society is similar to other family history societies. The growth of interest in family history in Northern Ireland, like the development of local history, reflects wider patterns of popular interest in the past. But, like local history, it operates in a context in which history in general is deeply politicized and family background—ancestry and religious denomination—is fundamental to the ways in which people define themselves and are categorized by others along the axes of ethnicity, political allegiance, and religion. The North of Ireland Family History Society operates in a context in which the question of which "side" people are from haunts everyday life. The apparently unselfconscious expression of the significance of their ancestral Irishness by some genealogical visitors contrasts with the protective dissembling, subtle reckoning, and cautious disclosure of background and identity that is part of social interaction in potentially "mixed" company in Northern Ireland. Questions of religion and politics are routinely avoided for fear of giving offense, creating tension, or being subject to aggressive or offensive reactions in "mixed company." At the same time, individuals are continually located by others through the clues of first name, surname, or school into one "side" or another. Yet family history research in Northern Ireland cannot *not* involve the issue of religious background since, especially in the absence of census or civil records, church registers of baptism and marriage are some of the most significant sources of genealogical information. The question of religion is inescapable. How then can a society devoted to supporting the exploration of family history operate when both history and "where people are from," in terms of religious background and cultural identity, are such delicate and potentially divisive subjects?

Family history societies, like local history societies in Northern Ireland, face the challenge of finding ways to effectively engage with the past, and to do so in "mixed" or "cross-community" organizations without alienating their members. One response to this challenge is to shield the practice from the question of politics. For some, family history, like local history, is best isolated from the polarized and irreconcilable historical narratives of traditional nationalism and unionism in Northern Ireland that potentially fracture tacitly "mixed" and nonpolitical social organizations like those of family history enthusiasts.[5] Instead, family history offers an alternative way of exploring the past, one that leads to a sense of the "ordinary" social and economic histories that have been neglected in the historical mythologies of both Orange and Green and their mutually opposed historical perspectives. Within nationalist accounts of Irish history, the Plantation of Ulster marks the defeat of the last of Gaelic Ireland and the final heroic failure of resistance in the north. It followed a long history of invasion, dispossession, oppression, and struggle that disrupted and destroyed a precolonial cultural golden age. The founding historical narratives of Ulster Protestant identities, in contrast, center on an image of a loyal, steadfast, civil people under siege from a hostile native Gaelic population and struggling to preserve the covenant of Protestant presence in Ulster.[6] Neither perspective on the past allows much room for "ordinary" family or local history.

If one strategy of collective support for family history in a society divided into two separate communities of denomination and descent—Catholic native and Protestant settler—is to avoid the question of religious and political difference because of its divisive effects, another strategy is to foster a culture of "safe" disclosure. The generous support that its members offer each other, and especially those new to family history, is central to the ethos of the North of Ireland Family History Society. Volunteers make the library collection open to members, help others in finding sources, and respond to overseas queries. One significant but unspoken dimension of this support is the absolutely matter-of-fact way in which the unavoidable issue of religious background is handled as members are directed to the relevant Catholic, Church of Ireland, Presbyterian, or other nonconformist church registers. This means that the society tries to create an oasis of relaxed openness in a social context in which the anxiety, hesitancy, and fear that surrounded the disclosure of information about personal background during the Troubles still continues. As one member put it to me, "People are very cagey about revealing anything about themselves until they know who they are dealing with. You can't talk about family history in Northern Ireland but you can in the Society."[7] The Family History Society does not offer a "neutral space"—a space unmarked by the dominance of one "side" advocated within some community relations policies—achieved through avoiding issues of religious or cultural difference but a space in which difference is less freighted and less fraught.

Yet these "safe" contexts are only achieved through the efforts of individuals to develop relationships of mutual support, and they depend on the particular composition of the group in which a discussion of family background may occur. Despite the commitment of some members to disinterested interest in helping other members and encouraging a sense of security, "people in the society are most relaxed about talking about where they come from as long as they are talking to their own side. They can feel threatened when they are asked to open up in other ways." This "safe" context is also qualified by the location of the society's library and its annual general meetings. Despite the genuine efforts of members to create a welcoming and open culture for all, the cultural complexion of the organization is inevitably interpreted through its location in Protestant east Belfast and in a building, a former hotel, shared with a Masonic lodge; Masons in Northern Ireland are strongly associated with Protestant unionism. Its cheap rental rates make maintaining the library possible for a voluntary nonprofit society, but the location and its interior decoration—visitors to the library pass a portrait of the queen—may deter potential members uneasy with these less-than-neutral symbols. One member joked to me that, as a Catholic, "being the only Fenian to get into a Masonic Lodge is a bit like Sinn Fein getting into Stormont." This location may be a legacy of the earlier history of the organization rather than reflecting its current composition and culture, but it undoubtedly significantly shapes how the organization is perceived.[8]

This "safe" context is also qualified by the degree to which the exploration of identity and heritage is effectively privatized. Though initial wariness about the question of people's backgrounds may dissipate with personal contact, there is still resistance among some members to the public presence of traditions from the "other side." An evening of songs about migration, for example, included those that were "too Irish" for some and that "didn't suit their persuasion." In contrast, other members argue strongly for the value of developing mechanisms to encourage people to share stories since "family history is a way of understanding what makes people the way they are." As one active member argued, "what is the point of being interested in family history unless you talk about it?" A greater public presence for the stories of family history within the Family History Society through talks and recorded memories could be a "way of understanding each other, of understanding the other side, understanding all kinds of background."[9] There are plans to develop projects for recording family history as memories of "ordinary" lives. Thus the generosity, supportiveness, and openness of the society coexists with strands of protective conservatism and risk-taking initiatives to challenge this resistance. As the society continues to work through the pragmatics of supporting family history in a divided society—in part at least by avoiding questions of identity and division—for many of its members, and for those outside of the society doing their family trees, their research involves personal explorations of the meanings of identity and descent in Northern Ireland. For some at least, this involves exploring their experience of being defined as "not belonging in an ancient land."

"Not Belonging in an Ancient Land"

Geoffrey Beattie's memoir *Protestant Boy*, published in 2004, opens with one of his visits home to his elderly mother and her familiar unhappiness about his distance from her and the working class, predominately Protestant area of north Belfast where she still lives and where he grew up. He has, she feels, forgotten where he comes from. He is no longer "a proper Belfast man" but has become "one of those English snobs."[10] *Protestant Boy* is an account of Beattie's relationship to her and to the family and place he has not forgotten. The significance of this home fuels his search for greater knowledge of his family's past as his "tenuous and faltering link with Northern Ireland was threatened by the mortality of those whom I loved, those who were my only link with my own past."[11] The negotiated continuities and dissimilarities of identity between the adult daughter or son who has left home—the locality or country as well as the parental household—and the parent who is left behind are entangled with the threat of the loss of the sense of cultural and historical location that a parent's knowledge of the family's past can provide. They are also entwined with the particular question of his cultural identity as a "Protestant Ulsterman." Beattie wants "a clearer sense of who I am and where I belong."[12] His attempt to know more about his family's past is not only shaped by the usual problems of recovering the history of "insignificant people" but also framed by the reduction of the history of these "much maligned"[13] Protestant people to a history of illegitimate presence and oppressive privilege. According to the categories of native and settler belonging, his surname alone undermines his claim to call Northern Ireland home. It offers the pleasures of possible connection with others who share the name but also delimits his place within those categories of identity and descent: "I love hearing of anyone with the same name, love to think that there might be some connection no matter how vague. . . . It's a Protestant name, part of that great Plantation of Ulster in the seventeenth century. My family probably came from the Lowlands of Scotland originally, so my name marks me out as a settler, an interloper, someone who does not really belong in Ireland, or perhaps anywhere for that matter."[14] Beattie's sense of his name as marker of unnatural presence echoes the feelings of a genealogist who told me that although he could trace his family in Northern Ireland back to 1714, his name defines him as different from those who naturally belong as "native Irish."

It seems to invalidate his right to feel he belongs. Genealogy for Ulster "Planter" families, he suggested, is a way of dealing with being defined as "not belonging in an ancient land."[15]

Questions of ancestry and origins are thus intimately interwoven with questions of identity and belonging. For Protestants in Northern Ireland, these questions are shaped by the ways in which the category British no longer seems secure, stable, or sufficient. The apparent disinterest on "the mainland" in the loyalty of British people in Ulster that the peace process has signaled for many Protestants in Northern Ireland is compounded by questions of Britishness raised by Welsh and Scottish assertions of cultural particularity and political autonomy and debates about postcolonial Englishness and the multicultural character of Britain.[16] Attitudes toward the cultural practices and political positions of Protestants in Northern Ireland who define themselves against Irishness are also inflected by the popularity of this ethnic identity worldwide. They are informed by the appeal of the match between ancestry, land, and cultural authenticity symbolized by the "native" in the face of the perceived threat of cultural globalization and by the political and cultural recognition of the histories of settler ill treatment of indigenous people and contemporary indigenous rights. Beattie recalls the explicitly anti-unionist and anti-Protestant attitudes of the intellectual elite of Cambridge (where he was a postgraduate student in the 1970s) who interpreted the conflict in Ulster in terms of

> good guys and bad guys: there were the native Irish, "driven out of their lands," and then there were the Protestant settlers. The Native Americans were fashionable at the time, so too were the aborigines of Australia, and the Catholic Irish seemed to fall into a similar category in some people's minds. Then there were the problems of civil rights and gerrymandering and discrimination. . . . The words they used were "discrimination," "persecution" and "deprivation" on the one side and "privilege," "elite" and "the ascendancy" on the other. But I didn't recognise my own experience in what they said. And I detected no understanding on their side of the psychology of these Protestant interlopers.[17]

His journey to find out about his working-class Protestant family history beyond the "bombast of politicians" and their "cries of No Surrender" is simultaneously a counterpoint to this discourse of native belonging and settler illegitimacy.

Beattie's exploration of family history in relation to the history of Northern Ireland and its questions of identity and difference is not exceptional. In contrast to the common observation that Northern Ireland is characterized by an obsessive concern with the past and the insistent presence of antagonistic nationalist and unionist histories, family history (like local history) is often motivated by a sense of lack of historical knowledge and desire for historical knowledge that can help make sense of the present and the recent past. This involves exploring personal and family relationships to the dominant communal narratives of oppression and besiegement and the "ordinary histories" that they neglect. It is part of a wider reconsideration of Protestant culture, heritage, and identity in Northern Ireland. For many, family history involves exploring the dimensions of family life that are conventionally insignificant and exploring the family's place within the historical events and processes that have shaped Northern Ireland.

A new "convert" to family history near Portadown in County Armagh told me of the different lines of his research. They include tracing the history of the family farm and the generations of his family and their relationships to each other, and exploring his possible descent from one of three brothers that arrived with King William III and were given land locally. This interest in proving a genealogical connection to the founding fathers of Planter families that arrived together as brothers, each establishing a lineage, is a familiar one that speaks both of long residence in Ulster and origin in Scotland or England. This also often extends to tracing the histories of ancestors who left Ulster and took part in the founding history of the United States. In this case, there is one possible ancestor who shares his name who took part in the American war of independence on the winning side. This is a pattern of genealogical research that reflects the wider interest in recovering historical connections with Scotland and the neglected histories of Presbyterian Ulster-Scots migration to North America. While the date of emigration of an ancestor from Ireland is the pivotal event from which family history stretches forward to the present and backwards in history for overseas visitors, for many Protestants in Northern Ireland the crucial date is the arrival of an ancestor in Ireland. This search for the connection back to Scotland by family historians is matched by efforts to rewrite histories of emigration from Ireland to include the mainly Presbyterian migrants who left Ulster in the eighteenth century, and to emphasize their significance in the foundation of the American state. These new accounts of eighteenth-century migration from Ulster, settlement, survival, and, for some, success in the new world can be motivated by desires to tell a more complex story of Irish migration and redress their neglect, or to recover a more distinctive, and sometimes more exclusive, Ulster-Scots history to match a newly asserted linguistic heritage.[18]

Until recently, this history of migration has been largely absent from the histories of the Irish diaspora that have been dominated by a focus on Catholic post-Famine migration. However, the attempts to redress this are evident in both recent published histories and in the heritage spaces of Northern Ireland. It is now possible to visit the humble rural homesteads of "Planter families" in Ulster who migrated to America and rose to political prominence and economic prosperity. The Ulster-American Folk Park in Omagh in County Tyrone recreates the Ulster village, emigrant journey, and Pennsylvania homestead of Presbyterian migrants from Ulster. It was established by the wealthy American Mellon family and constructed around the home of their ancestor Thomas Mellon, who had migrated with his parents from County Tyrone to western Pennsylvania in 1818. In November 1999, a new mural created by the Shankill Ulster-Scots Cultural Society was unveiled on the Protestant, working-class, loyalist Shankill Road in Belfast that celebrated a shared Ulster-Scots ancestry and its American achievements through the words of James Buchanan, president of the United States from 1857 to 1861: "My Ulster Blood is my most priceless heritage." The mural included the statement that "250,000 Ulster-Scots emigrated to American in the 1700's and were the driving force behind the American Revolution" (see figure 4).

The role of Ulster-Scots emigrants and those of Ulster-Scots ancestry in early American history—as revolutionary soldiers, frontiersmen, statesmen, and signatories to the Declaration of Independence—is central to the promotion of Ulster-Scottish heritage in Northern Ireland. One of the leaflets produced by the Ulster-Scots Agency/Tha Boord o Ulstèr-Scotch features the "Voyage to the New World" and tells "how the Ulster-Scots or Scots-Irish came to America"; another features the history of "Ulster-Scots in America." Its leaflet "Twenty Things You Didn't Know about . . . Ulster-Scots" is dominated by information about Ulster-Scots settlers as prominent figures in the early history of the United States and the Ulster-Scots roots of famous Americans—presidents, soldiers, businessmen, authors, and actors—and an "estimated 22 million people living in the United States [that] can claim Ulster-Scots roots" and help "make up the estimated 44 million Americans who today claim Irish extraction." This pride

4. Mural on Shankill Road, Belfast, Photograph © Dr. Jonathan
McCormick. Reproduced with permission of Jonathan McCormick,
from the CAIN Mural Directory.

in Ulster-Scots achievement in the United States features strongly in the movement to celebrate and preserve Scottish influences in speech, music, and dance
in Ulster more widely.[19] New interests in Ulster-Scots ancestry and heritage are
deeply tied to the different ways in which questions of collective and distinctive
cultural identities are being worked through in Northern Ireland. Ulster-Scots
history and culture can be aggressively asserted as an exclusive Protestant heritage and competitive counterpoint to Catholic Gaelic culture. Some accounts
of Ulster-Scots settlement in America are explicitly anti-Irish and anti-Catholic,

antagonistic assertions of a separate heritage and origin story.[20] For others, a focus on Scottish immigration to Ulster is a way of exploring one distinctive and hitherto neglected strand in a diverse cultural heritage that is shared by all in Northern Ireland.

Within family history in Northern Ireland, aspects of Protestant culture that are often associated with divided histories and sectarian traditions can be the focus of family pride, a pride that is not necessarily joined to a triumphalist celebration of the heritage of one "side." The involvement of grandfathers, uncles, or fathers in the Orange Order, for example, can be remembered as part of a family and community tradition, rather than being either suppressed or uncritically celebrated. The amateur family historian near Portadown talked to me of the sense of pride he feels in seeing his family name in official documents, both in discovering his name in land, taxation, and voting registers and seeing his grandfather's signature on the newly digitized online copy of the Ulster Covenant of 1912 signed by 471,414 men and women in Belfast and across Ulster pledging to defend the Union and expressing their collective opposition to Home Rule.[21] Another family historian living in Ballymena in County Antrim showed me the photograph of his grandfather standing outside the family farm wearing his Orange sash and talked of searching for the record of his service in the B-Specials, a category of the Ulster Special Constabulary established to protect Protestants in Ulster from attacks from the IRA in the 1920s, which came to be seen as a partisan Protestant army in Northern Ireland and was disbanded following their involvement in attacks on civil rights marchers in 1969. These family photos and service records are historical artifacts of a history whose injustices, he feels, need to be acknowledged. But they are not artifacts of a history that should be suppressed nor be viewed as a source of shame. His imaginative reconstruction of the country lane where his grandmother hung her washing to dry or the memory of his other grandmother insisting on not moving away from her Catholic neighbors as a Protestant women in the Catholic side of Londonderry are, for him, as significant as his family's connection to the organizations of Ulster Protestantism. Family history, he feels, is a way to better understand a troubled past.

This genealogical exploration of Protestant family histories can involve exploring the distinctive traditions of that past—Planter ancestors or family members in the Orange Order—but also involve the usual practices and sources shared by other local family historians and visitors. Beattie's investigation of his family's past takes him to street directories, land registers, graveyards, and on a car journey in search of the rural townland where his father's ancestors may have lived in preindustrial Northern Ireland. These are the sources, searches, and significant moments that feature too in the genealogical work of overseas visitors, who may hold quite different perspectives on the meaning of being of Irish descent or of Ulster stock but share this desire to "know where they came from." Beattie's description of standing for ages where his ancestors may have come from, moved and "slightly teary eyed," echoes the accounts of genealogical visitors who are several generations and thousands of miles removed from the ancestor who left Ireland. The desire of visitors to trace their roots in Northern Ireland as an exploration of the ancestral heritage that has shaped them can chime most strongly not with those who are conventionally defined as "native" but with those in Northern Ireland exploring their relationship to a place in which they are defined as not belonging, both by tracing their genealogy in Northern Ireland and their Planter origins elsewhere. These connections across differences of perspective between those who seek origins as diasporic Irish and those who are defined as not belonging in Ulster extend to parallels between two plural senses of cultural location. Despite usually being accompanied by different perspectives on the meaning of Irishness, a version of Ulster Protestant belonging that combines a sense of long presence in Ulster but also origins elsewhere resonates with the multiply located identifications of those who combine a sense of American belonging in the United States and ancestral connections across the sea to Ireland.

Yet the potent ideal of native belonging can continue to undermine a sense of home. One family historian explained his reasons for becoming interested in family history through his "sense of being not native to Northern Ireland" and "wanting to know where I belonged." His feeling of "not belonging in Ireland" and sense of not being able to feel that its cultural heritage can really ever be his, of "not being native," began as a child:

> It's hard to say. . . . When I was growing up—we are talking about before TV—and living in right in the country and listening to the radio, those old stories of Gaelic tales, the fairy tales on the children's hour—the banshee and stuff like that. And I thought "This is about my country." But the more I've gone into this I've realised the [family name] are not native in Northern Ireland. Alright they have been here centuries but

they were interlopers, if you like, originally, not native Irish in any sense
at all—Protestant, Planters and everything else.[22]

This feeling that he cannot legitimately enjoy the oral histories and material
landscapes of the place, clearly of great interest to him, persists despite his historical interests and family history research: "That feeling of not really being
native, that feeling of really not belonging. . . . The more I go out with a group
of friends who look at old stone circles, prehistoric monuments, things like that,
for the day usually, maybe a couple of times a year. And these things were here
centuries and centuries ago, long before any of my family ever came to this land,
there were people here. . . . It is hard to put into words, this feeling. It's strange."
He came to realize as a child that what he had thought was his was really somehow not his; he feels the material landscape of prehistoric Ireland cannot be part
of his heritage because his ancestors were not there when it was being shaped.
This suggests a deeply and painfully internalized model of native belonging. For
him, the parallels between the position of Protestant Planters as "interlopers"
in Northern Ireland and settler presence in other places are clear. His "feelings about Europeans v. native Americans, Canadians v. first nations etc." have
shaped his sense of "being like occupiers in a conquered country."

His sense of his own lack of roots, and the pattern of Protestant movement
away from areas in Ulster where his ancestors were present over a hundred years
ago, are matched by his impression that Protestants are gradually being displaced
in Northern Ireland:

My family seem to be itinerants, moving from one place to another.
They don't seem to have really put down roots. But maybe that's just
being silly. It is so long ago. But even now in Northern Ireland you are
seeing this movement of Protestants from the west to the east. You get
the feeling that eventually they'll move back to the mainland perhaps.
But maybe that's just my imagination. It's just the feeling I get. As the
west is becoming more Catholic the Protestants are gradually being
driven back again.

For him, family history has not provided an alternative to the model of native
belonging and settler presence but has intensified this feeling of personal and
collective displacement.[23] This was not expressed with bitterness but with sad

acceptance that for him the naturalness of native belonging in Ireland and in European settler contexts means Northern Ireland can never be home. Home can only be the place where your ancestors have always been.

Always, however, is a long, long time. In Northern Ireland, ancestry and belonging are also being reimagined through the idea that there never has been a people there who did not originally come from somewhere else. This understanding of Northern Ireland as a place shaped by long histories of immigration as well as emigration is a feature of recent cultural attempts to diminish the neatness of the divisive and damaging categories of "native" and "settler." In 2005 a major traveling exhibition organized by the Northern Ireland Museum's Council titled *Our People, Our Times: A History of Northern Ireland's Cultural Diversity* framed the history and contemporary character of Northern Ireland through an extended history of migration that "shows that we, or our ancestors, all arrived here at some point in history." It posed the question "Are we not all migrants or descendants of migrants to this land?"[24] to undermine the usual division in Northern Ireland between those who have apparently always been there and those who have settled. This focus on migration continues the emphasis of arguments about culture and identity in Northern Ireland developed by cultural commentators in the 1980s. Local historian Jack Magee, for example, long argued that "Celts, Vikings, Normans, Scots and English might be seen for what they actually were, successive waves of immigrants who intermingled and fused, and each have left their marks on our settlement patterns, our rural customs and traditions, our place-names and our colloquial speech."[25] Cultural critic Edna Longley famously refigured Northern Ireland as a "cultural corridor"—a place traversed by cultural flows—to replace the model of native purity and alien settlement.[26] Representations of Ulster's history in terms of waves of settlers situates the arrival of seventeenth-century English and Scottish planters within a longer history of settlement before and after the Plantation of Ulster.

Genealogy itself has been framed by ideas of mobility. The complex historical geography of migration into as well as away from Ireland was the theme of a genealogical conference and study tour organized by the Ulster Historical Foundation in 1999—"A Millennium of Migration: 1,000 Years of Invasion and Emigration" (figure 5). "Studying patterns of settlement from the Viking and Norman raiders to the returning émigrés of the 20th century," the event explored "the rich tapestry of civilization and migration as it developed in this millennium."

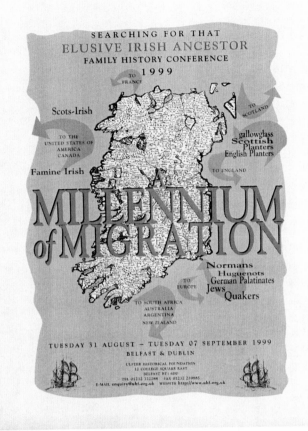

5. Conference Poster, "A Millennium of Migration: 1,000 Years of Invasion and Emigration" (Belfast: Ulster Historical Foundation, 1999). Reproduced with permission of the Ulster Historical Foundation.

Here Ulster is presented as a node in a complex history of inward and outward migration that includes the significant arrivals of "gallowglass, Scottish Planters and English Planters" and of "Norman, Huguenots, German Palatinates, Jews and Quakers," and the departures of "Scots-Irish and Famine Irish" to the United States of America and Canada and emigration to South Africa, Australia, Argentina and New Zealand. It also suggests the long histories of movement back and forth between Ulster, Scotland, England, Wales, and continental Europe.

An emphasis on shared histories of settlement and generations of family history in Northern Ireland can provide a model of belonging for Protestant descendants of English and Scottish settlers. However, this can recreate a distinction between the long settled and newly arrived. In order to both challenge the model of "native" and "settler" and foster inclusive attitudes to new immigrants, the *Our People, Our Times* exhibition included within its "migration timeline" and exhibits nineteenth-century Italian and Jewish immigration, twentieth-century Indian and Chinese settlement, and new patterns of immigration from Africa, the Middle East, and Eastern Europe. This is an intercultural history of Northern Ireland rather than a classification and catalogue of the most and least "native" and naturally belonging. It engages with and explores Northern Ireland as "diaspora space" inhabited "not only by those who have migrated and their descendants, but equally by those who are constructed and represented as indigenous."[27]

But migration also includes the internal displacements that are the product of a conflict premised on rigid ethnic and religious distinctions and their competing nationalisms. The exhibition's "migration timeline" includes a date and description that represents a significant point in a recent history of migration within Northern Ireland: "1971: Significant migration of families across and out of Belfast in response to civil unrest." Thus while an extended history of migration is promoted as a way of understanding Northern Ireland, doing family history here also means coming to terms with recent histories of forced and voluntary departure of people from areas where their families had lived in response to fear and intimidation over the course of the Troubles. In Geoffrey Beattie's research, street directories help him trace his grandfather's place of residence but also reminded him that the earlier generations of the Catholic family he knew as a boy and who moved away in the Troubles had also been his grandfather's neighbors. Family histories include earlier displacements. A family historian in County Down talked to me of his particular interest in his mother's side of the family, who had been well-off Protestant farmers in County Longford as far back as he could trace but left during the Irish Civil War because of intimidation. The family that remained now feel unwelcome in the South. Their experience suggests to him "that there is no place for Protestant Unionists in the South despite it being multicultural in other ways."[28] Undertaking family history can be a process of exploring the costs of the categories of cultural identity, religious denomination, and political affiliation in stories of displacement, bereavement, and broken relationships.

"No Such Thing as Purity of Blood"

Family trees can be diagrams of descent that complicate those categories of "Planter" and "Gael," "settler" and "native," when they include marriages and relationships that traversed what have come to be seen as the "two communities." These entangled genealogies are being uncovered in family history research and have featured in recent cultural explorations of identity. In 2000 and 2001, an exhibition titled *Local Identities: An Exploration of Cultural Identity,* organized by regional museum curators in Northern Ireland and funded by the Cultural Diversity Group of the Northern Ireland Community Relations Council, toured museums in Northern Ireland. Designed to encourage positive versions of cultural diversity as well as cultural interconnections at the local scale, the exhibition included a family tree among its panels of text and images.[29] This fictional family tree drew on museum professional and public intellectual Brian Turner's academic work on surnames and his exploration of surname histories with participants in local historical and community meetings. It showed three generations of an individual's genealogy whose eight great-grandparents' surnames were associated with Lowland Scots, French Huguenots from Lisburn, Anglo-Norman from east Down, Donegal Irish, English settlers, Highland Scots from Argyll and the Western Isles, Manx found in east Down, and Fermanagh Irish ancestors (see figure 6). This range of surnames is evidence of intermarriage, not just between the simple categories of native and settler but across diverse groups that reflect more complex local geographies and histories of migration. Though surnames are often taken as clues to an individual's background as Catholic or Protestant, the exhibit's family tree illustrates that an individual's surname can only stand for one ancestral line. Focusing a family history on one name reduces what counts as a genealogical connection to the past. Instead this is a genealogy of ancestral interconnections, of surnames that have historic associations with particular groups and are evidence of distinctive settlement histories, but cannot be used to simply locate an individual in one of those categories in the present. The different names in this family tree suggest hybrid alliances and liaisons that in different ways, with different costs and degrees of ease, crossed the boundaries between social, cultural, and religious categories.

Though this family tree was constructed as a illustrative device for the exhibition, it was neither improbable nor unrepresentative of common patterns

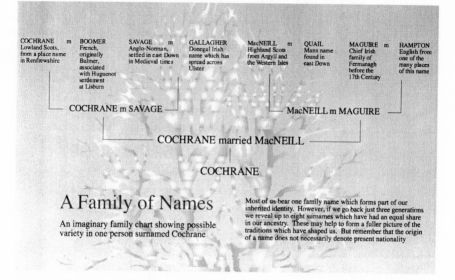

COCHRANE	m	BOOMER	SAVAGE	m	GALLAGHER	MacNEILL	m	QUAIL	MAGUIRE	m	HAMPTON
Lowland Scots, from a place name in Renfrewshire		French, originally Bulmer, associated with Huguenot settlement at Lisburn	Anglo-Norman, settled in east Down in Medieval times		Donegal Irish name which has spread across Ulster	Highland Scots from Argyll and the Western Isles		Manx name found in east Down	Chief Irish family of Fermanagh before the 17th Century		English from one of the many places of this name

└─── COCHRANE m SAVAGE ───┘   └─── MacNEILL m MAGUIRE ───┘

└─── COCHRANE married MacNEILL ───┘

COCHRANE

A Family of Names

An imaginary family chart showing possible variety in one person surnamed Cochrane

Most of us bear one family name which forms part of our inherited identity. However, if we go back just three generations we reveal up to eight surnames which have had an equal share in our ancestry. These may help to form a fuller picture of the traditions which have shaped us. But remember that the origin of a name does not necessarily denote present nationality

6. "A Family of Names." From *Local Identities: An Exploration of Cultural Identity* (Belfast: Northern Ireland Museums Council, Northern Ireland Regional Curators Group, 2000). Reproduced with permission of Brian Turner.

of diversity in Northern Irish genealogies. The discovery of intermarriage between Catholics and Protestants, and the religious conversion this often entailed, is a familiar experience for those pursuing their families' pasts. The need to accept the discovery despite its challenges to a family's or individual's sense of themselves was common advice from family historians in Northern Ireland. One was adamant:

> If you're doing family history I'm sure you realize you've got to be very broadminded, especially in Northern Ireland where you are Catholic or you're Protestant. Right. And if you're doing family history the first thing if you come to our society they'll say is "Can I just tell you before you start into this, you're going to get surprises and if you get surprises you're going to have to accept them because we're not all down the line like the way you think you are." I mean if you're going to come and find out such and such a thing and close the books and say "I'm not going to do my family history!" I mean you're not going to do it, full stop. So I mean I realized that most people here, very few people are not a mix of religions.[30]

As one genealogist put it to me, "There is no such thing as purity of blood existing in this country."

The personal encounters with "difference" through its presence in one's own family history can lead to new or renewed relationships across conventional divisions and new senses of identity. An elderly man living in Bangor, whose father had moved to Northern Ireland since he disapproved of the southern Irish state after independence, told me of his Huguenot ancestors, who came to Ireland from France in the 1690s, and of a family story of one who was caught up in the Siege of Derry. His genealogy has led to the rediscovery of, and renewed contact with, relatives in the south, including the family of his aunt, who had "married a Roman Catholic and been excommunicated" due to the Methodist family's "strong views on the Catholic Protestant thing," and her two daughters, who, he joked, "worse still," became Catholic nuns. He enjoys his family likeness and his shared interests with a Catholic monk who shares his name but whose exact genealogical connection is as yet unknown. This genealogically instigated knowledge of and contact with family in the South and travel south of the border—which for many Protestants in Northern Ireland would have previously been unthinkable—can lead to revised senses of identity. As one Protestant woman told me:

> I now feel more Irish. I now have an Irish passport. I used to class myself as British but I now say I am Irish or Northern Irish. I now feel partly Irish. When I lived in Manchester in the 1960s, I would have classed myself as British. People wouldn't understand Northern Ireland. They weren't used to Northern Ireland accents and would ask me if I came from Canada! We used to use a GB sticker on the car on holiday but we'd be attracted to those with IRL stickers. Through doing family history I would now have more liberal attitudes. I've now got roots in the South. As a child at school I'd play the card of being born in England, in ——, but just because that's where my father happened to be working. Not many children would have been able to say that. But now part of my family roots are from the South. I wouldn't class myself as Republican now but at the start of the Troubles I'd have been horrified at the thought of being in a united Ireland. But now I wouldn't be so bothered. I feel I live in the island of Ireland but I feel more Northern Irish when I am in the South.[31]

This example of a shifted sense of roots and identity as a result of research-ing family history is paralleled by an account of the new awareness of the Scot-tish planter family heritage for one Catholic man. The genealogical journey of Damian McAdam, a Catholic man brought up in a nationalist community in Derry, was the subject of the last of a series of television programs titled *Blood Ties* broadcast on BBC Northern Ireland in 2002. Each of the six half-hour epi-sodes focused on a genealogical investigation.[32] Most followed the experiences of visitors to Northern Ireland, sometimes paired with a local relation also ex-ploring their family's past. However, the last program in the series focused solely on Damian McAdam, whose great-grandfather, he explains, "jumped the fence" as "an adult convert" to Catholicism. This accounts for the dissonance between his background and his conventionally "Planter surname." It is this previously unknown "Planter" family history that he explores first in Northern Ireland, iden-tifying where the lowland Scots McAdams settled in the 1630s, and then where they came from in Ayrshire. The recent generations can be traced genealogically. Further back in time the connections are broad rather than documented ones but meaningful nonetheless.

In order to intensify the discovery story, the program makers offer him a ge-netic test to see whether he is connected to the bloodline of the chief of the Mc-Gregor clan to which the McAdams were historically linked. The results suggest a degree of connection, and he is offered honorary membership in the McGregor clan. His reaction is more reflective than dramatic, as his relationship to the Mc-Gregors is absorbed into a broad sense of the relationships between family his-tory and historical processes, and in particular how the entwining of a love story and the history of Scotland and Ulster has given him his name but distanced him, until now, from the history that name suggests. Against the backdrop of his ferry journey back to Northern Ireland from Scotland and a stroll past loyalist murals along curb-painted Derry streets, the program ends with his reflections:

> Well, the fact that I have royal blood as part of the McGregor clan, I've got to accept that as part of my history. History does this to families. Families will, depending on what circumstances are there at the time, what is happening in their area at the time, will make decisions to move, for example, the Plantation. I think it is fair to assume that our family, the McAdams, come with the Plantation. That was an event in history

that determined that some families took a decision to better themselves, or the promise of a better life from an undertaker or servitor, decided "yes, ok, we'll go with the Plantation in Ulster." And then history, itself, probably a love story, which decided where I am at. My great-grandfather being Presbyterian, deciding "ok, I want to marry a woman from the Brandymount area." And that very well, possibly is why he turned Catholic, and him doing that has changed the whole history of my current line of the McAdam line. That is the way genealogy is. And what I would say to anybody who is thinking of going down that way. You go it and you take it warts and all and you accept it. Not that I am saying there is anything wrong with it. I am absolutely delighted. I think it is an amazing story. I am quite sure and hope and trust that the rest of my family think the same because they are not aware of any of this at all.[33]

Traditionally in nationalist history, the Plantation is figured as the unjust dispossession of native Gaelic people from their lands by foreign usurpers, while in unionist history it is a divinely ordained cultivation of an ill-used land. In contrast, McAdam refigures this history of Plantation in terms of a narrative of family fortunes, opportunism, and hope for betterment. Centuries later, the family history swerves away from the Planter heritage with the conversion of his great-grandfather to Catholicism for marriage. For McAdam, this new knowledge enriches his sense of the country's past and the family's past. Like others, he argues that family history in Northern Ireland has to be done with an openness to what it may uncover.

Yet the hope expressed in Damian McAdam's final words suggests that the reaction of other family members to the discoveries in family histories cannot be guaranteed. Individuals who do not necessarily share an interest in pursing the family history are expected to accept its effects on their own understanding of their family's past. When the discoveries fundamentally alter long-held assumptions of a "purity of line," the responses of the wider family are even less certain. Sometimes news of intermarriage or religious change may be greeted with hostility. For one Protestant woman living in Portstewart, the discovery that she is tied, via her grandfather, to a noble Catholic Norfolk family was enormously enriching. For her, each ancestor's life is of value regardless of their wealth or title—for her, "family history is a great leveller"—so her interest in them is not dominated by their nobility but by her unexpected connection to a family of Catholic martyrs. An interest in family history leads to an attitude of openness to its results, she argues, but "people who weren't interested could be upset or dismissive about discoveries of ancestors of different religious background in their family tree. The staunch Orangemen in my family would not be willing to hear of or acknowledge the Catholic martyrs in their family past."[34] In other cases, resistance to family histories that challenge the family's cultural and political affinities is found not among local relatives but among diasporic relations where the certainties of affiliation persist, impervious to the shifts of identity "back home." One local family accepted a history of intermarriage, but their "Australian cousins" did not:

> In my family one widow married a Roman Catholic man and she was excommunicated from the family. . . . People here are comfortable with this in the family history but the family in Australia wouldn't have been. They'd left from Derry in 1920 having, as the family story goes, been burnt out by the IRA, though my father told me it was also because the father wasn't doing well as a farmer; the burning out is only half the story. The grandmother of the family would have been very bitter and very keen on the Orange side. When her grandson married a Roman Catholic they didn't tell her. When I visited them, the woman said that "her neighbours are very nice even though they are Roman Catholic." It was like you'd never left Northern Ireland![35]

The conflicting accounts of the family past that are common within all families are here complicated by the geographies of relatedness that stretch between the places of origin and diasporic settlement and the different attitudes to the politics of belonging, history, and religious identities they entail.

The frequent discoveries of intermarriage between Catholics and Protestants in family trees in Northern Ireland may enrich and expand the researcher's understanding of themselves and their family's past. But family histories of "mixed marriages" are also often painful stories of the policing of those categories of difference and the impact this has had on those transgressing those boundaries through relationships across religious divisions between Church of Ireland and Presbyterian as well as Catholic and Protestant. Though mixed marriages were common in the eighteenth and nineteenth centuries, this practice was deeply affected by the Catholic papal edict of 1908, the Ne Temere decree, that mixed marriages should only be conducted in a Catholic Church by a Catholic priest and that children born to mixed marriages should be brought up as Catholic. The edict was enforced in a period of intensified sectarian and political polarization, and it deepened antagonism to mixed marriages on both sides and often deeply damaged those relationships. Like the continued unhappy reactions to these discoveries by family members locally and abroad, family histories are also often histories of resistance to religious "miscegenation," of ostracized family members, forced separations, and competition over the religious upbringing of children.

Sometimes these are stories from generations in the past, like the account of "one woman who had married a Protestant man from the coast and had died leaving behind a child" whose family "kidnapped the child from the father in order to make sure it was brought up a Catholic." Some are more recent, like the story of a grandmother mourning a lost brother:

> I know that my grandmother . . . , who married my grandfather, . . . she had a brother. She lived in Omagh and she had a brother and now they were orphaned at an early age, but the story goes that she did have a brother who fell in love with a Catholic girl and possibly was hounded out of the town of Omagh by the local people there because he was changing his religion. Now I know my aunt has told me that that brother left the Omagh area and my grandmother mourned as it were for losing him and going away. And years later there was even a football match in Omagh where there was a linesman by the name of — who was coming from Belfast and she went along to the match to see afterwards, waiting near the changing rooms to see if this was the same man, her brother, but it wasn't.[36]

In family histories such as this, the effects of sectarianism echo through the generations and their effects are still being felt.

For one active family historian in County Tyrone, her research led her to surmise that her mother's coldness and emotional distance from her, and her hostility toward family history research, may be explained by her mother's anger and grief at being forced to end a relationship with a Catholic man and the likelihood that this meant also giving up their baby for adoption by his family:

it seems that my mother had went with a fella when she . . . before she met my dad. He was a Catholic, she was a Protestant. My grandmother was dead against Catholics and she put her out of the house. She would have if she hadn't got out of this relationship. So she broke off with him, but according . . . we never heard this, we didn't know . . . you talk about family history, my mother got married to my father, there was nothing told to us about her herself, she was saying about my aunts and uncles, where they lived. But personally my mother's history before that, we didn't know. We knew where she worked but nothing about . . . so she says, one day my aunt said, you know, "Did you know your mum went with a fella and she really, it was really, you know, true love type thing? But then my granny heard of it and they had to break it up."[37]

In other cases, intermarriage may have been tolerated within limits even if sectarianism fractured or tested the closeness of family relationships across religious difference. In Geoffrey Beatties's *Protestant Boy*, he recounts his response to the "inconceivable" revelation from another child that his much-loved uncle was Catholic: "It was Kevin who told me that my Uncle Terence was a Taig—his word not, not mine. A big fucking Taig just like him, the exact words fresh in my memory. The man who taught me to box, to tuck my head in right behind my fists, to fish with my hands, to stand up for myself on the street, that man was a Fenian bastard. All Kevin's words. I was ashen-faced all that day and night. It was as if one certainty in my life had been overturned."[38] Years later he realizes at his dying uncle's hospital bedside that, although his Uncle Terence was Beattie's father's best friend, this was the reason why he was not allowed to be present in the family home after his father's funeral. This is also why he "hadn't been allowed into the house of my Uncle Jack, who was a staunch Loyalist and had been married to my Aunty May, for nearly forty years. Forty fucking years. The years of fucking madness, I call them."[39]

Thus arguments for the value of family history in Northern Ireland do not suggest that family history is a pleasurable distraction from the tensions of division. It is a practice that can involve personal explorations of family histories that defy those divisions and uncover painful histories of their effects. As director of the Irish Genealogical Project in Northern Ireland in the early 1990s, John Winters argued in 1993 that the databases produced in the project could transcend their primary tourism purposes. Family history, he suggested, could "instil a knowledge and understanding about the interdependence of the different religious and cultural communities in Northern Ireland and the consequences of their integration and segregation." The Education for Mutual Understanding Programme established in schools in response to the Troubles emphasized "understanding and evaluating the shared, diverse, and distinctive aspects of cultural heritage," and for Winters, "it is within this arena that Irish Genealogy has a definite purpose. Perhaps with the means to explore ethnic identity in real terms a new generation can break out of inherent misconceptions and realise the positive benefits of family history."[40] Family trees in Northern Ireland may reflect centuries of marriages across the categories of family origin that are more diverse than the "two communities" suggest and that undermine the idea of pure descent within them, but that also have been shaped by attempts to constrain their intersection. Family trees may or may not record the family members lost to the other "side" as children or adults, relatives that could no longer count as family. These family histories challenge the absolutes of identity and belonging but also show the effects of those efforts to protect them in the intimate and private domain of family life. Family history in Northern Ireland complicates conventional categories of identity and descent and reveals the costs of attempts to preserve their fictional purity. Family histories of military service also reveal those costs and complicate those categories of difference.

Military Family Histories

In *Protestant Boy,* Geoffrey Beattie writes of quizzing his mother about her father's service in the British army in the late nineteenth and early twentieth centuries. She knows he was in India and South Africa, but he is frustrated that she can't answer the question of whether he was at the Somme: "I just wanted some concrete past, a past that I felt I knew a little about, and a survivor of the Somme for a grandparent would have done this. South Africa and India were too vague for me. Every boy in Belfast knew something about the Somme; the men not turning back, walking to their deaths in the service of the Crown, a true blood sacrifice, perhaps one of the greatest blood sacrifices of all."[41]

His grandfather turns out not to have served in World War I, but Beattie's interest in the Somme reflects the intense significance of this battle, and World War

I more generally, for Protestant working-class identity. Though the heavy losses suffered by the Thirty-sixth Division in the Somme were commemorated after the war by the Ulster Tower monument on the battlefield, over the last two decades and especially since the cease-fires of 1994, the Somme has become increasingly significant to Protestant identities in Northern Ireland.[42] This is reflected in the work of the Somme Association, which established the Somme Heritage Centre near Newtownards in County Down, and in loyalist murals in which the Somme has largely replaced the traditional iconography of Orangism. The Somme is a symbol of allegiance and sacrifice that was drawn on more specifically to legitimate the Ulster Volunteer Force formed in 1966 on the fiftieth anniversary of the battle. This loyalist paramilitary organization adopted the name of the force that was formed in 1913 to fight to maintain the union between Ireland and Britain and whose members volunteered to the newly formed Thirty-sixth Division, and adopted its motto, "For God and Ulster." Loyalist murals link the Battle of the Boyne, the Somme, and recent armed combat against the IRA.

However, as Beattie's memoir suggests, the Somme is also remembered as a distinctive part of a working-class Ulster Protestant past that is not "tainted by sectarianism" or dominated by the Orange Order and the middle-class Britishness of official unionism. This is a distinctly local, community, and family history of shared sacrifice and loss remembered by deprived local communities who now feel betrayed by Ulster unionism and the British state. As Brian Graham and Peter Shirlow have argued, "These communities are still defined by family traditions, lineages and sometimes a continuity of place not yet utterly destroyed by urban regeneration. Photographs of the dead are still to be found on mantle pieces and in family albums."[43] This memorializing is part of the making of collective Protestant identities beyond the limits of unionist Britishness and in response to the apparent security and success of Catholic nationalist culture.

But photographs of the dead and memories of wartime service and sacrifice are also found in other family albums and other family histories that challenge the conventional equations of loyalty and allegiance in Northern Ireland. In 1998 I wrote to each member of the Association of Ulster Genealogists and Record Agents as part of the research for this book. Mary Treanor, the mother of Edmund Treanor, one of the professional genealogists listed as a member of the association, replied to my letter to her son to tell me that he had been shot dead by loyalist gunmen in a random attack on Catholics in a bar in north Belfast on

New Year's Eve eight months before. The shooting was a reprisal for the murder of the loyalist terrorist leader Billy Wright in the Maze prison. Edmund would have liked to have met me, she wrote. When I visited her, she talked to me about her family and the deep love of family history that she and Edmund had shared, and of how this interest had led to his professional work helping others with their genealogical research.[44] His care in recording her stories, collecting the family memorabilia, and undertaking new research on the family's history had led to a rich archive that she is now left with but that would have been his inheritance.

The terrible loss of her son has not, however, changed the deep antisectarianism that has been a foundation of her personal relationships throughout her life and of her work in the 1980s in the community relations group that was active in the small mixed area of housing on the edge of a loyalist enclave in north Belfast, where she still lives. This is a perspective that is deeply shaped by her own family history that confounds the simplicities of the "either/or" categories of identity and affiliation in Northern Ireland. Edmund was killed by members of the Loyalist Ulster Defence Association who, she argues, could have no conception of the meaning of loyalty and honorable sacrifice. Not only does her family history include intermarriage and denominational changes, but her family's record of service in the British Army in the first and second world wars, she argued, challenged both sectarian loyalism and nationalist antipathy to the British state. Her brother's death at the age of twenty-one, who, having joined the RAF after the bombing of Belfast, was shot down over France, and the murder of her thirty-one-year-old son by terrorists—"who call themselves loyal"—were for her parallel losses in a family history that defied sectarianism and the simplicities of the absolute distinctions between who is native and who is loyal in Northern Ireland. In the years that have followed her son's death, she has worked with other members of WAVE, a grassroots, cross-community, voluntary organization supporting those bereaved and traumatized by the Troubles, and talked about her family history at the Ulster Museum. She has written to politicians including Senator George Mitchell and David Trimble encouraging them to find ways of making peace and to have the courage to take risks in the peace process as her brother, uncles, and mother's cousin had to do as servicemen in war. Despite her deep grief, she talked of finding the courage to speak out for an end to violence in Northern Ireland in the years following his death,[45] to use the inquest into his murder to accuse "his killers of betraying her family's sacrifice in the second world war," and to let her family history of sacrifice be a public statement of the real complexities of loyalty and identity that confound the categories of difference in Northern Ireland. The *Irish News* featured an extract from the inquest statement and the coroner's response on 28 November 1998:

> "My brother joined the RAF aged 19 after the Germans bombed Belfast," she said. "He flew over Germany and France. He was shot down after D-Day over France. He and four of his comrades are buried there. The resistance helped the other two back to England. My cousin was killed in Italy the following day. He survived Dunkirk and the African campaign. Their names are in the Book of Remembrance in St Anne's Cathedral, Belfast. The killers of Edmund betrayed the sacrifice that they made so we could live. If they have any conscience they should give themselves up. They would receive a short sentence, unlike the sentence they gave my son on New Year's Eve while having a drink with friends. Edmund was a good a caring person always willing to help others of any class or creed." Coroner John Lecky said he was moved by Mrs Treanor's words, saying it was sad reflection on society that nobody had been charged with the murder. "The people who murdered your son would claim to be loyalists," he said. "But the history of your family shows it is they who represent loyalism in the best and proper sense of the word. They were willing to give their lives for their country."[46]

This refusal to accept the model of "two communities"—each with "different ancestors, different anniversaries, different wars"[47]—in the face of profound personal loss is paralleled by wider moves to acknowledge the history of Irish service in the British army in both world wars. While the contribution of those who served in World War I in the Thirty-sixth Division became incorporated into a narrative of Protestant loyalty and sacrifice in Northern Ireland, the contribution of Irish men who fought in the two other new Irish divisions, the Sixteenth and Tenth, and in the existing Irish regiments was either ignored or derided in Irish nationalist culture. The Battle of the Somme in July 1916 had been preceded in Ireland by the Easter Rising and the executions of its leaders, which swung public opinion in support of independence. Those who opposed commemoration of wartime service in the immediate aftermath of World War I argued that it commemorated the presence of the colonial power, and this ambivalence about fighting for the colonial or former colonial power continued to shape attitudes to commemoration until recently.[48] Irish servicemen returned after the Great War to find themselves defined as traitors to the Irish nation, ostracized and intimidated. In some cases, they were murdered or expelled from Ireland on the threat of death.[49] This is the tragedy of forced exile as a result of nationalist definitions of loyalty and belonging that is so painfully conveyed in Sebastian Barry's novel *The Whereabouts of Eneas McNulty* (1998), in which Eneas makes the "mistake" not only of enlisting in the merchant navy but of joining the Royal Irish Constabulary on his return and is subject to a lifelong death threat from local Republican leaders.[50] Barry's more recent novel *A Long, Long Way* (2005), which tells the story of Irishmen in the first world war through the story of one solider from Dublin, continues his exploration of the experience of those caught in the net of nationalist absolutes. It is part of the recent acknowledgment of the contribution of all those from Ireland who served in both world wars.[51]

The IRA bombing of the November Remembrance Day service at the war memorial in Enniskillen in County Fermanagh in Northern Ireland in 1987 murderously demonstrated that commemoration of both world wars was held by many nationalists to be an expression of loyalty to a reviled British state. Outrage at the bombing began a process of exploring and commemorating Irish war dead that included restoring the neglected war memorials of Irish towns and that led to the first ceremony in Dublin during the D-Day commemorations in 1995 to honor the 10,000 men who fought in the British army in World War II, attended by all political parties in the South, representatives from the Ulster Unionist Party, and, significantly, Sinn Fein.[52] In 1998, President Mary McAleese in the company of Queen Elizabeth opened the Island of Ireland Peace Park at Messines in Belgium to commemorate the Battle of Messines Ridge, where Irish soldiers—who had been willing to fight to stop or fight to achieve Home Rule before the war—had fought a common enemy together.

These public and deeply symbolic memorials are paralleled by less prominent but no less significant gestures of reconciliation and commemoration. Two friends and family history enthusiasts in Larne, County Antrim, who share an interest in military history, and in the service of men from Ulster in World War I in particular, are researching and collating the family histories of the men whose names appear on the Larne cenotaph. This commemorative project also involves recovering the names and histories of the Catholic men who made up half of those from the town who died in the war but whose names were not recorded on its war memorial. One of them organizes coach trips to see the war graves in France and "would love to see more nationalist people on the bus." For these Protestant men, World War I is not an emblem of Protestant sacrifice but a shared history of loss.[53] So while military history is a specialist branch of popular history often associated with masculine militarism rather than reconciliation, when entangled with family history in Northern Ireland, it can reflect a quiet commitment to peace.

The new understanding and appreciation of the service of Irish men in the British army has mostly focused on those who fought in the two world wars rather than the history of Irish soldiers in the British army more widely. The two world wars, and World War II especially, can be seen as part of a shared and justified Allied cause. However, regular employment in the British army has a more ambiguous place in Irish history. Irish nationalism, as expressed in the Irish war of independence and the foundation of the state, reconfigured the meaning of family histories of employment in the British army as evidence of mistaken loyalty to the colonial power and treachery to the nation. In his memoir *The Speckled People* (2003), Hugo Hamilton tells the story of his German mother and ardently purist Irish nationalist father in Dublin in the 1950s and early 1960s. When he discovers his father has hidden the medals, letters, and photographs that reveal his grandfather's service in the British merchant navy, he realizes that his father's painfully rigid cultural code that crushes his mother and children has been based on the erasure of his own father from the family's past.[54] This personal denial and public derision of family histories of military service as result of nationalism's demands of purity of loyalty and identity was intensified through the Troubles, when the British military presence, initially welcomed by Catholics, became an army of occupation for the nationalist community. In a province whose recent history is of armed conflict over its very existence as a political entity and all the fear, loss, pain, and anger of those years, the theme of military service is deeply and bitterly politicized.

Yet as the Bloody Sunday tribunal continues its investigation of the army's shooting of protesting civilians in Derry, other investigations explore alleged collaborations between loyalist paramilitaries and the army, and the nationalist demands for the demilitarization in Northern Ireland are followed through, one former republican prisoner is now arguing for the value of exploring family histories of British military service. This local community activist is involved in community development and educational projects in the poor, working-class, Catholic, and strongly nationalist area of Ardoyne in north Belfast, and family history is central to his vision of conflict transformation.[55] In the local and family history classes he runs, he uses his own family history to encourage others to explore their personal and shared histories and gain a stronger sense of "where they come from." Although there is a stereotype in Northern Ireland of Catholics "having all the history"—being located through a strong sense of the past—he argues that both the dominance of the nationalist narrative and the teaching of history of "kings and queens" in schools severely neglects everyone's local and family history. The story he recounts is a story of avowed purity:

> In my house we had . . . well I suppose it is the same in every house. But there is this tradition of how you proved your purity, whether it is Republican purity or nationalist purity or religious purity, you know. So, the way it used to be anyway was that whenever my Ma and Da were ever arguing, my Da would say, "Well, at least there is no Protestant blood in my family." To which my Ma would reply, "Well, at least none of my brothers were in the British army." Blah, blah, right? And so it used to go on. But then I used to find that amazing, you know: "How, Da, do you know that when your father was an orphan and you don't even know who your Grandda is?"[56]

His family research undoes those avowals:

> So anyway, I found out then that my grandfather who was an IRA man who I'd assumed was Catholic was actually a Protestant. He was an orphan whose father was a Protestant and was in the British Army and was killed in the Boer War. His own grandfather served twenty-two years in the British Army in the West and East Indies, and they were all a big British regimental family who settled in Tyrone and they were Planters. And so my own grandfather who has told my Da about all these mad stories about Protestants [like] "never trust them" was actually one of them himself!

As a child in his republican community, he hated British soldiers, but he is now fascinated by the history of his Protestant army ancestors. Using his own family story, he encourages others to tap the military archives that they would have felt profoundly alienated from in the past in order to access the detailed information on ancestors that their records of service contain:

> Whenever I was explaining to people "It's brilliant if your great-grandfather or your great-great-grandfather was in the British army because they actually recorded who the next of kin was and not only that, what height you were, the colour of your eyes, the colour of your hair, what size you were." And so you can create this picture of who your great-grandparents were for people. And you know they'd go, "Gez, I've got blue eyes and black hair," and they make a link straight back to the past.

British military service records are thus refigured as resources for a progressive engagement with the past in republican Ardoyne, north Belfast.

This is an exceptional case in the degree to which this activist explicitly links family history to the politics of reconciliation and conflict transformation. But he insisted that the significance of his story is not that it is unusual but that it is very common. As he explained, "Every single person in the Ardoyne would have had someone in jail for the IRA or have a great-grandfather who fought in whatever war for the British army, and they'll all have Protestants related to them as well." Because it was an employment option for working-class men, family histories of military service in the British army are common in Catholic and Protestant working-class communities. Coming to terms with the history of Northern Ireland entails exploring military history as shared working-class history across the divisions of religion and loyalty. This recognition of commonality is, he suggests, potentially more constructive than "much of what passes for community relations now." Instead of being based on the premise that there are two groups who learn to respect each other, he argues that family history destroys ideas of the existence of two groups; it explodes myths of purity and instead teaches that "we are all the same":

> I can see how it could be used as a tool for reconciliation, because I really don't give any substance to what the community relations stuff is, you know. Even though we have a community relations project here, it is very much, I suppose, building up an infrastructure for single-identity stuff. It is not really actually making people understand that they are the same people. They are constantly saying, "you are the mirror of them" and not saying, "no, no, no, that's not the case at all." I'm saying, "we are

all the same, and the person who told us it was us and them, that's them."
There is no difference, and here is how you can prove it.

Unlike "single-identity work," which is the term used to describe a group's reflections on their own history and identity, ideally as a prelude to "cross-community work,"[57] family history, he argues, can prove "there is no difference" between those working-class communities that are so polarized by mutual mistrust and hatred. Recent museum exhibitions exploring the history of conflict and war in Northern Ireland, both by focusing on the history of World War II and by situating the Troubles in the history of war and conflict in Ireland over the course of the twentieth century, are part of continuing attempts to deal with issues of victimhood, memory, commemoration, and reconciliation.[58] This argument from a former republican prisoner that the recognition of shared histories of British military service within families whose members recently saw the British solider as a "legitimate target" in the armed struggle for a united Ireland is part of this process.

One exploration of questions of blame, responsibility, and the figure of the "enemy" through family history from over twenty years ago resonates with the issues raised by the recent past. In 1986 a radio program titled *The Wings of the Seraphim* was broadcast on BBC Radio Ulster as part of a series of programs for schools titled "Today and Yesterday in Northern Ireland."[59] The subject of this program, written and narrated by the radio and television producer Douglas Carson, is World War II told through the lens of Carson's memory of the war as a child in Northern Ireland and shaped by his subsequent explorations of his family's history. Born in 1938, he describes his first seven years as the worst in human history. Carson's narration is interspersed with extracts of recorded speeches by Hitler and Churchill. The program's sound effects are music and song—German classical and popular pieces, wartime songs—and the sound of bombs, sirens, and shelling. The narrative is accompanied by recitations from the passage in the Book of Revelation in which "seven angels are given seven golden vials full of the wrath of god." These extracts, solemnly recited by a woman and man, give the program its name and give the account an apocalyptic tone. The war is an unleashing of violence; misery and suffering stalk the land.

This is also a family story, a story of cousins dying from its start to its end. These are Carson's German cousins. At the beginning of the program, Carson introduces his place and his people, from Scotland originally but rooted in County Down:

My name is Carson and I come from County Down. My people crossed the sea from Scotland. These tidy acres were the promised land. My great-granduncle was called Israel. Imagine the round tower at Drumbo, a broken steeple and a church beside it. The night wind plays it like a flute. A lament for the dead, for the lost tribes of Israel. My father is here with his fathers before him. Uncles, aunts, and cousins, roots of bone. The flowers that grow out of them should be blue. They knew about flax for they sowed it and reaped it. Their lives were woven into linen. They married in linen.[60]

But this is not just a local linen family: a linen connection and a marriage extend the family to Germany. In 1922, Eliza, Carson's father's cousin, married Alfred Gruschwitz, a linen mill owner from eastern Germany, and moved to Silesia; Silesia was "Eliza's promised land." They had a large family—"seven of their children grew and married"—and the last of their thirty-two grandchildren was born in 1936. Carson's account of the war is an account of the deaths of his relatives in the war, dying as soldiers and civilians in France, Germany, Poland, and Russia. As Carson's Ulster family says good-bye to "a clutch of cousins" embarking for France in the British Army, their German cousins are fighting and dying "for the Reich"—the "Great War divided the family. At Ypres and Passchendael, we fought on both sides."[61] As Belfast is blacked out and bombed and eight hundred "citizens of Belfast" die in the air raids, his cousins are being killed as German soldiers in Russia. In *The Wings of the Seraphim,* sometimes their names are recited by Carson as litanies of loss; sometimes the circumstances of their deaths are given: soldiers dying in battle, a resistance fighter shot dead, casualties of Allied bombing and Russian advance.

> The Fuhrer sent his armies into Russia. "The world," he said, "will hold its breath." It did. Millions died. It was a war of slaughter.
>
> *The angel poured his vial and they gnawed their tongues for pain.*
>
> Alfred von Kessel, aged thirty five; Octavion von Gramon, twenty two; Dietrich von Cruben, aged twenty one. The great-grand-offspring of my ancestors were dying in sheughs at Krakow and Rjev. . . .
>
> In February Stalingrad surrendered. The Germans made their last advances. Four more cousins left their bones in Russia: Engelhard Spancken,

aged twenty-two; Eberhard von Kessel, aged twenty-seven; Hartvig von Cruben, aged twenty-five; his brother Claus von Cruben.

The British and Americans invaded France. The Germans were driven back to the Rhine. In June, Anton Spancken was killed in an air raid. His son Wolfgang Spancken had turned seventeen. He worked against the Nazis and they killed him. In the new year, the Russians invaded Silesia. The Russians were enraged and made a desert. Villages and farms were smashed to rubble. Silesia became part of Poland. A multitude of refugees went west. Among them were the remnants of the Gruschwitz family. Elizabeth Schmudebach, aged twenty-three, was expecting her first baby in February. Her daughter was born and died on the road. The Russians reached the suburbs of Berlin. Hitler was recruiting boys to guard it. Christopher von Kessel was a veteran at twenty. He was killed in the last stand of the Reich.

The history of the war is humanized by these named deaths. Carson's use of the local word for ditch—sheugh—in describing his cousins dying "at Krakow and Rjev," and his use of the County Down place-names—Drumbo and Ballylesson—juxtaposes the local and the distant through family ties. It brings the war home, but this is kinship with the "enemy." For Carson, the misery of millions and the deaths of millions of others as a result of the war and Nazi policy raise profound questions about the attribution of blame, responsibility, and the dehumanization of the "enemy." Two deeply reflective passages of poetry occur in an otherwise flat and factual narration. One, at the start, follows an account of the first death of one of his cousins and is a quiet poetic exegesis on the choices between recognizing or repressing a familial connection that is fractured by the antipathies of nations at war:

> In April 1940 I was two. The presents were a ration book, a gas mask, an identity card with a personal number. The Germans took Holland, Belgium, and Luxembourg. The first cousin gave his life for the Reich. He was Rainer von Gramon. He was aged twenty-three. I see him in uniform, a peaked cap, a pair of glossy jackboots and a swastika. The face is a familiar face. He looks like me.

> I will lock up my looking glass with his picture
> in the attic in a black frame face to the wall

in case his eyes get into my reflections.
His daylight is fading out of my reach
in sepia, in autumn, into old harvests,
mislaid in ripening fields at Ballylesson.

At the end of the program, Carson returns to this theme of accountability and recognition and reworks the poem's conclusion. In this second version, the decision of the first passage to suppress the implications of that recognition is replaced by questions: how should he respond to the recognition of likeness with another cousin that died at the end of the war? What does this familial connection imply about blame and responsibility?

Anton von Spancken was a prisoner of the Russians. They released what was left of him and he died. I see him in uniform with a swastika. His face is a familiar one. He looks like me.

Will I lock up the looking glass with his picture
in the attic in a black frame face to the wall
in case his eyes get into my reflections?
Or dig him up and ask him on whose head
he puts the blame for fifty million dead?
I have taken his fingerprints from the Rhine
and matched them in Drumbo. The match is mine.

The Nazis went into hiding in us. The blood of all the enemies is in our veins.

This is a likeness that embodies a family connection and that defies the dehumanized image of the enemy. His family history of Scottish origins, Ulster roots, and German relatives troubles the image of the enemy as an abstract "other"; it questions the attribution of blame. In acknowledging the "match" of fingerprints between his German cousin and himself, Carson suggests that the crimes of war as well as its routine conduct and the suffering of the enemy are carried out and experienced by "people like us," bound together by blood.

Written and broadcast in the mid-1980s in Northern Ireland, it is very likely that Douglas Carson's account of World War II and of family connections that cross the categories of ally and enemy would have resonated with the Troubles for the radio program's listeners. The archive summary suggests that the program used family history to explore the ways in which the history of Northern Ireland is connected to wider historical processes and events. It describes the subject as "the family history of Carson illustrating the complexity of family links around the world. Ancestors were burnt in Poland, cousins killed in France, Germans had family blood in their veins, others slaughtered in Russia, another killed in the last stand of the Reich, but all had roots or connections with Ulster."[62] At the same time, the program's list of young men's deaths and its sound track of shelling echo the regular news reporting of the Troubles before, during, and after the year this program was first broadcast. For Carson, the program was a distillation of his reflections on the historical subjects that had been the focus of his quarter of a century of progam making, and whose teaching in schools in Northern Ireland, which he witnessed, was refracted through the polarized perspectives of Northern Irish politics. In making connections between "bombing on the Eastern Front and in east Belfast," Carson's program is an exploration of the horrors that result from adherence to different forms of "perfect truths," fundamentalisms of different kinds. While the program's aesthetics evoke the biblical "truth" of his family background as Plymouth Brethren and the culture of Northern Irish Protestantism more widely, the dangers all forms of "perfect truth" are his subject—republican and loyalist, as well as those of Nazi Fascism and communist Marxism that the "immigrant side" of his family were "caught between."[63] Both the Troubles and World War II are the horrific results of devotion to "perfect truths."

Yet *The Wings of the Seraphim* is not a detached reflection on the effects of fundamentalism. Instead Carson invites the listener to consider, as he does, one's personal responsibility in the face of these fundamentalisms and the immunity of no one to their appeal and their energies. Carson's statement that "the Nazis went into hiding in us" is a challenging invitation to consider that the actions of those deemed to be the enemy could, in other circumstances, be our own. Its open ambiguity means that it may refer to an "us" in Northern Ireland or a wider human capacity for ideologically justified and normalized killing. However, his reflections on blame and accountability particularly prefigure recent attempts to deal with the trauma and loss of thirty years of violence in Northern Ireland. The final line of *The Wings of the Seraphim*—"the blood of all the enemies is in our veins"—challenges an image of the "two communities" as separate communities of descent. Thus, one particular and in some ways unusual family history of Ulster stock and dispersal, of entangled family histories of enemies and allies, can be projected back onto Northern Ireland order to understand the many family histories of interconnection and commonality that have been severed by sectarianism.

Conclusion

While Ireland is the subject of so much diasporic fondness, fervor, and affection, family history in Northern Ireland demonstrates in the most raw and painful ways the effects of divisive genealogical definitions of relatedness, belonging, identity, and difference and the inescapably political nature of all expressions of collective ancestry and origins. Those who visit Northern Ireland to explore their roots and find ancestral homes come to a place in which genealogy, for many, is also an exploration of the family's origins and location within its histories and categories of belonging and difference. Overseas visitors encounter local people also exploring questions of home and identity. Sometimes this can lead to expected connections that cut across different perspectives on the meaning of Irish descent: emphatic understanding of the pull of that longing to locate points of origin, uneasy realization of difference in diasporic and local approaches to the past and politics of Ulster, interconnected genealogies between those exploring Irish roots and those in Northern Ireland tracing Ulster-Scots connections via emigrant ancestors in the New World.

The social and personal dimensions of family history in Northern Ireland are inescapably framed by questions of division. Sometimes these are managed by emphasizing family history as an escape from the overtly political. For some, family history is an alternative to that politicized past and its sectarian versions, even if the subject of this hobby—family background and, by implication, religious and cultural identity—has been so heavily framed by the categories of identity within this divided society. In many cases, family histories are central to an individual and familial identity firmly located within one of the "two communities," as native Gaelic or as settler Planter stock. Yet, as the accounts of the practice of family history presented here show, family history can also be a way of exploring personal and familial relationships to those conventional categories of belonging. Family history may intentionally be or inadvertently become an exploration of the history of Northern Ireland through the lens of the personal and familial. The routine experience of discovering intermarriage or religious conversion within family trees challenges the image of the two communities of descent in the most intimate domain of the family. New understandings of shared experience including familiar family histories of Catholic and Protestant service in the British army similarly undermine the image of two communities who share no history but that of sectarian antagonism. Genealogy in action in Northern Ireland deserves attention not only because of what it suggests about the particular challenges of doing family history in a divided society and the wider politics of genealogical models of collective identity. It also demonstrates the innovative, practical, and potentially conciliatory responses to the demands of exploring personal and familial locations within and beyond the conventional categories of belonging in this place.

But if family history in Northern Ireland often uncovers the entanglements of native and settler ancestries that erode these categories, family history is also a record of the costs. Here the idea of native belonging deployed in political campaigns to redress the dispossession of indigenous groups produces an exclusive model of legitimate presence and cultural inheritance. This can be used to suggest that the real home of families who have been in Ulster for centuries, and whose genealogies are in any case entangled with those of the "native," is somewhere else or, at best, that they can be incorporated into a plural model of Irishness. Being defined as or defining oneself as "not belonging in an ancient land" is profoundly alienating. Interests in Ulster-Scots roots and diasporic achievement is one response to this charge of not being native. Family histories also show the costs of the policing of those categories of difference. Family trees that show intermarriage are often joined to family stories of the struggles to overcome hostility within their families and within their localities. Other family stories are of families that were fractured as members were ostracized because of their relationships with the "other side."

For Avtar Brah, diasporic spaces are characterized by "the entanglement, the intertwining of the genealogies of dispersion with those of 'staying put.'"[64] In Northern Ireland, these genealogical entanglements are between those who arrived and left in centuries of movement between these two islands on the edge of Europe, those who settled as part of early modern colonization, those who left in the eighteenth century and in the nineteenth century, those who return with very recent family connections and those with very distant roots in Ulster. Though diasporic interest in Irish ancestry is often based both on the appeal of Irishness and the appeal of that ultimate place of original belonging, and though the categories of settler and native, Planter and Gael remain potent and divisive, these intertwined genealogies suggest how these models of belonging and identity can be reworked as well as invoked. In the next chapter, however, I consider how ideas of the native and newcomer are mobilized within the technologies and interpretations of new research on "the genetic history and geography of Ireland" in ways that work against these potentially progressive entanglements.

6

Irish Origins, Celtic Origins

Population Genetics, Cultural Politics

In Brian Friel's play *The Home Place*, which opened in Dublin in February 2005, the setting is the house and garden of Christopher Gore, a "Planter" landlord in Ballybeg, County Donegal, in the summer of 1878.[1] His cousin Dr. Richard Gore, an English scientist, and his assistant are visiting en route to the Aran Islands as part of their anthropometric survey of "racial" types in Ireland. Their attempt to do some local measuring while guests at "The Lodge" comes just after the murder of an abusive local landlord. Christopher Gore tries to facilitate their work by encouraging his tenants to volunteer for measurement; Con Doherty, a local man, forces Dr. Gore and his assistant to leave. This local resistance precipitates a crisis in the household and threatens each individual's negotiations of their location within the local dynamics of late-nineteenth-century class, blood, and belonging in Ireland. For Christopher Gore, the Gore family "home place" in Kent never really was home; now Ballybeg can no longer be his home.

The Home Place dramatizes "the doomed nexus of those who believe themselves the possessors and those who believe themselves dispossessed"[2] and explores the way these categories have been shaped by ideas of inheritance, difference, and mixing—ancestral, cultural, material, and social. In the play, Friel engages with two entwined issues that were being worked through in late-nineteenth-century science, politics, and culture: the presence of the settler and the character of the native in both colonial racial typologies and nationalist accounts of spirit, blood, and race.

The printed edition of the play includes an extract of a scientific paper published in 1892 in the *Proceedings of the Royal Irish Academy* that presented the results of an anthropometric survey of the Aran Islands, County Galway, by Professor A. C. Haddon.[3] In 1891 Alfred Cort Haddon, one of the founding figures of British anthropology, had established Dublin's Anthropometric Laboratory to study the racial characteristics of Irish people.[4] His work with Charles R. Browne on the Aran Islands used new anthropometric techniques for the study of "racial types." But their interest in the Aran Islands was not novel. Their visit followed many others made by antiquarians, philologists, folklore collectors, writers, artists, and Irish languages enthusiasts and travelers from the early nineteenth century for whom the islands' isolation suggested a primitive nobility, organic community, and a pure Gaelic stock protected by distance from modernity and, for cultural nationalists, Anglicization.[5] Nevertheless, the work of Haddon and Browne was foundational for an extended history of scientists visiting Ireland to measure people and map patterns of physical variation across the island. *The Home Place*, like Friel's *Translations*, thus stages a moment in the history of the application of a rational science of survey and measurement in Ireland. In this case, the science is not in the direct service of the state, and it is people rather than topography being measured.

The twinned themes of native character and alien presence in *The Home Place* resonate with contemporary questions of belonging in debates about immigration, citizenship, and multiculturalism in Ireland and with the ways ideas of ancestral origins and allegiance are entwined in the conventional models of identity and difference in Northern Ireland. Friel's exploration of the history of the measurement of racial types in Ireland, the physiological categorization of the native and settler, and the historical and contemporary implications of these models of origins, ancestry, and belonging coincides with new work on the human population genetics of Ireland. Attempts to explore the genetic composition of the population and infer from it prehistoric origins and patterns of settlement today are less intrusive than the calipers and rulers of anthropometry. Cheek cells, from which DNA samples can be taken, are solicited from volunteers and sent back to laboratories by post.

Nevertheless, the play resonates not only with contemporary questions of belonging but also with the ways in which ideas of individual identity and human difference are being reshaped by genetic science. Friel has Dr. Richard Gore wonder whether

> black hair and strong chin and clear complexion . . . constitute an ethnic
> code we can't yet decipher? That they are signposts to an enormous

fault of genetic information that is only just beyond the reach of our understanding? Are they saying to us—these physical features—if only we could hear them—are they whispering to us: Crack our code and we will reveal to you how a man thinks, what his character traits are, his loyalties, his vices, his entire intellectual architecture.[6]

The allusions are not simply to late-nineteenth-century anthropometry but to the contemporary public presence of genetics as the "code of codes." Genes, as this metaphor implies, are commonly understood as the set of inherited instructions that determine all life as well as individual identity.[7] Although the public presentation of genomic science now places greater emphasis on the complex relationships between genes and environmental effects, genetic determinism continues to characterize a significant strand of scientific accounts of human society and human nature. And while people often incorporate ideas of genetic inheritance into their understandings of themselves and others in dynamic and flexible ways,[8] the genetic essentialism that Friel alludes to remains a powerful mode of explaining individual or collective attributes and behaviors. By focusing on nineteenth-century anthropometry in Ireland, *The Home Place* offers a critical commentary on both colonial and nationalist models of the biological patterning of difference, and on the contemporary appeal and problematic implications of genetic essentialism and genetic accounts of ethnic or cultural difference.

In 2000, a century after the work of Haddon and Browne was published in the *Proceedings of the Royal Irish Academy*, a new Royal Irish Academy research program titled "Irish Origins: The Genetic History and Geography of Ireland," initiated by its Genetic Anthropology Committee, was launched with Irish government National Millennium Committee funding (figure 7). The research included projects to explore contemporary genetic variation by sampling and examining genetic material from people in Ireland and Northern Ireland and using this material to reconstruct the prehistoric migration pathways to the island and the "origins" of its contemporary inhabitants. This project reflects the ways in which the exploration of the total genetic makeup of humans in the Human Genome Project has been paralleled by research focusing on human origins, prehistories of human migration, and contemporary patterns of human similarity and difference or "diversity."

Though the Human Genome Diversity Project, which sought to map global human genetic variation, was discredited because of its lack of sensitivity to the

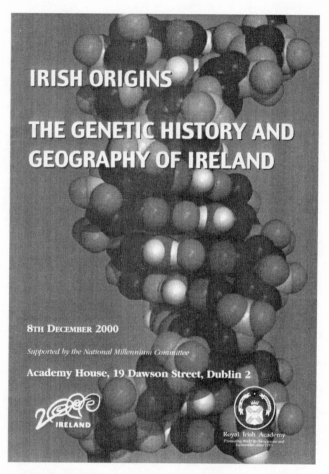

7. "Irish Origins: The Genetic History and Geography of Ireland." Royal Irish Academy conference booklet cover, 2000. Reproduced with permission of the Royal Irish Academy.

ethics and politics of collecting and categorizing human genetic material and thus human groups, numerous independent, national, and internationally coordinated projects exploring genetic variation within and between groups continue.[9] They are promoted through arguments about their potential value for biomedicine, national security, and forensic science and for reconstructing prehistoric geographies of migration and origin for human groups or humanity as a whole. The necessity for national genetic self-knowledge, like personal genealogical knowledge in many contexts, now seems normal and normative. The pursuit of personal and collective knowledge of Irish origins reflects these wider developments. Thousands of personal genealogical projects exploring Irish emigrant ancestry from afar are now paralleled by new research by geneticists in Ireland addressing the genetic composition of the population and using it to explore the prehistoric migrations that populated the island.

Despite its association with innovative scientific developments, the "Irish Origins" research program also evokes previous studies of ancient Irish origins whose history demonstrates the inescapably political nature of accounts of origins and settlement, the categorization of difference, and the construction of criteria of belonging and legitimate presence by descent. John O'Hart's late-nineteenth-century account of the origin and genealogy of the Irish nation in terms of the arrival of Milesian men from Spain who became the founding fathers of the Gaelic nation in *Irish Pedigrees* treated as fact a particular national origin story whose validity was the subject of heated scholarly dispute among antiquarians in the late eighteenth century.[10] As Clare O'Halloran has argued, interest in questions of the origin of the people of Ireland were both shared by Catholic and Protestant antiquaries and deeply shaped by their consciousness of the political dimensions of questions of settlement and arrival. Debates about origins were framed by divergent perspectives on the Anglo-Norman conquest and what was then the relatively recent history of sixteenth- and seventeenth-century Plantation. Different positions within these debates reflected different political imperatives of, on the one hand, achieving improved political and religious rights for Catholics or, on the other, of validating the attachments to the land of their birth and the legitimate presence of those whose family histories were of generations of "settler" residence in Ireland. Centuries on, the theme of ancient and historical settlement continues to be deeply political. Differing perspectives on the history of colonization and the validity and value of distinctions between "native" and "settler" have shaped contested professional and popular interpretations of Irish prehistory and history and are central to the cultural politics of identity and belonging in Ireland and Northern Ireland.

Two recent research papers on the human population genetics of Ireland by a research team of geneticists based in Dublin exemplify new developments in what is thus a long history of interest in the questions of who were the island's first people, when they arrived and where they came from, who followed and who were the original founding fathers of the Gaelic Irish nation. These new genetic descriptions of the population follow earlier efforts to scientifically describe and categorize people in Ireland. But opening this discussion of genetic accounts of prehistoric demography and the genetic composition of the contemporary population in Ireland and Northern Ireland with Friel's play is not to suggest an unbroken ideological chain between anthropometry, racial science, and research in human population genetics being carried out in genetic laboratories in Irish universities. To do so would not only miss their differences but also elide the contested authority of science, its internal heterogeneity, and the complex relationships between science and culture in both contexts. Instead, exploring the nature of this new work and its relationship to historical and contemporary perspectives on ideas of settlement and descent in Ireland, and the diverse deployments of these new genetic accounts of origins and difference, suggests their significant and complex implications for the politics of belonging in Ireland and Northern Ireland. The public figuring of this new work in human population genetics, in the media and among online audiences, is also a matter of postcolonial and diasporic cultural politics.

Irish Origins

In 2000 the popular magazine *Inside Ireland: Your Guide to All Things Irish,* produced in Dublin for a target audience in the United States, featured an article titled "More about Genes: The Irish Really Are a Race Apart." The article's author, Emmeline Hill, a geneticist at Trinity College, Dublin, explained the results of recent research completed by her and colleagues Daniel Bradley of Trinity College and Mark Jobling of the University of Leicester. The *Inside Ireland* article introduced the findings this way:

> Men with Gaelic surnames coming from the west of Ireland are descendants of the oldest inhabitants of Europe. In a recent study, scientists at Trinity College Dublin, created a new genetic map of the people of Ireland. By comparing this map to European genetic maps they have shown that the Irish are one of the last remnants of the pre-Neolithic hunters and gatherers who were living throughout Europe over 10,000 years ago, before the invention of agriculture. The Irish really ARE different.[11]

Hill explained how the research had found that a version of the Y chromosome associated with an ancient population in Ireland was found in greatest concentration in samples of men with Gaelic surnames, and especially those that are found most in the western province of Connaught. The results thus suggest that the human genetic composition of the west of Ireland has been least affected by in-migration after its early prehistoric settlement. "By comparison," Hill explained, "in the east of the country there has been a lot more mixing of genes coming from foreign sources."[12]

The research that Hill explained in *Inside Ireland* had been published earlier in 2000 in the science journal *Nature* in a paper titled "Y Chromosome Variation and Irish Origins: A Pre-Neolithic Gene Gradient Starts in the Near East and Culminates in Western Ireland."[13] In this paper, Hill, Jobling, and Bradley presented the results of their study of human genetic variation in Ireland and its relationship to patterns of European genetic diversity. This study applied new approaches in human population genetics that use surnames or family names as markers of patterns of direct descent and relatedness among men.[14] Unlike other genetic material that is inherited in the process of human reproduction, the Y chromosome is inherited directly and largely unchanged from father to sons. Small mutations that occur in the Y chromosome are passed on, leading to distinctive patterns of Y-chromosome nucleotides shared by men who share direct paternal descent. Thus in patrilineal surname systems where surnames also pass directly from father to sons, surnames can be taken as evidence of direct genetic descent. Making allowances for the occurrence of what are described as "non-paternity events," which result in surnames and genes not getting passed on together from father to son—illegitimacy or infidelity in marriage—surnames are taken as markers of genetic relatedness among men. Human population geneticists have used the combination of direct paternal Y-chromosome inheritance and patterns of variation due to mutation to explore the degree of genetic relatedness between men and within groups of men sharing a surname and for larger-scale studies of genetic variation. Variant forms of the Y chromosome that arise through mutation are used to distinguish between directly related and unrelated men, to estimate the most common recent ancestors of men sharing the same surname, and to reconstruct histories and prehistories of descent and relatedness: how closely or how directly individual men, groups of men, and by extension wider population groups are related to each other.[15]

In this case, the authors explored the distribution of a particular set of Y-chromosome genetic variants—haplogroup 1—that has a high frequency in the island of Ireland as a whole and examined its degree of concentration among men that were grouped according to the origin of their surname. Using Edward Ma-cLysaght's *The Surnames of Ireland*, that most well-known of guides to Irish surnames first published in 1957, the scientists derived seven surname groups.[16] Three were described as "diagnostic of historical influx":[17] Scottish, Norman/Norse, and English surname groups. The four others were based on surnames of Gaelic origin in the four ancient provinces of Ireland: Ulster, Munster, Leinster, and Connaught. Genetic samples were taken from 221 men who were grouped into one of seven surname categories. The scientists then looked at the percentage occurrence of that specific Y-chromosome type, haplogroup 1, in the full set of samples, in the combined Gaelic surname group samples, and then in each of the regionally distinguished Gaelic surname categories. They found the highest concentration of this Y-chromosome type among the samples taken from men with Gaelic surnames and in particular among those associated with counties in Connaught. Jobling, one of the authors, uses this project to demonstrate the wider value of Y-chromosome genetic studies:

> The general validity of the principle of associating Y chromosomes with surnames is shown by a study of Y chromosomal haplogroup diversity in Ireland. First, the Y chromosomes of 221 Irishmen were assigned to haplogroups. Then, to remove the effects of incursions from outside Ireland, chromosomes associated with surnames having English (e.g. Harrison, Kent), Scottish (e.g. Boyd, Knox), Norman (e.g. Bourke, Fitzgerald) or Norse (Doyle) origins were removed. The Y chromosomal haplogroup composition of the remaining men with Gaelic surnames was different from the undivided set, with a higher frequency of one haplogroup, hg 1, in particular. When the Gaelic surnames were further subdivided according to the four counties of Ireland in which they originated about 1000 years ago, further structure was revealed: the four groups were significantly different and the westernmost group (Connaught) showed near fixation (98.5%) of hg 1 chromosomes.[18]

The high concentration of haplogroup 1 in the samples taken from men with Gaelic names associated with the west of Ireland, they argue, extends a genetic gradient that runs across Europe from the Near East to the western seaboard and reflects the relative isolation of the pre-Neolithic populations in the west from the genetic effects of the migration of Neolithic farming groups from the Near East.

The lesser concentrations of haplogroup 1 in the "eastern Gaelic cohorts may be indicative of a prehistoric influx or of later gene flow across the linguistic barrier from historical migrant groups."[19]

This new work surveying the pattern of Y chromosomes among men across Ireland and using it to distinguish between the genetic trace of prehistoric migration and the genetic effects of historical migration extends a century of research on human biophysical variation in Ireland. The work of Haddon and Browne on the Aran Islands published in 1892 was the first of many studies of physical variation in Ireland, and, like the studies that followed, its methods and perspectives reflected the development of physical anthropology and population genetics. Ireland has been a significant field site for those interested in surveying "racial types" and in exploring the physical differences between what are taken to be original and settler groups. The body of research published from these studies is an index of the rise and revision of mid-twentieth-century racial science, which sought to give scientific credibility to racist taxonomies of human difference.[20] One of the most famous studies, the Harvard Irish Survey, or Harvard Irish Mission as it is also called, was undertaken between 1931 and 1936. Under the leadership of Earnest Hooton of the anthropology department at Harvard, the survey sought to investigate "the origins and development of the races and cultures of Ireland" by correlating three survey subjects: archaeology, physical anthropology, and social anthropology.[21] Its study of family and community in Ireland is most well known. But its anthropometric survey,[22] which measured variation in the physical characteristics of people across Ireland, has been followed in the subsequent decades by a steady stream of anthropologists and population geneticists mainly from the United States, whose studies include measuring freckles as supposedly "Celtic" phenotypical characteristics as well as the standard anthropometric markers of skin color, eye color, head shape, facial features, and other forms of physical difference.[23] Scientific interest in the Aran Islands also continued as the tradition of anthropometric measurements was replaced by, or supplemented with, studies of variation based on blood type in the mid–twentieth century.[24] Serological studies of the 1940s and 1950s focused on the Aran Islands, and other rural areas in the west of Ireland, and on blood type variation in general.[25]

This work was not only informed by the desire to describe and categorize human variation. It was also often driven by fascination with particular patterns of difference, especially in relationships between groups judged to be historically distinctive. Addressing the genetic effects of in-migration, or, more particularly, colonial settlement in Ireland, has been a recurrent research objective. Research undertaken by American physical anthropologists continues to reproduce the model of biological difference between an original population and various colonial settlers that framed much of the work on physical variation in Ireland over the twentieth century. In his account of his research in Ireland, the American physical anthropologist John Relethford describes first visiting Ireland as a graduate student in the summer of 1977 taking anthropometric and skin color measurements from school children in Longford, undertaking doctoral research on genetic variation in the west of Ireland, reanalyzing the anthropometric data collected in the Harvard survey of the 1930s, and returning to the question of the genetic distinctiveness of the Aran Islands that had been the focus of the work of Earle Hackett of Trinity College and M. E. Folan of University College, Galway.[26] In the late 1950s, Hackett published the results of his studies using the pattern of blood type frequencies to consider the genetic differences of what he described as the "two main racial components" in Ireland.[27] He and Folan used blood type frequencies to explore the local belief that the presence of a garrison of English soldiers on the Aran Island of Inis Mór since the seventeenth century had genetically influenced the local population.[28] Like Hackett and Folen, Relethford concluded that that "English gene flow" had affected the Aran Islands and the neighboring island of Inishbofin, a conclusion he reached by subjecting the anthropometric data collected by Haddon and Browne in 1892 to statistical analysis. Though the use of multivariate analysis of anthropometric data to explore genetic difference is contested within physical anthropology, research of this kind continues to be pursued. And though recent studies have dropped the language of racial types, the subjects of the research (the genetic evidence of the "major political-religious" boundary in Northern Ireland, for example[29]) and the methods employed (phenotypical variation as well as blood type and gene frequencies) suggest the legacy of earlier interests in tracing the correlation between the conventional categories of native and newcomer in Ireland and biological or racial difference.[30]

The research on Y-chromosome variation published in *Nature* in 2000 has a complex relationship to this history of studying the bodies and blood of people in Ireland. In an article in *Inside Ireland* that preceded her account of the "Y-Chromosome Variation and Irish Origins" project, Emmeline Hill located her research with Daniel Bradley and Mark Jobling within the history of studies of human biophysical variation in Ireland.[31] Yet building on this research also involves distancing their work at least from its most explicitly racialized accounts of difference. These days population genetics is most often presented as the ally of antiracism. The language and assumptions of mid-twentieth-century science have been replaced with claims that genetics disproves the racial logic of genetically distinctive and bounded human groups. Today the language of genetics is largely one of gradients in patterns of human genetic diversity rather than racial groups. Nevertheless, population geneticists continue to pursue questions of biological difference but through the lexicon of "diversity" and "variation." The term "population" has largely replaced "race." It is within a liberal, progressive, posteugenic genetics free from the taint of racial science that the authors of the paper in *Nature* situate their work. Yet the reactions of the authors to critical engagements with their research reveal the degree to which the authors knowingly play upon public interests in the relationships between ethnicity and genetic difference and, more significantly, fail to adequately understand the political implications of their figuring of genetic variation and genetic descent.

As in other contexts, the application of new approaches in molecular genetics to studies of human genetic diversity has generated significant debate. In Ireland, the most sustained discussion of the new research published in *Nature* and the new Royal Irish Academy "Irish Origins" research scheme took place at a conference to launch the program and afterwards in the popular but scholarly magazine *Archaeology Ireland*. The contested approaches to the migration of people, language, and material culture within the history of Irish archaeology made those archaeologists who engaged with the work especially attuned to the implications of the genetic study's language of migration, genetic mixture, and isolation. Though a newly professionalized archaeology replaced its antiquarian antecedents over the course of the twentieth century, political sensitivities regarding the interpretation and approach to themes of settlement and migration that characterized Irish antiquarianism in the late eighteenth century continued to inflect archaeology.[32] Of most relevance here is the tension between "invasionist" and "insular" models of explanation. Twentieth-century archaeology in Ireland has been dominated by attempts to find continental origins and influences for cultural styles and practices, reflecting a dominant view of development as the product of external stimulus and immigration. Despite its resonance with the national mythology of sequential invasions (with some, like the Celtic, seen as foundational, and others viewed as foreign), archaeologists who challenged the "invasionist" model pointed out the colonial dimensions of arguments that all aspects of prehistoric development could be attributed to the arrival of groups from outside Ireland. The "insular" school is criticized by others as narrowly nativist, seeking indigenous origins for all cultural forms and underemphasizing migration and cultural interconnection. Although the polarization between the "invasionist" and "insular" schools has passed, the national history of archaeology (in both its Irish nationalist and Ulster nationalist forms) is still evident in sensitivity regarding the degree to which prehistories of British, as opposed to other, sources of influence are acknowledged or emphasized.

The question of Irish origins that preoccupied antiquarians also still engages archaeologists, although they work with more sophisticated models of "origins." In 1984, for example, Irish archaeologists debated theories of the coming of Irish-speaking people to Ireland in a seminar held by the Irish Association of Professional Archaeologists.[33] The debate resurfaced in the early 1990s, and in 1998 archaeologists J. P. Mallory and Barra Ó Donnagháin engaged with new work being initiated in the field by population geneticists in their paper "The Origins of the Population of Ireland: A Survey of Putative Immigrations in Irish Prehistory and History," a contribution to the Royal Irish Academy efforts to secure government funding for the "Irish Origins" program.[34] Thus Irish archaeology's disciplinary history of debated explanatory paradigms of insularity and invasion and the recent work of archaeologists on prehistoric migration informed the most critical responses to the work that began to emerge from research on "the genetic history and geography of Ireland."

Firstly, archaeological critics were quick to identify the way the account of a gradient of an ancient genetic type from east to west across Ireland evokes images of both Irish isolation within Europe and the particular isolation of the west of Ireland that has been central to Irish cultural nationalism. For archaeologist Barra Ó Donnabháin, the view "that Ireland (or particular regions of Ireland) preserves some pristine or ancient gene pool that has been lost or diluted elsewhere in Europe" risks reinstating a now outmoded archaeological idea of Irish cultural and biological isolation.[35] The conclusion that the genetic survey suggests Ireland's relative isolation and the particular isolation of the west of the island dominates the research, despite the authors' awareness of the histories of settlement in Ireland, and indeed does so as a result of their methodological response to that history.

By categorizing the genetic samples they collected according to whether the men sampled have "Gaelic" surnames or those "diagnostic of historical influx," they are able to focus on prehistoric rather than historic migration. The gradient of genetic distinctiveness of an ancient haplotype that peaks in the west of Ireland has already been screened for the effects of "historic incursion." The gradient does not cover all genetic material; it is only a proxy for genetic variation and one that is only found in men. Nor does it account for historic migration. For geneticists, this is its value; the combination of Y-chromosome genetics and surnames makes it possible to extract the history of ancient migration from the genetic muddle that is the product of centuries of human migration and mixing. But their account of the relative genetic isolation of Ireland from Neolithic migration from Eastern Europe can be interpreted as an argument about the general isolation of Ireland from "foreign" genetic sources, as well as the relative isolation of the west of Ireland. The online version of the *San Francisco Chronicle*, SF Gate, reports:

> A genetic signature nearly as unique to the Irish as leprechauns and shamrocks is helping researchers to understand the origin of Ireland's earliest settlers and the prehistoric movement of people across Europe. The pattern is believed to be a genetic remnant of the first Western Europeans, but it is no longer common across the continent because of migrations and invasions from the Near East, researchers said. As an island, Ireland was not affected by the movement of people and the majority of its men retain the variation, researchers said in a study published Thursday in the journal Nature.[36]

Although it is prehistoric population movement that is being assessed in this genetic study, the image of isolation before the arrival of settlers from the Norse and Normans onwards conjures up an image of a native population enjoying an extended golden age after their much earlier arrival—an island "not affected by the movement of people."

Popular accounts of the research are thus reminiscent of those claims made a century ago for the pure Gaelic blood of the west of Ireland in contrast to the lamentable moral, cultural, and spiritual corruption of the Anglicized east. Inadvertently, this study evokes romantic nationalism's geographical imagination of purity and impurity, of idealized isolation and anxieties about pollution. When considered in light of recent efforts to reimagine Ireland and Irishness through themes of migration into and away from Ireland and through histories of inter-connection and exchange, this allusion to isolation regenerates the imagination of national purity after years of critical reappraisal. During the late 1980s and 1990s, this idea of Ireland as an isolated island ideally sheltered from the corruptions of modernity and Anglicization, which informed the broadly isolationist and pro-tectionist approach to culture in the first decades of new state, was challenged because of its production of a repressive and exclusionary ideal of social, cultural, and religious homogeneity. Echoing the traditional trope of the Book of Invasions but rejecting its association with Gaelic nativism, recent academic and popular accounts of "the people of Ireland" in terms of waves of settlers, including new immigrants, have questioned those persistent categories of "native" and "settler."[37] New cultural discourses of mobility, mixing, and interconnection challenge an isolationist account of Irish identity in which all outside influences are viewed as threatening. In some cases, these arguments have addressed ideas of biological or racial purity directly by positing the liberating recognition "that we are all happily mongrelized, interdependent, impure, mixed up."[38] Geneticists use the language of gradients and clines rather than genetically distinguished and genetic "pure" groups. Yet, unlike these deliberately reappropriated ideas of impurity and mongrel mixtures, gradients can suggest poles of difference at either end.

At the same time, the language of gradients and admixture used by human population geneticists turns out to be easily compatible with their method of dif-ferentiating men according to their surnames and supposed descent from the old categories of "native" and "newcomer" in Ireland. Distinguishing lines of paternal ancestry through surnames enables the geneticists to use the Y chromosomes of men with Gaelic surnames today as sources of information about the genetics of the population of Ireland prior to early medieval immigration. The gradient that they find in their results is the product of purifying the sample to achieve the subsample of "native" men. The gradient of the haplogroup 1 that Hill et al. identify is based on screening out the samples of "ultimate origin outside Ireland" from the account of prehistoric genetics. At one level, this is simply an artifact of the process. Only genetic samples from men with Y chromosomes directly inher-ited from prehistoric or, more accurately, pre-Neolithic forefathers in Ireland can be used to explore prehistoric population genetics from contemporary samples. Screening out the nonnative genetic material allows the authors to study an "older geography" of Y-chromosome variation. By implication, if not by intention, they thus produce a genetic distinction between those of "native" descent and those "of ultimate origin outside Ireland." The implications of this methodology for understandings of genetics, ethnicity, and descent emerge most strongly in considering their approach to surnames and paternal descent in light of other engagements with surname histories and ancestry in Ireland and, especially, Northern Ireland.

Surnames: Signs of Difference and Shared Plurality

The account of "Y-Chromosome Variation and Irish Origins" is not problematic only because of the ways it remobilizes ideas of isolation and genetic difference in describing prehistoric migration and the contemporary population in Ireland. The analytical strategy of exploring the incidence of haplotype 1 in groups of samples organized according to the historical origins of surnames is both fundamental to the research and its most problematic feature. For Hill, Bradley, and Jobling, the categorization of surnames according to their historical origins allows them to examine genetic differences between groups who have different paternal ancestries in or beyond Ireland and to explore the genetic variations among those of Gaelic paternal ancestry. The obvious implication of this methodology is that surnames really do stand for different unbroken lineages and that genetic differences among men in Ireland and Northern Ireland correspond to the historic origins of their names. To follow this chain of interpretation, the surnames that geneticists categorize into the groups of Gaelic, Scottish, Norman/Norse, and English names describe the men who carry them according to those categories of "native" and "settler" descent. Though this is the intrinsic logic of their research, the geneticists involved rejected this reading of the implications of their work.

In commenting on the *Nature* paper, archaeologist Gabriel Cooney argued that future work using genetics in studies of prehistoric patterns of migration and settlement would need to be more "historically and archaeologically situated and be more sensitive to the wider implications of issues such as origins, ethnicity and cultural identities."[39] In response, Dan Bradley and Emmeline Hill insisted that the categorization of surnames was geographical not ethnic. Gaelic surnames, they explain, were categorized into four groups that correspond to the four provinces in Ireland; the three others groups "indicate an ultimate origin outside the island." This distinction between the geographical and the ethnic only holds if ethnicity is detached from the geographical imaginations of origins or homelands through which, along with ideas of shared descent and shared cultural heritage, ethnicities are constituted. In their defense, the authors also pointed out that the *Nature* paper makes no direct connections between the identities of the living men whose genetic material is ordered into these four groups of "prehistoric, Gaelic origin" and three groups "diagnostic of historical influx (Scottish, Norman/Norse and English)." Yet, as Cooney argued, "research which is based on identifying gene variation between those bearing surnames regarded as being of Gaelic, Scottish, Norman/Norse or English origin has to be viewed as creating a connection between ethnic affiliation and genetics."[40] Nevertheless, challenging the criticism that their categorization suggests a correlation between genetic and ethnic affiliation, Bradley and Hill replied in the "spirit of this caution" about linking surnames, and via surnames, genetics with ethnic identity.[41] They point out that "even if one proposed that genetics should in some way serve to define ethnicity (and, emphatically, we do not ascribe to this view), the surname is only a poor marker of overall ancestry. Even if one goes back, say, a mere four generations, only one sixteenth of one's genetic heritage is contributed by the great-grandfather who bequeathed a surname. All our volunteers were Irish, and there is no mention, or presumption in our work of their ethnic or cultural affiliations."[42]

So although the authors locate their work within an established tradition of interest in surnames in Ireland, they also qualify the significance of surnames as markers of ancestry by pointing out their relation to direct paternal descent alone. Yet their argument that Irish surnames were simply grouped geographically ignores the historically freighted ethnic and cultural associations that inform their own distinctions between Gaelic and Scottish, Norman/Norse, and English surnames. They conclude their riposte with three reasons why "modern genetic findings do not encourage the identification of ethnicity with genetic character." Firstly, they argue, the genetic composition of a population changes much more slowly than language or culture, so there is a temporal dissonance between genetics and "the myriad other factors which influence and define identity." Secondly, genetic research reveals gradients rather than sharp boundaries between groups. And thirdly, as is often argued in defense of studies of human genetic variation, there is greater genetic diversity within rather than between groups, and "the knowledge that all humans share quite a recent common ancestry, emphasizes the triviality of our differences."[43] Nevertheless, it is those trivial differences that are the focus of their research.

This persistent focus on difference has precedents in earlier anthropological studies, some of which used surnames as indices of native and settler descent in Ireland. In 1898 John Beddoe, author of *The Races of Great Britain*, published his reflections "On Complexional Differences Between the Irish with Indigenous and Exotic Surnames Respectively." For Beddoe, "the two great sections of the Irish people" were defined "for the sake of brevity, indigenous and exotic respectively; these names are convenient, and though their correctness may easily be impugned, they are every way better than those of Celt and Saxon, which are too commonly employed." He explained, "By indigenous I should mean, if it were possible to separate them, the descendants of the people who where at home in Ireland, before the days of Thorgils, and Olaf, and Sigtryg, Silkbeard and Magnus Barefoot, and by Exotics the Danes, Norwegians, English, Welsh, Scotch, Huguenots and Palatines who have settled there at various times subsequently."[44] While acknowledging the "constant intermixture of blood between the 'indigenous' and the 'exotic' during all this period of a thousand years," Beddoe sought to assess the degree to which the "exotic" groups could be differentiated from the "indigenous" on the basis of hair and eye color, using his "index of nigrescence." (The "indigenous," he observed, were generally dark haired and light eyed.) Surnames were a means of doing so, he argued, but with qualifying caveats:

> What we really can do is to institute a comparison between the bearers of indigenous and those of exotic surnames. Of course the utmost one would be entitled to assert of the latter is that they have some exotic blood in their ancestry, whereas there is no evidence that the others have any such admixture. Even that would be too much to assert in every case, as we know that some Irishmen, especially within the pale, did adopt, in accordance with the law, surnames of English form. Still, I am disposed to think too much has been made of this.[45]

Unlike Beddoe, the geneticists exploring Y-chromosome genetics in Ireland are not exploring observable differences between those of different paternal descent. Nor do they use his language of race. Yet contemporary population genetics does share his attention to those categories of difference. In other work, Beddoe presented a distinctive Gaelic Irish "Africanoid" type; here at least he was conscious of the limits of differentiation. For contemporary population geneticists, a focus on the Y chromosome and direct descent happily resolves the need to take account of thousands of years of "interbreeding" or "admixture." The Y chromosome stays "true" as an unaltered record of direct descent. Taking Y-chromosome variation as an indicator of wider genetic variation makes these studies in human population genetics possible, but also makes those categories of "indigenous" and "exotic" appear more real than even Beddoe would allow.

Though the geneticists' work can be located within a current revival of interest in surnames as sources for historical demography and migration studies,[46] it departs in significant ways from other recent approaches to surnames and, via surnames, questions of identity and relatedness in Ireland and Northern Ireland. It does so in three ways: firstly in the premise that surnames are reliable indicators of distinctive categories of descent. Hill et al. argue that the well-established surname system in Ireland dating from about AD 950 supports the use of surnames as proxies of direct paternal descent. Yet archaeologists and historians have pointed to the complicated dynamics of the adoption and evolution of surnames that contrasts strongly with the assumption of their unbroken patrilineage. In the *Archaeology Ireland* debate, Gabriel Cooney was particularly critical of using naming patterns that, he argues, were part of a much more complex and active process of making kin distinction in the "culturally fluid world" of medieval Ireland to infer patterns of migration thousands of years before.[47] Since surnames are significant markers of identity and affiliation, changing surnames is a common way of repositioning a family or individual socially, culturally, and politically. As many recent commentators have noted, Irish history is full of this strategic surname fluidity as well as more ordinary mutations of surnames before they became more fixed by modern forms of civil registration and literacy.[48] Historian Jonathan Bardon has argued, for example, that as the numbers of people in Ireland who could speak Irish in the nineteenth century dropped dramatically, many Gaelic names were anglicized, translated, or "pseudo-translated," so names that now appear similar may have different etymological evolutionary pathways. With patterns of intermarriage and religious conversion in Ulster from the seventeenth century, family names did not remain fixed to one category of "native" or "planter." Drawing on Robert Bell's *Book of Ulster Surnames*,[49] he highlights how

> Some names were easily confused and amalgamated, such as the Scottish Border surname Kerr and the Irish surname Carr, and anglicisation either of the Co. Donegal Mac Giolla Chathair, "son of the devotee of

(St) Chathair" or the Co. Monaghan Mac Giolla Cheara, "son of the devotee of (St) Ceara." The Carrolls or O'Carrolls of Dromore almost all changed their surname to Cardwell. Most of the Ulster sept of Ó Dreáin anglicized to Adrian but some, in a pseudo-translation, converted to Hawthorne, *drioghean* in Gaelic meaning "blackthorn" or "hawthorn." Many members of the MacAree family in Co. Monaghan changed their name to King, assuming their surname derived from Mac an Ríogh, "son of king," though it is more likely to come from Mac Fhearadhaigh, "son of the many one." Even the dropping of a prefix could invalidate conclusions of regional origin, in the absence of other evidence: the common Ulster surname Neill is borne by people who could descend from the Scots Neilsons or MacNeillies; from the MacNeills of the Isles; from any branch of the Ulster O'Neills; or from Mac an Fhilidh, "son of the poet," which had also been anglicized as MacNeilly, Neely, MacAnelly, MacAnilly and MacNeely.[50]

In contrast, in the research by Hill et al., surnames are taken as accurate evidence of indigenous and exogenous ancestry despite the relatively recent development of inherited surname system within the temporalities of prehistoric migration used in human population genetics and historical evidence of the instability of surnames.

The political implications of treating surnames as markers of direct descent and clues to religious, cultural, and political backgrounds are most overt in Northern Ireland. Yet surnames do not neatly correlate with one or another religious or political category. Recently, both popular and scholarly accounts of Ulster's history have used surnames as evidence of intermarriage and intermixing to challenge the notion of two absolutely separate and ethnically distinct cultural groups in Northern Ireland. Bardon's account dispels the idea of two communities of descent—Gaelic, Catholic, and native, or British, Protestant, and planter. Similarly, in his explorations of the place of those of Scottish ancestry in Ulster and the long histories of migration between Ulster and Scotland, Michael Hall argues, "Nothing highlights better the absurdity of any notion that Ulster is a land of two quite distinct and separate communities, than the surnames of its inhabitants. Contrary to the popular belief that all Ulster's Catholics are related to the Gaels, and all Ulster's Protestants to the Planters, the rich assortment of surnames should prove just how much intermingling has occurred throughout our history."[51] The relatively recent historical use of surnames as indicators of different descent follows a much longer history of "intermingling." Jim Mallory is similarly skeptical about using the genetics of modern populations divided according to surname origins to talk about prehistoric populations: "If Ireland was settled by 8000 BC that means that there has been thousands of years of mixing before you can label someone Irish on the basis of their surname."[52]

Secondly, the genetic approach to surnames and descent is one that obscures this "intermingling" in its concentration on direct descent. Though geneticists often combine their accounts of the natural significance of surnames with accounts of how patrilineal surnames only parallel a very tiny proportion of a man's genetic inheritance, in practice the Y chromosome is overworked. It is made to stand for much broader patterns of relatedness, difference, divergence, migration, and origins—individual, collective, human. Though only based on genetic patterns in men and only then focusing on the Y chromosome, the results are often taken as standing for the genetic history and contemporary genetic character of the population as a whole, and the genetic geography of humanity as a whole. In explaining his work to me, Daniel Bradley was very clear in acknowledging that Y-chromosome studies can signal patterns of descent and difference but that they do not tell the "whole story":

> What we are saying is despite all the mixing that's gone on we can still pick up a signal. We're not saying this is the whole story. We're saying there *is* a signal despite the undoubted mixing, historical and pre-historical. But just because we find the signal doesn't mean we find the whole story. There are other stories as well, there are multiple stories and in a sense different genes tell different stories. They have different histories because the very basis of genetic heritage is that it is mixed. That's what mating is all about—mixed in every generation.[53]

But because Y-chromosome studies by their nature only trace direct male-line descent, they cannot encompass that mixing "in every generation." When Bradley and Hill wrote in *Archaeology Ireland* that "it does not take specialist knowledge to propose that a Y chromosome possessed by a man named Burke may be of ultimate Norman ancestry, that one from a Mr Byrne may also have been around in a more ancient Leinster, and that the O'Sullivan patrilineages stretch back to the south-west," they were writing of Y-chromosome inheritance and not genetic ancestry more widely.[54] But this acknowledged narrowness does not get passed on as research findings move to other domains of knowledge production and consumption. Mr. Burke, Mr. Byrne, and Mr. O'Sullivan also have thousands and thousands of other sources of their genetic inheritance that upset those seven surname and Y-chromosomal ancestry categories. Only by eliding all these other sources can men bearing Gaelic surnames be said to be direct descendants of pre-Neolithic men in Ireland.

The account of the genetic isolation of the west of Ireland is thus based on only "one story" of genetic inheritance. This assignment of descent is based solely on direct paternal ancestry. All the other sources of genetic material along the ever-branching family tree—from all four grandparents, all eight great-grandparents, and so on—and all those other names in the family tree are ignored in favor of the direct paternal ancestral line—of son, father, grandfather, and so on backwards in time over thousands of years. This reckoning of ancestry masks diversity in family trees: a man can only have one line of direct Y-chromosome descent and so only one genetically significant surname and, despite the geneticists' desire to keep genetics and ethnicity apart, only one category of ethnic origin. Those who argue that understanding the nature of human demography undermines any claim for the biological bases of cultural, national, or ethnic difference sometimes suggest that current genetic research may support this perspective.[55] However, judging by the "Y-Chromosome Variation and Irish Origins" paper, it is more likely that Y-chromosome genetics provide support for differentiating between those whose names suggest "native" and "nonnative" direct male-line descent.

At the end of her book on the ways in which aristocrats in Ireland have been traditionally defined through those distinctions between Gaelic and colonial nobility, Anne Chambers features one possibility for reimagining Ireland not in terms of a community of native descent and alien presence but of continuous mixing—"a sea fed by many streams"—and the expectation that this will supported by new genetic evidence.[56] Yet the "mixing" of genes in all human reproduction and the "mixing" of people through intermarriage cannot feature in Y-chromosome human population genetics because the method of analysis is solely based on direct paternal descent. National genetic surveys are designed in ways that screen out the "nonnative." Studies based on so-called nonnative surnames as straightforward markers of nonnative descent, that assume the stability of surname inheritance, and that discount all other sources of genetic material cannot register the long prehistories and histories of "genetic exchange" that follow complex and multidirectional patterns of migration. Although the geneticists acknowledge that "there are difficulties in constructing an ancient patrilineal geography,"[57] the strikingly limited nature of this model of descent remains understated.

However, its limits are obvious to some. In explaining to me his sense of the potential of genealogy to complicate understandings of communal identity and difference in Northern Ireland, a community activist in the republican working-class area of Ardoyne in north Belfast argued that for family history to really help people understand "where they come from," it has to follow both male and female lines and not just "the paternal thing." He stressed both the relatively recent origins of surnames and the limits of genealogical projects that focus on one surname and ignore the others that could link them to the "other side," and thus foreground interconnections and complexities that challenge the idea of "two tribes" in Northern Ireland:

> For anyone trying to understand where all this is coming from then it doesn't do you any favours just to follow the father's line. . . . There's all those people that made you, not just one line right through there. It is all to do with how you organize what you have been told. And it's not that it's wrong; it's wrong if you take it in isolation of all those other things. That helps people unpack even their own family unit. The respect should be for both sides not just for one, you know, from your father. I am just thinking, you can apply Section 75 and everything to it![58]

Section 75 is a part of the Good Friday/Belfast agreement that charges government in Northern Ireland to promote equality between men and women as well as between people of different cultural, religious, and ethnic backgrounds. Family history can be a route to a different politics of gender as well as reconciliation and conflict transformation. In contrast, in Y-chromosome population genetics, women are only conduits for the transfer of names and genes between men.[59]

Thirdly, the approach to surnames in these studies of the human population genetics of Ireland contrasts strongly with more innovative approaches to surnames especially in Northern Ireland. The assumptions and understated limits of Y-chromosome genetics do not mean that an interest in surnames is necessarily framed by ideas of patrilineal descent and genetic distinction. Surnames, and the histories they index, can be resources for other approaches to identity and collective heritage. From his earliest research on the distribution of surnames in Ulster, Brian Turner has argued for the value of surnames as sources for exploring the complex history of the region and that this should entail a broadening of family name research.[60] "Perversely the very strength of Gaelic consciousness about family names," he argued, "has to some extent stunted the progress of surname study in Ireland." For Turner, a reliance on

> medieval sources when dealing with modern themes . . . may lead to a peculiar time lag in many scholarly works about family distribution. A lot has happened in the last four hundred years, particularly in Ulster. Gaelic society has been destroyed and an enormous influx of names, mainly from England and Scotland, has been introduced throughout the province. If we are to explore the full relevance of the study of family names then we need to take into account not only the origins of Irish names, but the great population movements of the last four hundred years. If we are to use family names as pathways into the past then we need to study the distribution of names. We need to expand our knowledge of where the names were and when and why they moved . . . because where the name was, there was the life, the person, the family, the tradition, and the community.[61]

This argument about the need to consider all names rather than confine research to Gaelic names is really an argument for an historical understanding of the region that considers these histories of settlement as part of the history rather than simply the problem of history in Northern Ireland. Turner advocates the value of mapping the historical and contemporary geography of surnames as a way of exploring the "various strands which have wound together to make our community."[62]

Thus in his essay to accompany his map of the *Surname Landscape in the County of Fermanagh* (figure 8), published in 2002, Turner writes, "The people of Fermanagh have over 2000 surnames and all of them have stories to be told. Each individual may be identified by only one name, but a look back through the generations will reveal many more which have contributed to that person. So it is with the county. Its surname landscape can contribute to a developing understanding of how it has come to be, and help identify the various strands of history which have come together in this place."[63] Individual family trees are encompassed within a

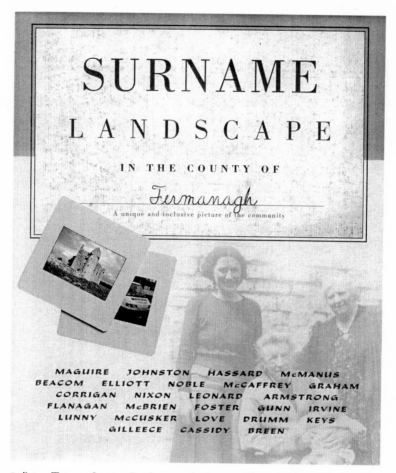

SURNAME
L A N D S C A P E
IN THE COUNTY OF

Fermanagh

A unique and inclusive picture of the community

MAGUIRE   JOHNSTON   HASSARD   McMANUS
BEACOM   ELLIOTT   NOBLE   McCAFFREY   GRAHAM
CORRIGAN   NIXON   LEONARD   ARMSTRONG
FLANAGAN   McBRIEN   FOSTER   GUNN   IRVINE
LUNNY   McCUSKER   LOVE   DRUMM   KEYS
GILLEECE   CASSIDY   BREEN

8. Brian Turner, *Surname Landscape in the County of Fermanagh* (Downpatrick: Turner Circle, 2003). Reproduced with permission of Brian Turner.

shared sense of collective diversity. This is a map of surnames framed by ideas of a complex shared heritage of settlement and residence in Northern Ireland. It maps "strands of history" that are evident in personal genealogy and in the surname geography of the county instead of pure lines of descent and absolute ethnic categories. Using surnames as markers of direct genetic descent cannot register these more complex stories of migration, cultural contact, and intermarriage.

Turner's project is thus not one of erasing the historical origins of surnames in an effort to challenge their use as sectarian markers in the present but of exploring those origins as part of a collective history. This can counter the dangerous "misunderstanding, and half understanding" that haunt the "subconscious mental landscape" of "our names and those of our neighbours."[64] Individuals' interest in their own names can be a starting point for a wider interest in surnames as indicators of "historical development, population movement, and settlement."[65] In a similar spirit to the multicultural family tree that Turner prepared for the *Local Identities* exhibition (figure 6), a series of programs on surnames titled "What's in a Name?" were broadcast on BBC Radio Ulster in 2000 and 2001.[66] They also offered a different way of thinking about surnames, inheritance, and heritage. In these programs, Turner and Irish language advocate Aodán Mac Póilin talked through examples of surname histories and responded to phone-in queries. They tapped people's personal interest in their own surnames. But in the stories they told of surname origins and geographies, surnames became windows into a complex history of settlement and migration that was presented as *everyone's* history. An individual interest in an individual surname was the starting point for sense of a shared heritage of settlement reflected in the variety of surnames within a personal family tree and within society. Surnames were explored as clues to a complex and rich heritage in Northern Ireland rather than markers of ethnically pure, ancient, and distinct "communities of descent."

This point is made more explicitly in a recent essay on the history of settlement in Fermanagh from the Scottish and English borderland in the early seventeenth century, in which Turner uses the contemporary prevalence of originally borderer family names to complicate accounts of settlement, dispossession, and "such dangerously simplistic notions as 'The native Irish,' 'The two traditions,' or the 'Ulster Scots.'"[67] He writes,

> Gaelic Ireland has a proud tradition of interest in genealogy and family history. This tradition of Catholic and aristocratic Ireland lamented the disruption caused by conquest and settlement in the seventeenth century. It was natural for poets and scholars to express bitter feelings of political and cultural defeat, and we can learn much from appreciating the feelings of that time. What is not defensible is that, even in our own day, some local histories can still speak of Irish people who bear surnames formed in Britain as if they were aliens in their own land, and collude accordingly.[68]

Taking one family name, Turner uses it to explore the history of the settlement of the border county of Fermanagh. But he warns once again that tracing the histories of surnames is not to suggest that the bearers of those names are inheritors of the categories of the past or their modern simplified forms as Planter and Gael: "the Armstrongs and Elliots of today are not the Anglo-Scottish borderers of yesterday. Centuries of intermarriage and a myriad of relationships has made them a product of this land."[69] Tracing the histories and geographies of particular names is thus not meant to shore up their use as distinguishing markers of ethnic difference in the present. The reference to historic groups referred to in surname studies should not be taken to mean that contemporary surnames stand neatly for these category distinctions in the present. As Turner argued in one of his earliest published pieces on family names, "One important point remains to be made. Throughout this article I have referred to 'settler' names and families. By this I do not imply distinction between the people of present day Fermanagh. Because of the fact that each of us is heir to many surnames the terminology used in family name study must refer to the historical elements within the community rather than within the individual."[70] The multiplicity of names and origins in any family tree, unless that tree is pruned back to one male line of direct descent, is mirrored in wider patterns of plurality. As he put it to me: "There are different strands are out there in society but they are within us too."[71]

Daniel Bradley would most likely agree, conscious of the partial nature of the genetic story and what he sees as the dissonance between the temporalities of genetic evolution and social and cultural change: "We're made up of separate strands of ancestry. Now the thing is these different strands can correlate and give a consistent story, that's why this is powerful . . . because we've looked at different strands and say different strands telling the same stories will give much more credibility to the story. But we're not saying it's the only story."[72] Nevertheless, scholarly and popular accounts of population genetics do not foreground these caveats, and the genetic and ethnic slide into much closer symmetry. This is partly the result of simple assumptions about family naming systems; it is also due to the ways in which the genetic studies both evoke and elide complex issues of descent in relation to categories of "native" and "settler" origin and collective heritage. Even if presented with the conventional detachment and disinterest of scientific deliberation, decisions about how surnames can be used and what can be concluded from the results are inescapably political. Geneticists knowingly make use of the cultural significance of patronyms, but this very significance means that their work is sticky with the politics of history, identity, and difference. But this chapter, thus far, is itself a partial account of population genetics and the cultural politics of ancestry and belonging. It is just one origin story, and of a certain sort. New accounts of the human population genetics of Ireland are also entangled in the postcolonial politics of cultural condescension and contemporary competing claims to ancient belonging.

Celtic Origins

Four years after the publication of the "Y-Chromosome Variation and Irish Origins" paper, the work of geneticist Daniel Bradley and colleagues in Trinity, Leeds, and Cambridge gained media coverage again, this time in the Irish *Sunday Times* under the heading "The Irish Are Not Celts, Say Experts."[73] The research reported upon this time had just been published in a paper in the *American Journal of Human Genetics* that argued that there is no genetic evidence for the migration of a Celtic population from Eastern Europe to Ireland.[74] The results of the "Y-Chromosome Variation and Irish Origins" paper in *Nature* evoke a mythology of cultural isolation and a nationalist gradient of intensified Irishness across the island from east to west. The subsequent paper by Bradley and colleagues, in part funded through the Royal Irish Academy *Irish Origins* program and published in 2004, is population genetics in a demythologizing mode. The target of this research was the theory that the origins of the Celtic peoples are in central Europe and that the Celtic origins of Ireland are explained by the migration or invasion of Celts from a Celtic homeland around 2,500 years ago.

In order to assess the genetic evidence for this theory, the authors undertook a systematic analysis of previously published genetic sequences in Europe and new genetic samples from an additional 200 Irish volunteers. Y-chromosome markers were supplemented by analysis of mitochrondrial DNA (mtDNA), which is passed on from a mother to her children directly and, like the Y chromosome, can be distinguished through the variations that result from mutation over time. Other genetic markers with different modes of inheritance were also used. While the results of the mtDNA analysis do not show the same degree of east to west variation in Ireland as the Y-chromosome study showed, the results confirm the broader east-west cline of genetic variation across Europe.[75] However, the principal conclusion of the paper is that the analysis of multiple genetic markers does not reveal genetic similarity between Celtic people and those living in the hypothesized "Celtic" homeland of central European that the migrationist theory would suggest. The study concludes therefore that there is no genetic evidence for a Celtic migration to Ireland. Instead, the genetic "affinities of the areas where Celtic languages are spoken, or were formerly spoken, are generally with other regions in the Atlantic zone, from northern Spain to northern Britain."[76] So while the earlier paper implied genetic distinctions between those of Gaelic and non-Gaelic descent, this research suggests a broader level of genetic similarity along the sweep of Atlantic geography. This sort of identification of connections and differences at different resolutions and scales of analysis is common to human population genetics. Those who are defined as related at one scale are genetically distinguished at another.

The 2004 paper contributes to the flourishing field of European population genetics as well as to research on Irish prehistoric population geography. But in different ways and with different effects, it also disseminates out into the public culture of ethnic identification and the making of ethnic distinction. It takes up the idea of "the Celtic" with all its cultural resonances and simultaneously takes up a long-standing theme in Irish archaeology. By the late nineteenth and early twentieth centuries, late-eighteenth-century Catholic antiquarian accounts of the origin of the Celts in central Europe had become central to Gaelic cultural nationalism. In 1919, the influential historian and Gaelic revivalist Eoin MacNeill published his history of early Ireland, which "recognised the Celts as a late pre-historic people who had introduced the Irish language, conquered the pre-Celts and established a rural decentralised society that was given the spirit of national-ity by the introduction of Christianity, which united the Irish people, prepared the ground for a national monarchy and brought about a situation where Ireland became a European centre for religious and secular learning."[77] Though this ac-count of the arrival of a new population of Celtic people has been largely rejected by archaeologists, it has remained part of the way in which Irish prehistory and history is popularly understood. In their discussion document prepared for the initiation of the Royal Irish Academy "Irish Origins" funding program, J. P. Mal-lory and Barra Ó Donnagháin summarized what is known and unknown about Irish population history and in doing so presented current archaeological ap-proaches to the idea of a Celtic incursion c. 300–100 BC. Drawing on the earlier work of archaeologist Richard Warner and reflecting on recent interests in the "physical and genetic characteristics of the Celtic people of Britain and Ireland" among geneticists, Mallory and Ó Donnagháin reiterate the lack of evidence for the arrival of a large Celtic population, and thus the "general assumption that the 'celticization' of Ireland" was not "the product of mass immigration but rather a small-scale intrusion," and emphasize the difficulty of sustaining "an argument for any genetic trait that was found to unite the Celtic 'residue' of Britain and Ireland to the exclusion of other populations."[78] The origins of the Irish language and cultural forms described as Celtic, it is argued, are unlikely to have been accompanied by the in-migration of large numbers of Celtic people but by small groups of Irish-speaking Celts who became powerful and thus influential in the gradual process of language change.

However, just as Irish archaeologists do not need the genetic evidence to disprove an idea of the arrival of significant numbers of Celtic people that has already been discarded, contemporary popular associations of the Celtic do not necessarily need to locate the prehistoric origins of Celtic people in central continental Europe as did antiquarians in the late eighteenth century. Though popular accounts of the ancient origins of the Irish and British still appear, sometimes echoing earlier accounts of Phoenician origins,[79] the question of the origins and migration routes of the Celts that preoccupied late-eighteenth-century antiquarians has less contemporary salience.[80] Yet debates about patterns of Celtic settlement within Britain and Ireland continue, and in particular are caught up in the dynamics of collective identity making in Northern Ireland. But where the Celts came from is less important to many "Celtic" North Americans, New Zealanders, and Australians than where their own ancestors came from historically. Most people who identify themselves as Celtic from diasporic distance look to Celtic origins in Scotland, Wales, Ireland, or Brittany, not to ancient Celtic origins in continental Europe. For many, Celtic origins in Celtic countries are enough. Although the genetic research by Bradley and colleagues suggests an expanded Celtic region, it effectively confirms a genetic correlation between countries already popularly described as Celtic. The report on the research that reached the online MSNBC News via Reuters reflected the media interest in a dramatic story of mistaken origins but, despite its headline—"Famous 'Celtic' Nations May Be Misnamed: Genetic Studies Hint at Unexpected Origins of Clans"—the report suggested the inconsequential nature of the research for popular conceptions of the Celtic. The account of the research that followed this headline did not refer at all to "clans" and ended with the final comment that the research, as Daniel Bradley must have made clear, "could not determine whether the common genetic traits meant 'Celtic' nations would look alike or have similar temperaments." Yet disproving the idea of the arrival of the Celts does not necessarily discredit the category of the "Celtic." As Daniel Bradley put it to me, "Now that doesn't say we're not Celts."[81] The term Celtic, he suggests, can still name a cultural category but one that correlates with "genetic affinity" between traditionally Celtic nations rather than genetic descent from Celtic invaders. Here the genetic profile is detached from the ethnic category, yet it simultaneously is used to affirm historical connection between "Celtic" countries. This genetic study chimes with recent archaeological approaches in disproving the idea of Celtic invasions from central Europe, but it does so because it sets out to assess and ultimately discredits an idea that, as the authors acknowledge, archaeologists have largely left behind. At the same time, it may have little effect on the diasporic popularity of the Celtic in which ancestral origin in Ireland is more significant than some anterior origin in central Europe.

Yet, in a twist in the tale of the dispersal of this origin story, the results can also be reported in ways that suggest another dimension to the relationship between population genetics and postcolonial cultural politics. The issues here are not only the potential refiguring of nationalist accounts of ancestral distinction and collective descent, but the cultural relationships that reflect the hangover of a British and Irish colonial past. For Bradley, the reporting of the results of the study in the Irish version of the British *Sunday Times* under the headline "The Irish Are Not Celts, Say Experts"[82] was familiar sensationalist misreporting. But more particularly it reflects what he detects as a "certain distain" in the British press toward Irish subjects. This disdain, he argues, accounts for the tendency of the less liberal press to "latch onto" stories that question or qualify the tenets of Irish national history. Bradley recalled being goaded by a journalist for a British tabloid newspaper to respond to the claim that the genetics was "just about the Irish trying to be different." Though ideas of difference were central to colonial discourse, and later to Irish nationalism, celebratory expressions of difference and assertions of cultural autonomy can also be taken as an affront to the former colonial power. Evidence for a misguided sense of Irish cultural distinction is read, by some at least, as proof of the foolishness of the former colony. Thus new research that may be part of an internally contested postcolonial process of rethinking history, belonging, and identity may become part of a different sort of postcolonial politics in which the former colonial power works through its relationship to the former colony through a mixture of comedy, caricature, and condescension.

This sensitivity to the predilections of a certain sort of English audience has precedents in late-eighteenth-century Irish antiquarian concerns that English reviewers of their work would not provide a "just account of the work, but merely attempt to raise a laugh at the expense of the Irish."[83] But it also has more recent grounds. In 1999 Richard Warner, archaeologist at the Ulster Museum in Belfast, made a speech to the Irish Association for Cultural, Social, and Economic Relations in which he argued against notions of ethnic or racial purity based on ideas of a genetically Celtic stock of native inhabitants. Warner traces the origins of the idea of a northern European Celtic people in classical literature and the adoption of this term in early antiquarianism to describe Iron Age Ireland, and in Irish nationalism to define Irish cultural and racial distinctiveness, and argues against the persistent use of the label *Celtic* in spite of the lack of archaeological evidence for the arrival of a Celtic people in Ireland.

Warner's criticism is driven both by his commitment to archaeological accuracy and by his impatience with the use of terms like *Celtic*, which imply that contemporary categories of identity have their basis in distinctive ancestral origins and thus biological difference.[84] However, Warner's robustly debunking style of address provided good copy for the *Times*, which, under the headline of "Irish Eyes Are English Not Celtic," quoted him as saying, "In round terms, the image of the Irish as a genetically Celtic people, in fact the whole idea of a Celtic ethnicity and of Celtic peoples, Irish, Welsh and all the rest of it, is a load of complete cock and bull. . . . The average Irish person probably has more English genes than Celtic."[85] In his speech to the Irish Association, a cross-border organization established in 1938 whose main aim is "the promotion of communication, understanding, and co-operation between all the people of Ireland both North and South through dialogue and debate,"[86] Warner exposed the fabricated nature and political function of myths of origin, including those that suggest the distinctive descent of contemporary political and cultural groups in Northern Ireland. He is especially critical of the ways the current political strategy of "parity of esteem" for different cultures lends legitimacy to the idea of separate communities of descent.

However, it was his knowingly provocative and knowingly oversimplified aside that provided the material for the *Sunday Times* Irish joke, that exemplified the postcolonial belittling to which Bradley referred. As Warner explained to me, "It was a sort of silly throw away that reporters love and they made quite a bit out of that one."[87] Irish history and culture is figured in this newspaper report as the stuff of farce and foolish fiction. Its misrepresentation of Warner's argument unsurprisingly elicited this response in the humorous section of *Archaeology Ireland*:

> Archaeology, language, genetics and contemporary politics form a dangerous cocktail when mixed together. Perhaps the authorities in Ireland should be cautious about allowing archaeological material to fall into the hands of geneticists or archaeologists who appear to cling to the dangerous racial prejudices which typified twentieth-century Europe. Furthermore, the IACESR [Irish Association for Cultural, Social and Economic Relations], if it entertains Warner's proposals should drop the adjective "Irish" from its title.[88]

This comment is framed by skepticism about reconstructing population history through genetics that Warner hoped would be a demythologizing method. But misrepresented through the anti-Irishness of this particular organ of the British press, Warner's work is misinterpreted as supporting rather than challenging "racial prejudices."

The anti-Irishness of responses to research like this can be even less subtle. Soon after it appeared, the *Sunday Times* account of Warner's speech was reproduced almost in full in the British National Party's journal, *Spearhead*, which took particular delight the newspaper article's final paragraph: "There is a final irony in Ireland's 'Celtic' origin. The Aran islands off Galway, whose population is partly descended from a settlement of Cromwell's soldiers, is one of the last refuges of the Irish language. 'Aran is going to be the last bastion of spoken Irish' said Warner, so the Irish language will die in the mouths of the English."[89] Thus Warner's attempt to question myths of national purity or national genetic distinctiveness by evoking the blood type frequency studies of the 1950s can find a ready audience in a group whose racism and xenophobia extends to attacks on Irish nationalism whose claims for difference are interpreted as an insult to Britishness.

Soon after the publication of the *Times'* newspaper report, Warner's work also appeared on the Web site of the Scottish Loyalists, an ultra-Loyalist sectarian group in Northern Ireland. Here Warner's account of the recent origin of the idea of Celtic ethnicity in nineteenth-century romantic nationalism was used to "badly dent the theory of distinct Celtic ethnicity which forms an important part of the basis of Irish Nationalism." The Web site text also featured the work of archaeologist Jim Mallory, whose argument that the spread of Celtic languages was not accompanied by the arrival, as tradition suggests, of Celtic peoples, is used to further the Scottish Loyalists' efforts to discredit Irish nationalist culture. The proof of the untruth of Irish nationalism will be found, the article suggests, in new work by population geneticists in Ireland. Drawing support from the report of Warner's speech to the Irish Association, the Web site text asserts that "Warner believes his case will be proved next year when the Royal Irish Academy completes its genetic map of Ireland. Thousands of DNA samples will be analysed and compared with genes from skeletons found by archaeologists."[90] For significantly different reasons both Warner and Scottish loyalists in Northern Ireland look to genetics to disprove myths of Irish Celtic identity. Yet the content and reception of the two research papers on Irish origins and Celtic origins by Bradley and colleagues suggests that genetics can be used to both reinforce ideas of genetic isolation, distinguish between people of the basis of native and foreign descent, and to undermine other equally politically charged ideas of ancestral distinction.

But if the genetic undoing of the idea of the Celtic is a source of satisfaction for some loyalists, it has quite different implications for others. In exploring new sources of identity, some loyalists have reclaimed a Celtic heritage from its association with Catholic nationalism in the present and with native Gaelic people in the past to assert a British Celtic rather than Irish identity in Northern Ireland. Deploying complicated arguments about prehistoric settlement and language, they have claimed that a British Celtic-speaking group inhabited Ireland before the arrival of Gaelic Celtic speakers. The rightful indigenous people and those deprived of their cultural property—the Irish language in speech and place names—are native British rather than Irish in Northern Ireland.[91] This new account of Celtic origins follows the trope of ancient return to origins that was central to the idea of the Cruthin as predecessors of Plantation settlers first elaborated by Ian Adamson in the 1970s.[92] In this version of Irish prehistory and ancestral origins, the Cruthin were a pre-Celtic tribe driven out of Ulster to Scotland by the Celts; they are the ancestors of those that returned "home" as Scottish settlers in the Plantation. Rather than being defined as culturally alien

and illegitimate invaders, according to nationalist nativism, Protestants are rede-
fined as emigrant returnees.

These attempts to forge alternative narratives of native presence that define
contemporary Protestant people in Northern Ireland as descendants of the province's earliest inhabitants suggest the persistent potency and problematic politics
of this idea of being indigenous. A culture of competitive indigeneity refigures
the mutual antagonism between those usually defined as "settlers" and those who
continue to be defined as "native." The power of the idea of native and natural
belonging is harnessed here, but by challenging Irish national claims to be the
original people, the model of the first people as rightful claimants to land and
culture is preserved. Genetically deconstructing the idea of Celtic migration to
prehistoric Ireland can have ambiguous results for those proposing a native British Celtic or pre-Celtic presence in Ulster. Warner's work, in particular his argument that there is archaeological evidence for the presence of Roman soldiers in
Ireland, has been read by some as an implicitly unionist case for long integration
of Ireland into the English kingdom, indirectly "feeding ammunition to the English for use as anti-Irish propaganda and of stirring the Irish sectarian pot." But his
critique of Cruthinism, on the same grounds as his critique of Celticism—that is,
its historical inaccuracy and the divisiveness of its notion of separate origins and
descent—has led him to be dubbed a Gaelic apologist by Adamson.[93]

Yet just as genetics are lauded for their potential to undo the mythologies of
native Gaelic or Celtic origin by those conventionally defined as "alien" by those
mythologies, they are also turned to in new constructions of identity and belonging in Northern Ireland. In July 2004 *The Ulster Scot*, the official publication
of the Ulster-Scots Agency (Boord o Ulstèr-Scotch), contained an article featuring a new project to use Y-chromosome genetics to explore the "deep ancestry"
of those whose surnames are associated with the Border Reivers, many of who
moved from the Scottish borderland to parts of Ulster, especially Fermanagh, in
the seventeenth century. The project, as the article explained, seeks to explore
the degrees of relatedness among borderer descendants "on an individual and
family level."[94] This attempt to address the history of the borderlands between
northern England and southern Scotland as part of a strategy to promote the
region is caught up in a local exploration of ancestry and identity in Northern
Ireland in the Ulster-Scots movement—a movement that in its most positive
versions celebrates the hitherto overlooked Scottish influence on dance, song,

and dialect in Ulster and in its most malign aspects is a form of loyalist cultural nationalism defined in aggressive and bitter opposition to Gaelic nationalist culture. When compared with Brian Turner's approach to exploring the distinctiveness of this history of settlement, and especially his insistence that "the Armstrongs and Elliots of today are not the Anglo-Scottish borderers of yesterday. Centuries of intermarriage and a myriad of relationships have made them a product of this land,"[95] the use of Y-chromosome genetics in borderer surname studies is more likely to reinforce polarized categories and communities of descent in Northern Ireland.

It is also likely that this project will appeal to those interested in their Scotch-Irish or Ulster-Scots heritage in Canada and the United States, just as Turner's map of surnames in County Fermanagh as evidence of the complex settlement of this region will become a resource for single surname societies undertaking genetic surname studies using Y-chromosome genetics. So while arguments about the deep prehistoric and historic connections between southwest Scotland and northeast Ireland have been used to challenge the projection of contemporary categories of nation and ethnicity back into the past,[96] accounts of prehistoric migration and origins are simultaneously used to generate new responses to those potent categories of "native" and "settler." The animosity expressed in arguments generated in online discussion forums about the histories of settlement in Ulster from Scotland and the origin of Ulster-Scots suggest that these local disputes about settlement and legitimate presence, ownership and appropriation are never only local but circulate in extended chains of identification and differentiation.[97] The political effects and implications of population genetics cannot be contained as scientific, political, and cultural projects addressing questions of ancestry and descent cross-fertilize. Accounts of ancient and more recent origins and settlement are clearly deeply tied to questions of cultural and political identity.

Conclusion

Setting the subjects of population genetics and cultural politics side by side and tracking their mutual effects does not produce a simple account of the implications of these new scientific versions of origins, settlement, and genetic difference. Instead it shows the complex relationship between genetics and the postcolonial dynamics of identity and difference. Geneticists frequently argue for the significance of their work for resolving questions of collective and human origins, yet they distance themselves from its social consequences. But as these Irish and Celtic origin stories show, questions of origins and descent never float freely above the politics of making categories of difference and reckoning relatedness. This new research on genetic variation in the contemporary population of the island of Ireland has to be considered in relation to the inescapably political nature of any account of settlement or human biological or genetic variation in Ireland and Northern Ireland. When geneticists differentiate men according to whether their research subjects have "ultimate origins outside Ireland," they inevitably, even if inadvertently, evoke the long history of defining native belonging though ancestral links to an ancient Gaelic past in the most strict reckonings of Irish nationhood. When translated into genetic measures of who is "most Irish of the Irish," population genetics is enmeshed in the most potent politics of sovereignty, identity, and citizenship. This is a politics in which questions of the historic place of those outside the category of Gaelic, Catholic, and native—Jewish people, Huguenot settlers, the "Anglo-Irish," English and Scottish Planters in Ulster, recent immigrants—are threaded together. The nationalist reinscription of colonial categories of difference and anxiety about corruption haunt contemporary cultural politics in Ireland.[98]

In 2004 during the controversial and heated debate on the referendum to remove the rights to citizenship of children born in Ireland to non-national immigrant parents, one commentator writing in the *Irish Times* charged those in favor of the constitutional amendment to consider the implications of the legislation:

> What this referendum seeks to do therefore, is to insert a claim into the heart of the Irish ethos to the effect that normal principles of citizenship can be suspended in the case of those who are not properly "one of us." It tells people in the starkest terms (rendered more stark because of the intentional choice to amend the Constitution) that we do not wish them to know a sense of belonging. It says that our land is under no circumstances to be a land of new starts and fresh chances but rather that genetic connection to the pure Irish race is a necessary pre-requisite of Irishness.[99]

As this critique of geneticized belonging suggests, genetic accounts of the native and nonnative, however careful to avoid overtly geneticizing ethnicity, are never immune from being interpreted as evidence for who has most and least rights to belong, legally as well as symbolically.

Although the geneticists involved want to distance their work from questions of race, nation, and ethnicity, their choice of research projects and practices of public dissemination suggest a strategy of generating public interest but disavowing responsibility for its interpretation. In this model of the relationship between science and society, scientists are the innocent party whose work is vulnerable to media distortion and public misunderstanding. The language of population genetics, with its use—however cautious and qualified—of ethnic categories and less cautious language of "ultimate origin," genetic "isolation" and "admixture," is readily translated by journalists into simplified forms that make much more overt connections between genetics, race, surnames, and degrees of Irishness. Geneticists both know this and sometimes supply the press with the material to do so, even while claiming they are innocent parties in the process. So while Bradley and Hill insisted in *Archaeology Ireland* that they had no intention of linking genetics and ethnicity, the *Inside Ireland* report by Hill on the research featured the headline "the Irish really are a race apart" and subheadings announcing that "Men with Gaelic names are more ancient" and "Connaught men are the most Irish of the Irish." Her earlier article framed population genetics with questions of identity; its title was "Who Are We? It's in the Genes."[100] Popular accounts of genetic research like this feed interest in personal and collective origins and fascination with newly geneticized accounts of who is related to whom as they cut across or confirm categories of race, ethnicity, and nation. Thus, although these authors do not use the language of ethnicity or race in their academic publications, the wider associations of genetics with identity that result both from the publicity strategies of scientists themselves and the research institutions and from the translation of the work by the media mean that their research cannot be isolated from the implications of its accounts of genetic difference and degrees of relatedness.

For genetic maps of difference and degrees of relatedness quickly become material for the making and revision of national and diasporic ethnic distinctions. Accounts of genetic variation based on unknowing and knowing reductions—especially in the approach to surnames and the focus on paternal descent—can be both subjects of critique and sources for different sort of projects of identity making, personal and collective: some challenging the geneticization of identity, others (from fundamentally different positions) using genetics to question particular accounts of ethnic or national difference. Claims about who is who and who comes from where made in one domain—academic genetics—spill over into another—popular culture. Local investigations of belonging infect others, and at difference scales: attempts to refigure Ireland through the idea of a mongrel population and histories of migration, family trees and maps of interconnected roots and shared complexity in Northern Ireland, lingering low-level but insidious colonial condescension, resurgent and novel forms of loyal Britishness, diasporic identifications with "Irish" or "Scotch-Irish" surnames and ancestries. Taking these two research papers and locating their accounts of Irish and Celtic origins within this extended network of meanings and uses exposes the potent and intimate webs of influence and effect between population genetics and cultural politics.

But there is more to explore. The genetics laboratory in Trinity College in Dublin where Daniel Bradley leads his research team working on population genetics in Ireland does not undertake commercial genetic testing, though it has undertaken selected studies of surname and clan names with external funding from one enthusiastic benefactor. Many commercial enterprises have been established in the United States and Britain using new genetic data and techniques, including the use of Y-chromosome research, to provide genetic tests for popular genealogy. Since Y-chromosome tests can estimate degrees of relatedness among men, they are especially of interest to groups—single surname or clan-name societies—who focus on a specific named lineage. Many of these groups use commercial genetic testing companies to explore the lines of descent among groups of men who share surnames but may be dispersed across the geographies of Irish emigration. What happens when diasporic genealogy meets population genetics, and what these tests mean for those involved in terms of personal, national, ethnic identity and relatedness, for questions of belonging in Ireland and Northern Ireland, and for the figuring of the global Irish diaspora, is the subject of the next chapter.

7

Irish DNA

Genetic Distance and Connection in Diasporic Genealogies

In January 2006, the findings of a new research paper on the human population genetics of Ireland were reported widely in newspapers in Ireland and the
United States. The *New York Times*, for example, featured the research in a piece
headlined "If New York's Irish Claim Nobility, Science May Back Up the Blarney." Nicolas Wade, the newspaper's science reporter, began the feature with the
advice to "listen more kindly to the New York Irishmen who assure you that the
blood of early Irish kings flows in their veins. At least 2 percent of the time, they
are telling you the truth, according to a new genetic survey." This figure of 2
percent is based on research that claims that "about one in 50 New Yorkers of
European origin—including men with names like O'Connor, Flynn, Egan, Hynes,
O'Reilly and Quinn—carry the genetic signature" linked to a fifth-century Irish
high king, Niall of the Nine Hostages, thought to be the ancestor of the large
numbers of men with a particular genetic "signature" in northwest Ireland.[1] Two
to three million men worldwide, the paper reported, are estimated to share this
Y-chromosome haplotype, and so also descend from this noble lineage.

This account of the prodigious fertility of a mythologized Gaelic king and
the noble lineage of his descendants made for arresting headlines: the Irish *Sunday Times* titled its report "High King Niall: The Most Fertile Man in Ireland"; the
Los Angeles Times chose "An Irish King Rules Gene Pool"; the story in the *Belfast
Telegraph* was of "The True Father of Ireland"; the *New Scientist* report was titled
"Medieval Irish Warlord Boasts 3 Million Descendants."[2] The findings reported
on by Wade and many others had just been published in the *American Journal of
Human Genetics* and were the results of research undertaken by Laoise T. Moore
and written up with Brian McEvoy and the team led by Daniel Bradley in the
Smurfit Institute of Genetics, Trinity College, Dublin.[3] The authors argue that a

"previously unnoted model haplotype that peaks in frequency in the northwestern part of the island . . . shows a significant association with surnames purported to have descended from the most important and enduring dynasty of early medieval Ireland, the *Uí Néill*."[4]

The research also reached a more specialized audience. Members of the online discussion list Irish-DNA hosted by RootsWeb.com alerted other members to the findings. Irish-DNA is an e-mail forum for discussing the use of genetics in genealogy and, in particular, research on Irish ancestry.[5] Its members vary in their level of involvement and interest. Some members coordinate projects that use new genetic tests that have been developed for family history and genealogy in their clan association or surname studies. Clans of Ireland, Ltd., currently lists twenty-two DNA studies being undertaken by its clan associations; similar projects are being undertaken by unaffiliated Irish clan groups.[6] Other members of the Irish-DNA list who are interested in learning more about what the genetic tests can do seek the advice of those with more understanding of the scientific basis of the tests and more expertise in the complex interpretive techniques that these genetic projects entail. Much of the e-mail communication is members exchanging the results of their genetic tests, conventional genealogical material, and historical information and using these combined sources to establish connections with others, find specific clan or family origins in particular parts of Ireland, and work out the genealogical relationships between premodern Gaelic clans. Members of the Irish-DNA list vary in their takes on Irish history and ancestry. The case of the *Uí Néill* genetic lineage was met with both skepticism and speculative reflection on its significance for list members' particular surname studies.

The research also features on the Web site of the Texas-based company Family Tree DNA, one of the largest and most successful commercial providers of genetics tests for genealogy, which heavily promotes the use of Y-chromosome tests in surname studies including, but not limited to, those focusing on Irish surnames. Those customers who have already undertaken one of the Y-chromosome tests on offer can see whether they "match the profile" of the *Uí Néill* signature; potential customers are encouraged to order a test to see if they do. They can order a kit at a reduced rate if their surname is one that is associated with the *Uí Néill* lineage and if their surname is already the subject of a group study being hosted by Family Tree DNA. A genetic connection to the *Uí Néill* is, the Web site suggests, a royal connection, an ancestral link to the descendants of Niall who "were the most powerful rulers of Ireland until the 11th century."[7] Members of the Irish DNA Heritage Project, which was launched in December 2005 to link together individual Irish surname genetic projects and provide a "home" for those who have done a genetic test and have an Irish surname that is not yet the focus of a group study, were also directed to the new research.[8]

These new developments feed and reflect the current public interest in human origins and ancestry and more personalized senses of ethnic or familial descent, evident both in the growth of genealogy as a hobby and in the relatively new but now well-established genre of television documentaries on human prehistoric origins and celebrity and ordinary genealogies.[9] The incorporation of the findings of the *Uí Néill* research paper on the patterns of Y-chromosome haplotypes in Ireland and their supposed association with descent from Niall into the cultures and commerce of genetic genealogy is a specific example of the recent application of new techniques in human population genetics to popular genealogy. The tests offered by companies such as Family Tree DNA have been developed directly from the technologies of extraction, analysis, and interpretation developed in the study of human population genetics, and the introduction of more refined tests and more refined interpretations of test results in genetic genealogy closely follows the research findings of scientists in this field. Enthusiasts for the usefulness of genetics in genealogy herald the new availability of scientific tests as a breakthrough in the field. Genealogy, they argue, is no longer limited by the availability of documentary sources. Those who have reached a dead end due to the lack of recorded information can turn to genetics by paying for a testing kit and collecting, as instructed, a sample of cells on a brush or swab from the insides of their mouth, placing the swabs in solution in the supplied glass or plastic vial, and sending them in a padded envelope to a testing laboratory. The online culture of genealogy now includes Web sites as well as discussion lists developed by amateur genealogists devoted to providing guidance, explanatory material, and examples of the use of genetics in genealogy.

Single surname associations that focus on the genealogical relationships between men sharing a surname and their collective ancestral connection to an original homeland provide an ideal customer base for companies selling Y-chromosome tests. In the case of Irish clan societies, this interest in genealogical connection and the histories of migration that have shaped the name's current distribution is also framed by the attractive associations of Irishness in general and the appeal of distinctive descent from particular and often noble, ancient Irish families. These new commodities are advertised in ways that invoke both new accounts of genes as fundamental to, if not determining of, individual identity, biology, character, and abilities, and older understandings of shared descent and shared substance—blood—as central to family, ethnic group, race, and nation. At the same time, these potent products cut across the less deterministic, less biologically exclusive and more flexible, more dynamic ways in which individual and collective identities are performed and group membership is negotiated.[10] Exploring these new practices of using genetic tests in researching Irish ancestry and origins—and the ways they are inflecting those issues of ethnic identity, possession and belonging, diasporic connection and distinction—means addressing several questions: What versions of shared Irish descent and what sorts of relatedness result from the complex interpretative efforts that produce accounts of genetic similarity, genetic connection, and "genetic distance"? What are the implications of these small-scale collective studies and their personalized results for senses of belonging within existing associations and in relation to categories of belonging in Ireland, Northern Ireland, and the United States? How are Irish diasporic attachments and affiliations expressed and tested through new genetic technologies? What version of a global Irish diaspora is produced through the use of genetic tests in Irish surname studies?

Genetic Irish Surname Studies: Getting Started and Getting Results

Genetic Irish surname studies typically involve genetic research units in universities in Ireland and the United States, commercial laboratories, and transatlantic and transnational organizations based on shared descent from Gaelic Irish clans. The Smurfit Institute of Genetics in Trinity College, Dublin, for example, does not provide commercial genetic testing services, but, as the *Uí Néill* paper illustrates, their research findings have been used by Family Tree DNA in encouraging a market for these tests, and by individuals and groups involved in Irish genetic surname studies. Key individuals have also played a role in the development of this strand of Irish genealogy. Patrick Guinness, of the Guinness brewing family in Ireland, has been a central figure in supporting the work of the Smurfit Institute, encouraging interest in their work and informally advising other enthusiasts. Having already explored the origins of the Guinness family through conventional documentary genealogy, he contacted Daniel Bradley after the publication of the "Irish Origins" paper in *Nature* in 2000 prompted his interested in the wider potential of the new genetic techniques. He subsequently funded the doctoral research of Brian McEvoy on the genetics of Irish clan groups because of his interest in the Guinness family origins and in the genealogical relationships between Gaelic Irish clans more widely.[11] This work is beginning to be published and made use of in genetic Irish clan and surname studies.[12]

Most of these projects are coordinated by a "Group Administrator" who encourages members of existing clan associations or newly established groups to buy tests directly through Family Tree DNA and who communicates and, with some help from the company advisors, interprets the results for those who have participated and for other interested members. Like most of the other genetic genealogy companies, Family Tree DNA offers two main types of tests, one based on the Y chromosome and one based on mitochondrial DNA or mtDNA. As Web site primers and new books on genetics in genealogy explain, unlike the other genetic material that is mixed and combined in the process of human reproduction, the Y chromosome is passed largely unchanged directly from fathers to sons. Similarly, mtDNA, which is contained in mitochrondria in the cell cytoplasm rather than nucleus, comes from the mother's ovum and is inherited by her children, both daughters and sons, unchanged. Nevertheless, mutations in both mtDNA and the Y chromosome occur over time, leading to distinctive arrangements of nucleotides in the genetic sequence of mtDNA and along the Y chromosome. Those who share these patterns are thought to be related, and the degree to which sequences "match" each other is used to estimate degrees of relatedness. Those whose Y-chromosome or mtDNA sequences match are said to share a paternal or maternal ancestor, respectively, at some time in the near or distant past. The closer the match, the more recent the genealogical connection.

Many companies offer several sorts of Y-chromosome tests that differ in their depth of analysis. The "marker" in twelve-marker, twenty-five-marker, and thirty-seven-marker tests refers to particular sections of the Y chromosome that have been identified as most variable. The more markers that are examined, the more expensive the test and the more detailed the results. The results come as a set of numbers that correspond to the number of repeated sets (or short tandem repeats) of the four bases (adenine, cytosine, thymine, and guanine, or A, C, T,

3 9 3	3 9 0	1 9	3 9 1	3 8 5 a	3 8 5 b	4 2 6	3 8 8	4 3 9	3 8 9 -1	3 9 2	3 8 9 -2	4 5 8	4 5 9 a	4 5 9 b	4 5 5	4 5 4	4 4 7	4 3 7	4 4 8	4 4 9	4 6 4 a	4 6 4 b	4 6 4 c	4 6 4 d
13	25	14	11	11	13	12	12	12	13	14	29	17	9	10	11	11	25	15	18	30	15	16	16	17

9. *Uí Néill* genetic signature. After detail from Family Tree DNA's Web page "Matching Niall Nóigiallach—Niall of the Nine Hostages," http://www.family treedna.com/matchnialltest.html.

and G) counted at particular segments of the Y chromosome. The *Uí Néill* genetic signature, or at least the values for the twenty-five markers that represent a portion of the total Y-chromosome sequence, for example, appears on the Family Tree DNA Web page in this standard format (figure 9).[13]

Men who undertake the Y-chromosome test receive their results in this format. The numbers in bold in the first row are often given the prefix DYS, which stands for DNA Y-chromosome segment, numbered according to an internationally agreed standard in order to allow to the comparison and collation of results in both population genetics and genetic genealogy.[14] The results of surname group projects usually take the form of tables that list the participants according to their test kit number and sometimes the individual's name and/or the name, date of birth and death, and location of their most distant known male-line ancestor. The results are tabulated for each individual for each of the twelve, twenty-five, or thirty-seven Y-chromosome markers. The tables are presented and explained on the society or association Web sites as well as on individual project Web pages on the Family Tree DNA site. Most are publicly accessible.

But the genetic patterns may also be represented graphically in diagrams that depict the numbers of individuals in each group and their genetic distinctiveness in terms of differently colored and sized circles and lines that correspond to degrees of genetic connection. This representational and analytical device—a phylogenetic tree—is used both in genetic research papers and increasingly within Y-chromosome genetic genealogy.

It is this technique of sequencing selected areas of the Y chromosome, comparing the results with broad patterns of Y-chromosome distribution produced by population geneticists, comparing the results of individual men, and using the estimated rates and sequence of mutations to statistically describe relations between them that is central to the surname studies that Family Tree DNA facilitates and encourages.[15]

Research Questions: Irish Origins, Irish Descent

Like Irish clan associations themselves, these projects are often coordinated by individuals in the United States or in other places of Irish emigration, sometimes in collaboration with individuals in Ireland. And like clan associations, these projects are shaped by diasporic affiliations and desires. The broad goal of these projects is to allow a man with an Irish name, and thus assumed paternal Irish ancestry, but no knowledge of where in Ireland his ancestor came from to locate a place of origin in Ireland. In order to make this possible, these studies attempt to refine and geneticize existing maps of Gaelic surname distributions by establishing the "genetic signature" of a surname or clan group, and of distinctive subgroups, septs, or branches. Sometimes the projects are established in order to explore the histories and mythologies of a surname's origins in relation to known historical or semimythological figures as described in medieval annals and genealogies, and as popularized by O'Hart, and to see if supposed descent from these noble figures can be traced in the Y-chromosome markers of male clan members.

This new technology is presented as a way of making up for lost knowledge of genealogical origins or simply the nonexistence of sources that could link modern and medieval genealogies. The McMahon Surname DNA study introduces the project in this way:

> Many of us whose ancestors emigrated from Ireland are uncertain where we came from—either County Monaghan or County Clare, the two places in Ireland where the Mac Mahon surname arose. But our ancestors have sometimes come from Dublin, or Scotland or perhaps emigrated elsewhere, to Europe or Australia. There are also two or more separate septs of Mahon who originate in Ireland and may now be known as McMahon in the US or elsewhere and there are variations of the McMahon name. . . . We have on our site the MacMahon Genealogy for the Monaghan MacMahons from the time of the Collas up to the 1640s and in some cases have been able to construct additional family lineages beyond that decade. But due to many events pertaining to turmoil in our

homeland there are essentially no records between the 1640s and the early 1800s, leaving us with a nearly 200 year gap to fill. This is often impossible to accomplish.

Many descendants of émigrés then do not know whether their roots are with the Ulster sept of MacMahons in County Monaghan or with the Clare sept of one of the Mahon septs.[16]

These genetic techniques are thus seen to offer ways of linking modern and medieval genealogies and of clarifying the geography of origins. Introductions to projects explain on their Web sites that the studies may enable the group to genetically distinguish between different branches of the name that are associated with particular regions, as well as explore the connections between clans that are thought to be historically linked by genealogy and geography. The O'Donaghue Society Y-DNA Project locates the Ó Donnchadha tribes, from which the surname derives, within the "macro tribal history" of Ireland and as descendants of the "the tribes of the second migration, the Milesian (the Gaels or Goidels), [who] carry names like Eóghanachta (descendants of Eoghan) or Connachta (descendants of Conn)." It explains that there are "eight known O'Donoghue ancient tribal areas in Ireland. They were in Munster: Tipperary, Cork/Kerry—Leinster: Kilkenny, Wicklow/Dublin, Meath, Cavan—Connaught: Galway, Mayo/Sligo. Considerable migration took place over the centuries and family groups took root in many other counties (eg Clare, Limerick, Waterford, Roscommon and others), which would today be recognised as their areas of origin."[17] The goal of the O'Donaghue project, like others, is to "build a data base of DNA patterns for the different origin locations across Ireland, providing directional guidance for those who do not know where their ancestors came from."

The goal then is not simply to find a single origin place for the ancient tribe, but to provide a differentiated geography of origins within which diasporic descendants can be precisely located. The tests thus offer a precise place of Irish ancestry, a singular and local place of origin in Ireland that is the dream of diasporic genealogy. But rather than simply provide a genetic profile for men worldwide who share a surname that originated in Ireland, and thus share a particular line of Irish descent, these projects explore degrees of genetic and historical separation and connection. The description of the project focusing on Byrne names on the Family Tree DNA Web page explains the way the project is informed by the work of the geneticists in Trinity College, Dublin, and its interests in identifying distinctive lines and ancestral locations: "Many people of Irish descent have surnames similar to Byrne and believe they are descended from the Clan O'Bryne of the Wicklow area. A recent Trinity College study revealed that only about one-third of the Byrne men tested are connected to a Wicklow cluster, while the other two-thirds may have no relationship, or be offshoots." The three goals of the project are

1. To separate the various Irish groups with surnames phonetically similar to Byrne.

2. To connect each members to this appropriate sept, such as the O'Byrne clan of Leinster, the O'Beirne clan of Roscommon, the Muinte Birne of Tyrone, the MacConboirne of Mayo, the O'Braoin/O'Breen of Westmeath, the Mac Braoin/MacBreen sept of Na Clanna, Kilkenny, etc.

3. To find the MRCA [most recent common ancestor] of each.[18]

The Clan Ó Cléirigh DNA Project established by Ultan Cleary of Ireland and Jason S. Clary of the United States to "prove or disprove family traditions and historical notions of the relationships between families bearing variations of the name in many countries" is strongly focused on "the 9th Century Irish Prince Cléireach Mac Ceadadhach and this son Maolfabhaill Mac Cléirigh (who's sons were Ó Cléirigh)." The questions they intend to answer include

How many of us are actually directly descended from Cléireach Mac Ceadadhach?

Are there any living descendants of the last most senior member of the clan who can claim "Chief of the Name" and register the clan arms with the Chief Herald of Ireland?

Is the popular theory that Desiree Clary, Queen of Sweden, and certain Clary populations in France were descended from Ó *Cléirigh* descendants who emigrated to France in the 16th and 17th Century true?

Are any of the 18th Century and later immigrants to America, Canada and other counties from France related?

Which, if any, of the Clark/Clarke families around the world are related?

Are the Milesian Genealogies which trace descendants of the early Irish kings to King Galam "Mil Espania" of Spain (Basque or Galicia) possible or even probable?

Do individuals in the Hines project descendants of the O'Heynes, a family traced to Cléireach's other son Eidhin, match up with our project and can we get a viable haplotype for Cléireach himself using data from descendants of both of his sons?[19]

The Clary project is framed by questions of collective direct descent, explorations of genetic evidence of "chiefly" lineage, the possibility of reconstructing a haplotype of a ninth-century prince, the study of connections among O'Clearys and variant names worldwide, as well as the wider question of Gaelic Milesian origins. In these projects, the rationalities of science are not counterposed to the romance of myth; instead the wonder of science and the mysticism of ancient origins are combined. Some projects begin with more mundane genealogical intentions. The McCabe DNA Surname Project, for example, began as an "attempt to find the father of an 1840's orphan in the U.S."[20] Like Irish diasporic genealogy more widely, interests in recent and ordinary ancestry are often twinned with fascination with ancient and noble descent.

Ordering Genetic Similarity and Difference

Genetic surname studies are simultaneously a matter of exploring commonality and difference. They may begin, as with the Clan Ó Cléirigh DNA Project's hope of working out a princely haplotype, in anticipation of establishing a single genetic signature for the name or clan as a whole. Yet their techniques for doing so involve exploring degrees of genetic difference and degrees of genetic similarity among participants. Establishing genetic patterns and corresponding geographical locations for specific clans, septs, or genetically distinctive lines within a particular surname group involves comparing the Y-chromosome genetics of individual men, who as participants in these projects have bought the test and whose Y chromosome has been analyzed (in most cases) by Family Tree DNA. Group administrators collate the results, and after familiarizing themselves with the complex interpretative techniques and new developments in the field, and often considerable reading in early Irish history and mythology, present the results in the form of tables that list the participants by name and or kit number and, as in the example of the Uí Néill haplotype, tabulate the allele values for each of the markers that have been established.

But the results are also grouped, and it is the identification and interpretation of these groups that are central to these projects. The groups categorize participants according to degrees of genetic similarity. But they are also ordered in particular ways, usually by their degree of similarity to what is established as a characteristic haplotype for the group. There are two techniques for establishing this haplotype: one based on numerical frequency and the other on verified genealogy and in some cases geographical location. The O'Shea DNA Project, for example, adopts the first approach, the "ancestral modal method." As the project administrator makes clear in explaining the results, the alleles for each of the thirty-seven markers that are found most commonly among participants are taken as the ancestral modal, the *"Haplotype* of the unidentified hypothetical common ancestor of all O'Sheas." However, the explanation also makes clear this is not a fixed or static "genetic signature": "The Ancestral Modal is recalculated every time a new result is processed and thus the figures presented may change with new issues of this article. The relatively small number of results at hand to date may currently be giving an unrepresentative *Ancestral Modal,* but hopefully the addition of further results will correct this."[21] The groups that result from comparison of the participants with this ancestral modal are thus continuously subject to revision and dependent on both the size of the sample and the genetic profiles of those who get involved. A different set of O'Sheas could produce entirely different groups.

They are also deeply dependent on the size of the sample. Though the aims of the projects are very big, the number of men involved are often very small. Many projects have less that ten participants and very few have more than thirty. Often the sample group includes close paternal relatives—fathers and sons, cousins and uncles—who share a particular haplotype whose significance is thus exaggerated. The O'Neill study, established in August 2005, exemplifies the degree to which the results reflect the size and profiles of those who get involved. Focusing on "the O'Neills [who] were kings of Ireland for about 500 years and are the oldest traceable surname in Western Europe, the name going back about 1,000 years," the project now has six participants, one of which claims descent from the sixteenth-century chief Shane O'Neill. The Family Tree DNA project

Web page reports that "to date, two participants have 25/25 matched (a father and son) while the other have no close matches yet in the project."[22] This is a relatively new project, so the small size is not necessarily representative, yet like more established projects, the summaries of the data include warnings from project coordinators that the results may be revised as more people get involved. So although genetics seems to offer a precision and exactitude that can assuage the usual unknowability of several centuries of paternal lineage to ancient origins, the results are qualified from the start. Group administrators are more or less explicit about the degree of difficulty in making sense of the results as well as their provisional nature, but most acknowledge that the results are the best current interpretations and may be revised. Following the epistemology of "good science," participants are given results that carry the promise of scientific truth but are advised that these results are current truths subject to the normal process of scientific progress. These warnings of their contingency do not, however, frame the promotion of the tests by commercial companies or enthusiasts. Nor do the cautious interpretations of at least most project coordinators accompany the wider announcement of the results in media reports.

The O'Shea DNA Project is "actively seeking more Irish based participants with proven ancient family histories, particularly in Co Kerry, that can be used as bench marks" and so is also interested in making use of a second method of establishing the "baseline" haplotype. This involves taking the Y-chromosome profile of participants who have a verified genealogy that links them to an area and an established lineage in Ireland as closest to the ancient type. Sometimes these genetic reference points can be men who live in areas in Ireland that are defined most strongly as the heartland of the name, and who are encouraged to participate by project members. However, men in Ireland who are potential bench marks for diasporic genetic studies may have a lot less enthusiasm for donating cheek cells to these projects. The attractions of rootedness and clan relatedness are crosscut by the geographically differentiated significance of being of Irish descent. Having Irish ancestry matters differently in different places. The taken-for-granted rootedness of the "native" is an ideal of belonging, lost and longed for by some. But a sense of "native" location that makes questions of ancestry irrelevant for some can thwart the achievement of ancestral connection for others. A taken-for-granted sense of ancestral location perhaps means the "rooted" are not necessarily motivated to donate cheek cells to aid other people's search for origins.

The author of the summary of the O'Shea project results writes, "Of the twenty five current participants, fourteen are based in the US, six in Ireland, three in Australia and one each in Canada and South Africa," and expresses surprise that "we still have not attracted anyone from Britain or any other European country as one would imagine O'Sheas there, would be as interested in their roots as their kinsmen in the US or Australia." He reports that "voluntary participants have also been scarce on the ground within Ireland and the few recent additions have been due to pestering by and financial support of, the committee members of the Clan Society."[23] Family Tree DNA encourages groups to set up funds from donations by project members to pay for the testing of key individuals. Those participating in the Driscoll of Cork DNA Project, for example, are invited to "Contribute to our General Funds which is used to purchase kits for non-genealogically originated DRISCOLL whose lineage is of interest to the group as a whole because they come from a historically interesting family key to our origins."[24] These men may simply be those that are defined as ordinary sources of genetic samples of unbroken descent and domicile in the surname's heartland. In other cases, they are thought to be of noble descent. Some recognized Chiefs of the Name are being invited to have their DNA tested as part of genetic clan projects.

The MacTighernan DNA Test, for example, combines an intense and detailed attempt to find the geographical "centre of origin" for each of the groups that have been identified among participants and connect individuals within those groups genealogically, with an interest in establishing whether, as according to "Irish history [as] it was written c. 1100s in the Annals of the Four Masters that the MacTighernans descend from both The O'Rourkes who were kings of Drumahaire and The O'Conors, who were past high kings of Ireland." When visiting Ireland, Michael Patrick McTiernan, of Chester County, Pennsylvania, a key figure in the MacTighernan project, met Patrick Guinness in Dublin who encouraged him to explore the possible links to the chiefly O'Rourke line, and subsequently encouraged the London-based businessman Philip O'Rourke, The O'Ruairc of Bréifne, to undertake the genetic test for the MacTighernan project. O'Rourke's results are included in the project and compared with MacTighernan results. The outcome is equivocal. As McTiernan explains, "So far, Philip's test scores are beyond the threshold of genetically relating to any of the 9 MacTighernan DNA groups. In the future there may be a 10th or 11th MacTighernan DNA group that has a match with Philip." But he has written to "Desmond O'Conor, The O'Conor Don, whose ancestors were the past high kings of all of Ireland" to "see if he would do the DNA test which might once and for all prove if the MacTighernans descend from the O'Conors as stated in Irish history some 900 years ago."[25]

In some cases, genetic tests for paternal ancestry are being used to create formal distinctions within clan organizations based on genetic connection to ancient Gaelic "bloodlines." The O'Donoghue Society, like many similar associations, offers encouragement and support to those exploring O'Donoghue ancestry worldwide. Its Web site suggests an inclusive welcome to all those who share interest in gaining a "deeper understanding of the individual family histories of those that carry or have carried the O'Donoghue name, and its many variants."[26] But the results of the Society's Y-DNA Project have been used as the basis for a more exclusive association. The Royal Order of Ónaghts Ó Donnchadha was established in 2004 as a response to the genetic study's findings. As the official launch document explained, the results have

> enabled the participants to clearly identify their lineage within the different Septs of the Eoghanaght lines. There are two clear Kerry lines in this descent, the O Donoghues Mor and the O Donoghues of the Glens. The O Donoghue of the Glens has a current acknowledged Chief of the Name in the person of Geoffrey Paul The O Donoghue of the Glens residing in Offaly. However, after the fall of The O Donoghue Mor in 1583 during the Desmond rebellion, that line faded into relative obscurity. Family tradition and historical evidence show that the Mor line did not, however, die out, and the yDNA results support that conclusion. This study indicates the existence of a number of O Donoghues who are legitimate heirs to that honour and lineage.[27]

Membership in the Royal Order is open to those who can "show relationships through yDNA to either of these lines." The launch document acknowledges the "obvious question of how such an organization based on ancient Gaelic traditions is valid in today's Republic," but states that the order hopes to "create an active group which will engender a sense of kinship, seek consequential causes to support and set goals to disseminate a better understanding of the unique, ancient culture that once was the Gaelic/Celtic heritage to our kinsmen and the broader population."[28] This is a sense of kinship based upon genetic similarity and one whose value depends on it being exclusive to those who possess the Y-chromosome profiles to qualify for membership. The Royal Order thus formally excludes those who may possess the name and sense of affiliation but not the corresponding haplotypes.

Genetic Mismatches

The O'Donaghue Society is unusual in the degree to which genetic test results are used as formal criteria for membership in this newly established order. But distinguishing between participants is fundamental to all these projects even if the effect of the production of categories of belonging and relatedness within them are less formal than the O'Donaghue Royal Order, and handled with more circumspection. The grouping of individuals can suggest some men have chiefly descent and other men are not even distantly related to the clan group. Patrick Guinness acknowledges the appeal of chiefly genetic ancestry but reminds those involved that in the past many men shared the name of the royal dynasties as members of the wider group who served them. Using the example of his own Guinness group turning out to be unrelated to the chiefly lineage, he is at pains to point out to the individuals and groups he advises that most people's ancestry is ordinary and that most are descended from "plebs." But for him, the association via names and degree of genetic connection to a tribal group and region is still a valuable source of historical knowledge of origins:

> Well, what I say to people who don't belong, people like me, for example, who don't belong to the royal lineages: it doesn't matter. You can still say that you are from that part of Ireland even if you are in the Un-termenshen group. You still helped build those castles, maintain those churches; your ancestors are buried in those graveyards. So this was your stomping ground. Yes, you were a peasant; yes, life was nasty, brutish, and short; yes, you made no decisions; they were made by somebody else; yes, you didn't marry the prettiest girls. But here you are, you are alive, you survived and you know it's still part of your background.[29]

Here "plebeian" descent can be accommodated within broad regional clan groups. But how are cases of those whose haplotypes suggest that they are only distantly related, if at all, to the other men in the genetic surname project represented in explanations of project results? When those interpreting the results do so in relation to established clan histories derived from the histories, mythologies, and genealogies of early Gaelic society, some project participants can be informed of their likely connections to specific historical figures and specific places. In contrast, other members are located in a provisional limbo awaiting classification, as in this example from the O'Donaghue results:

> One individual who comes from Clare has alleles that match either one or the other of the Kerry tribes, and his TMRCA (Time to the Most Recent Common Ancestor) would indicate a connection back to the founding of the separate tribes by the sons of Corc in the 5th century, when Oengus Mac Nad Friach sent a contingent from Cashel to Clare to control the local population there. That group developed into the Eoghanacht Ninussa, and we suspect that we have a member of that Eoghanacht tribe as well.
>
> There are several individuals whose haplotype is significantly different from any of the established tribal haplotypes we have identified. While they are listed in the main spreadsheet A, their alleles do not match any of these ancestral haplotypes closely enough, nor is their TMRCA close enough to other participants, to be able to identify the tribe to which they belong. We await the addition of new participants to broaden our database and hopefully identify more of the O'Donoghue tribes.[30]

In other cases, men whose results do not place them within the main groups are defined as outlier groups with the explanation that they may be reclassified or these groups may become more significant as more men participate and more results arrive from Family Tree DNA. Sometimes these newly defined groups are groups of one. Instead of simply being told they are not related, individual men are described, when possible, as a "group" among the range of groups, even if they do not fall within the groups taken to be, or taken to be closest to, the ancestral modal haplotype. However, those men whose Y-chromosome markers bear no relation to those that are established as typical for the surname or clan group cannot be grouped in this way. So while these tests locate all participants in the project in terms of degrees of similarity rather than on the basis of the possession of a single "signature," they do differentiate between those with at least some degree of connection and those with none. Participants thus always face the prospect that their tests will reveal that what may be their long and deeply held attachment to a name, ancestry, Gaelic heritage, culture, place, and origin does not match their genes (or at least their genetic patrilineage). The promise of affirmation of ancestral identity has to have as its corollary the threat of refutation.

Some involved are matter of fact about this. Others suggest that a discovery that one's surname doesn't match the established haplotype for that name is fortunate since it prevents an individual wasting more time on researching the mistaken lineage. The O'Brien project Web site FAQs includes this answer to the question "Should additional family members be tested?"

> Ideally, yes. About 2–5% of people turn out—through hidden adoption or paternity—not to be who they believe themselves to be. By having a related descendant tested (e.g. a cousin or uncle with the same presumed male-line ancestry), such unexpected paternity can be revealed. In which case, several more family members could be tested to resolve who in the family is or is not actually O'BRIEN/etc. Note that the test would, sooner or later (as more surname projects are undertaken), reveal the individual's *true* ancestry, so unexpected results should be seen as a breakthrough, not a loss. It also underscores why one would want to get the testing done as soon as possible—*before* spending years researching the *wrong* surname![31]

Men who are interested in a particular project but don't bear the particular surname being studied through direct paternal descent are often encouraged to find another group or to begin one themselves. The implication is that discovering nonbelonging in one group opens the possibilities of discovering true belonging in another, so no one is left completely outside a genetic collective. At the same time, the criteria of membership with a clan or surname association shifts, at least symbolically. Clan membership, which is often open to those who are interested in the name because of its presence within their family trees but not bearers of it, is implicitly tightened to those whose genetic results support their direct male-line descent. The senses of collective descent that suffuse these societies could potentially withstand these new genetic distinctions, but the significance that is afforded to shared ancestry within them, which may be greater when it is genetically verified, can fracture previously untested senses of affinity and affiliation. The claim that participating in a surname DNA project provides "a sense of camaraderie with all who participate in the Family Project, which is particularly strong for those who share a genetic ancestry" suggests by extension that those who do not share genetic ancestry have no natural basis for senses of connection and commonality. Those involved often talk of a strong sense of affinity with those that match genetically even if these matches are fairly distant, and they explain this affinity through a positive or at least benign sense of family ties. But extended to its ultimate logic, this attitude implies increasing antipathy with increasing genetic difference. References to shared membership in a "World Family" are weak counterpoints to the problematic potency of ideas of genetic kinship.[32]

The responses of men who discover that their Y-chromosome pattern doesn't correspond to the patterns that have been ascribed to the name are largely absent from the online domain of genetic Irish surname studies. Group administrators report the e-mail communication that stops abruptly after results of this kind. Unsurprisingly, there is no place for the expression of loss, disappointment, or even skepticism when the public forum of online discussion groups is defined through being part of and invested in and not outside the shared community of descent. This silence is unsurprising too when failing to match is not just a matter of fractured senses of fraternity but of suspected illegitimacy in the recent or distant past.

The explanations provided on project Web sites and in accounts of project results of why a man's test might show that they do not bear the haplotype of the surname do suggest at least some care over the communication of "sensitive" results. The idiom of explanation is characterized by new "neutral" terms and old proprieties over ordered sex and marriage. The McManus Clan Association home page explains that "where we use the term 'interruption' here, it is intended to mean a break in the direct lineage between a person and the commonly accepted progenitor of the family. In some cases this progenitor might not be known or documented, but the DNA analysis performed uncovers the fact that the inherited DNA of a person does not indicate a close kinship with person whose DNA derives from an 'established' lineage."[33] A "non-paternity event" is the other frequently used term to describe a range of reasons why a man may inherit his biological father's Y chromosome but not his name. The list of events includes adoption, but most often refers to women's infidelity in marriage or women having children outside marriage who take her name. An earlier version of the McManus home page presented a less guarded list of reasons that, along with fosterage, legal name change, and rare sudden mutations, included "A *non-linear event* interrupting the supposed genealogical lineage to the 'documented' common ancestor. This could be caused by extra-marital affairs, *prime nocte* (the medieval right of a manorial lord to bed a newly married bride on the 'first night' of her marriage), surrogate partners, rape, or other event which caused the father not to be the one stated on the record" and "*Patriarchal Interruption*—where a child is born out of wedlock and the mother's family name is used as the child's surname."[34] Failure to match as expected in genetic surname studies is thus framed more or less explicitly by questions of men's abilities to order and violently disorder the "proper" arrangements of women, sex, and reproduction.

At the same time, the acknowledged causes of "interruptions" in the New World can, by contrast, conjure up an Old World of uninterrupted continuities:

> Outside of families still living in traditional "homelands" where there is long continuity of family—and the handful of records that are left in Ireland—only a very few can link up with their ancestral link within this surname group. Add to this the fact that sometimes the surname was changed during immigration (for many varied reasons), non-related orphan children taking on the surname of their adoptive parents, assumption of the surname of their master by slaves and other ways of having the surname (or not) and not knowing how one is linked to the surname. Now there is a way for some, when coupled with conventional research, to determine if they are linked to which of the McManus origins with some degree of certainty.[35]

However, "interruptions" of various kinds are also presumed to have happened in the distant past, too. In one case, the explanation for one participant whose results fell completely outside the group was that they had an ancestor who was genetically unrelated to the clan but who "must has done something special to be allowed to adopt the name." Or an unexpected genetic similarity between clans that were thought to be distinct is conjectured to have been caused by "an O'Neall male" parenting "a male MacMahon child who retained the name MacMahon and from whom Monaghan MacMahons now descend. A rather delicate topic, but quite possible." If this sexual misdemeanor in the remote past is figured as a matter of delicacy, it is all the more likely that a recent "interruption" is interpreted by the participant and by others as an embarrassment as well as a threat to their sense of clan relatedness.

The question of named lineages in these genetic studies is also a matter of the histories and contemporary imaginaries of race. The McManus site lists verified or suspected examples of "interruptions of a McManus lineage" that are not the product of disordered reproduction but of men's deliberate use of an alias or legal name changes. It also includes examples of the "creation of new McManus lineage from another non-related lineage." The examples, again some proven and some surmised in family genealogies, include cases of adoption. But they are largely those of men and women who are named McManus and described in the records as "negro" slaves who have been given or have taken the name by virtue of their slave status. It is most likely that this list of examples is devised to help explain how names do not always follow genes, and there is no intention of explicitly distinguishing Irishness in racial terms. However, the implication is that the genetics can help to distinguish the original, white Irish McManus lineage from "new" McManus lineages. It would be possible to argue that genetics can point to the ways relationships and genealogies cross racial lines, since men conventionally located within the categories of black and white can have identical Y-chromosome haplotypes by virtue of shared paternal descent. Yet rather than Y-chromosome genetics being used to at least trouble the correspondence between the lines of ancestry and lines of race, here genetics seems to be presented as a way of clarifying who really has Irish ancestry from among those who might be thought to do so because of their Irish surnames. Other project coordinators report on men with Irish surnames who have haplotypes that are described by geneticists as African, who therefore cannot be encompassed within the newly geneticized clan collective and sometimes appear as outlier results at the bottom of those numerical tables of results. Others talk of genetic tests disabusing African American men of their myths of descent from white Irish plantation owners. In the famous Jefferson-Hemmings case, Y-chromosome genetic tests, whose results were published in 1998, suggested that Thomas Jefferson was the father of one of Sally Hemming's sons, and thus pointed to the entanglements of sex and slavery at the heart of the nation's founding narratives.[36] Although it is likely in many cases that slave owners did father those slave children who bore their names, the McManus site emphasizes cases where slaves acquired their owners' names alone, as an example of the "interruptions" that can mean men who share surnames don't always share Y-chromosome genetic descent. In Irish surname studies, genetic tests seem to be

presented as a way sorting out lineages rather than at least potentially complicating who can legitimately claim Irish descent.

Making Sense of Connections

However, the meaning of genetic similarity is not straightforward even for those
who are judged to fall within the groups based on their nearness to the bench-
mark haplotype. The language of comparison upon which the interpretations of
relatedness between individual men and their place within the overall findings
are based is a complex one. Comparison involves describing and analyzing the
significance of genetic matches, genetic difference, and current accounts of rates
of genetic mutation in general and the rates of mutation of specific markers. Family Tree DNA has developed a system of estimating the number of generations or
time to the most recent common paternal ancestor (TMRCA) of any two men.
But the results are described not in a language of certainties but of estimates and
statistical probabilities. This extract from the Driscoll project is typical:

> David Dean and Edward Joseph Driscoll match 22 of 25 markers. The
> implication is that they share a common ancestor but too long ago to be
> found in the paper records. Specifically, the probability that they share
> a common ancestors within:
>> 200 years is 10%
>> 400 years is 45%
>> 600 years is 74%
>
> On the other hand, David Dean and Richard Driscoll are definitely re-
> lated. They match 34 of 37 markers. The probability that they share a
> common ancestors within:
>> 8 generations or about 200 years is 48%
>> 16 generations or about 400 years is 91%
>> 24 generations or about 600 years is 99%[37]

Those who buy Family Tree DNA tests are also encouraged to allow their results to be entered on a searchable database that allows them to look for genetic
"matches" with "genetic cousins" and find out the self-defined "ethnic or geographical origins" of those they match, and potentially be identified as a "genetic

cousin" by other customers.[38] So these projects entail not only calculating degrees of Y-chromosome genetic relatedness among participants. Those involved who agree to their results being accessible in this way also are likely to receive regular e-mail updates from Family Tree DNA of the names and e-mail addresses of men who match and whose degree of genetic closeness can be calculated and who can be contacted to discuss possible genealogical connections. Some project results are tabulated according to Family Tree DNA's method of estimating "genetic distance," which is a measure of the number of differences in the number of repeats of A, T, G, and C at each of the twenty-five or thirty-seven loci. The fewer the number of differences, the smaller the genetic distance. Project participants can thus scan the tables to see who they are genetically closest to according to these Y-chromosome markers.

It is hard to know to whether these sorts of statistical probabilities are satisfying or frustrating results. E-mail discussion lists at least suggest the demands of trying to understand them and relate them to personal genealogies and clan histories. These lists are dominated by appeals for guidance, speculative interpretation, advice, clarifications, corrections of misunderstandings, and explanations of the most basic basis of the tests and the most complicated analytical approaches. But it is clear that the probabilities and the different temporalities of ancestry and spatialities of origin n project reports do not always supply simple answers to quests for origins. Many of the results suggest instead different orders of origins and different registers of relatedness. At one level of analysis, the results may be interpreted as regionally rooting the clan, sept, or surname group in Ireland. At another, they suggest a much more temporally and geographically distant original place. References to early Irish history appear in project reports alongside accounts of prehistoric population movements. A "close-knit relationship" between a geographically bounded group is juxtaposed to a much larger scale and generalized sense of relatedness, as in the explanation of group 1 of the MacCurtain study:

> Group 1 is the largest group with 23 out of 42 people tested so far. Every one in the main portion of Group 1 show complete matches, or no genetic differences at this level of testing. Since they all are from the same region, the area where Counties Clare, Cork, and Kerry join this should not be surprising. Most of this region is mountainous, and has many isolated valleys and towns, leading to a close knit relationship

over the years. The one surprising finding is the Haplogroup J2. . . . This Haplogroup did not expand out of the Middle East until about 3000 to 5000 years ago.

The Haplogroup J is found primarily in Middle Eastern and North African populations. This group was carried by the Middle Eastern traders into Europe, central Asia, India, and Pakistan. It also contains the Cohen model lineage. This is the line of the Jewish priesthood. The J2 sub clade originated in the Northern portion of the Fertile Crescent where it spread throughout the Mediterranean area, Central Asia, and India. One member has had the J2 Haplogroup tested and confirmed. This sub clade is indicative of a Neolithic farmer origin. (A map of Europe showing where people who have tested for Haplogroup J2 can be found at http://www.ysearch.org/haplomap_europe.asp?haplo=,J2)

Group 1 shows that at 200 years (8 generations) they have a 55% probability of a common ancestor, and at 400 years (16 generations) the probability increases to 80%.[39]

Group 1 are thus bound together by their degree of Y-chromosome genetic matching (even if probabilities of common ancestors remain probabilities) that is thought to reflect the topography of their shared locality in Ireland. At the same time, however, one member has a haplogroup that is shared with millions of others, but also close to that identified with Jewish priestly men, and "found primarily in Middle Eastern and North African populations."[40] Similarly, the results of the MacTighernan study at one order of analysis suggest genetic diversity among the MacTighernan men and at another point to a very extended sense of genetic relatedness: "With the tests completed so far we 29 MacTighernans fall into nine separate unrelated and different DNA groups. . . . Based on what I have read there are 153 distinct genetic population haplogroups in the world, with all of us falling in the R1b haplogroup as well as 70% of all those tested at the FamilytreeDNA lab. Most or a large part of western Europe's population is also in the R1b haplogroup."[41] This combination of differentiation at one scale of analysis and generalized connection at another is a striking feature of genetic genealogy.

Genetic surname project coordinators encourage potential participants and existing project members who have not yet done so to take the more expensive but more informative Y-chromosome tests. The twelve-marker tests explore too few markers to do more than locate the individuals within the broad Y-chromosome haplogroups that population geneticists have identified and named for different regions of the world. A twelve-marker test would thus only ascertain the direct paternal European descent of men interested in their Irish origins. Tests that include more markers, the twenty-five- or thirty-seven-marker tests, are those that are used to explore relatedness and origins within same-surname groups. However, project results often describe those involved in terms of both broad haplogroups and more refined groups of haplotypes specific to the project members. This means that the projects often produce different sorts of relatedness and different origins at different degrees of resolution. The result of comparing the Y-chromosome markers of the men involved in the MacCurtain study to the current population genetics of prehistoric human migration, for example, suggests that the MacCurtains have "three different origins" that relate to three different broad haplogroups, named and mapped by geneticists. This genetic reckoning of origin and relatedness does not seem provide an image of primordial rootedness in Ireland but diverse origins and extended temporalities of migration.

Genetic surname studies thus are demanding not only in their scientific basis and statistical complexity. Those who try to relate the results of the genetic studies to their prior sense of ancestry, origin, and descent have to cope with not only the coexistence of different registers of relatedness—some specific and some very general—different timescales, and different geographies. They also have to cope with the incommensurability of genetic and genealogical time. Though clan genealogies stretch back into prehistory, most personal family trees are not complete or even partially complete beyond four or five generations. Genetic mutation rates that allow for differentiation between lineages as well as estimates of most common recent ancestors usually calibrate connections within much longer time spans, up to and more than 600 years ago. Prehistorical migration pathways derived from the mapping of broad Y-chromosome haplogroups are described in terms of tens of thousands of years. For some participants, these awkward incommensurabilities between ordinary genealogy and its geneticized forms, like the degrees of speculation and qualification involved in interpreting results, are ignored, overlooked, or deemed to be irrelevant in light of the promise of scientific confirmation of clan ancestry and origins.

However, sometimes those most committed to the projects and most close to the interpretative work they require are those most vexed by the illogics that are accepted by others. Michael McTiernan does not shy away from unresolved, and in many ways, fundamental questions:

> the remaining mystery in our DNA test group is if one of us is off a specific baseline by 3 or 4 mutations or rather mutation events which implies that you are in a whole separate and distinct DNA group and you do not genetically relate to that baseline or your common ancestor is well beyond 2000 years or 70 generations back in time then that leaves the question of how we all ended up with identical surnames, if surnames only began in the year 1120. A guess is that way back in time before surnames came into use there existed in or around Cos Leitrim, Roscommon, Sligo or Cavan a tribe or clan whose leader was called MacTighernan. In Gaelic, MacTighernan means "son of Lord." When surnames first started all the male warriors might have just taken the chief's name for themselves which might be a reasonable explanation or guess as to how we all ended up with nine different genetic groups from one small area of Connacht, Ireland all with the same surname.[42]

In this case, the surname, that key sign of descent, turns out to be a much less reliable index of relatedness that those promoting these studies suggest. Indeed, the likelihood of genetic diversity being discovered within Irish clan or surname studies has led to concerns that the results could lead to clan associations splitting along the lines of these genetic groups. Three clan societies, all three sharing a surname but each having a distinctive genetic profile, could, for example, replace the one that formerly included them all. Thus the genetic projects not only involve new criteria for inclusion and belonging within the clan and within diasporic communities of Irish descent, but they also create new distinctions and new connections within those imaginative and virtual communities. The effects of these studies will depend on the degree to which participants' senses of ancestral affiliation are playful, important, or fundamental to their sense of themselves and their ethnicity, and the relative significance of shared ancestry within their patterns of sociability, on and off line.

Like conventional genealogical research on Irish ancestry, geneticized genealogy in Irish surname studies is often undertaken as a collective endeavor by people who vary considerably in their attitudes to and degree of knowledge of Ireland. In Irish surname DNA projects, different degrees of expertise and understanding are also a matter of knowledge of molecular genetics, statistics, and interpretative techniques. Some people have more time and interest in reading up in these areas; others are happy to be guided by the experts. So there is a greater range of expertise and a greater reliance on trust between the authoritative and the amateur in these projects. But as in ordinary genealogy, efforts to trace clan lineage via genetics often involve a geography of knowledge in which those provocative issues of imaginative possession, authenticity, and the disjunctures between the figuring of the Irish past and understandings of the Irish present in Ireland, Northern Ireland, and the diaspora regularly surface. Patrick Guinness, for example, frequently has to explain to Americans who have used O'Hart's *Irish Pedigrees* as a source for exploring their surname's location within Gaelic chiefly lineages that O'Hart is viewed as a example of late-nineteenth-century nationalist foolishness in Ireland:

> Again, a lot of Irish Americans who sent me e-mails looking for advice about this, that, and the other quote O'Hart, and I have to say, "I'm sorry but it is a load of bollocks, and nobody in Ireland takes O'Hart seriously except as a sort of comic turn you know. Oh that's what he said, ha, ha." It's treated as an example of how gullible people could be in the 1800s, and—but again, if you've been studying O'Hart for the last thirty years and you've been basing all your notes and your research on that, it comes as a bit of a blow to hear that he is not highly respected.[43]

These relationships between the "misguided" and "enlightened" are not always configured in terms of the "misguided abroad" and the "enlightened in Ireland." In some cases, new genetic techniques are being used in diasporic DNA surname projects to question clan genealogies "cooked up" in the medieval past and more recent misplaced ethnic affiliations in the United States and Northern Ireland. The McCain-McKane-O'Kane DNA Testing Project is a particularly rich example of the ways in which new genetics technologies are being adopted and applied to questions of ancestral origin, ethnic difference, and belonging in places linked by migration to and from Ulster.

McCain-McKane-O'Kane DNA Testing Project

This project using the newly available testing services of Family Tree DNA to explore the history of the McKane clan was established in September 2003. The

three most active figures in the project have been project coordinator Barra Mc-
Cain of Oxford, Mississippi, whose ancestors had migrated from Ulster to the
American colonies in 1730, project webmaster Jim McKane who lives in Water-
loo, Ontario, and descends from mid-nineteenth-century immigrants, and Joe
McKane, who was born in County Antrim in Northern Ireland and now lives in
Chattanooga, Tennessee. Though Barra McCain and Joe McKane were already
interested in the potential of the new tests, and Barra McCain had already done
in-depth documentary research on the McCain origins, the initial impetus for
the project was an invitation to join another being established in 2003 by Len
Keane of Wakefield, Massachusetts, who also wanted to proclaim himself chief
of the O'Kane clan. The McCain-McKane-O'Kane DNA Testing Project was
established as an alternative genetic and historical project to "sort out the Ulster
McKanes" that would be detached from this claim to chiefly status.[44] Its aim has
been "to test and categorize the Kane surnamed people from Ireland, Scotland
and the Isle of Man and to classify them by paternal blood kinship. Then when
possible to ascertain the history of these blood clans." The "Kane" surname in
this description is shorthand for series of names—McCain, McCaine, McKane,
McKain, McKean, McKeen, O'Kane, Kane, McCaughhan, McCann, Keane,
Cain, Kain, and Keen—that are anglicized versions of one or more Gaelic names
such as Mac Catháin, O Catháin, and Mac Céin. The project has been using
Y-chromosome genetic tests taken by participants, many of whom have been
actively recruited by Barra McCain, to explore the degree of relatedness between
men with these surnames. The aim is to explore the clan histories of early modern
Ulster and especially those historically linked to the Route District between the
Bush and Bann Rivers of northern County Antrim.[45]

For Barra McCain, the DNA project is part of his long-term and detailed
exploration of his own ancestry as "a native Mississippian" with Ulster roots and
the place of this diasporic history in the histories of Ulster, Irish migration, and
the processes through which categories of identity and difference have been
shaped in Ulster and the United States. This exploratory journey began as a boy
of nine or ten and the realization that his name was not English, the questions to
his grandparents that followed, the answers that revealed that the family came
from Ireland, and his discovery of the existence of the Gaelic language from
which his surname derived. A trip to Ireland in his early twenties was the first
of many visits that have been informed by a degree in history, years of personal

historical research, and growing fluency in Irish. While family histories and popular surname guides suggested Scots-Irish origins of the McCains—migration
from Ulster but ultimate roots in Scotland—his documentary research pointed
to native Gaelic rather than Scots-Irish origins. The results of the genetic studies,
including his high-resolution match to fellow project director Joe McKane of Bal-
lywatt, County Antrim, confirm that the "old histories of the McCains generated
in America circa 1900 to the present were largely fabrications, bits and pieces
of pop history strung together with spoon-fed Ulster Protestant myths which
did not make sense, did not check out chronologically, did not check out with
the local history of the Bann Valley." Discovering that Joe McKane is "blood
kin"—a "cousin"—confirmed his thoughts about "the real McCain history and
our place in Irish and Ulster History." For Barra McCain, the accepted "pseudo-
histories" obscure a more complex history of a native Gaelic family in Ulster,
many of whose members converted to Presbyterianism in the second half of the
seventeenth century and migrated to the New World in the late seventeenth and
early eighteenth centuries.

For Barra McCain, this is a history that challenges the accepted accounts of
Scots-Irish-American history as well as contemporary efforts to underpin Ulster-
Scots identities in Ulster with alternative histories of origins in Scotland and distinctive Scottish descent. This attention to the question of Scots-Irish migration
is not an attempt to redress the formerly overlooked significance of pre-Famine
migration from Ulster in the history of Irish migration but a claim that the complexity of this earlier migration is elided under the title of Scots- or Scotch-Irish:
the account of migration being challenged here is not the dominance of the Catholic post-Famine migration histories but the dominance of a particular version
of Scotch-Irish or Scots-Irish heritage in the United States. The creation of the
category "Scotch-Irish" in the United States in order to differentiate earlier settlers from Ireland from the poor Catholic post-Famine migrants in terms of religion, class, and ancestry has, Barra McCain argues, resulted in an myth of earlier
migrant groups as homogenously Scottish in ancestry and Protestant in religious
affiliation. The false family history of the McCains, like others, he argues, derives
from late-nineteenth-century efforts of earlier settlers to disavow ancestral and
ethnic connections with the poor, newly arrived Irish and to construct a collective history that would align them with an Anglo-Saxon and Protestant America.
For him, the popular association of the McCain families in the United States with

the Scottish McCains of Glencoe, and thus dispossessed Highland chiefs, is a hangover from a Victorian craze for Scottishness and a romantic attraction to a particular story of the defeat, massacre, and exile of Scottish McCains. The notable McCain figures of the past that are claimed as Scots-Irish in the United States and as Ulster-Scots in Northern Ireland, such as Thomas McKean, a signatory of the American Declaration of Independence, Barra McCain argues, are more likely to be descendants of native Irish McCains.

The results of the genetic project appear to uphold this contention of the native Gaelic origin of the McCains. However, those who want to hold on to a Scots-Irish identity in the United States, including Senator John McCain, a 2008 presidential candidate whose popular books celebrate his Scots-Irish roots as well as American patriotism, are reluctant to be genetically tested. This is especially the case for those who have paid to be members of clan associations. As Barra McCain explains, some McCains believe that the McCains were a subgroup of the Scottish clan McDonald and so are related to

> these lost Highland chiefs, but we know now through DNA testing that those people are not Gaelic in ancestry. They [the McDonalds] are not R1b Irish Gaelic but they are R1a and they are Norse in ancestry. So you get a lot of McCains testing wanting to prove that they are these descendants of Highland chiefs, and we wind up proving they are the opposite, that they are not. You know, they are just Irish guys like us. So with some of them it is ok with them, but some of them get very angry because they've got these $800 kilts and you know they've put a lot of time in this and been in this Highland clan and they find out, well, "sorry, son, you are not, you know. You're just from County Antrim and that's it, you know."

Others accept new versions of their ancestral origins, McCain continues: "There are McCains that believe the late Victorian accounts of Ulster history and families that are not factual. This presents a problem. [But] the more educated McCains grasped fairly quickly the pan-Gaelic nature of the Irish Sea people and the ebb and flow of Gaels in Ireland and the Hebrides and understood that modern concepts of nationality did not really fit McCain history."[46] At the same time, there is resistance among some Protestant McCains in Northern Ireland, including some prominent unionist politicians and the pro-unionist families Barra McCain

is related to via Joe McCain, to being tested because of the risk of being genetically located within this "pan-Gaelic" community of descent. He understands
their fears of being genetically linked to an originally Gaelic Catholic family that
converted to Protestantism in the late seventeenth century.

However, Barra McCain also reports on being contacted in the late 1990s by
"radical unionist groups" in Northern Ireland interested in finding a distinctive
haplotype to match the theory of Scottish settlers in the Plantation being descendants of the Cruthin people or Picts native to Ulster. This is a search not only for
genetic distinction that correlates to ethnic difference but for genetic proof of
original and prior presence and native belonging to counter the political and cultural potency of ideas of native Gaelic belonging, rights to land, and the natural
legitimacy of the Irish nation. The search for a genetic signature of original native
status or for a distinctive Ulster-Scottish haplotype, he argues, misinterprets the
relationship between genetics and identity in terms of contemporary national and
ethnic divisions. For Barra McCain, Y-chromosome genetics studies point instead
to a shared ancient ancestry across the Irish sea that undermines, at one level,
ideas of genetic homologies with contemporary divisions. But at another level,
they reveal old tribal groups within the islands whose haplotypes stretch across
modern state borders. The descendants of both natives and settlers, Catholics
and Protestants "are all what they call R1b Atlantic mobile, typical Atlantic western European types that evolved into what we now know as Celtic peoples, there
is no difference in them." Geographical proximity means genetic connections:

> The East Coast of Antrim is only twelve miles over there to the Mull of
> Kintyre, and you can look out and see Islay, and you know our people—
> you know these Irish, these Gaelic Celtic people, proto Celts—you
> know we've been traveling back and forth over that twelve miles for
> 5,000 years, so you are going to have DNA patterns, you know, on both
> sides, you know, and the Picts were just one more tribal group in them
> of Irishmen or of Celts or whatever you want to call them. So there is
> not going to be us and them. It is going to be us. They are just a different
> tribal group in there, and that's what the DNA is suggesting. But they
> are going to find out more and more about tribal groupings. It is not go-
> ing to be a divisive thing, though; it is going to be merely a tool and a
> mechanism to get really precise with studying Dark Age Irish History.

It is not going to be something you can politicize and turn into and use
it in modern Northern Irish politics. It's just not possible to extract that
sort of agenda from it.[47]

He envisages a "very neat little tidy tribal map of Ireland via DNA that will tell
you which tribal group you belong to" becoming available in the future. For him,
the newly published haplotype associated with Niall of the Nine Hostages is a
major step toward that tribal genetic geography of Ireland.

This is a deeply considered and carefully researched version of genetic commonality and distinction that challenges contemporary ideas of "two tribes" in
Northern Ireland. Barra McCain is adamant that genetics "is not something you
can politicize" and clearly wants to undermine the crude application of ideas of genetic difference to "Northern Irish politics." Yet his account of genetic commonality across the islands and of genetic tribal distinctiveness has subtle but significant
political implications. Beneath a generalized Y-chromosome genetic similarity are
genetically distinctive patterns that reflect, he suggests, old tribal groups. Thus,
rather than deconstruct the idea of genetic patterns in contemporary populations
as reflections of ancient tribal groups, ideas of genetic distinctiveness and ancient
clan lineages are reinforced. As in Y-chromosome genetics more widely, these
projects sieve out the effects of centuries of intermarriage in the historic past
in their focus in direct patrilineage alone. The resulting geography of genetic
relatedness is based on ancient tribal patterns and more ancient shared descent
tracked through patrilineal descent rather than genealogical interconnections,
those "mixed marriages" that emerge through ordinary family history.

This model of genetic relatedness is also one that subsumes any claim to the
distinctiveness of Ulster Protestant heritage in Northern Ireland into an inclusive
but dominant pan-Celticism. Ireland in this genetic imaginary is fundamentally
Celtic. While this is a Celticism that spans the Irish Sea, it still figures those people defined as non-Celtic in the past and in the present as ultimately belonging,
via ancestral origins, elsewhere. Y-chromosome genetics may point to a shared
ancient Celtic ancestry that undermines the idea that genetic difference follows
contemporary political affiliations and cultural identities, but at the same time,
its sole focus on direct male-line descent produces a model of distinctive ancient
clan lineages that persist in the present. Within this schema, a man born in Ireland
but whose surname and paternal line is non-Celtic has ultimate genetic origins

elsewhere. There is no suggestion that genetics should be applied to the legal and cultural organization of national belonging in this account. Yet these potent genetic geographies of origins are readily available for political appropriation. They could easily be used to support a more overtly geneticized version of nationhood. Though the value of Y-chromosome genetics, for many, is its use in differentiating descent within the pan-Celtic collective, a prospective genetic atlas of tribal Ireland seems more likely to reinforce rather than undermine the model of the nation as community of shared Gaelic descent and support notions of the unnatural presence of the nonnative. It would also be a map of male descent.

Gender and the Genetic Diaspora

By their nature, Y-chromosome genetic surname studies not only differentiate between men but can only apply to men. Men can have their DNA analyzed in two ways, through both Y-chromosome and mtDNA tests. Since women have two X chromosomes rather than the XY of men, they only have mtDNA to test. A considerable number of the exchanges on online discussion lists are devoted to explaining to women who are interested in the new techniques that the tests and the studies focus on male genetic lineages alone. Many of the project Web sites contain similar explanations in the answers they provide to "frequently asked questions." In some cases, the guidance notes for project participants graphically figure those whose genetic material can and cannot count as genetically significant (figure 10).

The frequently answered questions section of the O'Brien clan project uses a family tree, which identifies the direct male O'Brien descent that a test individual must have, in order to illustrate their answer to the question "Does the person being tested have to be a male O'BRIEN? Yes. Only males surnamed O'BRIEN (or some variation), ones who have a direct-line male O'BRIEN ancestry as shown in the chart below, can meaningfully participate in the O'BRIEN Y-Chromosome DNA Surname Project. . . . If you are a female O'BRIEN descendant or if you are a male O'Brien descent who is not surnamed O'BRIEN, you will need to find a male O'BRIEN relative who is a direct-line O'BRIEN descendant to be tested for you."

As the O'Driscoll Web site explains:

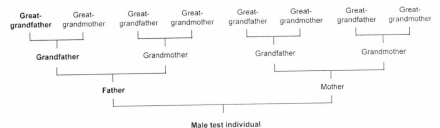

10. The common form of diagram used to highlight direct male-line descent within recent generations of a family tree used as an explanatory device in genetic surname projects.

FAQ

Q: My 4th great-grandfather is Denis Driscol born 1745 in Ireland, As I am female, could one of my sons do the test?

A: No, the surname testing is based on the "Y" chromosome which is a paternal test and thus all the samples must be derived from a male surnamed DRISCOLL or a variant thereof.[48]

So while the Irish clan and surname organizations now using genetic tests in their attempts to genetically sequence a clan identity or identify branches within clan groups are usually open to women as well as men, women cannot be directly involved as participants in Y-chromosome genetic surname studies. As in the O'Brien advice above, women are often encouraged by the genetic testing companies and by genetic clan and surname project coordinators to have their father, brother, or other male relative from the paternal side tested to provide genetic knowledge of their father's line. Women are thus offered a sort of Y-chromosomal ancestry by association even if the genetic tests are based on a version of ancestry that has no genetic presence within them. Alternatively, as in conventional genealogy, some women are interested in pursing genetic research on their husband's or partner's paternal line because of its significance for their children. Many women accept the validity of Y-chromosome genetics and follow the advice offered by Family Tree DNA and project administrators to ask a male paternal relative to have the test done in order to gain genetic knowledge of their father's lineage even if that lineage is traced by a chromosome they do not have and whose connection to them cannot be embodied.

DNA project administrators are mostly men, but there are women active in the field as well. Their enthusiasm for genetic genealogy and involvement in clan associations suggest that they have little or no problem with the profoundly masculinist basis of patrilineal descent groups and patrilineal surname systems. Their acceptance of this historical tradition of patrilineage extends to its geneticization. Like mtDNA tests, Y-chromosome tests only explore a tiny proportion of a person's ancestry. But since Y-chromosome tests, unlike mtDNA, correspond with a patrilineal naming convention, for many their narrowness is an acceptable and even welcome reduction. Yet the answers to the frequently asked questions such as those provided by the O'Brien and O'Driscoll project sites and the volume of correspondence in online discussion lists devoted to explaining the focus of surname studies on male genetic lineages alone suggest that for many women, their involvement and interest in these projects rests on an acquired acceptance of their basis on patrilineal descent. However, there are hints of dissension. One project administrator reported being accused of being sexist.[49] A women elected as honorary chief by one clan was upset to discover that the appeal to participants at a clan gathering for donations of cheek cells to the genetic clan project could not include her.[50]

Some, but not many, projects try to include women in other ways by featuring the results of mtDNA tests that have been taken by women (and some men). Women and men who buy mtDNA tests also receive their results in a numerical and tabulated form. In these tests, a customer's pattern of mtDNA at particular section of the total sequence known as the hypervariable control region (HVR1) is compared to a standardized sequence known as the Cambridge Reference Sequence (CRS). (Those who want to and can afford to can pay for a more in-depth test that includes a second hypervariable control region—HVR2—or have their total mtDNA sequenced). A customer's mtDNA is identified with a letter that denotes a particular named pattern also known as a haplogroup and sets of letters and numbers that indicate where and how their sequence differs from CRS. Family Tree DNA gives an example of the form of the results in a short and extended table.[51] The short version lists a fictional customer's results as HVR1 Haplogroup H, HVR1 Differences from CRS: 16162G, 16209C, 16519C.

The difference between the interpretations of mtDNA results and the familiar form and content of family history is striking. While the temporalities and statistical probabilities of Y-chromosome descent have to be interpreted laboriously in order to have any resonances with conventional genealogy, this labor is futile with mtDNA results. This is partly a function of the rate of mutation of mitochrondrial DNA. The mitochondrial "molecular clock" is thought to tick more slowly: these longer average rates of mutation have resulted in less genetic diversity within patterns of mtDNA, and it is argued therefore that mtDNA is a blunter tool for tracing ancestry. While the temporalities of most common recent paternal ancestor have to be stretched and squeezed to match the historical emergence of surnames, the timescales of mtDNA difference are far greater than historical time. So mtDNA tests have neither the symmetry between patrilineal surnames and Y chromosomes nor an easily meaningful temporality. The results of the tests locate the maternal origins of those tested not in Ireland at all, let alone a specific region in Ireland, but in an early prehistoric origin and migration pathway. Attempts to name mtDNA lineages and construct senses of collective mtDNA descent by drawing on the language of clans and named maternal progenitors by geneticist Bryan Sykes and others suggests their semantic shallowness in comparison to the cultural potency of the familiar models of descent and relatedness in diasporic Irish clan associations. In his popular account of human mtDNA lineages, Bryan Sykes gave women's names such as Tara, Helena, and Jasmine to seven forms of mtDNA common in Europe and provided fictional accounts of the prehistoric lives of each of these "founding mothers."[52] His genetic testing company Oxford Ancestors encourages people to join e-mail discussion lists for each maternal "clan," and his names for the lineages have been adopted more widely.

In the O'Driscoll study, for example, mtDNA results are included and explained, but the contrast between the genetic descriptions and the individual family histories of participants that are also included in the Web page presentation of the results are striking. These are the genealogical details of one participant, Eileen:

> My father's grandmother was Esther (or Hester) Driscoll. She was the daughter of Jeremiah Driscoll & Margaret Donovan of Scilly, Kinsale, Co. Cork. She and her sister appear in the baptismal records for Kinsale:
> 1836/05/29, Esther, sponsors: Tim Hayes & Bess Allen
> 1839/06/15, Norry, sponsors: George Driscoll & Joanna Leary

Esther married William Alcock in Kinsale, Cork with whom she had 5 children: Jane b. 1864, Honora b. 1866, Margaret b. 1868, William Francis b. 1876 and Jeremiah Joseph b. 1877.

Jane married Dennis Fives in Kinsale and had a son William Joseph b. 8 May 1886.

Esther and her children Jane (with her husband and son), Nora, William, and Jere emigrated to New York about 1888 (perhaps on the City of New York), where most of the family became active in the telegraph business.

The results of her genetic test are explained in this way:

Eileen's prehistoric maternal ancestor is Tara or haplogroup T. Tara originates in the Near East some 45,000 years ago. Eileen's subgroup is T3 and they are said to have entered Europe around 9,000 years ago. Once in Europe, these sub-lineages underwent a dramatic expansion associated with the arrival of agriculture in Europe. In Ireland her descendants are a small minority.[53]

The difference between the historic and prehistoric; the time of generations and the time of ancient demography; between named individuals whose lives are known through those documented dates of birth and death, named children and the place names of towns and cities—Kinsale, Cork, New York—and mythical mother Tara and ancient and generalized origins in the Near East; between the few of the family tree and the thousands that are included even in a "small minority" intensifies the dissonance between genealogy and mtDNA genetic descent. MtDNA is neither equivalent to, nor offers a compensation for, the happy coincidence of Y chromosomes and Irish surnames, and despite the inclusion of mtDNA results in the new Irish DNA Heritage Project, it is relatively insignificant in the world of geneticized Irish genealogy. Despite all the qualifiers and caveats that frame the interpretation of Y-chromosome studies, these projects and the research papers that inform this field reinforce a reductive and narrow version of descent via patrilineage alone. Not only does this edit out the potential genealogical significance of the men on all those maternal lines that are ignored in this version of descent, but it also makes meaningful ancestry profoundly masculine. The world of exploring Irish descent via DNA is one in which direct patrilineal descent carries the truth of science and the symbolic significance of founding father figures and sons.

Barra McCain and I discussed the issue of the focus on direct male-line descent:

> CN: Some people say the tests are narrow because they only test a portion of your ancestry and you obviously have lots of other men you descend from. What do you think of that?
>
> BMcC: Well actually that's not quite true, you only have one male line back. If you think about it this is where it gets metaphysical and cosmic and if you really think about it, your paternal line, you only have one back at the beginning. It doesn't dilute. You only have one Y chromosome. So there is only one McCain line whereas your maternal line, you've got many, and I was sitting here thinking about that one day and it just sort of floored me. If you think about the construction of the universe, that's a very profound thing. Not only is it extremely useful for the historian, but its very profound that you are talking about one man in a cave in Northern Spain and you are a direct descendant of him and that's the only male line you have and if your male line dies it is gone forever. If your maternal line dies, well, you have other maternal lines to fall back on. So it is an interesting perspective. I don't know any way to express it more than that. It is very profound because you only have one male line, and I don't know what that means, but there it is. So there is no other way to say it. You only have one masculine line, so, looked at with that perspective, it becomes extremely important to know about your clan. All the men in the group that match, we know we all go to one man that lived; we can tell by the DNA that he lived around the year 1200 to 1300, and he took the name or some form of the name Cain.[54]

Some of those involved are more inclined to acknowledge the partiality of locating origins via direct male-line descent alone, but they argue nevertheless that Y-chromosome genetics coupled with clan histories can provide a sense of ancestral location. Patrick Guinness is most explicit:

> But of course this is all in the male line—it is surname denominated—and so the question is, you say to yourself, well actually that's a very fine

identifier, the further back you go, and so doesn't really mean anything at all and that is the million dollar question. But if it is your only sense of identity, if you are from County Cork and your surname is O'Sullivan, which is a local surname, it seems to indicate in your mind's eye that at least one branch of your ancestry as well as your physical grandparent are from the same part of Ireland, and so instead of just giving you an Irish identity, it gives you a local identity also. . . . But of course, the reality is although we can say it is just a tiny, tiny shave, shaving of your genetic makeup—the further back you go it halves—and you know before you get to 1000 AD, it becomes less than a thousandth part of what you might be.[55]

From this perspective, it is the knowingly narrow nature of this version of descent that makes it useful for locating local origins. In most accounts of genetic geographies of origin in Ireland and other places, the partial and particular nature of this form of ancestral origins is thus, usually, a known and acceptable or an unconsidered reduction.

Y-chromosome genetics in genealogy often involve male fantasies of a past and more simple world of sex and power. This is evident in what are presented as historically informed interpretations of research findings in population genetics, and more overtly in the media reporting of this research. But it is also often expressed by those involved in genetic surname projects. The media reporting of the *Uí Néill* research paper clearly played upon an imagination of the past in which powerful men enjoyed unlimited access to uncomplicated sex with women who were simply the objects of male power. Newspaper reports deployed the language of evolutionary psychology with its accounts of fundamentally different and biologically determined natural goals of women and men in reproduction, and in particular the idea that men are driven to sexual promiscuity to guarantee the reproduction of their genes. At the same, time the reports evoke masculinist escapist fantasies of an ancient or medieval world of patriarchal power, combat, and honor. The report on the project in the Irish *Sunday Times* opened with the statement, "Geneticists have identified Ireland's most successful alpha male."[56] Many reports compared the results to a similar claim by geneticists that contemporary patterns of Y-chromosome genetics in Asia suggest that the thirteenth-century Mongol emperor Genghis Khan is the genetic father of 16 million descendants.[57]

The report on the research, published by National Geographic online, situated the account of the supposed fertility of Niall of the Nine Hostages in a history of the sexual power of powerful men: "one 15th-century nobleman with *Uí Néill* lineage, Turlough O'Donnell, is known to have had 18 sons with 10 different women. His sons gave him 59 grandsons." A grandson of Genghis Khan, "Kubilai Khan, who established the Yuan Dynasty in China, had 22 legitimate sons and was reported to have added 30 virgins to his harem each year."[58] Web log jokes about sex and status in response to news of the research suggest the appeal of these accounts of power and progeny; members had fun with knowing references to "fruitful loins" and claims that today "the male of the species isn't allowed to do what it was programmed to do."[59] The news reporting of Irish Y-chromosome genetic studies is framed by and feeds a deeply masculinist culture of naturalized asymmetries of sexual power and men's compulsion to "pass on their genes."

Yet this association between sex, progeny, and power was not simply a media distortion of a research paper but an extension of its central claims that the genetic results demonstrated the demographic effects of the relationship between, as the authors put it, "profligacy and power." The references to Genghis Khan were made in the paper itself and by Daniel Bradley in interviews with journalists, and the use of both these stories of powerful men are clearly designed to generate media interest. The speculative nature of the reference to Niall in the paper is lost in most of the news reporting. But as in other scientific research, those involved often make conjectures knowing that the ensuing reporting will not represent the speculative tone—and then claim innocence in their part in the process of dissemination. However, the problem with research of this kind is not just the way it is presented ripe for journalistic distortion and wide dissemination, but in assumptions that their authors do not imagine to be subjects of contention.

Questions of reproduction as well as migration are central to population geneticists' work on prehistoric and medieval demography. Interpretations of genetic surveys are therefore frequently framed by the geneticists' understandings of the social organization of sex. The *Uí Néill* research paper clearly seeks to extend the purchase of research in population genetics and to position the research as culturally informed work at the interface between science and history. However, like the "Irish Origins" paper discussed in chapter 6, its research methodologies effectively screen out the effects of the complex prehistories and histories of migration between Ireland, Britain, and further afield. The problem is not that the samples are small, although the contrast between sample sizes and estimates of descendants are surprising. In this case, the greater incidence of the haplotype among men with surnames associated with the *Uí Néill* clan used as the basis for the estimate that 3 million men worldwide descend from Niall of the Nine hostages is based on tests conducted on fifty-nine men in Ireland with these names.

But sample size is not the problem. Research of this kind concentrates on patrilineal descent and then promotes particular models of native and nonnative ancestry. The reduction of descent to patrilineage and the idea of geneticized singular ethnic ancestry this promotes is joined to a reductive imagination of premodern relationships between power and male fertility. The result of the effort to produce historically informed and culturally informative interpretations of genetic research findings is a crude correlation between the cultural and the biological that reduces social life to sex and power. It is based on a particular understanding of sex and the nature of relationships between women and men that is assumed to have been universal in the premodern past. The authors of the paper framed their analysis of Irish Y-chromosome patterns by their interest in exploring the "biological legacy" of the "sociocultural features" of "highly patriarchal and pastoralist" medieval Irish social order and conclude that their "results do seem to confirm the existence of a single-medieval progenitor to the most powerful and enduring Irish dynasty. They also lend support to the veracity and remarkable knowledge preservation of the genealogical and oral traditions of Gaelic Ireland and give a powerful and specific illustration of the link between profligacy and power in one European society within the past 2 millennia."[60] So although the authors acknowledge that the Irish medieval genealogies were shaped by the desire to validate power by fabricating ancestral connections to the ancient dynasties, their results suggest a correlation between traditional genealogical and genetic accounts of powerful ancestral progenitors. Suggesting that this figure could be Niall of the Nine Hostages, whose power came with unlimited sex and thus large numbers of descendants, effectively cloaks a myth of masculinity with the credibility of both historical scholarship and genetic science.

Those who are most enthusiastic about what genetics can reveal about the past are sometimes matter-of-fact about what they take to be the undeniable facts of the past. Though often prefaced by a liberal acknowledgment of the more progressive present, these uncompromisingly blunt statements of an idea of the

Gaelic Irish past when things were more brutal and more simple, when the currencies of power were "silver, cattle and women slaves" inadvertently suggest a vicarious frisson of male sexual power.[61] The Irish-American author and actor Malachy McCourt, enlisted for his views about the research for the *New York Times* report, is sanguine about claims to nobility, since there were so many clan kings and they would have had many children because "they didn't mind who they slept with, and they had first dibs."[62] References to the particular social and cultural conventions of specific medieval societies become evidence for a universal human history that is fundamental and foundational. Accounts like this suggest a nostalgic longing for that premodern imagined past of male sex and power unconstrained by modern morality, family commitments, and feminism.

However, these fantasies of men's sexual license expressed through the "facts" of the past also involve investments in women's sexual fidelity. The "natural" double standard, beloved of evolutionary psychologists, in which men are driven to reproduce their genes but who anxiously police the behavior of the women they support to avoid investing resources in children that are not theirs, seems to lurk behind apparently benign statements of satisfaction when the genetic results suggest that women have been reliable conduits for men's names and genes.[63] Y-chromosome genetics is all about men but can be read as a measure of women's sexual fidelity, or, as Patrick Guinness puts it, commenting on one case, "All the wives have been, or for those particular conceptions, appear to have been faithful to their husbands. So even though we don't have their DNA, it tells us a little bit about their sort of fidelity at the time of those conceptions anyway."[64] The geneticized extended Irish family, then, is one in which descent is fundamentally patrilineal. As in the conventions of nationhood, women matter, but their worth is measured according to a heteronormative and familial sexual politics of male dominance and male descent.[65]

Conclusion

There is no genetic test for Irishness. Unlike the tests on sale that claim to identify African, Native American, and Jewish origins by companies that include Family Tree DNA, these businesses do not sell genetic tests with the explicit promise of establishing Irish ancestry. However, these tests are premised on the deeply problematic presumption that there is a direct correlation between genetic markers, ancestral origins, and ethnicity. Being of Irish—and more specifically, being of Gaelic Irish—descent is figured as a property that can be genetically tested. Ethnic affiliation is genetic; ethnic groups are genetically distinctive. But new genetic versions of Irish descent are not framed by older ideas of genetic purity. Nor do they come with a language of ethnic proportions. This is because the focus on direct male-line descent is already exclusive. The focus on the paternal descent alone effectively means that a language of ethnic fractions or mixing is unnecessary since the focus on direct paternal descent is itself a sort of purification. Despite the general significance accorded to genetic inheritance, these accounts of genetic connection back to chiefly surname progenitors oddly overlook or disregard all the rest of the genetic material that is mixed and passed on in human reproduction. For recent generations, this focus on direct paternal descent alone foregrounds one grandfather out of two, one great-grandfather out of four; extended backwards to the timescales of Y-chromosome mutation rates and estimates of most recent common ancestors, direct male-line descent alone becomes increasingly narrow. Logically, the further back in generations you go, the less a contemporary Y-chromosome profile can say about the expanding group of past people that are ancestors. Yet the Y chromosome seems to be the only one that matters in terms of relatedness, origins, and even personality. A man may describe himself in terms of his maternal and paternal genetic haplotype and genetic origins, but the logic of the Y chromosome, that "one male line," suggests that a man can only have one genetic ancestry. The ideal of Irish origins via DNA is thus not the older idea of purity of blood but of "uninterrupted descent" from a Gaelic chiefly line.

Direct male-line descent in Y-chromosome genetic genealogy not only geneticizes and narrows the meaning of ancestry and ethnicity. It is also deeply gendered. The link backwards from son to father to grandfather that is extended genetically through the Y chromosome borrows the apparent natural legitimacy of patrilineal naming patterns and leaves unquestioned the cultural order of patriarchy from which it derives. Although the documentary sources of family history reflect the historical marginalization of women, in practice genealogy is now seldom confined to interest in male lineage alone. In contrast, the dominance of Y-chromosome genetics in the contemporary culture of genetic genealogy produces a version of the national and globally extended diasporic Irish family that is defined through male descent. After decades of critical feminist challenges to the ways in which women have been rendered marginal in accounts of both the Irish nation and diaspora,[66] Y-chromosome surname studies return to a regressive masculinist imaginary in which women socially and sexually service the intergenerational transfer of men's names and genes.

But though these tests imply that women and men occupy fundamentally different places in the imaginaries of genetic genealogy and collective ancestral origins, the tests also differentiate between men. Genetic Irish surname projects are established to confirm origins and shared descent and to genetically refine old maps of surname distributions and so provide more accurate and specific regional ancestral homes for their diasporic participants. For those who belong to these globalized and transnational associations, they promise a local point of origin. The appeal of this single line of descent and singular place of origin, which can be determined not through documents but from new technologies applied to cheek cells, evokes an older version of genealogy simplified to patrilineage. Part of its appeal lies in the contemporary temporality of the Irish diaspora. As the time since the arrival of nineteenth-century and earlier Irish migrants grows, for many descendants the details of their place of origin in Ireland have been lost, forgotten, and hard to find. The family trees of descendants reflect generations of intermarriage between Irish and other migrant groups that could suggest multiple ethnic origins for those that now identify as Irish-American. For some faced with both a lack of knowledge of a singular place of origins and the complexity of their ethnic ancestry, the promise of a genetically verified Irishness becomes more attractive. The appealing authority of science is joined to a particular cultural condition of diasporic longing.

Yet though these projects may be informed by a desire to have a single ethnic affiliation genetically confirmed and a single place of origin genetically located, in practice they produce new genetic distinctions within those imaginative and virtual communities that challenge existing assumptions of relatedness, collective identity, and belonging. The outcomes of genetic surname projects are tables of degrees of similarity and difference, degrees of genetic distance, and the identification of different lineages even within clans. Their results can suggest not belonging as well as belonging within the diasporic clan and sometimes within the broader category of Irish descent, and so have ambiguous and uneven effects for participants and for wider imagined communities. For men with Irish names and the corresponding haplotypes being identified in these projects, genetics confirms a simple and singular ethnic origin. For men who also identify with Ireland through descent but whose particular family histories of intermarriage mean that they do not have the supposedly appropriate surname and or corresponding haplotype, the genetic results refute their Irish ethnic identification.

For each account of the pleasure of belonging confirmed and genetic cousins discovered, there are untold stories of dissatisfaction, bemusement, deep disappointment, and exclusion for those who are genetically defined as outside the collective in Ireland as well as within the diaspora. Some may respond by rejecting the model of ancestry that underpins these tests. However, for others, the scientific aura and authority of genetics make it difficult to dismiss the reductiveness of these tests. So for many, the pursuit of the promise of Irish ancestry affirmed produces the upsetting effect of not belonging in the clan and within the diasporic community of descent. The new use of genetics to explore Irish origins by transnational communities based on assumptions of shared Gaelic descent suggest a growing geneticization of the diasporic, extended Irish family and its informal but effective rules of membership. They produce new scientifically assisted definitions of both collective descent and distinctive ancient lineages within the diasporic community.

So while these diasporic projects point to diversity within the diaspora, they ultimately do so by geneticizing difference within the "homeland" and diaspora in problematic ways. But new interests in genetically exploring Irish clan ancestry in this strand of diasporic genealogy are not just a matter of diaporic ethnic identifications but of understandings of identity and difference in Ireland and Northern Ireland, too. The genetic atlas of Irish ancestry that these projects may produce would effectively be an atlas of Gaelic Irishness. At one genetic resolution of relatedness, this atlas would be a map of genetic similarity and shared distant ancestry across the two islands of the British Isles. At another resolution, when more markers are compared, it differentiates between the two islands and differentiates specific Gaelic tribal lineages. For most Irish surname projects, the geography of genetic relatedness—of similarity and difference at different resolutions—that matters is still a map of Gaelic genetics. According to the logics of patrilineage, men in Ireland as well as men in the diaspora who identify themselves as Irish or as of Irish descent but do not have Gaelic names and the corresponding haplotypes are deemed to have genetic origins elsewhere. Unlike the possible understandings of interconnection opened up by family history in Northern Ireland, the genealogical imaginary of Y-chromosome genetics is not one of mixing, which renders those old categories of pure native and settler descent nonsensical in the present, but one of single direct ancestral lines and old tribal groups. The message of broad genetic similarity—even if based on a narrow model of paternal descent—that could challenge the idea that cultural or ethnic groups have some basis in genetics may seem less compelling than the message of distinctive clan ancestries that can be genetically described and identified from an individual's sample of cheek cells or saliva. Genetic Irish clan and surname projects involve reckoning degrees of genetic similarity and difference between men and using the resulting genetic groupings within clan and surname groups to establish premodern tribal geographies of lineage and location. In doing so, they geneticize ethnicity and refigure both nation and diaspora as fundamentally communities of masculine, patrilineal, and Gaelic descent.

8

Conclusion

This book has been about the making of connections through shared ancestry and origins across a geography shaped by the history of emigration from Ireland in the second half of the nineteenth century. This is a geography whose networks of attachment and affiliation reflect the particular and changing interpretations in Ireland, Northern Ireland, and the places that Irish emigrants settled of that period of migration and of the patterns of migration from and to Ireland that preceded it and followed. But as each chapter demonstrates, the making of connections is as much about the assertion of distinctions and the negotiation of difference as it is an expression of the significance of collective identity. At the same time, a sense of shared identity that accommodates difference is central to the theorization of a diasporic consciousness. Here I return to questions of belonging and possession to foreground what has emerged through attending to the conceptual and practical challenges of a diasporic imagination of pluralism and collective identity, and to the entanglements of personal and collective explorations of national, ethnic, and diasporic identity via descent and their interconnected cultural geographies. Behind the different dimensions of the contemporary meanings, explorations, and practices of being of Irish descent considered here are profoundly political questions of who counts as Irish, who belongs in Ireland, and to whom does Ireland belong in terms of citizenship and sovereignty as well as imaginative possession.

Engaging with the meanings of being of Irish descent has involved exploring the political and cultural reimagining of Irishness as an extended diasporic family, the meaning of Irish ancestry, return and relatedness within diasporic genealogy, arguments about noble descent in the diaspora and in the postcolonial republic, the exploration of "native" and "settler" ancestry in Northern Ireland, and the geneticization of difference and connection in human population genetics in Ireland and in transnational Irish clan and surname projects. Underlying my engagement with each is an argument that all accounts of descent must be considered in terms of the political implications of the narrowness or breadth of different definitions of Irishness. The implications of these versions of Irishness for the politics of belonging in relation to the old categories of "native" and "settler"; configurations of race, ethnicity, and nationhood; and the new questions of immigration both in Ireland and Northern Ireland and in Irish diasporic locations become apparent in all their complexity by tracing the intersections between different approaches to questions of Irish ancestry and origins. What also emerges through a focus on Ireland as a node in a network of identifications is a geography of both locally distinctive and mutually informing versions of being of Irish descent. My consideration of the meaning of Irish ancestry in Northern Ireland, in the Republic of Ireland, and in relation to multiculturalism in North America, and more specifically in the United States, is a partial exploration of that network. Other dynamics of connection and difference would emerge through an expanded focus on other diasporic locations—Canada, New Zealand, Australia, Britain—but this book offers an interpretive framework that could be productively extended to that wider geography. The result of this geographical analytical lens is a map of locally specific versions of being of Irish descent that reflect the particular place of Irishness in these countries' histories of migration and contemporary configurations of categories of ethnicity, race, indigeneity, nationhood, and belonging that can intersect, collide, and cross-fertilize as they are set in motion and mobilized.

The popularity of Irishness and the public prominence of Irish-American culture in the United States, especially, have been drawn on in efforts to formulate and foster the idea of the Irish diaspora as a particular model of collective affinity and cultural pluralism in Ireland at the turn of the twenty-first century. The official and popular discourse of the diaspora in Ireland, in turn, offers both a model of diasporic plurality and affinity and a welcome to match diasporic desires for reunion and return, even if some ancestral "homecomings" are motivated more by the appeal of a primordial, rather than plural, version of Irishness. Similarly, the significance of the idea of Irish origins outside Ireland undoubtedly frames new genetic research on Irish population history and at the same time furnishes a market for new genetic explorations of Irish clan ancestry. Transnational projects using genetic techniques to order the relationships between clan members, establish geographies of origin in Ireland, and explore the relationships between clans themselves feed back into accounts of difference and ancient clan origins in Ireland. However, overseas interests in Irish clan ancestry can also intersect with debates about the status of Gaelic titles in a republic, the authenticity of clan gatherings, and claims to ownership of clan insignia that foreground the tension between different versions of Irishness and different models of noble descent. But diasporic interests in ancestral links to Gaelic ancient nobility also coincide with more inclusive accounts of noble ancestry. Ideas of noble and aristocratic lineage can be used to differentiate between native and colonial nobility in Ireland. Yet the complex noble family histories beginning to be brought to public attention in recent popular accounts point to the degree of genealogical interconnection between these categories of belonging and to the shared experience of those who some would see as diametrically opposed on either side of a boundary between Irish and English or between native and colonial settler. Locally situated approaches to Irish ancestry can travel with significant effects on the dynamics of identity and difference in other places.

As I have demonstrated in this book, different conceptions of ethnicity run through the culture of Irish diasporic genealogy. The ways in which Irishness is often prioritized over other ancestral connections in the genealogies of those who identify with Ireland in the United States can reinforce a model of singular ethnicity that denigrates more mixed or plural senses of cultural affiliation both in the United States and in Ireland and Northern Ireland. But the valorization of a singular ethnic inheritance can come from Ireland too. Though ideas of plurality were central to the most fully elaborated and politically progressive versions of the Irish diaspora, the celebration of global affinities via descent can encourage a model of single ethnic ancestry. When the singular ethnic identity avowed as a diasporic collective inheritance is more specifically Catholic and Gaelic, this has the effect of reproducing a model of Irishness that not only excludes those who are conventionally defined as the descendants of colonial settlers but new immigrants too. The search for places of original belonging in response to the political challenge of indigenous rights and the cultural appeal of the harmonious alignment of place of domicile and descent—of being ancestrally at home—can lead to investments in ideas of ancient presence whose logics imply that more recently arrived immigrants ultimately belong elsewhere. This includes those deemed newly arrived in Ulster in comparison to prehistoric native presence, other historical settler groups in Ireland, and new immigrants in Ireland, Northern Ireland, and the United States. However, local currencies of nation, race, ethnicity, or native belonging are not absolutely overdetermining.

People differently situate their own explorations of ancestry and identity in relation to the wider politics of belonging. This book has explored interests in Irish ancestry and origins with these questions of diasporic and national belonging in mind, but has done so by attending to these entanglements and intersections, and to the diversity and mutability that characterize the practices and the politics of exploring Irish descent.

This book has tried to describe that diversity and capture the critical but contingent politics of the different investments in descent as the basis for personal and collective identities. It has also been an interrogation of the specific and wider implications of those twinned themes of a diasporic consciousness: difference and connection. A diasporic sense of collective identity challenges the model of the nation as a geographically bounded community of cultural sameness and shared descent and ideally encompasses plurality and hybridity. It is constituted through what is shared and what is distinctive across the geographies of the original homeland and the homes made through migration. This diasporic consciousness rejects a narrative of original purity and the anxieties of cultural corruption. Yet this consideration of the possibilities of a diasporic imagination, through a focus on the relationships between people living Ireland and Northern Ireland and those interested in Irish ancestry outside Ireland, demonstrates the challenges of realizing a reconciliation of collective identity and difference. The encounters between those visited as relatives in Ireland and their guests and new relations researching their Irish ancestors foreground the ways in which cultural, class, and attitudinal differences are actively negotiated and cut across or qualify the significance of shared ancestry, especially when the differences that become apparent are over the relevance of genealogical knowledge and the nature of Irish identity. Wider sensitivities about the ways in which Irish-American culture is interpreted in Ireland in relation to ideas of cultural authenticity and cultural appropriation frame these personal experiences of connections and difference.

But questions of difference are fundamental to the practices of Irish ancestral identification in other ways. The identification with Irish descent outside Ireland is often simultaneously a dis-identification with other possibilities of ethnic categorization, especially when this choice is made in a context in which ethnic particularity within a multicultural polity is normative. However, identification with a distinctive collective ethnic identity does not mean that difference is only delimited by the boundaries between these imagined communities. For running though the culture of Irish diasporic genealogy are assertions of difference and distinction *within* that collective. Assertions of the distinctiveness of individual or selective group identities within the wider global Irish community may be based on the nature and number of ancestors from Ireland; on having an identified connection with a particular region, locality, or home in Ireland; and the depth of knowledge, commitment, and quality of continued relationships with people in Ireland, in contrast to the supposed superficiality of others. Claims to being descended from ancient noble families clearly locate individuals in more distinctive and special communities of shared descent. But differentiation also happens in the ways some with interests in Irish ancestry dissociate themselves from the cultural forms or political associations of the popular culture of diasporic Irishness. The Irish diaspora can thus be imagined as a global community but one more riven with different sorts of claims to distinction and sensitivities about difference than a harmonious balance of commonality and diversity.

If the plurality of the diaspora is characterized by the assertion of distinction and negotiation of difference, what then is the nature of the connections that constitute the diasporic community? The idea of diaspora detaches collective identity from the conventional cultural geography of the nation in which a community of shared descent inhabits a natural homeland. But the dominance of discourses of shared ancestry suggest that the diaspora remains constituted through ties of descent that link the generations that follow dispersal to each other and to the original homeland. The description of an Irish global community as an extended family reflects the potent model of kinship through descent that remains central to the conceptualization of the diaspora. So while the diaspora stands as an alternative to the idea of the national family, it also carries with it the problems of that figuring of the nation as family: the grading of closeness and distance within the family according to the ways kinship is reckoned in relation to some founding line or figure, the naturalization of hierarchical relationships of authority and subordination, including their most patriarchal forms, and most problematically the prioritization of biological closeness through shared "blood" or "genes" as the basis for solidarity or care. Valorizing the family as the natural basis of human relationships stifles alternative models of relatedness based on shared goals, senses of interdependence, and the negotiation of difference. The ways in which ideas of descent are figured within diasporic identifications cannot be considered in isolation from the political implications of figuring biological connection as the fundamental basis of human relatedness.

The approaches and perspectives that have been explored in this book suggest that the culture of Irish diasporic genealogy both challenges and reinforces the idea of Irishness "born and bred." Though genealogy is often motivated by the appeal of that ideal of purity and rootedness, the diaspora's extended geography of Irishness challenges place of birth as the qualification for belonging. Yet the twinned term—"bred"—remains undisputed in all its potent and problematic dimensions. Diasporic connection is genealogical connection with all the positive associations the bonds of kinship carry. However, the corollary of celebrating genealogical connection is the idea of an increasing natural antipathy between people with increasing genealogical distance. Diasporic genealogy may challenge a geography of national belonging, even if it is often motivated by the appeal of indigeneity, but it can also reproduce national and racialized models of naturalized patterns of antipathy and affinity. Contemporary interests in pursuing knowledge of Irish origins and ancestry via genealogy, population genetics, and geneticized genealogy also need to be situated within, and critically addressed in relation to, the current resurgence of ideas of human relatedness and difference reckoned according to genetically distinctive lines of descent.

But if ideas of descent and blood connection suggest such strongly essentialist and potentially divisive, exclusive models of identity and relatedness, genealogy in practice—the purposeful exploration of personal family past in all its archival, online, and social dimensions—can itself be a process that throws into question the naturalness of genealogical connection and assumptions of ancestral location. The popular culture of Irishness in the United States and the emphasis on ethnic particularity within multiculturalism may encourage an identification with Irish ancestry that negates all other connections with different emigrant origins. A family story of Irish emigrant origins can be the defining family narrative at the expense of acknowledging or appreciating the emigrant origins of other ancestors who only seem to be insignificant grafts on the Irish line. Yet, for a significant number of those exploring their genealogy, the empirical emphasis and encyclopedic impulses of genealogy can lead to new senses of the complexity of roots and the contingencies of ethnic affiliation.

This new appreciation is paralleled by the ways in which genealogy in Northern Ireland reveals the degree of interconnection across what are taken to be two discrete communities of descent—native, Catholic, and nationalist or settler, Protestant, and unionist. Family trees chart patterns of intermarriage across religious division, not only between Catholics and Protestants but between Anglicans, Presbyterians, and other Protestant denominations. And as those with most enthusiasm for the constructive potential of genealogy in Northern Ireland argue, the ordinary family histories of working-class people can highlight the shared patterns of experience of inner-city working-class life and men's military service in the British army that challenge the idea of the absolute cultural difference and immutable loyalties of the "two communities." At the same time, family histories are also often histories of the policing of those boundaries: they register the costs for those whose relationships were deeply strained or destroyed by familial and wider social pressure to keep to one's own "side."

The practice of genealogy can have unanticipated effects even if its starting points and premises appear unpromising. Though the idea of ancestral origins and the return to roots is often enveloped in a blood mysticism of belonging that promises an intense and transformative moment of reunion, in practice the experience of return is often strongly characterized by the negotiation of connection and difference. Both the qualified sense of mutual recognition of connection and the realization of the work involved for both parties in the achievement of reciprocal bonds suggest that the existence of genealogical connections in themselves does not guarantee that those who share them naturally feel like family or share a view of their significance. The asymmetries between the investment in being of Irish descent and the importance of genealogy for genealogical visitors and those they encounter in Ireland suggest that the pluralism central to the model of the diaspora includes a plurality of attitudes to the meaning of shared descent.

Unexpected commonalities can also emerge. The interests in Irish ancestry and origins of those in the United States can resonate most strongly not with those who are defined as native but those who are defined as settlers in Northern Ireland. The unexpected and often deeply felt senses of communion between those doing their genealogy based in shared interests in the significance of ancestry rather than shared descent suggest alternative forms of relatedness. Like the effort of doing kinship between those genealogically connected, these family-like relationships between fellow researchers can undermine the potency of the blood connection. Being related can come to matter less, and sometimes less than the quality of these family-like relationships. In practice, popular genealogy is both underpinned by and can undermine the "genealogical model" of the primacy of inheritance and collective descent.

Furthermore, genealogical visitors do not only return to Ireland with versions of Irish history that, in their anticolonial fervor, can jar with the attitudes of those they encounter. They also come to uncover the stories of ancestors whose emigrant lives expose the costs of the nationalist model of absolute loyalty, cultural purity, and sexual morality. Their interests in recovering the history of those who were made to feel that they had no place in the nation complicate the conventional explanations of emigrant exile as product of colonial oppression. Irish diasporic genealogies can challenge as well as reproduce the politics of national belonging. Interest in Irish ancestors may be prompted by the wider cultural interest in genealogy and the cultural significance of indigenous belonging in the United States but may lead to new attention being given to the lives of those who failed to meet the most exclusive and demanding criteria of Irish national belonging. As the meanings of genealogy travel with genealogical tourists and though electronic networks, the political implications of genealogical practices and identifications can mutate so that what may be a politically regressive turn to ideas of white European ancestry in one context can, in another, productively unsettle exclusive versions of belonging.

The most obvious and accessible versions of interest in Irish roots in the United States seldom register the deeper and more differentiated approaches to ethnic identification that those involved bring to and derive from their research. A sweeping critique of genealogy's most essentializing, reductive, and narrow models of ethnic origin does not acknowledge the expression of its more reflexive and potentially politically progressive forms. Running through these pages are cases of individuals and groups whose innovative and imaginative perspectives on family history challenge its use by others to delimit separate and primordial communities of descent. This book chronicles these approaches since they not only suggest the different ways ideas of ancestry and descent can be mobilized—with their different sorts of political implications—but also because they furnish inspiring models for others reflecting on what it means to situate oneself historically and geographically through genealogy. They offer an alternative idiom for critically engaging with the meaning of shared descent for those who feel frustrated that the dominant framing of the meaning of roots does not match their sense of its significance.

This book has focused on genealogy as a popular practice rather than as a Foucauldian mode of exploration attentive to the historical contingencies and social origins of ideas elevated to the status of natural truths. Yet reading Michel Foucault somewhat against the grain, with questions of ancestry and descent in mind, suggests that he also was thinking of genealogy "in its own right." He writes,

> The search for descent is not the erecting of foundations: on the contrary, it disturbs what was previously considered immobile; it fragments what was thought unified; it shows the heterogeneity of what was imagined consistent with itself. . . . The purpose of history, guided by genealogy, is not to discover the roots of our identity but to commit itself to its dissipation. It does not seek to define our unique threshold of emergence, the homeland to which metaphysicians promise a return; it seeks to make visible all of those discontinuities that cross us. . . . If genealogy in its own right gives rise to questions concerning our native land, native language and the laws that govern us, its intention is to reveal the heterogeneous systems which, masked by the self, inhibit the formation of any form of identity.[1]

Popular genealogy and Foucauldian genealogy can do similar work, undermining the foundational fixity and singularity that "identity" implies.

But the emerging culture of genetic genealogy that is made possible and encouraged by new work in human population genetics in and beyond Ireland tempers any argument about the progressive potential of particular strands of popular diasporic genealogy. For each aspect of genealogical practice that can unsettle the ideas that often frame and motivate research into ancestral origins is countered by geneticized genealogy's renewal of old reductive imaginations of descent and the creation of new notions of genetic origin and genetic distance. Both human population genetics and geneticized genealogy concentrate heavily, and in the case of Irish surname and clan projects almost exclusively, on patterns of direct paternal descent. This means that the genealogical interconnections between conventional categories of difference that are so significant to those "mixed" genealogies are irrelevant in comparison to the idea of an ultimate and singular place of origin and an ultimate and single shared common ancestor.

As those involved argue, you can only have one line of paternal ancestry. The ordinary effort of doing relatedness is replaced with the promise of a scientific truth of genetic connection. Since geneticized genealogy is concerned with "deep ancestry" beyond recent generations, it is far removed from the research on ancestors' lives that can enrich understandings of the past and uncover hidden histories of those socially and cultural marginalized in, or excluded from, the nation. Furthermore, Y-chromosome genetics in Irish diasporic genealogy make the lines of ancestral connection that link the diasporic to the homeland fundamentally ones of male descent. In this emerging version of the extended diasporic family, being of Irish descent is reckoned according to the direct paternal inheritance of surnames, genes, and Irishness. The meanings of being of Irish descent can thus range from the most fluid, inclusive, and reflexive to the most narrowly delimited and divisively fixed.

Notes

Bibliography

Index

Notes

1. Introduction: Origin Stories

1. John O'Hart, *Irish Pedigrees; or, The Origin and Stem of the Irish Nation* (London, Glasgow, and New York: James Duffy and Co., 1892), first published in one volume in Dublin in 1876.

2. The Google search engine identified 109,000 Web sites when I entered the words "O'Hart's Irish Pedigrees" on 7 December 2005. Most of those listed on the first ten pages of results that I looked at were personal or group genealogical Web sites or Web sites giving guidance to sources for Irish genealogical research.

3. Review of the third edition of *Irish Pedigrees* reprinted in John O'Hart, *The Irish and Anglo-Irish Landed Gentry When Cromwell Came to Ireland; or, A Supplement to Irish Pedigrees*, 1st ed. (Dublin: M. H. Gill and Son, 1884), 766.

4. O'Hart, "Preface to the Second Edition," reprinted in *Irish Pedigrees*, 5th ed., xiv.

5. Anthony D. Smith, *The Ethnic Origin of Nations* (Oxford: Basil Blackwell, 1986), 24–25; Anthony D. Smith, *Myths and Memories of the Nation* (Oxford: Oxford Univ. Press, 1999), 3–65.

6. Fergus Gillespie, "Irish Genealogy and Pseudo-Genealogy," in *Aspects of Irish Genealogy, Proceedings of the First Irish Genealogical Congress* (Naas: First Irish Genealogical Congress Committee, 1993), 123–37, 134.

7. T. F. O'Rahilly, *Early Irish History and Mythology* (Dublin: Dublin Institute for Advanced Studies, 1946), 194. See also Aodán Mac Póilin, "'Spiritual Beyond the Ways of Men': Images of the Gael," *Irish Review* 10 (1994): 2.

8. O'Rahilly, 194.

9. R. V. Comerford, *Inventing the Nation: Ireland* (London: Arnold and Oxford Univ. Press, 2003), 51–84, 55. See also John Carey, *The Irish National Origin-Legend: Synthetic Pseudohistory*, Quiggen Pamphlets on the Sources of Mediaeval Gaelic History, Department of Anglo-Saxon, Norse, and Celtic (Cambridge: Univ. of Cambridge, 1994).

10. Nicholas Canny, *Making Ireland British, 1580–1650* (Oxford: Oxford Univ. Press, 2001).

11. Clare O'Halloran, *Golden Ages and Barbarous Nations: Antiquarian Debate and Cultural Politics in Ireland, c. 1750–1800* (Cork: Cork Univ. Press, 2004).

12. O'Halloran, 7.

13. Review of the third edition of *Irish Pedigrees* reprinted in O'Hart, *The Irish and Anglo-Irish Landed Gentry*, 1st ed., 763.

14. Elizabeth Grubgeld, "Anglo-Irish Autobiography and the Genealogical Mandate," *Éire-Ireland: An Interdisciplinary Journal of Irish Studies* 32, no. 4, 33, no. 1, and 33, no. 2 (1997/1998): 96–115.

15. The history of Irish ethnicity and racialization in the United States has been an important strand of ethnic history and whiteness studies. See James R. Barrett and David Roediger, "Inbetween Peoples: Race, Nationality, and the 'New Immigrant' Working Class,'" *Journal of American Ethnic History* 16 (1997): 3–44; Theodore W. Allen, *The Invention of the White Race*, vol. 1, *Racial Oppression and Social Control* (London: Verso, 1994); Noel Ignatiev, *How the Irish Became White* (London: Routledge, 1995). I discuss these issues in chapter 2.

16. Elizabeth A. Povinelli, "Notes on Gridlock: Genealogy, Intimacy, Sexuality," *Public Culture* 14, no. 1 (2002): 215–38.

17. Alex Haley, *Roots: The Saga of an American Family* (Garden City, N.Y.: Doubleday, 1976).

18. Matthew Frye Jacobson, *Special Sorrows: The Diasporic Imagination of Irish, Polish, and Jewish Immigrants in the United States* (Berkeley: Univ. of California Press, 2002), 243.

19. For accounts of the cultural practice of Irish ethnicity in the United States and in other countries of significant Irish immigration, see J. J. Lee and Marion R. Casey, eds., *Making the Irish American: History and Heritage of the Irish in the United States* (New York: New York Univ. Press, 2006); Patrick O'Sullivan, ed., *The Creative Migrant* (Leicester: Leicester Univ. Press, 1994).

20. Diane Negra, "The Irish in Us: Irishness, Performativity, and Popular Culture," in *The Irish in Us: Irishness, Performativity, and Popular Culture*, ed. Diane Negra (Durham, N.C.: Duke Univ. Press, 2006), 1–19.

21. Ken Gelder and Jane Jacobs, *Uncanny Australia: Sacredness and Identity in a Postcolonial Nation* (Melbourne: Melbourne Univ. Press, 1998).

22. Liisa Malkki, "National Geographic: The Rooting of Peoples and the Territorialisation of National Identity among Scholars and Refugees," *Cultural Anthropology* 7, no. 1 (1992): 31.

23. James Clifford, *Routes: Travels and Translation in the Late Twentieth Century* (Cambridge, Mass.: Harvard Univ. Press, 1997); Caren Kaplan, *Questions of Travel: Postmodern Discourses of Displacement* (Durham, N.C.: Duke Univ. Press, 1996).

24. Gilles Deleuze and Félix Guattari, *A Thousand Plateaus: Capitalism and Schizophrenia* (Minneapolis: Univ. of Minnesota Press, 1988), 8 and 11.

25. Caren Kaplan, "Deterritorializations: The Rewriting of Home and Exile in Western Feminist Discourse," *Cultural Critique* 6 (1987): 187–98; Janet Wolff, "On the Road Again: Metaphors of Travel in Cultural Criticism," *Cultural Studies* 7, no. 3 (1993): 224–39.

26. Sara Ahmed, Claudia Castañeda, Anne-Marie Fortier, and Mimi Sheller, "Introduction: Uprootings/Regroundings: Questions of Home and Migration," in *Uprootings/ Regroundings: Questions of Home and Migration*, ed. Sara Ahmed, Claudia Castañeda, Anne-Marie Fortier, and Mimi Sheller (Oxford: Berg, 2003), 1–19.

27. Paul Gilroy, "Diaspora and the Detours of Identity," in *Identity and Difference*, ed. Kath Woodward (London: Sage in association with the Open Univ., 1997), 317. See also Paul Gilroy, "Nationalism, History, and Ethnic Absolutism," *History Workshop Journal* 30 (1990): 114–20; Paul Gilroy, "Roots and Routes: Black Identity as an Outernational Project," in *Racial and Ethnic Identity: Psychological Development and Creative Expression*, ed. Herbert W. Harris, Howard C. Blue, and Ezra E. H. Griffith (London: Routledge, 1995), 15–30; Paul Gilroy, "Route Work: The Black Atlantic and the Politics of Exile," in *The Post-colonial Question: Common Skies, Divided Horizons*, ed. Iain Chambers and Lidia Curti (London: Routledge, 1996), 17–29.

28. Gilroy, "Diaspora and the Detours of Identity," 327.

29. Stuart Hall, "New Ethnicities," in *Stuart Hall: Critical Dialogues in Cultural Studies*, ed. David Morley and Kuan-Hsing Chen (London: Routledge, 1996), 441–49.

30. Tim Ingold, "Ancestry, Generation, Substance, Memory, Land," in his *The Perception of the Environment: Essays on Livelihood, Dwelling, and Skill* (London: Routledge, 2000), 132–51.

31. Ingold, 149.

32. Walter Benn Michaels, "Race into Culture: A Critical Genealogy of Cultural Identity," *Critical Inquiry* 18 (1992): 655–85; Walter Benn Michaels, "The No-Drop Rule," *Critical Inquiry* 20 (1994): 758–69.

33. Daniel and Jonathan Boyarin recognize in his critical dismissal of a genealogically based identity, a highly individualistic, voluntaristic notion of the autonomous self (Boyarin and Boyarin, "Diaspora: Generation and the Ground of Jewish Identity," *Critical Inquiry* 19 [1993]: 693–725). In contrast, Ingold's critical engagement with the "genealogical model" offers an alternative thoroughly relational model rather than the idea of individualistic self-fashioning.

34. Stuart Hall, "Cultural Identity and Diaspora," in *Identity: Community, Culture, Difference*, ed. Jonathan Rutherford (London: Lawrence and Wishart, 1990), 224. See also Stuart Hall, "Old and New Identities, Old and New Ethnicities," in *Culture, Globalization and the World-System: Contemporary Conditions for the Representation of Identity*, ed. Anthony D. King (Basingstoke: Macmillan, 1991), 41–68.

35. Gilroy, "Diaspora and the Detours of Identity," 328.

36. Sarah Franklin and Susan McKinnon, "Relative Values: Reconfiguring Kinship Studies," in *Relative Values: Reconfiguring Kinship Studies*, ed. Sarah Franklin and Susan McKinnon (Durham, N.C.: Duke Univ. Press, 2001), 1–44; Mary Bouquet, "Family Trees and Their Affinities: The Visual Imperative of the Genealogical Diagram," *Journal of the Royal Anthropological Institute* (n.s.) 2 (1994): 43–66.

37. Povinelli, 217.

38. Akhil Gupta and James Ferguson, "Beyond 'Culture': Space, Identity, and the Politics of Difference," *Cultural Anthropology* 7, no. 1 (1992): 10.

39. Avtar Brah, *Cartographies of Diaspora: Contesting Identities* (London: Routledge, 1996), 180.

40. Julia Watson, "Ordering the Family: Genealogy as Autobiographical Pedigree," in *Getting a Life: Everyday Uses of Autobiography*, ed. Sidonie Smith and Julia Watson (Minneapolis: Univ. of Minnesota Press, 1996), 297–323.

41. Marilyn Strathern, *After Nature: English Kinship in the Late Twentieth Century* (Cambridge: Cambridge Univ. Press, 1998).

42. Jeanette Edwards and Marilyn Strathern, "Including Our Own," in *Cultures of Relatedness: New Approaches to the Study of Kinship*, ed. Janet Carsten (Cambridge: Cambridge Univ. Press, 2000), 149–66; Jeanette Edwards, *Born and Bred: Idioms of Kinship and New Reproductive Technologies in England* (Oxford: Oxford Univ. Press, 2000).

43. David Lowenthal traces the relationships between ideas of individual and collective heritage and inheritance in *The Heritage Crusade and the Spoils of History* (Cambridge: Cambridge Univ. Press, 1998).

44. John O'Hart, preface to *The Irish and Anglo-Irish Landed Gentry When Cromwell Came to Ireland; or, A Supplement to Irish Pedigrees*, 5th ed. (Dublin: James Duffy, 1892), xi.

45. O'Hart, preface to *Irish Pedigrees*, 5th ed., x.

46. O'Hart, *The Irish and Anglo-Irish Landed Gentry*, 1st ed.; emphasis in original.

47. O'Hart, *Irish Pedigrees*, 5th ed., "Dedication to The Right Honourable The Earl of Aberdeen," xxiii–xxx, xxiv.

48. O'Hart, preface to *Irish Pedigrees*, 1st ed., vii.

2. Special Affinities: Ethnic Origins and Diasporic Irishness

1. Northern Ireland Office, *The Agreement: Agreement Reached in the Multi-party Negotiations* (Belfast: Northern Ireland Office, 1998).

2. Article 2 of the 1937 constitution, which asserted sovereignty over the whole of the island and thus denied the legitimacy of partition, was seen to provide the formal justification for the campaign to end the British rule in the "six counties." Revising this constitutional claim was integral to the attempt to ensure that the principle of self-determination would be central to any change in the political status of Northern Ireland. The other strands of the agreement established the basis of devolved power sharing in Northern Ireland in the new Northern Ireland Assembly and Northern Ireland Executive; put in place the North-South Ministerial Council, British-Irish "Council of the Isles," and the British-Irish Intergovernmental Conference that acknowledged the interests of both the British and Irish governments in the future of Northern Ireland; and addressed issues of rights and equality, decommissioning, security, policing, justice, and prisoners release.

See Brendan O'Leary, "The Nature of the British-Irish Agreement," *New Left Review* 233 (1999): 66–96.

3. Northern Ireland Office, 4.

4. Quoted in Ailbhe Smyth, "'A Great Day for the Women of Ireland': The Meaning of Mary Robinson's Presidency for Irish Women," *Canadian Journal of Irish Studies* 18, no. 1 (1992): 61–75.

5. Government of Ireland, *The Irish Genealogical Project, Comptroller and Auditor General Report on Value for Money Examination*, no. 14 (Dublin: Stationery Office, 1996), iii. This all-island project was funded by the Irish government training and employment agency, FÁS, and the International Fund for Ireland, a body set up by the Irish and British governments to promote "economic and social development" and to encourage "contact, dialogue and reconciliation between communities in both parts of Ireland" financed by the European Union, the United States, Canada, Australia, and New Zealand (Government of Ireland, 7). The project was established in 1988 to coordinate the computerized indexing of local genealogical records that had begun throughout Ireland in the late 1970s and 1980s. The Irish Family History Society was formed in 1984 to bring together those involved in local parish register indexing projects often linked to youth employment and training schemes and to manage the Family History Centres. The Irish Genealogical Project was initiated by the Family History Council of Ireland, which established the objectives, organizational framework, guidelines, and standards of practice for Family History Centres in 1986, and involved public sector agencies in the Republic and Northern Ireland, local voluntary groups, the Association of Professional Genealogists in Ireland, the Association of Ulster Genealogists and Record Agents, and the Irish Family History Foundation. See Michael Byrne, "Irish Parish Register Indexing Projects," *Irish Family History* 1 (1985): 19–26; Michael Byrne, "Report on Research Activities in Ireland 1985–1986," *Irish Family History* 2 (1986): 7–22; Michael Byrne, "Irish Family History News," *Irish Family History* 3 (1987): 5–9; John Tunney, "The IGP: A Tourist Agenda for Genealogy," *Irish Family History* 6 (1990): 61–65.

6. Mary Robinson, "Cherishing the Irish Diaspora," address to the Oireachtas, 1995.

7. See Jacobson for his insightful accounts of the making of Irish diasporic nationalism and its complex relations to the politics of assimilation in the United States and in relation to U.S. foreign policy.

8. James S. Donnelly Jr., "The Construction of the Memory of the Famine in Ireland and the Irish Diaspora, 1850–1900," *Éire/Ireland* 31, no. 1 and 2 (1996): 26–61.

9. The Great Irish Famine Curriculum, http://wwwvms.utexas.edu/~jdana/history/famine.html; Irish Famine/Genocide Committee, http://www.ifgc.org/. For a useful critical discussion of the different approaches adopted in recent public school curricula in New York and New Jersey, see Catherine M. Eagan, "'Still 'Black' and 'Proud': Irish America and the Racial Politics of Hibernophilia," in *The Irish in Us: Irishness, Performativity, and Popular Culture*, ed. Diane Negra (Durham, N.C.: Duke Univ. Press, 2006), 40–50.

10. Cormac Ó Gráda, *Black '47 and Beyond: The Great Irish Famine in History, Economy, and Memory* (Princeton: Princeton Univ. Press, 1999); Mary Daly, "Revisionism and Irish History: The Great Famine," in *The Making of Modern Irish History: Revisionism and the Revisionist Controversy*, ed. D. George Boyce and Alan O'Day (London: Routledge, 1996), 71–89; Colm Tóibín, *The Irish Famine* (London: Profile Books, 1999); Graham Davis, "The Historiography of the Irish Famine," in *The Meaning of the Famine*, ed. Patrick O'Sullivan (Leicester: Leicester Univ. Press, 1997), 13–39.

11. Kerby A. Miller, "Emigration, Capitalism, and Ideology in Post-Famine Ireland," in *Migrations: The Irish at Home and Abroad*, ed. Richard Kearney (Dublin: Wolfhound Press, 1990), 91–108, 90.

12. David Fitzpatrick, "Emigration, 1871–1921," in *A New History of Ireland, vi. Ireland under the Union, II, 1870–1976*, ed. W. E. Vaughan (Oxford: Oxford Univ. Press, 1996), 606.

13. David Cairns and Shaun Richards, *Writing Ireland: Colonialism, Nationalism, and Culture* (Manchester: Manchester Univ. Press, 1997), 58–65.

14. Kerby Miller's important work on Irish migration and emigrant experience both challenges traditional nationalist interpretations and furnishes material for popular accounts of the trauma of Irish emigration. His emphasis on the class dimensions of Irish migration is accompanied by an account of a Catholic, Gaelic culture characterized by passivity, communality, and dependency rather than individualism, which resulted in emigration being perceived as banishment and exile (Kerby A. Miller, *Emigrants and Exiles: Ireland and the Irish Exodus to North America* [New York: Oxford Univ. Press, 1985]). For a critique of the argument that this cultural background made Irish emigrants disadvantaged in terms of social mobility in their emigrant destinations, see Donald Harman Akenson, "Irish Migration to North America, 1800–1920," in *The Irish Diaspora*, ed. Andy Bielenberg (Harlow: Pearson Education, 2000), 111–38, which is reprinted from an earlier version: Akenson, "The Historiography of the Irish in the United States," in *The Irish World Wide: History, Heritage, Identity*, ed. Patrick O' Sullivan, vol. 2 of *The Irish in the New Communites* (Leicester: Leicester Univ. Press, 1992), 99–127. See also Akenson, "The Irish in North America," *Éire-Ireland* 21, no. 1 (1986): 122–29.

15. Richard Kearney, *Postnationalist Ireland, Politics, Culture, Philosophy* (London: Routledge, 1997), 5.

16. Ibid., 99.

17. Patrick O'Sullivan, "The Displacement of Identity: On Being Irish," *Political Geography* 13, no. 3 (1994): 270–78.

18. Kevin Kenny, "Diaspora and Comparison: The Global Irish as a Case Study," *Journal of American History* 90, no. 1 (2003): 134–62; available at http://www.historycooperative.org/journals/jah/90.1/kenny.html. Kenny's argument for a necessary attentiveness to the diverse historical geographies of Irish emigration and Irish immigrant communities echoes earlier calls and is being met by new work exploring this diversity. See Cecil J. Houston and William J. Smyth, *Irish Emigration and Canadian Settlement: Patterns, Links, and*

Letters (Toronto: Univ. of Toronto Press, 1990), and the contents and introduction to the special issue of *Immigrants and Minorities*, Enda Delaney and Donald M. MacRaild, "Irish Migration, Networks, and Ethnic Identities since 1750: An Introduction," *Immigrants and Minorities* 23, no. 2–3 (2005): 127–42.

19. Kenny, "Diaspora and Comparison"; see also Jacobson, 22–32.

20. Kenny, "Diaspora and Comparison," paragraph 44.

21. See Andy Bielenberg, ed., *The Irish Diaspora* (Harlow: Longman, 2000), and the multivolume *Irish World Wide: History, Heritage, Identity* series edited by Patrick O'Sullivan, which includes *Patterns of Migration* (Leicester: Leicester Univ. Press, 1992); *The Irish in the New Communities* (Leicester: Leicester Univ. Press, 1992; *The Creative Migrant* (Leicester: Leicester Univ. Press, 1994); *Irish Women and Irish Migration* (Leicester: Leicester Univ. Press, 1995); *Religion and Identity* (Leicester: Leicester Univ. Press, 1996), and *The Meaning of the Famine* (Leicester: Leicester Univ. Press, 1997).

22. Breda Gray, "Unmasking Irishness: Irish Women, the Irish Nation, and the Irish Diaspora," in *Location and Dislocation in Contemporary Irish Society: Emigration and Irish Identities*, ed. Jim Mac Laughlin (Cork: Cork Univ. Press, 1997), 209–35; Mary Hickman and Bronwen Walter, "Deconstructing Whiteness: Irish Women in Britain," *Feminist Review* 50 (1995): 5–19; Bronwen Walter, "Irishness, Gender, and Place," *Environment and Planning D: Society and Space* 13 (1995): 35–50; Bronwen Walter, *Outsiders Inside: Whiteness, Place, and Irish Women* (London: Routledge, 2001). See also O' Sullivan, ed., *Irish Women and Irish Migration*.

23. Mary Hickman, "'Locating' the Irish Diaspora," *Irish Journal of Sociology* 11, no. 2 (2002): 8–26.

24. David Fitzpatrick, "Emigration, 1801–70," in *A New History of Ireland*, vol. 5, *Ireland Under the Union, I, 1801–70*, ed. W. E. Vaughan (Oxford: Oxford Univ. Press, 1989), 562–607; David Fitzpatrick, "Emigration, 1871–1921," 606–37; and David Noel Doyle, "The Irish in North America, 1776–1845," in *A New History of Ireland*, vol. 5, *Ireland Under the Union, I, 1801–70*, ed. W. E. Vaughan (Oxford: Oxford Univ. Press, 1996), 682–725, and David Noel Doyle, "The Remaking of Irish-America, 1845–80," in *A New History of Ireland*, vol. 6, *Ireland Under the Union, II, 1870–1976*, ed. W. E. Vaughan (Oxford: Oxford Univ. Press, 1996), 725–63.

25. Akenson, "Irish Migration," 111–38.

26. Alan O'Day, "Revising the Diaspora," in *The Making of Modern Irish History*, ed. D. George Boyce and Alan O'Day (London: Routledge, 1996), 194–95.

27. David Noel Doyle, "Scots Irish or Scotch-Irish," in *Making the Irish American: History and Heritage of the Irish in the United States*, ed. J. J. Lee and Marion R. Casey (New York: New York Univ. Press, 2006), 151–70; Kerby A. Miller, "'Scotch-Irish' Myths and 'Irish' Identities in Eighteenth- and Nineteenth-Century America," in *New Perspectives on the Irish Diaspora*, ed. Charles Fanning (Carbondale: Southern Illinois Univ. Press, 2000), 75–92; Kerby A. Miller, "'Scotch-Irish,' 'Black Irish,' and 'Real Irish': Emigrants and Identities in the Old South," in *The Irish Diaspora*, ed. Andy Bielenberg (Harlow: Longman, 2000),

139–57; Kerby A. Miller, "Ulster Presbyterians and the 'Two Traditions' in Ireland and America," in *Making the Irish American: History and Heritage of the Irish in the United States*, ed. J. J. Lee and Marion R. Casey (New York: New York Univ. Press, 2006), 255–70.

28. Akenson, "Irish Migration," 114.

29. David Brett, *The Construction of Heritage* (Cork: Cork Univ. Press, 1996), 118.

30. Richard Kearney, "Thinking Otherwise," in *Across the Frontiers: Cultural, Political, Economic Ireland in the 1990s*, ed. Richard Kearney (Dublin: Wolfhound Press, 1988), 21; emphasis in the original.

31. See, for example, the contrasting perspectives of Declan Kiberd and Edna Longley in Declan Kiberd, "Strangers in Their Own Country: Multi-Culturalism in Ireland," in Edna Longley and Declan Kiberd, *Multi-Culturalism: The View from the Two Irelands* (Cork: Cork Univ. Press, 2001), 45–74; and Edna Longley, "Multi-Culturalism and Northern Ireland: Making Differences Fruitful," in Longley and Kiberd, *Multi-Culturalism*, 1–44.

32. Breda Gray, "The Irish Diaspora: Globalised Belongings(s)," *Irish Journal of Sociology* 11, no. 2 (2002): 123–44.

33. See, for example, William Crotty, "Introduction: The Irish Way in World Affairs," in *Ireland on the World Stage*, ed. William Crotty and David E. Schmitt (Harlow: Longman, 2002), 1–23.

34. Peadar Kirby, Luke Gibbons, and Michael Cronin, eds., introduction to *Reinventing Ireland: Culture, Society and the Global Economy*, (London and Sterling, Va.: Pluto Press, 2002), 16; see also their "Conclusions and Transformations," 196–208.

35. Kirby, Gibbons, and Cronin, 13.

36. Gray, "The Irish Diaspora," 126.

37. Michael Cronin, "Speed Limits: Ireland, Globalisation, and the War against Time," in *Reinventing Ireland: Culture, Society and the Global Economy*, ed. Peadar Kirby, Luke Gibbons, and Michael Cronin (London and Sterling, Va.: Pluto Press, 2002), 54–66. For other critical engagements with inequality with "global Ireland," see Ethel Crowley and Jim Mac Laughlin, eds., *Under the Belly of the Tiger: Class, Race, Identity, and Culture in Global Ireland* (Dublin: Irish Reporter Publications, 1997).

38. Jim Mac Laughlin, "Emigration and the Construction of Nationalist Hegemony in Ireland: The Historical Background to 'New Wave' Irish Emigration" and "The Devaluation of 'Nation' as 'Home' and the De-politicisation of Recent Irish Emigration," in *Location and Dislocation in Contemporary Irish Society: Emigration and Irish Identities*, ed. Jim Mac Laughlin (Cork: Cork Univ. Press, 1997), 5–35 and 179–208.

39. Reginald Byron, *Irish America* (Oxford: Clarendon Press, 1999) and Reginald Byron, "Ethnicity at the Limit: Ancestry and the Politics of Multiculturalism in the United States," *Anthropological Journal of European Cultures* 8, no. 1 (1999): 9–30.

40. Desmond King, *Making Americans: Immigration, Race, and the Origins of the Diverse Democracy* (Cambridge, Mass.: Harvard Univ. Press, 2000), 264.

41. David R. Colburn and George E. Pozzetta, "Race, Ethnicity, and the Evolution of Political Legitimacy," in *The Sixties: From Memory to History*, ed. David Farber (Chapel Hill and London: Univ. of North Carolina Press, 1994), 119–48.

42. King, 263.

43. Mary C. Waters, *Ethnic Options: Choosing Identities in America* (Berkeley: Univ. of California Press, 1990).

44. Reginald Byron, *Irish America*, 159. Byron is referring particularly to the work of Michael Hout and Joshua Goldstein, "How 4.5 Million Irish Immigrants Became 40 Million Irish Americans: Demographic and Subjective Aspects of the Ethnic Composition of White Americans," *American Sociological Review* 59 (1994): 64–82.

45. Byron, *Irish America*, 146–47.

46. Donald Harman Akenson, *The Irish Diaspora: A Primer* (Belfast: Institute of Irish Studies, 1993), 10.

47. Byron, *Irish America*, 274.

48. In August 2000, I posted a set of questions about the meaning, practice, and experience of genealogy on general Irish and Irish-county-based e-mail discussion lists to supplement interviews conducted in Ireland and Northern Ireland in 1998 and 1999. In drawing on the interview material and the 167 e-mail replies to my posting, I have not included the names of people to maintain the anonymity of the respondents. In this chapter and the others, I have not given respondents pseudonyms, either, as these names could be read as ethnically significant. This is especially the case in the material on family history in Northern Ireland. Respondents are only identified by date of reply (many were received on the same day, especially 2 August 2000), gender (if possible), and country of residence. Though leaving place names unchanged could lessen the anonymity of the responses, I have not changed or omitted them in any quoted material here and in chapter 3 since they vividly demonstrate the local and global geographies of origins and relatedness that genealogy entails.

49. E-mail response from woman in Canada, 2 August 2000.

50. E-mail response from woman in the United States, 3 August 2000.

51. Ingold, 132–51.

52. Edwards and Strathern, 149–66.

53. Negra, 3.

54. E-mail response from woman in the United States, 2 August 2000.

55. E-mail response from woman in the United States, 6 August 2000.

56. E-mail response from woman in Australia, 2 August 2000.

57. E-mail response from woman in the United States, 2 August 2000.

58. Byron, *Irish America*, 267.

59. Richard D. Alba, *Ethnic Identity: The Transformation of White America* (New Haven: Yale Univ. Press, 1990).

60. David Roediger, "Reflections on 'Whiteness and Ethnicity in the History of "White Ethnics" in the United States,'" in *Race Critical Theories*, ed. Philomena Essed and David T. Goldberg (Maldon, Mass.: Blackwell, 2002), 495.

61. E-mail response from woman in the United States, 3 August 2000.

62. E-mail response from woman in Canada, 2 August 2000.

63. David T. Goldberg, "The Semantics of Race," *Ethnic and Racial Studies* 15 (1992): 543–69.

64. L. Perry Curtis, *Apes and Angels: The Irishman in Victorian Caricature* (1971; Washington: Smithsonian Institution Press, 1997). See also Jim Mac Laughlin, "'Pestilence on Their Backs, Famine in Their Stomachs': The Racial Construction of Irishness and the Irish in Victorian Britain," in *Ireland and Cultural Theory: The Mechanics of Authenticity*, ed. Colin Graham and Richard Kirkland (London: Macmillan, 1999), 50–76.

65. Chris Morash, "Celticism: Between Race and Culture," *Irish Review* 20 (1997): 29–36, 44–45.

66. Cairns and Richards, 42–57.

67. Theodore W. Allen and David Roediger argue this most carefully and convincingly. See Allen, *The Invention of the White Race*; David Roediger, *The Wages of Whiteness: Race and the Making of the American Working Class* (London: Verso, 1991) and David Roediger, *Towards the Abolition of Whiteness: Essays on Race, Politics, and Working Class History* (London: Verso, 1994). See also Ignatiev, *How the Irish Became White*, which illustrates Allen's original argument through a series of empirical case studies.

68. Sallie Marston, "Who Are 'the People'? Gender, Citizenship, and the Making of the American Nation," *Environment and Planning D: Society and Space* 20 (1990): 449–58.

69. Barrett and Roediger, 3–44.

70. E-mail response from woman in Canada, 2 August 2000.

71. Mary C. Waters, *Ethnic Options: Choosing Identities in America* (Berkeley: Univ. of California Press, 1990), 163.

72. Roediger, "Reflections," 495.

73. Reactions to immigration have included anti-immigration campaigns, general anxiety, and racist attacks, but also the development of immigrant and asylum support organizations and academic engagement with questions of race and nation. See Bryan Fanning, *Racism and Social Change in the Republic of Ireland* (Manchester: Manchester Univ. Press, 2002); Ronit Lentin, ed., *The Expanding Nation: Towards a Multi-Ethnic Ireland* (Dublin: Trinity College, 1999); Ronit Lentin, ed., *Emerging Irish Identities* (Dublin: National Consultative Committee on Racism and Interculturalism, 2000); Robbie McVeigh, *The Racialisation of Irishness: Racism and Anti-Racism in Irish Society* (Belfast: Centre for Research and Documentation, 1996); Ronit Lentin and Robbie McVeigh ed., *Racism and Anti-Racism in Ireland* (Belfast: Beyond the Pale, 2002).

74. The cartoon was reproduced in Edward MacLysaght's memoir where he describes researching the pedigrees of two men with the O'Malley name to determine which was

The O'Malley, the Chief of the Name (see chapter 4). He was both amused and embarrassed to see the cartoon appear in case it might be interpreted as a joke at the expense of the O'Malley family in Ireland (Edward MacLysaght, *Changing Times: Ireland since 1898* [Gerrards Cross: Colin Smyth, 1978], 193).

75. Ronit Lentin, "Responding to the Racialisation of Irishness: Disavowed Multiculturalism and Its Discontents," *Sociological Research Online* 5, no. 4 (2001). Available at http://www.socresonline.org.uk/5/4/lentin.html.

76. Eithne Luibhéid, "Childbearing against the State? Asylum Seeker Women in the Irish Republic," *Women's Studies International Forum* 27 (2004): 335–49.

77. Angeline D. Morrison, "Irish and White-ish: Mixed 'Race' Identity and the Scopic Regime of Whiteness," *Women's Studies International Forum* 27 (2004): 385–96.

78. Mairtin Mac an Ghaill, "Beyond a Black-White Dualism: Racialisation and Racism in the Republic of Ireland and the Irish Diaspora Experience," *Irish Journal of Sociology* 11, no. 2 (2002): 99–112.

79. Kevin Kenny, "Race, Violence, and Anti-Irish Sentiment in the Nineteenth Century," in *Making the Irish American: History and Heritage of the Irish in the United States*, ed. J. J. Lee and Marion R. Casey (New York: New York Univ. Press, 2006), 364–78; Mary Hickman, "The Irish in Britain: Racism, Incorporation and Identity," *Irish Studies Review* 10 (1995): 16–20; Mary Hickman, "Reconstructing Deconstructing 'Race': British Political Discourses about the Irish in Britain," *Ethnic and Racial Studies* 21, no. 2 (1998): 288–307.

80. Mairtin Mac an Ghaill and Chris Haywood, "Young (Male) Irelanders: Postcolonial Ethnicities—Expanding the Nation and Irishness," *European Journal of Cultural Studies* 6, no. 3 (2003): 386–403; Breda Gray, "From 'Ethnicity' to 'Diaspora': 1980s Emigration and 'Multicultural London,'" in *The Irish Diaspora*, ed. Andy Bielenberg (Harlow: Longman, 2000), 65–88; Breda Gray, "'Whitey Scripts' and Irish Women's Racialised Belonging(s) in England," *European Journal of Cultural Studies* 5, no. 3 (2002): 257–74.

81. Eithne Luibhéid, "Irish Immigrants in the United States' Racial System," in *Location and Dislocation in Contemporary Irish Society: Emigration and Irish Identities*, ed. Jim Mac Laughlin (Cork: Cork Univ. Press, 1997), 271.

82. Interview, Dublin, 27 July 1998.

83. E-mail response from woman in Canada, 2 August 2000.

84. Rebecca Solnit, *A Book of Migrations: Some Passages in Ireland* (London: Verso, 1997), 117–18.

85. Stephanie Rains makes a similar point about the acceptance of mixed descent in Irish-American genealogy through her reading of recent accounts of Irish-American ethnicity. See Stephanie Rains, "Irish Roots: Genealogy and the Performance of Irishness," in Diane Negra, ed., *The Irish in Us: Irishness, Performativity, and Popular Culture* (Durham, N.C.: Duke Univ. Press, 2006), 130–60.

86. E-mail response from woman in the United States, 23 August 2000.

87. E-mail response from man in United States, 2 August 2000.

88. E-mail response from woman in the United States, 2 August 2000.

89. E-mail response from woman in Canada, 2 August 2000.

90. Eagan, 50. See also Negra.

91. Breda Gray, "Remembering a 'Multicultural' Future through a History of Emigration: Towards a Feminist Politics of Solidarity across Difference," *Women's Studies International Forum* 27 (2004): 413–29.

92. E-mail response from woman in the United States, 2 August 2000.

93. Katharine Brown, "Reflections on Family History: The Musings of an Irreverent Colonial," *Familia* 12 (1996): 25–35.

94. Interview, Dublin 28 July 1998.

95. Mary Robinson, "Address by An tUachtarán, Mary Robinson at the Dinner of the First Irish Genealogical Congress on Tuesday 24 September 1991," in *Aspects of Irish Genealogy, Proceedings of the First Irish Genealogical Congress* (Naas: First Irish Genealogical Congress Committee, 1993), 8.

96. Maryann Gialanella Valiulis, "Power, Gender, and Identity in the Irish Free State," *Journal of Women's History* 6 (1995): 117–36.

97. David Lloyd, "Epilogue, 'Living in America': Politics and Emigrations," in *Ireland after History*, David Lloyd (Cork: Cork Univ. Press, 1999), 101–8.

3. Irish Roots and Relatives: Return, Reciprocity, and Relatedness

1. Thomas Lynch, *Booking Passage: We Irish and Americans* (London: Jonathan Cape, 2005), 34.

2. Ibid., 10, 62.

3. Ibid., 10.

4. This chapter, like chapter 2, is based on research conducted in Dublin and Belfast in the summer of 1998, in Belfast in 1999, and through an online appeal for responses to a set of open questions about the meaning and experience of tracing Irish ancestry posted on genealogical e-mail discussion groups in August 2000. I am very grateful to the staff of the National Library's then newly opened Genealogical Research Centre for allowing me to observe and talk with visitors and to the Ulster Historical Foundation for allowing me to adopt this research role as participant of their conference and study tour in 1999, to all those visitors and professional genealogists who agreed to be interviewed, and to all those who e-mailed me questionnaire responses.

5. James Murphy, "Finding Home: Aughkiluberd, 1969," *New Hibernia Review/Iris Éireannach Nua* 8, no. 3 (2004): 12–17.

6. Interview with American woman, Dublin, July 1998.

7. Lynch, 78.

8. Ibid., 35.

9. Ibid., 36.

10. Ibid., 81–82.

11. E-mail response from woman in New Zealand, 2 August 2000.

12. Interview Dublin, 17 July 1998.

13. Malkki, 38.

14. See, for example, Frank Gannon, *Midlife Irish: Discovering Family and Myself* (New York: Warner Books, 2003); Christopher Koch, *The Many-Coloured Land: A Return to Ireland* (London: Picador, 2002); Joan Mathieu, *Zulu: An Irish-American's Quest to Discover Her Roots* (Edinburgh: Mainstream Publishing, 1998); John Moss, *Invisible among the Ruins: Field Notes of a Canadian in Ireland* (Dublin: Univ. College Dublin Press, 2000).

15. Solnit, vii.

16. Ibid., 5.

17. Ibid., 68.

18. Ibid., 6.

19. Ibid., 78.

20. Ibid., 67.

21. Ibid., 8.

22. E-mail response from women in the United States, 4 September 2000.

23. Paul Gorry, "Tradition and Television," *Irish Roots* 4 (1994): 9.

24. E-mail response from woman in the United States, 4 August 2000.

25. Quoted in Lynch, unpaginated first pages.

26. Interview with professional genealogist, Dublin, 11 August 1998.

27. Interview with visitor to the library, Dublin, 10 August 1998.

28. David Fitzpatrick, "Emigration, 1801–70," 566–67.

29. Aidan Arrowsmith, "Fantasy Ireland: The Figure of the Returnee in Irish Culture," *Moving Worlds: A Journal of Transcultural Writing* 3, no. 1 (2003): 101–14. See also Philip O'Leary, "Yank Outsiders: Irish Americans in Gaelic Fiction and Drama of the Irish Free State, 1922–1939," in *New Perspectives on the Irish Diaspora*, ed. Charles Fanning (Carbondale: Southern Illinois Univ. Press, 2000), 253–65.

30. *Home*, from *Capuchin Annual* (Dublin: Capuchin Annual, 1940), 84.

31. Interview with professional genealogist, Dublin, 11 August 1998.

32. James Murphy, 17.

33. Lynch, 20.

34. E-mail response from woman in the United States, 1 August 2000.

35. E-mail response from woman in the United States, 1 August 2000.

36. E-mail response from woman in the United States, 2 August 2000.

37. E-mail response from woman in Canada, 1 August 2000.

38. E-mail response from woman in the United States, 1 August 2000.

39. E-mail response from woman in New Zealand, 2 August 2000.

40. Marilyn Strathern, "Cutting the Network," *Journal of the Royal Anthropological Institute* (n.s.) 2 (1996): 517–35.

41. E-mail response from woman in Canada, 1 August 2000.

42. E-mail response from woman in the United States, 2 August 2000.

43. E-mail response from woman in the United States, 4 August 2000.

44. E-mail response from woman in the United States, 29 February 2000.

45. E-mail response from woman in the United States, 3 August 2000.

46. Interview with American woman, Dublin, August 1998.

47. Interview with professional genealogist, Dublin, 11 August 1998.

48. E-mail response from man in Canada, 16 August 2000.

49. E-mail response from woman in the United States, 3 August 2000. The comment on the destruction of records refers to the fire in the public record office in 1922 that resulted from shelling by pro-Treaty forces at the beginning of the Irish Civil War, and that largely destroyed the 1821, 1831, 1841, and 1851 census records, recorded wills, and many Church of Ireland parish registers and the earlier destruction of the 1861, 1871, 1881, and 1891 census records by order of the government during World War I. The reason for the earlier destruction of records remains disputed.

50. E-mail response from woman in Canada, 1 August 2000.

51. E-mail response from woman in Canada, 1 August 2000.

52. E-mail response from woman in Australia, 2 August 2000.

53. E-mail response from woman in the United States, 2 August 2000.

54. E-mail response from woman in the United States, 2 August 2000.

55. Franklin and McKinnon.

56. E-mail response from woman in the United States, 19 August 2000.

57. E-mail response from woman in Canada, 2 August 2000.

58. Edwards and Strathern.

4. Postcolonial Nobility, Diasporic Distinction, and the Politics of Recognition

1. Hugh Montgomery-Massingberd, ed., *Burke's Introduction to Irish Ancestry*, London: Burke's Peerage, Ltd., 1976; *Burke's Irish Family Records* (London: Burke's Peerage, Ltd., 1976). Irish titled and "non-titled" families continue to be included in Burke's Landed Gentry Series.

2. Montgomery-Massingberd, preface to *Burke's Irish Family Records*, vii–xiv, viii.

3. Montgomery-Massingberd, *Burke's Irish Family Records*, xiii.

4. William F. Marmion, "Nobiliary Titles in the Republic," *Irish Roots* 3 (1995): 6.

5. Pierre Bourdieu, *Distinction: A Social Critique of the Judgement of Taste* (London: Routledge, 1986).

6. The O'Neill's opening words were followed by an opening lecture by the Hon. Fionn (O'Neill) Morgan, Raymond O'Neill's sister. The O'Neill Summer School took place from Wednesday, 15 June to Saturday, 18 June 2005, at Shane's Castle, County Antrim. The quotations from speeches and descriptions of events are from my notes from attending the event.

7. Kathleen Neill, *O'Neill Commemorative Journal of the First International Gathering of the Clan, 20–27 June 1982,* (Belfast: Irish Genealogical Association, 1982), 3; "O'Neills Proclaim New Chieftain," *Belfast Telegraph,* 23 June 1982.

8. The Clans of Ireland, Ltd., http://www.theclansofIreland.ie/ (accessed 14 November 2004). See also Tony McCarthy, "A Link with our Ancient Past," *Irish Roots* 3 (1993): 22–23.

9. The Clans of Ireland, Ltd., http://www.theclansofIreland.ie/ (accessed 14 November 2004).

10. Thomas Matthews, *The O'Neills of Ulster: Their History and Genealogy* (Dublin: Sealy, Bryers and Walker, 1907).

11. Paul Gorry, "Clanassic Park," *Irish Roots* 3 (1993): 23–24.

12. Ray Ryan, "Reunion of Clans 'Uplifts Nation,'" *Examiner,* 12 August 1996, 2.

13. Though these events are popularly known as inaugurations, Fergus Gillespie argued that they are symbolic rather than actual inaugurations, for to claim to inaugurate a chief, a political leader, within a state's jurisdiction would be tantamount to treason (interview with Fergus Gillespie, 9 September 2005).

14. Speech by Hugo, The O'Neill of Clanaboy, at the launch of The O'Neill Summer School initiative in 2004. Available at http://www.oneillsummerschool.com/main.html.

15. Lord O'Neill, "The O'Neill Family," in *Shane's Castle and Nature Reserve: Official Guide* (Shane's Castle, Antrim: Lord O'Neill, 1987), n.p.

16. Terence O'Neill, Baron O'Neill of the Maine, *The Autobiography of Terence O'Neill* (London: Rupert Hart-Davies, 1972), 1.

17. Peter Beresford Ellis, *Erin's Blood Royal: the Gaelic Noble Dynasties of Ireland* (London: Constable, 1999), 239.

18. Attempts to explore the past in "cross-community" local history societies in Northern Ireland often carefully balance the desire to tackle sensitive subjects with the risk of alienating some participants and fracturing the social relationships developed through shared interests in "safer" historical subjects. I discuss this in more depth in "Local Histories in Northern Ireland," *History Workshop Journal* 60 (2005): 45–68.

19. Richard Warner, "Who Are the O'Neills." Paper presented at the O'Neill Summer School, 16 June 2005.

20. Brian Lacey, "The Northern Ui Neill, Ancestors of the O'Neills." Paper presented at the O'Neill Summer School, 16 June 2005.

21. Sean O'Faolain, *The Great O'Neill: A Biography of Hugh O'Neill, Earl of Tyrone, 1550–1616* (London: Longmans, Green. 1942).

22. Ibid., 144.

23. Brian Friel, *Making History* (London: Faber, 1989). Friel undoubtedly took up O'Faolain's suggestion: "If anyone wished to make a study of the manner in which historical myths are created he might well take O'Neill as an example, and beginning with his defeat and death trace the gradual emergence of a picture at which the original would have gazed from under his red eyelashes with a chuckle of cynical amusement and amazement. Indeed, in those last years in Rome the myth was already beginning to emerge, and a talented dramatist might write an informative, entertaining, ironical play on the theme of the living man helplessly watching his translation into a star in the face of all the facts that had reduced him to poverty, exile, and defeat" (O'Faolain, v). See also Barry Sloan, "'The Overall Thing': Brian Friel's *Making History*," *Irish Studies Review* 8 (1994): 12–16.

24. Hiram Morgan, "Patriot or Traitor: The Career of Hugh O'Neill, Great Earl of Tyrone." Paper presented at the O'Neill Summer School, 16 June 2005.

25. O'Faolain, 4.

26. Walter J. P. Curley, *Vanishing Kingdoms: The Irish Chiefs and Their Families* (Dublin: Lilliput Press, 2004), 28–29. Curley does not include Joyce in his list, since he is of Anglo-Norman descent, although this chief was formally recognized by the chief herald in 1990. This list is based on Curley's account, but its accuracy is subject to the death of chiefs and the transfer of title. For example, the death of Terence Maguire was reported in February 2005.

27. Susan Hood, *Royal Roots, Republican Inheritance: The Survival of the Office of Arms* (Dublin: Wolfhound Press, 2002), 105.

28. *Irish Times*, 24 March 1943, quoted in Hood, *Royal Roots*, 167.

29. Susan Hood, "Chief Herald," *Irish Times*, 10 October 1995.

30. Terence MacCarthy, The MacCarthy Mór, Prince of Desmond, *Ulster's Office 1552–1800, A History of the Irish Office of Arms from the Tudor Plantations to the Act of Union* (Little Rock, Ark.: Gryfons, 1996), 234.

31. Ibid., 235.

32. Ibid., 236.

33. Hood, 207.

34. MacLysaght, *Changing Times*, 190.

35. Edward MacLysaght, "The Irish Chieftainries," in *Burke's Introduction to Irish Ancestry* (London: Burke's Peerage, Ltd., 1976), 45–46.

36. MacLysaght, *Changing Times*, 191.

37. Gerard Crotty, "Chiefs of the Name," in *Aspects of Irish Genealogy II, Proceedings of the Second Irish Genealogical Congress*, ed. M. D. Evans (Dublin: Irish Genealogical Congress Committee, 1996), 20–32.

38. Ibid., 31.

39. Eoghan McNarey, "'I've Got a Little List . . . ': Gaelic Chiefship and the Irish Republic," *Irish Roots* 4 (1993): 14.

40. Ibid.

41. Gerard Crotty, 29.

42. Terence MacCarthy, *Ulster's Office*, 238.

43. McNarey, 15.

44. Karnbach, William Francis Marmion, Lord of Duhallow, *Gaelic Titles and Forms of Address: A Guide in the English Language* (Kansas City: Irish Genealogical Foundation, 1997).

45. Terence MacCarthy, *Ulster's Office*, 236.

46. MacLysaght, *Changing Times*, 199.

47. Terence MacCarthy, *Ulster's Office*, 236; emphasis in original.

48. Gerard Crotty, 30–31.

49. McNarey, 15.

50. Gerard Crotty, 31–32.

51. Ibid., 24.

52. McNarey, 15.

53. Terence MacCarthy, *Ulster's Office*, 238–39.

54. Peter Berresford Ellis, *Erin's Blood Royal: The Gaelic Noble Dynasties of Ireland* (New York: Palgrave, 2002). The first edition of this book, published by Constable in 1999, contained a foreword by MacCarthy. MacCarthy's strategy echoes an earlier hoax or delusional claim that Edward MacLysaght exposed. MacLysaght recounts the case of Raymond Moulton O'Brien, who "for the greater part of his life devoted his undoubted talents to building up a facade of such verisimilitude that he had, for a time at least, an almost unprecedented success in imposing not only upon the ignorant and credulous but also upon many responsible people whose acceptance of his pretentious claims is almost incredible, or would have been has not the facade been so cleverly erected" (MacLysaght, *Changing Times*, 211). O'Brien arrived in Ireland at the beginning of the second world war, claiming he was Earl of Thomond and The O'Brien and supported by a Mexican court judgment and newspaper reports. He called himself Prince on his children's birth certificates, faked a court case of slander against him, faked a chivalric order, attempted to get postage stamps issued for the principality of Thomond, claimed he had an embassy in Dublin, and had a report in a French newspaper state that the principality was an independent state in Ireland with its own currency (MacLysaght, *Changing Times*, 211–20).

55. Terence MacCarthy, MacCarthy Mór, Prince of Desmond, *The Niadh Nask, History, and International Roll, 1996* (Clonmel: Niadh Nask, 1996); the Count of Clandermond, *Links in a Golden Chain: A Collection of Essays on the History of the Niadh Nask or the Military Order of the Golden Chain* (Little Rock, Ark.: Gryfons, 1998).

56. Sean Murphy has contributed to and traced the controversy about the recognition of Gaelic titles and the MacCarthy case and gathered evidence for other allegedly false claims to title. This extensive material is available on his website, http://homepage.eircom.net/~seanjmurphy/chiefs/index.htm, and in his publications: Sean Murphy, *Erin's Fake Chiefs* (Bray: Centre for Irish Genealogical and Historical Research, 2001) and Sean J. Murphy, *Twilight of the Chiefs: The MacCarthy Mór Hoax* (Dublin: Maunsel, 2004).

57. Charles Lysaght, foreword to Curley, *Vanishing Kingdoms*, 16.

58. "Scottish and Irish Chiefs are appearing in *Burke's Peerage and Baronetage* for the first time, apart from those who have been listed before because they have also been peers or baronets. However, they represent an ancient aristocracy, part Gael, part Norse and part Fleming or Norman, and are generally of longer pedigree than the peers and baronets they are joining. Moreover most of the ancestors of the chiefs who are also peers or baronets were chiefs long before they acquired their other titles" (Hugh Peskett, "Scottish and Irish Chiefs," in *Burke's Peerage, Baronetage and Knightage, Clan Chiefs and Scottish Feudal Barons*, 107th ed., ed. Charles Mosley [Stokesley: Burke's Peerage and Gentry, 2003], li–lii).

59. Curley, 47.

60. Quoted in ibid., 27.

61. Anne Chambers, *At Arm's Length: Aristocrats in the Republic of Ireland* (Dublin: New Island, 2004), 17.

62. Ibid., 17.

63. Charles Lysaght, "The Irish Peers and the House of Lords—the Final Chapter," in *Burke's Peerage and Baronetage*, 106th ed., ed. Charles Mosley (London: Fitzroy Dearborn, 1999), xli–xlii.

64. Ronald P. Gadd, *The Peerage of Ireland, with Lists of All Irish Peerages Past and Present* (Dublin: Irish Peers Association, 1985).

65. Interview with Fergus Gillespie, Dublin, 8 September 2005.

66. Curley, 60–61.

67. Ellis, *Erin's Blood Royal*, 252.

68. Curley, 180.

69. Chambers, i–ii.

70. Ibid.

71. Grubgeld.

72. Chambers, 187.

73. Ibid., 188–89.

74. Ibid.

75. Several decades of Irish feminist history have followed the important early work establishing the field, which includes Margaret MacCurtain and Donncha O Corráin, ed., *Women in Irish Society: The Historical Dimension* (Dublin: Arlen House, 1978).

76. Montgomery-Massingberd, ed., *Burke's Irish Family Records*, xiv.

5. Of Ulster Stock: Native, Settler, and Entangled Roots in Northern Ireland

1. Longley; see also Máiréad Nic Craith, *Plural Identities, Singular Narratives: The Case of Northern Ireland* (New York and Oxford: Berghahn Books, 2002), and *Culture and Identity Politics in Northern Ireland* (Basingstoke: Palgrave Macmillan, 2003).

2. Ronnie H. Buchanan, "Ulster: Exploring the Common Ground," *Familia* 2 (1989): 52.

3. Jonathan Bardon, *A History of Ulster* (Belfast: Blackstaff Press, 1992), 400.

4. North of Ireland Family History Society, http://www.nifhs.org/.

5. This was evident in the concern that my research could damage the relationships built up through the careful management of the problem of religious or political difference or discomfort the members by raising questions of politics and identity, and it remains a risk as I write about it. This chapter draws on interview material from family history enthusiasts in Northern Ireland who were not members of the North of Ireland Family History Society as well as society members. I have not included any personal or family names for the sake of preserving anonymity. Nor have I used pseudonyms since doing so would be inappropriate given the loaded associations of both given and family names.

6. Alan D. Falconer, "Remembering," in *Reconciling Memories*, ed. Alan D. Falconer and Joseph Liechty (Dublin: Columba Press, 1998), 11–19; Frank Wright, "Reconciling the Histories of Protestant and Catholic in Northern Ireland," in *Reconciling Memories*, ed. Alan D. Falconer and Joseph Liechty (Dublin: Columba Press, 1998), 128–48; and Peter Pyne, "The Teaching of History to Adults in a Culturally Divided Society: A Northern Ireland Case Study (1)," *Etudes Irelandaise* 12 (1989): 171–91.

7. Interview, Donaghadee, 8 January 2005.

8. The North of Ireland Family History Society was first located at the back of Craigavon House, the former home of the unionist leader Edward Carson where Ulster Volunteers reputedly drilled in the years leading up to the first world war, and it was associated with loyalist paramilitary and cultural organizations in the 1980s.

9. Interview, Belfast, 21 February 2005.

10. Geoffrey Beattie, *Protestant Boy* (London: Granta, 2004), 8 and 6.

11. Ibid., 15.

12. Ibid., 9.

13. Ibid., 14.

14. Ibid., 10.

15. Interview, Belfast, 18 August 1998.

16. Peter Shirlow and Mark McGovern, "Introduction: Who Are 'the People'? Unionism, Protestantism, and Loyalism in Northern Ireland," in *Who Are 'the People'?: Unionism, Protestantism, and Loyalism in Northern Ireland*, ed. Peter Shirlow and Mark McGovern (London: Pluto Press, 1997), 1–15.

17. Beattie, 12, 13.

18. Máiréad Nic Craith, "Politicised Linguistic Consciousness: The Case of Ulster Scots," *Nations and Nationalism* 7, no. 1 (2001): 21–38.

19. Popular accounts serve this heightened interest such as those by Billy Kennedy, which include *Faith and Freedom: The Scots-Irish in America* (Belfast: Ambassador Productions, 1999); *Heroes of the Scots-Irish in America* (Belfast: Ambassador Productions, 2000); *The Making of America: How the Scots-Irish Shaped a Nation* (Belfast: Ambassador Productions, 2001); *Our Most Priceless Heritage: The Lasting Legacy of the Scots-Irish in America* (Belfast:

Ambassador Productions, 2005); and his regional accounts of the Scots-Irish in Tennessee, the Shenandoah Valley, Pennsylvania, and Kentucky, all published by Ambassador Productions, Belfast, and Emerald House, Greenville, S.C. As this list indicates, interest in Protestant migration from Ulster within the Ulster-Scots movement focuses predominantly on migration to the American South and much less, if at all, on migration from Ulster to Canada and the rest of North America.

20. Rory Fitzpatrick, *God's Frontiersmen: The Scots-Irish Epic* (London: Weidenfeld and Nicolson, 1989).

21. Women signed the parallel declaration. The digitized material can be accessed through the Public Record Office of Northern Ireland site: http://www.proni.gov.uk/ulster covenant/index.html.

22. Interview, Bangor, 7 March 2005.

23. This lack of "sense of place" is an example of wider Protestant reflections on their relation to a model of native belonging and the lack of an alternative model of collective connection to land and landscape. See Brian J. Graham, "No Place of the Mind: Contested Protestant Representations of Ulster," *Ecumene* 1, no. 3 (1994), 257–81.

24. David Hanson, foreword to *Our People, Our Times: A History of Northern Ireland's Cultural Diversity* exhibition catalogue, Northern Ireland Museums Council, 2005, 2, 25.

25. Jack Magee, untitled contribution to *Cultural Traditions in Northern Ireland: Varieties of Irishness*, ed. Maurna Crozier (Belfast: Institute of Irish Studies, 1989), 37.

26. Edna Longley, "Pulling Down the Cultural (De)fences," *Fortnight* 279 (1989): 30.

27. Brah, 208.

28. Interview, County Down, 6 January 2005.

29. *Local Identities: An Exploration of Cultural Identity*, Belfast: Northern Ireland Museums Council, Northern Ireland Regional Curators Group, 2000.

30. Interview, Omagh, 24 February 2005.

31. Interview, Bangor, 11 January 2005.

32. *Blood Ties*, BBC Northern Ireland, produced by Michael McGowan, Brian Waddell Productions, 2002.

33. The quotation comes from my transcription of episode 6 of *Blood Ties*.

34. Interview, Portstewart, 7 January 2005.

35. Interview, Bangor, 11 January 2005.

36. Interview, Ballymena, 16 February 2005.

37. Interview, Omagh, 24 February 2005.

38. Beattie, 51.

39. Ibid., 174.

40. John Winters, "Irish Genealogical Project: Genealogy in Ulster," *Irish Family History* 9 (1993): 26.

41. Beattie, 44.

42. Brian Graham and Peter Shirlow, "The Battle of the Somme in Ulster Memory and Identity," *Political Geography* 21 (2002): 881–904.

43. Ibid., 898.

44. I am very grateful to Mary Treanor for sharing her memories of Edmund, her family history, her perspectives, and her experiences with me and for letting me include this material here. We talked in her home in Belfast first in July 1998, again in 2001, and most recently in December 2005.

45. "Murder victim's family plead for an end to the killings," *Irish News*, 3 January 1998, 1; "Victim's mother pleads for peace," *Irish News*, 3 June 1999, 5.

46. Martin Anderson, "Killers Betrayed Their Own Country," *Irish News*, 28 November 1998, 5.

47. Buchanan, 52.

48. Jane Leonard, "The Twinge of Memory: Armistice Day and Remembrance Sunday in Dublin since 1919," in *Unionism and Modern Ireland: New Perspectives on Politics and Culture*, ed. Richard English and Graham Walker (Dublin: Gill and Macmillan, 1996), 99–114; see also Keith Jeffery, "The Great War in Modern Irish memory"; in *Men, Women, and War*, ed. T. G. Fraser and Keith Jeffery (Dublin: Lilliput Press, 1993), 136–57; Keith Jeffery, "Irish Culture and the Great War," *Bullán* 1, no. 2 (1994): 87–96; and Nuala C. Johnson, "The Spectacle of Memory: Ireland's Remembrance of the Great War, 1919," *Journal of Historical Geography* 25, no. 1 (1999): 36–56.

49. Myles Dungan, *They Shall Grow Not Old: Irish Soldiers and the Great War* (Dublin: Four Courts Press, 1997), 39–41.

50. Sebastian Barry, *The Whereabouts of Eneas McNulty* (London: Picador, 1998).

51. See, for example, Myles Dungan, *Irish Voices from the Great War* (Dublin: Irish Academic Press, 1995).

52. D. Sharrock, "Irish Factions Unite to Remember the Dead: Enmity Put Aside as Republic Honours Those Who Died in British Uniform," *Guardian*, 11 November 1995.

53. Interviews, Larne, 26 January 2005, and Belfast, 27 January 2005.

54. Hugo Hamilton, *The Speckled People* (London: Fourth Estate, 2003).

55. This term has recently been adopted by both loyalist and republican community activists to describe not the resolution of conflict but the process of changing the relationships, beliefs, and structures that support its continuation. See Peter Shirlow, Brian Graham, Kieran McEvoy, Félim Ó hAhmaill, and Dawn Purvis, *Politically Motivated Former Prisoner Groups: Community Activism and Conflict Transformation, a Research Report Submitted to the Northern Ireland Community Relations Council*.

56. Interview, Belfast, 2 March 2005.

57. I discuss the development of this policy in response to criticisms of forced or failed "cross-community" initiatives and debates about its potential to shore up ideas of fixed and singular collective identity in "Equity, Diversity, and Interdependence: Cultural Policy in

Northern Ireland," *Antipode* 37, no. 2 (2005): 272–300. It is argued that the terms of the peace process and the implementation of the Good Friday/Belfast Agreement have reinforced rather than undermined the polarization of the "two communities." See Peter Shirlow and Brendan Murtagh, *Belfast: Segregation, Violence, and the City* (London: Pluto Press, 2006).

58. Recent exhibitions include *War and Conflict in Twentieth-Century Ireland: A Travelling Exhibition from the Ulster Museum* in 2000, and *Conflict: The Irish at War*, Ulster Museum, 2004. See T. Parkhill and M. Ferguson, *Conflict: The Irish at War*, Belfast: Ulster Museum, National Museums and Galleries of Northern Ireland, 2004; and for his insightful reflections on commemoration, see Michael Longley, "Memory and Acknowledgement," *Irish Review* 17/18 (1995): 153–59.

59. *The Wings of The Seraphim*, Today and Yesterday in Northern Ireland Series, BBC Radio Ulster. Produced by Pat Loughrey and Douglas Carson and written and narrated by Douglas Carson. First broadcast on 12 November 1986, archived in BBC Northern Ireland Community Archive, Ulster Folk and Transport Museum, Cultra, County Down, Northern Ireland. For an account of the development of historical resources for schools on radio in Northern Ireland, see James Hawthorn, "Above Suspicion or Controversy? The Development of the BBC's Irish History Programme for Schools in Northern Ireland, a Personal Recollection," in *Broadcasting in a Divided Community: Seventy Years of the BBC in Northern Ireland*, ed. Martin McLoone (Belfast: Institute of Irish Studies, 1996), 51–65.

60. All quoted extracts are based on my transcription of the program. The extract from the Book of Revelation spoken by an unnamed woman is italicized.

61. This quotation comes from a short written version of the radio program. Douglas Carson, "The Wings of the Seraphim," in *Remembrance*, ed. Gordon Lucy and Elaine McClure (Belfast: Ulster Society Publications, 1997), 28.

62. Summary included in the archival record.

63. Conversation with Douglas Carson, 18 May 2007.

64. Brah, 208.

6. Irish Origins, Celtic Origins: Population Genetics, Cultural Politics

1. Brian Friel, *The Home Place* (Loughcrew: Gallery Books, 2005).

2. Ibid., 68.

3. A. C. Haddon and C. R. Browne, "The Ethnography of the Aran Islands, County Galway," *Proceedings of the Royal Irish Academy* 3rd series, 2 (1893): 768–830. This paper was one of pair that resulted from work by Haddon and Browne on the Aran Islands. See also A. C. Haddon, "Studies in Irish Craniology: The Aran Islands, Co. Galway," *Proceedings of the Royal Irish Academy* 3rd series, 2 (1893): 759–67.

4. D. J. Cunningham and A. C. Haddon, "The Anthropometric Laboratory of Ireland," *Journal of the Anthropological Institute of Great Britain and Ireland* 21 (1892): 35–39.

5. Scott Ashley traces the intimate relationships between romanticism and anthropology in the work of Haddon and Browne in "The Poetics of Race in 1890s Ireland: An Ethnography of the Aran Islands," *Patterns of Prejudice* 35, no. 2 (2001): 5–18. Ashley argues that the ambivalences in Haddon and Browne's work on the Aran Islands and its avoidance of a discourse of Irish racial inferiority reflected both this romanticism and Haddon's own equivocations on the question of race. He later coauthored an important critique of ideas of racial purity: Julian Huxley, A. C. Haddon, and A. M. Carr-Saunders, *We Europeans: A Survey of "Racial" Problems* (London: Jonathan Cape, 1935). Greta Jones also addresses the neglected significance of Haddon's early work in Ireland and demonstrates the tensions between the primitivism of Haddon's progressive evolutionism and the primitivism of antiquarian and later cultural nationalist celebration of Gaelic culture. However, in situating Haddon's work within Ireland's scientific and intellectual community, she makes the important point that "it would be wrong to pit a typically 'Irish' view of the primitive past, represented by the enthusiasts for Gaelic culture, and an 'English' view encapsulated by Haddon's evolutionary progressivism. The contested territory was not between England and Ireland but within Ireland itself" (Jones, "Contested Territories: Alfred Cort Haddon, Progressive Evolutionism, and Ireland," *History of European Ideas* 24, no. 3 [1998]: 205). The work of both authors suggests that if Friel loosely modeled his Dr. Gore on Haddon, then the prescience of his engagement with familiar and emerging accounts of biological difference is at the expense of doing justice to complexity of Haddon's position. The history of science in Ireland is occluded by Friel's simple model of colonial power and knowledge.

6. Friel, *The Home Place*, 36.

7. Donna J. Haraway, *Modest_Witness@Second Millennium_FemaleMan©_Meets_OncoMouse™: Feminism and Technoscience* (London: Routledge, 1997).

8. Nikolas Rose, "The Politics of Life Itself," *Theory, Culture, and Society* 18 (2001): 1–30; Carlos Novas and Nikolas Rose, "Genetic Risk and the Birth of the Somatic Individual," *Economy and Society* 29 (2000): 485–513.

9. Corrine Hayden, "A Biodiversity Sampler for the Millennium," in *Reproducing Reproduction: Kinship, Power, and Technological Innovation*, ed. Sarah Franklin and Helene Ragoné (Philadelphia: Univ. of Pennsylvania Press, 1998), 173–203; Jonathan Marks, "'We're Going to Tell These People Who They Really Are': Science and Relatedness," in *Relative Values: Reconfiguring Kinship Studies*, ed. Sarah Franklin and Susan McKinnon (Durham N.C.: Duke Univ. Press, 2001), 355–83.

10. O'Hart, *Irish Pedigrees*.

11. Emmeline Hill, "More about Genes: The Irish Really Are a Race Apart," *Inside Ireland: Your Guide to All Things Irish* 90 (Autumn 2000): 6. Also available as sample article at http//www.insideireland.com/sample19.htm.

12. Ibid., 6.

13. Emmeline Hill, Mark A. Jobling, and Daniel G. Bradley, "Y Chromosome Variation and Irish Origins: A Pre-neolithic Gene Gradient Starts in the Near East and Culminates in Western Ireland," *Nature* 204 (23 March 2000): 351–52.

14. Mark A. Jobling and Chris Tyler-Smith, "Fathers and Sons: The Y Chromosome and Human Evolution," *Trends in Genetics* 11 (1995): 449–56; Mark A. Jobling, "In the Name of the Father: Surnames and Genetics," *Trends in Genetics* 17, no. 6 (2001): 353–57.

15. Mark A. Jobling and Chris Tyler-Smith, "The Human Y Chromosome: An Evolutionary Marker Comes of Age," *Nature* 4 (2003): 598–612.

16. Edward MacLysaght, *The Surnames of Ireland* (1957; Dublin: Irish Academic Press, 1997).

17. Hill et al., 351.

18. Jobling, 354.

19. Hill, Jobling, and Bradley, 351.

20. Nancy Stepan, *The Idea of Race in Science: Great Britain 1800–1960* (London: Macmillan, 1982); Elazar Barkan, *The Retreat of Scientific Racism: Changing Concepts of Race in Britain and the United States between the World Wars* (Cambridge: Cambridge Univ. Press, 1992).

21. See Anne Byrne, Ricca Edmondson, and Tony Varley, introduction to *Family and Community in Ireland*, by Conrad M. Arensberg and Solon T. Kimball (1940; Ennis: CLASP Press, 2001), i–ci.

22. E. A. Hooton, "Stature, Head Form, and Pigmentation of Adult Male Irish," *American Journal of. Physical Anthropology* 26 (1940): 229–49; E. A. Hooton, and C. W. Dupertuis, *The Physical Anthropology of Ireland*. Papers of the Peabody Museum of Archaeology and Ethnology, Harvard Univ., 30, no. 1 and 2, (Cambridge, Mass.: Peabody Museum of Archaeology and Ethnology, Harvard Univ., 1955).

23. J. H. Relethford, "Genetic Structure and Population History of Ireland: A Comparison of Blood Group and anthropometric Analyses," *Annals of Human Biology* 10 (1983): 321–34; J. H. Relethford, "Effects of English Admixture and Geographic Distance on Anthropometric Variation in Nineteenth-Century Ireland," *American Journal of Physical Anthropology* 76 (1988): 111–24; J. H. Relethford, "Genetic Drift and Anthropometric Variation in Ireland," *Human Biology* 63 (1991): 155–65; J. H. Relethford, F. C. Lees, and M. H. Crawford, "Population Structure and Anthropometric Variation in Rural Western Ireland: Migration and Biological Differentiation," *Annals of Human Biology* 7 (1980): 411–28; J. H. Relethford, F. C. Lees, and M. H. Crawford, "Population Structure and Anthropometric Variation in Rural Western Ireland: Isolation by Distance and Analysis of the Residuals," *American Journal of Physical Anthropology* 55 (1981): 233–45; J. H. Relethford and M. H. Crawford, "Anthropometric Variation and the Population History of Ireland," *American Journal of Physical Anthropology* 96 (1995): 25–38.

24. Browne pursued his interests in the racial characteristics of "isolate populations" in the west of Ireland, especially in County Galway and County Mayo over the next decade.

25. W. E. R. Hackett, G. W. P. Dawson and C. J. Dawson, "The Pattern of the ABO Blood Group Frequencies in Ireland," *Heredity* 10 (1956): 69–84.

26. John H. Relethford, *Reflections of Our Past: How Human History Is Revealed in Our Genes* (Boulder: Westview Press, 2003), 187–206. See also John H. Relethford, "Anthropometric Data and Population History," in *Human Biologists in the Archives: Demography, Health, Nutrition, and Genetics in Historical Populations,* ed. D. Ann Herring and Alan C. Swedlund (Cambridge: Cambridge Univ. Press, 2003), 32–52.

27. W. E. R. Hackett, "A Rough Estimate of Two Main Racial Components in the Republic of Ireland Based on an Analysis of ABO Blood Group Frequencies," *Journal of the Irish Medical Association* 42 (1958): 86–88.

28. W. E. R. Hackett and M. E. Folan, "The ABO and Rh Blood Groups of the Aran Islanders," *Irish Journal of Medical Science* (June 1958): 247–61.

29. A. H. Bittles and M. T. Smith, "ABO and Rh(D) Blood Group Frequencies in the Ards Penninsula, Northeastern Ireland: Evidence for the Continuing Existence of a Major Politico-Religious Boundary," *Annals of Human Biology* 18 (1991): 253–58.

30. For a general account of pre-molecular-genetic studies, see E. Sunderland, D. Tills, C. Bouloux, and J. Doyle, "Genetic Studies in Ireland," in *Genetic Variation in Britain,* ed. D. F. Roberts and E. Sunderland (London: Taylor and Francis, 1973), 141–59. Martin Paul Evison argues that the "discovery of genetic variation at the DNA level has not made past migrations to the British Isles transparent, but it has served to indicate the complexity of population structure. Paradoxically, historical interpretations of genetic evidence tend to be couched in terms which indicate that romantic views of history continue to influence the scientific agenda" ("All in the Genes? Evaluating the Biological Evidence of Contact and Migration," in *Cultures in Contact: Scandinavian Settlement in England in the Ninth and Tenth Centuries,* ed. Dawn M. Hadley and Julian D. Richards [Turnhout, Belgium: Brespols, 2000], 277).

31. Emmiline Hill, "Who Are WE? It's in the Genes," *Inside Ireland: Your Guide to All Things Irish* 88 (Spring 2000): 22.

32. Gabriel Cooney, "Building the Future on the Past: Archaeology and the Construction of National Identity in Ireland," in *Nationalism and Archaeology in Europe,* ed. Margarita Días-Andreu and Timothy Champion (London: Univ. College London Press, 1996), 146–63; Gabriel Cooney, "Theory and Practice in Irish Archaeology," in *Theory in Archaeology: A World Perspective,* ed. Peter J. Ucko (London: Routledge, 1995), 263–77; Peter C. Woodman, "Who Possesses Tara? Politics in Archaeology in Ireland," in *Theory in Archaeology: A World Perspective,* ed. Peter J. Ucko (London: Routledge, 1995), 278–97.

33. J. P. Mallory, "The Origins of the Irish," *Journal of Irish Archaeology* 2 (1984): 65. This paper reports on the seminar held by the Irish Association of Professional Archaeologists on 5 May 1984. As Mallory, professor of archaeology at Queen's University in Belfast, reported, the question put to the seminar was when did the Irish first arrive in Ireland? "For the purposes of discussion, an Irishman was defined as one who spoke either the

earliest attested form of the Irish language or a language immediately ancestral to it. Such a definition then pertains to the appearance of Irish-speaking Celts and is not attendant on any other features such as physical type, material culture, or, obviously, is to be confused with the arrival of the first people in Ireland."

34. J. P. Mallory, "Two Perspectives on the Problem of Irish Origins," *Emania* 9 (1991): 53–58. Volume 9 of the archaeological journal *Emania* was devoted to papers on "Irish origins." J. P. Mallory and Barra Ó Donnagháin, "The Origins of the Population of Ireland: A Survey of Putative Immigrations in Irish Prehistory and History," *Emania* 17 (1998): 47–81, is a revised version of the discussion document prepared by the authors as part of the Royal Irish Academy initiative to seek government funding for the "Irish Origins" program.

35. Barra Ó Donnabháin, "aDNA and Archaeology," *Archaeology Ireland* 15, no. 2 (2001): 34–35.

36. Matthew Fordahl, "Scientists Use Irish Genes to Uncover Europe's Past," SF Gate. com, 23 March 2000. Available at http://www.sfgate.com (accessed 10 February 2004).

37. Patrick Loughrey, *The People of Ireland* (Belfast: Appletree Press, 1988).

38. Kearney, *Postnationalist Ireland*, 188.

39. Gabriel Cooney, "Genes and Irish Origins," *Archaeology Ireland* 14, no. 2 (2000): 29.

40. Gabriel Cooney, "Is It All in the Genes?" *Archaeology Ireland* 15, no. 1 (2000): 34–35, 35.

41. In contributing to the *Archaeology Ireland* debate, David T. Croke, of the department of biochemistry at the Royal College of Surgeons in Dublin, defended the work of Hill et al. from charges of geneticizing ethnicity. The criticisms by archaeologists, he argued, result from a "careless reading of research papers in human population genetics" that mistakes the use of ethnic categories in labeling samples for a belief in the genetic significance of those ethnic labels: "In short, geneticists place no greater credence in surnames or concepts of 'ethnicity' than do our colleagues in other disciplines" (David T. Croke, "Genetics and Archaeology: Synergy or Culture-Clash?" *Archaeology Ireland* 5, no. 4 [2001]: 37). But if academic archaeologists can be "careless" in their reading, wider "misreading" is also likely. According to this defense, geneticists can claim the credit for public engagement from the degree of media interest they generate but are absolved of responsibility of their work.

42. Dan Bradley and Emmeline Hill, "What's in a Surname? Geneticists Reply," *Archaeology Ireland* 14, no. 4 (2000): 23.

43. Ibid., 23.

44. John Beddoe, "On Complexional Differences between the Irish with Indigenous and Exotic Surnames Respectively," *Journal of the Anthropological Institute of Great Britain and Ireland* 27 (1898): 164.

45. Ibid., 166. Beddoe's sources were police gazette lists of deserters from the army, navy, and marines. The results suggested the "exotics" were much closer to the "indigenous" in eye color but not in hair color. Beddoe explained this in a convoluted fashion,

claiming that mixing led to greater environmental influence, with the result that those of mixed "exotic" and "indigenous" ancestry had lighter hair than the "indigenous" since Irish "climatic conditions are supposed to be favourable to bloods."

46. In Ireland, this is being led by historical and cultural geographer William J. Smyth. See his recent essay "Excavating, Mapping and Interrogating Ancestral Terrains: Towards a Cultural Geography of First and Second Names in Ireland," in *Surveying Ireland's Past: Multidisciplinary Essays in Honour of Anngret Simms*, ed. Howard B. Clarke, Jacinta Prunty, and Mark Hennessy (Dublin: Geography Publications, 2004), 243–80. A new research project to produce a new atlas of surnames in Ireland is underway under his leadership in the geography department of University College in Cork. Among its aims, it seeks to "i. map and analyse the changing distribution of a representative sample of Irish surnames since the 17th century plantations and 19th century migrations through to the early 21st century; ii. Establish the ethnic diversity of Irish society via an analysis of selected key family names and forenames." For details of the "Atlas of Irish Names" project, see http://www .ucc.ie/research/atlas/. Surnames are also being used in new isonymic studies of migration. A three-year isonymic study of Irish migration to the north of England in the second half of the nineteenth century has been undertaken in the department of anthropology of the University of Durham funded by the Economic and Social Research Council and led by Dr. Malcombe Smith.

47. Cooney, "Genes and Irish Origins," 29.

48. James C. Scott, John Tehranian, and Jeremy Mathias, "The Production of Legal Identities Proper to States: The Case of the Permanent Family Surname," *Comparative Studies in Society and History* 44, no. 1 (2002): 4–44.

49. Robert Bell, *The Book of Ulster Surnames* (Belfast: Blackstaff Press, 1988).

50. Bardon, 400–401.

51. Michael Hall, *Ulster: The Hidden History* (Belfast: Pretani Press, 1996), 68.

52. In discussion with Jim Mallory, 17 February 2005, Belfast.

53. Interview with Daniel Bradley, 25 January 2005, Dublin.

54. Bradley and Hill, 22.

55. In a footnote to his critique of oversimplified postcolonial interpretations of Irish history and politics, Stephen Howe comments that "it is extremely likely (so far as one can judge on the patchy available evidence) that for instance, a very high proportion of Catholic Nationalists in Northern Ireland today can trace their ancestry partly to Scots or English 'planters,' whilst at least as many Protestant Unionists have some 'Gaelic Irish' ancestry; and that—to go further back—there is a grain of probable truth in Ian Adamson's claims that many of the seventeenth-century Lowland Scots migrants to Ulster had distant Irish family origins. Within the next decade the Human Genome Diversity Project may shed some new light on these questions—but one may safely predict that it will not offer much support to anyone's nationalist claims" (Stephen Howe, *Ireland and Empire: Colonial Legacies in Irish History and Culture* [Oxford: Oxford Univ. Press, 2000], 278). Similarly, newspaper

reports sometimes present hopeful accounts of the potential of genetics to disprove ideas of fundamental difference between the "communities" in Northern Ireland, by showing that groups who "clearly have a different historical background" may "have a greater relatedness than might be assumed." See Dick Ahlstrom, "Groups Set to Research the Genetic Origins of the Irish," *Irish Times*, 31 July 2000. But Y-chromosome genetic studies are based on using surnames as indicators of different ancestry corresponding to these groups. Ethnicity is thus geneticized even if the geneticists overtly reject this as an interpretation of their work.

56. "'What constitutes the new emerging Irish nation adheres to a theory expressed back in the 1940s of being 'a sea fed by many streams.' 'My children are Irish, but they also have Red Indian blood. . . . So if we did a national DNA test in Ireland, you might come out with pretty bizarre results,' Henry Mount Charles maintains. 'It is all about understanding the complexities of what the Irish nation is about'" (Chambers, 190).

57. Bradley and Hill, 23.

58. Anonymous interview, Belfast, 2 March 2005.

59. I further discuss ways in which paternal and maternal descent and masculinity and femininity feature in Y-chromosome and mtDNA human population genetics in "Genetic Kinship," *Cultural Studies* 18, no. 1 (2004): 1–34.

60. Brian S. Turner, "Distributional Aspects of Family Name Study Illustrated in the Glens of Antrim" (Ph.D. dissertation, Queen's Univ., Belfast, 1974); Brian S. Turner, "Family Names: Notes and Queries on Derry's Top Ten," *Templemore: Journal of the North West Archaeological and Historical Society* 3 (1990): 46–48.

61. Brian S. Turner, "Distributional Study of Family Names," *Ulster Local Studies* 8, no. 3 (1983): 5–9, 6.

62. Brian S. Turner, "Scottish Borderers on an Irish Frontier: The Transformation of Lancie Armstrang," in *The Debateable Land: Ireland's Border Counties*, ed. Brian S. Turner (Belfast: Ulster Local History Trust in Association with the Heritage Council, 2002), 47.

63. Brian Turner, *Surname Landscape in the Country of Fermanagh* (Downpatrick: Turner Circle, 2003).

64. Brian Turner, review of Robert Bell, *The Book of Ulster Surnames* (Blackstaff Press, 1988), *Ulster Folklife* 35 (1989): 137–38.

65. Turner, "Distributional Study," 5.

66. Brian Turner and Aodán Mac Póilin, "What's in a Name," BBC Radio Ulster, 2001 and 2002.

67. Turner, "Scottish Borderers," 49.

68. Ibid., 48.

69. Ibid., 49.

70. Brian S. Turner, "An Observation on Settler Names in Fermanagh," *Clogher Record* 8, no. 3 (1974): 289.

71. Interview with Brian Turner, 23 October 2000.

72. Interview with Daniel Bradley, 25 January 2005, Dublin.

73. Jan Battles, "The Irish Are Not Celts, Say Experts," *Sunday Times,* 5 September 2004, 6.

74. Brian McEvoy, Martin Richards, Peter Forster, and Daniel G. Bradley, "The *Longue Durée* of Genetic Ancestry: Multiple Genetic Marker Systems and Celtic Origins on the Atlantic Facade of Europe," *American Journal of Human Genetics* 75 (2004): 693–702.

75. This may reflect the fact that you cannot sample mtDNA in a way that avoids mtDNA inheritance derived from "incursions" from outside, as Hill et al. do for Y chromosomes using patrilineal surnames.

76. McEvoy et al., "The *Longue Durée* of Genetic Ancestry," 699. Similar claims are made in other studies using the Y chromosome and which, again, select volunteers to give samples on the basis of having "Irish Gaelic surnames" ("Genes Link Celtic to Basques" BBC News Online, 3 April 2001, http://news.bbc.co.uk/1/hi/Wales/1246894.stm [accessed 1 March 2004]).

77. Cooney, "Building the Future on the Past," 155.

78. Mallory and Ó Donnagháin, "The Origins of the Population of Ireland," 62. Richard B. Warner, "Cultural Intrusions in the Early Iron Age: Some Notes," *Emania* 9 (1991): 44–52.

79. Lorraine Evans, *Kingdom of the Ark: That Startling Story of How the Ancient British Race Is Descended from the Pharaohs* (New York: Simon and Schuster, 2000).

80. Joep Leerson traces the multiple meanings of the Celtic since it earliest constructions in the early eighteenth century. See Joep Leerson, "Celticism," in *Celticism,* ed. Terence Brown (Amsterdam: Rodopi, 1996), 1–20.

81. Interview with Daniel Bradley, 25 January 2005, Dublin.

82. Jan Battles, "The Irish Are Not Celts," 6.

83. This quotation comes from a letter by Edward Lethwich to the *Dublin Chronicle* in 1788 and is quoted in O'Halloran, 67.

84. Interview with Richard Warner, 14 June 2005.

85. Liam Clarke and Richard Woods, "Irish People Are More English Than Celtic," *Sunday Times* [Ireland] 14 November 1999, 3.

86. Http://www.irish-association.ie/welcome.htm (accessed 16 May 2003). Warner's speech to the association followed earlier engagement with questions of difference. In 1967 the historical geographer Estyn Evans delivered a speech on "the Irishness of the Irish" that also argued that "a pure race is a nationalist myth," although he was interested in how "the proportions of the various racial elements in the mixture vary from one region to another," and he undertook anthropometric studies to explore this variation. E. Estyn Evans, *The Irishness of the Irish* (Belfast: Irish Association for Cultural, Economic, and Social Relations, 1967).

87. Interview with Richard Warner, Belfast, 14 June 2005.

88. "Genetically Modified Archaeology," *Archaeology Ireland* 13, no. 4 (1999): 45.

89. "Nationalist Myth Challenged: John Tyndall Comments on Some New Evidence," *Spearhead*, http://www.spearhead-uk.com/0001-jt3.html (accessed 16 March 2003).

90. Http://www.scottishloyalists.com/myth.htm (accessed 2 February 2005).

91. Nic Craith, *Plural Identities*, 83–88.

92. Ian Adamson, *The Cruthin: The Ancient Kindred* (Newtownards: Nosmada Books, 1974). See Nic Craith, *Plural Identities*, 93–113.

93. Interview with Richard Warner, Belfast, 14 June 2005. In 1996 a controversy arose over reports in the British *Sunday Times* of evidence of Roman presence in Ireland that drew in part on Richard Warner's work and was framed by a similar anti-Irish condescension. Richard Warner, "De Bello Hibernico: A Less Than Edifying Debate," *Archaeology Ireland* 10 (1996): 38–40.

94. "Trace Your Border Reiver Roots by DNA!" *Ulster Scot*, July 2004, 6.

95. Turner, "Scottish Borderers," 49.

96. Andrew Murphy, "Ireland and Ante/Anti-colonial Theory," *Irish Studies Review* 7, no. 2 (1999): 153–62.

97. The heated debate that took place on the History Channel online discussion list in March 2005 is one example of the depth of feeling that can be invested in these categories and histories (http://www.thehistorychannel.co.uk/site/_debate/index3.php?BBsite=HISTORY_&forum_id=2&topic_id=8644 [accessed 30 May 2005]).

98. Lentin, "Responding to the Racialisation of Irishness."

99. Neville Cox, "Referendum on Citzenship," letter to the editor, *Irish Times*, 10 May 2004.

100. Hill, "Who Are WE?" 22.

7. Irish DNA: Genetic Distance and Connection in Diasporic Genealogies

1. Nicolas Wade, "If New York's Irish Claim Nobility, Science May Back Up the Blarney," *New York Times*, 18 January 2006.

2. Jan Battles, "High King Niall: The Most Fertile Man in Ireland," *Sunday Times* [Ireland], 15 January 2006, 3; David McKittrick, "The True Father of Ireland; Niall of the Nine Hostages: 1,500 Years after His Death, He Has up to 3 Million Descendants," *Belfast Telegraph*, 21 January 2006, 22–23; "Medieval Irish Warlord Boasts 3 Million Descendants," *New Scientist*, 18 January 2006; "An Irish King Rules Gene Pool," *LA Times*, 21 January 2006. Other reports on the research included the online *National Geographic News* where the study featured in the report by James Owen, "Millions of Men May Be Descended from Irish King, Study Says," 20 January 2006, available at http://news.nationalgeographic.com/news/2006/01/0120_060120_irish_men.html (accessed 7 February 2006), and the MSNBC Web site, which featured a Reuters report by Siobhan Kennedy with the headline "Irish King Left a Wide Genetic Trail: Scientists Say 3 Million Men Are Descended

from Niall of the Nine Hostages." Available at http://msnbc.msn.com/id/10892117/ (accessed 7 February 2006).

3. Laoise T. Moore, Brian McEvoy, Eleanor Cape, Katharine Simms, and Daniel G. Bradley, "A Y-Chromosome Signature of Hegemony in Gaelic Ireland," *American Journal of Human Genetics* 78 (2006): 334–38.

4. Ibid., 334.

5. Irish-DNA is one of hundreds of general and specialized discussion lists hosted by RootsWeb.com. It was founded in October 2004. List discussions are archived at http://archiver.rootsweb.com/th/index/IRISH-DNA/. Yahoo also hosts a similar list devoted to discussions of the use of genetic tests in tracing Irish roots also called Irish-DNA (http://groups.yahoo.com/group/Irish-DNA/).

6. Clans of Ireland, Ltd., http://www.theclansofireland.ie/dna.html (accessed 5 January 2006).

7. "Matching Niall Nógiallach—Niall of the Nine Hostages," http://www.family treedna.com/matchnialltest.html (accessed 7 February 2006).

8. Irish Heritage DNA Project, http://homepage.eircom.net/~ihdp/ihdp/index.htm (accessed 5 January 2006).

9. These programs include documentaries on new genetic research on human origins such as *The Human Journey* by National Geographic screened in the United States in 2004, the two BBC television series on celebrity genealogies, *Who Do You Think You Are?* of 2005 and 2006, the U.S. PBS series on the genetic ancestry of prominent African Americans *African American Lives* screened in February 2006, and the documentary on the genetic exploration of the ancestry of black British people *Motherland: A Genetic Journey* shown on BBC television in 2003.

10. Debora A. Bolnick, "'Showing Who They Really Are': Commercial Ventures in Genetic Genealogy," paper presented at the American Anthropological Association Annual Meeting, 22 November 2003; Paul Brodwin, "Genetics, Identity, and the Anthropology of Essentialism," *Anthropological Quarterly* 75 (2002): 323–30; Carl Elliott and Paul Brodwin, "Identity and Genetic Ancestry Tracing," *British Medical Journal* 325 (2002): 1469–71; Bob Simpson, "Imagined Genetic Communities: Ethnicity and Essentialism in the Twenty-first Century," *Anthropology Today* 16 (2000): 3–6; Richard Tutton, "'They Want to Know Where They Came From': Population Genetics, Identity, and Family Genealogy," *New Genetics and Society* 23 (2004): 105–20.

11. Interview with Patrick Guinness, Furness, County Kildare, Ireland, 20 February 2006.

12. Brian McEvoy's thesis was completed in 2005 and is being published in jointly authored papers on population genetics in Ireland. See Brian Patrick McEvoy, "Genetic investigation of Irish ancestry and surname history" (Ph.D. dissertation, Trinity College Dublin, 2005).

13. "Matching Niall Nógiallach."

14. HUGO Gene Nomenclature Committee is the international standard body based in University College, London, which controls and oversees the numbering of human genes, chromosomes, and chromosome segments including Y-chromosome segments or loci. See http://www.gene.ucl.ac.uk/nomenclature/.

15. The first page of the company website publicizes the "2805 Surname projects" being undertaken and the "36773 unique surnames" that are being explored through their Y-chromosome tests (http://www.ftdna.com; accessed 15 February 2006).

16. Clan McMahon, http://mcmahonsofmonaghan.org/mcmachon_dna_project.html (accessed 6 January 2006).

17. O'Donoghue Society, http://www.odonoghue.co.uk/guests/projects/view_project .php?ProjID=1 (accessed 15 February 2006).

18. Byrne DNA Project, http://www.byrneclan.org/phylogen_chart_1.htm (accessed 12 May 2006).

19. Clan Ó Cléirigh DNA Project, http://www.familytreedna.com/public/ocleirigh (accessed 6 January 2006).

20. McCabe DNA Surname Project, http://www.familytreedna.com/public/McCabe/ (accessed 6 January 2006).

21. O'Shea DNA Project, http:// www2.smumn.edu/uasal/DNAWWW/overview.html (accessed 7 June 2004).

22. O'Neill Project, http://www.familytreedna.com/public/oneill (accessed 6 January 2006).

23. O'Shea DNA Project.

24. Clan O'Driscoll DNA Project, http://www.odriscolls.me.uk/dna_project.htm (accessed 6 January 2006).

25. MacTighernan DNA Test, http://www.mctiernan.com/dnatest.htm (accessed 15 February 2006).

26. O'Donoghue Society, http://www.odonoghue.co.uk/guests/society/society.php (accessed 15 February 2006).

27. The Royal Order of Onaghts O Donnchadha, Official Launch Document, http:// www.odonoghue.co.uk/guests/history/tribes.php (accessed 15 February 2006).

28. The Royal Order of Onaghts O Donnchadha, Official Launch Document.

29. Interview with Patrick Guinness.

30. O'Donoghue Society, http://www.odonoghue.co.uk/guests/projects/view_project .php?ProjID=1 (accessed 15 February 2006).

31. O'Brien Clan, http://www.obrienclan.com/DNA.htm#FAQs (accessed 17 January 2006).

32. WorldFamilies.net, http://www.worldfamilies.net/surnames/o/neal/disc.html (accessed 6 January 2006).

33. McManus Family History, http://members.aol.com/manus/mcmanus_frames.htm (accessed 15 January 2006).

34. Ibid.

35. Ibid.

36. E. A. Foster et al., "Jefferson Fathered Slave's Last Child," *Nature* 396 (5 November 1998): 27–28.

37. Clan O'Driscoll DNA Project.

38. *Ysearch* and *mitosearch* are free public databases run by Family Tree DNA that allow those who have done tests though Family Tree DNA and other testing companies to search for "genetic matches." See http://www.ysearch.org and http://www.mitosearch .org.

39. Curtin Clan DNA Project, http://home.comcast.net/%7Enealcurtin/genetic genealogy.htm (accessed 15 January 2006).

40. The claim by geneticists to have identified a haplotype for the Cohanim Jewish priestly caste is one of the famous cases in the field. The research was based on examining the Y chromosome of men with the Cohen surname associated with the Cohanim group and establishing a haplotype based on the most commonly found markers. Though the research has been criticized both for its statistical assumptions and for its conflation of a cultural group with a biological lineage, it has nevertheless led to Family Tree DNA and other companies offering to tell whether a male customer has Jewish ancestry. For a critique of the Cohanim study, see Marks, 355–83.

41. MacTighernan DNA Test.

42. Ibid.

43. Interview with Patrick Guinness.

44. Interview with Barra McCain, Oxford, Mississippi, 7 March 2006.

45. For further details, see the project Web site at http://freepages.genealogy.roots web.com/~mccaindna/ (accessed 9 January 2006).

46. Interview with Barra McCain.

47. Ibid.

48. Clan O'Driscoll DNA Project.

49. E-mail message to author from an Irish surname project co-ordinator, 12 February 2006. Details changed to protect author's anonymity.

50. Interview with Patrick Guinness.

51. http://www.ftdna.com/(0ikehdik13wx3m45aghshs55)/mtResDisplay.aspx? (accessed 13 January 2006).

52. Bryan Sykes, *The Seven Daughters of Eve* (London: Bantam Press, 2001). I discuss his work and gendering of geneticist's accounts of genetic lineage in "Genetic Kinship."

53. Clan O'Driscoll DNA Project. I am forcing the comparison here. The genealogical details were not presented alongside the interpretation of the mtDNA results in the

way I have presented them here for the sake of contrast. The genealogical details were accessed through a hyperlink on a table of participants.

54. Interview with Barra McCain.

55. Interview with Patrick Guinness.

56. Battles, "High King Niall."

57. T. Zerjal et al., "The Genetic Legacy of the Mongols," *American Journal of Human Genetics* 72 (2003): 717–21.

58. Owen, http://news.nationalgeographic.com/news/2006/01/0120_060120_irish_men.html.

59. "SciGuy: A science blog with Eric Berger," 18 and 19 January 2006, http://blogs.chron.com/sciguy/archives/2006/01/to_the_victors.html (accessed 7 February 2006).

60. Moore et al., 338.

61. Interview with Patrick Guinness.

62. Wade.

63. Susan McKinnon, *Neo-liberal Genetics: The Myths and Moral Tales of Evolutionary Psychology* (Chicago: Prickly Paradigm Press, 2005).

64. Interview with Patrick Guinness.

65. The use of Y-chromosome genetics in Irish clan associations effectively reinforces the masculinist implications of diaspora's etymological association with dissemination as argued by Stefan Helmreich, "Kinship, Nation, and Paul Gilroy's Concept of Diaspora," *Diaspora* 2 (1993): 243–49.

66. There is now an extensive literature on gender, sexuality, and Irish history. Breda Gray's work has developed existing scholarship on the social history of women in the diaspora through her sophisticated engagements with the gendering of home and migration. See Breda Gray, *Women and the Irish Diaspora* (London: Routledge, 2004).

8. Conclusion

1. Michel Foucault, "Nietzsche, Genealogy, History," in *Language, Counter-Memory, Practice: Selected Essays and Interviews*, trans. Donald F. Bouchard and Sherry Simon, ed. Donald F. Bouchard (Ithaca, N.Y.: Cornell University Press, 1977), 147, 162.

Bibliography

Adamson, Ian. *The Cruthin: The Ancient Kindred*. Newtownards: Nosmada Books, 1974.

African American Lives. Thirteen/WNET New York and Kunhardt Productions, screened on PBS February 2006.

Ahlstrom, Dick. "Groups Set to Research the Genetic Origins of the Irish." *Irish Times*. 31 July 2000.

Ahmed, Sara, Claudia Castañeda, Anne-Marie Fortier, and Mimi Sheller. "Introduction: Uprootings/Regroundings: Questions of Home and Migration." In *Uprootings/Regroundings: Questions of Home and Migration*, edited by Sara Ahmed, Claudia Castañeda, Anne-Marie Fortier, and Mimi Sheller, 1–19. Oxford: Berg, 2003.

Akenson, Donald Harman. "The Historiography of the Irish in the United States." In *The Irish in the New Communities*. Vol. 2 of *The Irish World Wide: History, Heritage, Identity*, edited by Patrick O'Sullivan, 99–127. Leicester: Leicester Univ. Press, 1992.

———. *The Irish Diaspora: A Primer*. Belfast: Institute of Irish Studies, 1993.

———. "The Irish in North America." *Éire-Ireland* 21, no. 1 (1986): 122–29.

———. "Irish Migration to North America, 1800–1920." In *The Irish Diaspora*, edited by Andy Bielenberg, 111–38. Harlow: Pearson Education, 2000.

Alba, Richard D. *Ethnic Identity: The Transformation of White America*. New Haven: Yale Univ. Press, 1990.

Allen, Theodore W. *Racial Oppression and Social Control*. Vol. 1 of *The Invention of the White Race*. London: Verso, 1994.

Anderson, Martin. "Killers Betrayed Their Own Country." *Irish News*. 28 Nov. 1998, 5.

Arrowsmith, Aidan. "Fantasy Ireland: The Figure of the Returnee in Irish Culture." *Moving Worlds: A Journal of Transcultural Writing* 3, no. 1 (2003): 101–14.

Ashley, Scott. "The Poetics of Race in 1890s Ireland: An Ethnography of the Aran Islands." *Patterns of Prejudice* 35, no. 2 (2001): 5–18.

Bardon, Jonathan. *A History of Ulster.* Belfast: Blackstaff Press, 1992.

Barkan, Elazar. *The Retreat of Scientific Racism: Changing Concepts of Race in Britain and the United States between the World Wars.* Cambridge: Cambridge Univ. Press, 1992.

Barrett, James R., and David Roediger. "Inbetween Peoples: Race, Nationality, and the 'New Immigrant' Working Class." *Journal of American Ethnic History* 16 (1997): 3–44.

Barry, Sebastian. *The Whereabouts of Eneas McNulty.* London: Picador, 1998.

Battles, Jan. "High King Niall: The Most Fertile Man in Ireland." *Sunday Times.* [Ireland] 15 Jan. 2006, 3.

———. "The Irish Are Not Celts, Say Experts." *Sunday Times.* [Ireland] 5 Sept. 2004, 6.

Beattie, Geoffrey. *Protestant Boy.* London: Granta, 2004.

Beddoe, John. "On Complexional Differences between the Irish with Indigenous and Exotic Surnames Respectively." *Journal of the Anthropological Institute of Great Britain and Ireland* 27 (1898): 164–70.

Bell, Robert. *The Book of Ulster Surnames.* Belfast: Blackstaff Press, 1998.

Bittles, A. H., and M. T. Smith. "ABO and Rh(D) Blood Group Frequencies in the Ards Peninsula, Northeastern Ireland: Evidence for the Continuing Existence of a Major Politico-Religious Boundary." *Annals of Human Biology* 18 (1991): 253–58.

Blood Ties. BBC Northern Ireland. Produced by Michael McGowan, Brian Waddell Productions, 2002.

Bolnick, Debora A. "'Showing Who They Really Are': Commercial Ventures in Genetic Genealogy." Paper presented at the American Anthropological Association Annual Meeting, 22 Nov. 2003.

Bouquet, Mary. "Family Trees and Their Affinities: The Visual Imperative of the Genealogical Diagram." *Journal of the Royal Anthropological Institute* (NS) 2 (1994): 43–66.

Bourdieu, Pierre. *Distinction: A Social Critique of the Judgement of Taste.* London: Routledge, 1986.

Boyarin, Daniel, and Jonathan Boyarin. "Diaspora: Generation and the Ground of Jewish Identity." *Critical Enquiry* 19 (1993): 693–725.

Bradley, Dan, and Emmeline Hill. "What's in a Surname? Geneticists Reply." *Archaeology Ireland* 14, no. 4 (2000): 23.

Brah, Avtar. *Cartographies of Diaspora: Contesting Identities.* London: Routledge, 1996.

Brett, David. *The Construction of Heritage.* Cork: Cork Univ. Press, 1996.

Brodwin, Paul. "Genetics, Identity, and the Anthropology of Essentialism." *Anthropological Quarterly* 75 (2002): 323–30.

Brown, Katharine. "Reflections on Family History: The Musings of an Irreverent Colonial." *Familia* 12 (1996): 25–35.

Buchanan, Ronnie H. "Ulster: Exploring the Common Ground." *Familia* 2 (1989): 52–59.

Byrne, Anne, Ricca Edmondson, and Tony Varley. Introduction to *Family and Community in Ireland*, by Conrad M. Arensberg and Solon T. Kimball. 1940; Ennis: CLASP Press, 2001.

Byrne, Michael. "Irish Family History News." *Irish Family History* 3 (1987): 5–9.

———. "Irish Parish Register Indexing Projects." *Irish Family History* 1 (1985): 19–26.

———. "Report on Research Activities in Ireland 1985–1986." *Irish Family History* 2 (1986): 7–22.

Byron, Reginald. "Ethnicity at the Limit: Ancestry and the Politics of Multiculturalism in the United States." *Anthropological Journal of European Cultures* 8, no. 1 (1999): 9–30.

———. *Irish America*. Oxford: Clarendon Press, 1999.

Cairns, David, and Shaun Richards. *Writing Ireland: Colonialism, Nationalism, and Culture*. Manchester: Manchester Univ. Press, 1997.

Canny, Nicholas. *Making Ireland British, 1580–1650*. Oxford: Oxford Univ. Press, 2001.

Carey, John. *The Irish National Origin-Legend: Synthetic Pseudohistory*. Quiggen Pamphlets on the Sources of Mediaeval Gaelic History, Department of Anglo-Saxon, Norse, and Celtic, Univ. of Cambridge, Cambridge, 1994.

Carson, Douglas. "The Wings of the Seraphim." In *Remembrance*, edited by Gordon Lucy and Elaine McClure, 28–30. Belfast: Ulster Society Publications, 1997.

Chambers, Anne. *At Arm's Length: Aristocrats in the Republic of Ireland*. Dublin: New Island, 2004.

Clarke, Liam, and Richard Woods. "Irish People Are More English Than Celtic." [Ireland] *Sunday Times*. 14 November 1999, 3.

Clifford, James. *Routes: Travels and Translation in the Late Twentieth Century*. Cambridge, Mass.: Harvard Univ. Press, 1997.

Colburn, David R., and George E. Pozzetta. "Race, Ethnicity, and the Evolution of Political Legitimacy." In *The Sixties: From Memory to History*, edited by David Farber, 119–48. Chapel Hill: Univ. of North Carolina Press, 1994.

Comerford, R. V. *Inventing the Nation: Ireland.* London: Arnold and Oxford Univ. Press, 2003.

Cooney, Gabriel. "Building the Future on the Past: Archaeology and the Construction of National Identity in Ireland." In *Nationalism and Archaeology in Europe,* edited by Margarita Días-Andreu and Timothy Champion, 146–63. London: Univ. College London Press, 1996.

————. "Genes and Irish Origins." *Archaeology Ireland* 14, no. 2 (2000): 29.

————. "Is It All in the Genes?" *Archaeology Ireland* 15, no. 1 (2000): 34–35.

————. "Theory and Practice in Irish Archaeology." In *Theory in Archaeology: A World Perspective,* edited by Peter J. Ucko, 263–77. London: Routledge, 1995.

Count of Clandermond. *Links in a Golden Chain: A Collection of Essays on the History of the Niadh Nask or the Military Order of the Golden Chain.* Little Rock, Ark.: Gryfons Publishers and Distributors, 1998.

Cox, Neville. "Referendum on Citizenship." Letter to the editor. *Irish Times.* 10 May 2004.

Croke, David T. "Genetics and Archaeology: Synergy or Culture-Clash?" *Archaeology Ireland* 15, no. 4 (2001): 36–37.

Cronin, Michael. "Speed Limits: Ireland, Globalisation, and the War against Time." In *Reinventing Ireland: Culture, Society, and the Global Economy,* edited by Peadar Kirby, Luke Gibbons, and Michael Cronin, 54–66. London and Sterling, Va.: Pluto Press, 2002.

Crotty, Gerard. "Chiefs of the Name." In *Aspects of Irish Genealogy II, Proceedings of the Second Irish Genealogical Congress,* edited by M. D. Evans, 20–32. Dublin: Irish Genealogical Congress Committee, 1996.

Crotty, William. "Introduction: The Irish Way in World Affairs." In *Ireland on the World Stage,* edited by William Crotty and David E. Schmitt, 1–23. Harlow: Longman, 2002.

Crowley, Ethel, and Jim Mac Laughlin, eds. *Under the Belly of the Tiger: Class, Race, Identity, and Culture in Global Ireland.* Dublin: Irish Reporter Publications, 1997.

Cunningham, D. J., and A. C. Haddon. "The Anthropometric Laboratory of Ireland." *Journal of the Anthropological Institute of Great Britain and Ireland* 21 (1892): 35–39.

Curley, Walter J. P. *Vanishing Kingdoms: The Irish Chiefs and Their Families.* Dublin: Lilliput Press, 2004.

Curtis, L. Perry. *Apes and Angels: The Irishman in Victorian Caricature.* 1971; Washington, D.C.: Smithsonian Institution Press, 1997.

Daly, Mary. "Revisionism and Irish History: The Great Famine." In *The Making of Modern Irish History: Revisionism and the Revisionist Controversy*, edited by D. George Boyce and Alan O'Day, 71–89. London: Routledge, 1996.

Davis, Graham. "The Historiography of the Irish Famine." In *The Meaning of the Famine*, edited by Patrick O'Sullivan, 13–39. London: Leicester Univ. Press, 1997.

Delaney, Enda, and Donald M. MacRaild. "Irish Migration, Networks, and Ethnic Identities since 1750: An Introduction." *Immigrants and Minorities* 23, no. 2–3 (2005): 127–42.

Deleuze, Gilles, and Félix Guattari. *A Thousand Plateaus: Capitalism and Schizophrenia*. Minneapolis: Univ. of Minnesota Press, 1988.

Donnelly, James S., Jr. "The Construction of the Memory of the Famine in Ireland and the Irish Diaspora, 1850–1900." *Éire/Ireland* 31, no. 1 and 2 (1996): 26–61.

Doyle, David Noel. "The Irish in North America, 1776–1845." In *A New History of Ireland*. Vol. 5 of *Ireland under the Union, I, 1801–70*, edited by W. E. Vaughan, 682–725. Oxford: Oxford Univ. Press, 1989.

———. "The Remaking of Irish-America, 1845–80." In *A New History of Ireland*. Vol. 6 of *Ireland under the Union, II, 1870–1976*, edited by W. E. Vaughan, 725–63. Oxford: Oxford Univ. Press, 1996.

———. "Scots Irish or Scotch-Irish." In *Making the Irish American: History and Heritage of the Irish in the United States*, edited by J. J. Lee and Marion R. Casey, 151–70. New York: New York Univ. Press, 2006.

Dungan, Myles. *Irish Voices from the Great War*. Dublin: Irish Academic Press, 1995.

———. *They Shall Grow Not Old: Irish Soldiers and the Great War*. Dublin: Four Courts Press, 1997.

Eagan, Catherine M. "'Still 'Black' and 'Proud': Irish America and the Racial Politics of Hibernophilia." In *The Irish in Us: Irishness, Performativity, and Popular Culture*, edited by Diane Negra, 20–63. Durham, N.C.: Duke Univ. Press, 2006.

Edwards, Jeanette. *Born and Bred: Idioms of Kinship and New Reproductive Technologies in England*. Oxford: Oxford Univ. Press, 2000.

Edwards, Jeanette, and Marilyn Strathern. "Including Our Own." In *Cultures of Relatedness: New Approaches to the Study of Kinship*, edited by Janet Carsten, 149–66. Cambridge: Cambridge Univ. Press, 2000.

Elliott, Carl, and Paul Brodwin. "Identity and Genetic Ancestry Tracing." *British Medical Journal* 325 (2002): 1469–71.

Ellis, Peter Berresford. *Erin's Blood Royal: The Gaelic Noble Dynasties of Ireland.* London: Constable, 1999.

———. *Erin's Blood Royal: The Gaelic Noble Dynasties of Ireland.* New York: Palgrave, 2002.

Evans, E. Estyn. *The Irishness of the Irish.* Belfast: Irish Association for Cultural, Economic, and Social Relations, 1967.

Evans, Lorraine. *Kingdom of the Ark: That Startling Story of How the Ancient British Race Is Descended from the Pharaohs.* New York: Simon and Schuster, 2000.

Evison, Martin Paul. "All in the Genes? Evaluating the Biological Evidence of Contact and Migration." In *Cultures in Contact: Scandinavian Settlement in England in the Ninth and Tenth Centuries,* edited by Dawn M. Hadley and Julian D. Richards, 277–94. Turnhout, Belgium: Brespols, 2000.

Falconer, Alan D. "Remembering." In *Reconciling Memories,* edited by Alan D. Falconer and Joseph Liechty, 11–19. Dublin: Columba Press, 1998.

Fanning, Bryan. *Racism and Social Change in the Republic of Ireland.* Manchester: Manchester Univ. Press, 2002.

Fitzpatrick, David. "Emigration, 1801–70." In *A New History of Ireland.* Vol. 5 of *Ireland under the Union, I, 1801–70,* edited by W. E. Vaughan, 562–607. Oxford: Oxford Univ. Press, 1989.

———. "Emigration, 1871–1921." In *A New History of Ireland.* Vol. 6 of *Ireland under the Union, II, 1870–1976,* edited by W. E. Vaughan, 606–37. Oxford: Oxford Univ. Press, 1996.

Fitzpatrick, Rory. *God's Frontiersmen: The Scots-Irish Epic.* London: Weidenfeld and Nicolson, 1989.

Fordahl, Matthew. "Scientists Use Irish Genes to Uncover Europe's Past," SF Gate.com, 23 Mar. 2000. Available at http://www.sfgate.com.

Foster, E. A., M. A. Jobling, P. G. Taylor, P. Donnelly, P. de Knijff, R. Mieremet, T. Zerjal, and C. Tyler-Smith. "Jefferson Fathered Slave's Last Child." *Nature* 396 (5 Nov. 1998): 27–28.

Foucault, Michel. "Nietzsche, Genealogy, History." In *Language, Counter-Memory, Practice: Selected Essays and Interviews,* translated by Donald F. Bouchard and Sherry Simon and edited by Donald F. Bouchard, 139–64. Ithaca, N.Y.: Cornell Univ. Press, 1997.

Franklin, Sarah, and Susan McKinnon. "Relative Values: Reconfiguring Kinship Studies." In *Relative Values: Reconfiguring Kinship Studies,* edited by Sarah Franklin and Susan McKinnon, 1–44. Durham, N.C.: Duke Univ. Press, 2001.

Friel, Brian. *The Home Place.* Loughcrew: Gallery Books, 2005.

———. *Making History.* London: Faber, 1989.

Gadd, Ronald P. *The Peerage of Ireland, with Lists of All Irish Peerages Past and Present.* Dublin: Irish Peers Association, 1985.

Gannon, Frank. *Midlife Irish: Discovering Family and Myself.* New York: Warner Books, 2003.

Gelder, Ken, and Jane Jacobs. *Uncanny Australia: Sacredness and Identity in a Postcolonial Nation.* Melbourne: Melbourne Univ. Press, 1998.

"Genes Link Celtic to Basques." BBC News Online. 3 Apr. 2001. Available at http://news.bbc.co.uk/1/hi/Wales/1246894.stm.

"Genetically Modified Archaeology." *Archaeology Ireland* 13, no. 4 (1999): 45.

Gillespie, Fergus. "Irish Genealogy and Pseudo-Genealogy." In *Aspects of Irish Genealogy, Proceedings of the First Irish Genealogical Congress*, 123–37. Naas: First Irish Genealogical Congress Committee, 1993.

Gilroy, Paul. "Diaspora and the Detours of Identity." In *Identity and Difference*, edited by Kath Woodward, 299–346. London: Sage in association with the Open Univ., 1997.

———. "Nationalism, History, and Ethnic Absolutism." *History Workshop Journal* 30 (1990): 114–20.

———. "Roots and Routes: Black Identity as an Outernational Project." In *Racial and Ethnic Identity: Psychological Development and Creative Expression*, edited by Herbert W. Harris, Howard C. Blue, and Ezra E. H. Griffith, 15–30. London: Routledge, 1995.

———. "Route Work: The Black Atlantic and the Politics of Exile." In *The Postcolonial Question: Common Skies, Divided Horizons*, edited by Iain Chambers and Lidia Curti, 17–29. London: Routledge, 1996.

Goldberg, David T. "The Semantics of Race." *Ethnic and Racial Studies* 15 (1992): 543–69.

Gorry, Paul. "Clanassic Park." *Irish Roots* 3 (1993): 23–24.

———. "Tradition and Television." *Irish Roots* 4 (1994): 9.

Government of Ireland. *The Irish Genealogical Project, Comptroller and Auditor General Report on Value for Money Examination*, no. 14, Dublin: Stationery Office, 1996.

Graham, Brian, and Peter Shirlow. "The Battle of the Somme in Ulster Memory and Identity." *Political Geography* 21 (2002): 881–904.

Graham, Brian J. "No Place of the Mind: Contested Protestant Representations of Ulster." *Ecumene* 1, no. 3 (1994): 257–81.

Gray, Breda. "From 'Ethnicity' to 'Diaspora': 1980s Emigration and 'Multicultural London.'" In *The Irish Diaspora*, edited by Andy Bielenberg, 65–88. London: Pearson, 2000.

———. "The Irish Diaspora: Globalised Belongings(s)." *Irish Journal of Sociology* 11, no. 2 (2002): 123–44.

———. "Remembering a 'Multicultural' Future through a History of Emigration: Towards a Feminist Politics of Solidarity across Difference." *Women's Studies International Forum* 27 (2004): 413–29.

———. "Unmasking Irishness: Irish Women, the Irish Nation, and the Irish Diaspora." In *Location and Dislocation in Contemporary Irish Society: Emigration and Irish Identities*, edited by Jim Mac Laughlin, 209–35. Cork: Cork Univ. Press, 1997.

———. "'Whitey Scripts' and Irish Women's Racialised Belonging(s) in England." *European Journal of Cultural Studies* 5 no. 3 (2002): 257–74.

———. *Women and the Irish Diaspora*. London: Routledge, 2004.

Grubgeld, Elizabeth. "Anglo-Irish Autobiography and the Genealogical Mandate." *Éire-Ireland: An Interdisciplinary Journal of Irish Studies* 32, no. 4; 33, no. 1; and 33, no. 2 (1997/1998): 96–115.

Gupta, Akhil, and James Ferguson. "Beyond 'Culture': Space, Identity, and the Politics of Difference." *Cultural Anthropology* 7, no. 1 (1992): 6–23.

Hackett, W. E. R. "A Rough Estimate of Two Main Racial Components in the Republic of Ireland based on an Analysis of ABO Blood Group Frequencies." *Journal of the Irish Medical Association* 42 (1958): 86–88.

Hackett, W. E. R., and M. E. Folan. "The ABO and Rh Blood Groups of the Aran Islanders." *Irish Journal of Medical Science* (June 1958): 247–61.

Hackett, W. E. R., G. W. P. Dawson, and C. J. Dawson. "The Pattern of the ABO Blood Group Frequencies in Ireland." *Heredity* 10 (1956): 69–84.

Haddon, A. C. "Studies in Irish Craniology: The Aran Islands, Co. Galway." *Proceedings of the Royal Irish Academy* 3rd Series, 2 (1893): 759–67.

Haddon, A. C., and C. R. Browne. "The Ethnography of the Aran Islands, County Galway." *Proceedings of the Royal Irish Academy*, 3rd series, 2 (1893): 768–830.

Haley, Alex. *Roots: The Saga of an American Family*. Garden City, N.Y.: Doubleday, 1976.

Hall, Michael. *Ulster: The Hidden History*. Belfast: Pretani Press, 1996.

Hall, Stuart. "Cultural Identity and Diaspora." In *Identity: Community, Culture, Difference*, edited by Jonathan Rutherford, 222–37. London: Lawrence and Wishart, 1990.

―――. "The Local and the Global: Globalization and Ethnicity." In *Culture, Globalization, and the World-System: Contemporary Conditions for the Representation of Identity*, edited by Anthony D. King, 19–39. Basingstoke: Macmillan, 1991.

―――. "New Ethnicities." In *Stuart Hall: Critical Dialogues in Cultural Studies*, edited by David Morley and Kuan-Hsing Chen, 441–49. London: Routledge, 1996.

―――. "Old and New Identities, Old and New Ethnicities." In *Culture, Globalization, and the World-System: Contemporary Conditions for the Representation of Identity*, edited by Anthony D. King, 41–68. Basingstoke: Macmillan, 1991.

Hamilton, Hugo. *The Speckled People*. London: Fourth Estate, 2003.

Hanson, David. Foreword to *Our People, Our Times: A History of Northern Ireland's Cultural Diversity* exhibition catalogue, 2. Belfast: Northern Ireland Museums Council, 2005.

Haraway, Donna. *Modest_Witness@Second Millennium_FemaleMan©_Meets_Onco-Mouse™: Feminism and Technoscience*. London: Routledge, 1997.

Hawthorn, James. "Above Suspicion or Controversy? The Development of the BBC's Irish History Programme for Schools in Northern Ireland, a Personal Recollection." In *Broadcasting in a Divided Community: Seventy Years of the BBC in Northern Ireland*, edited by Martin McLoone, 51–65. Belfast: Institute of Irish Studies, 1996.

Hayden, Corrine. "A Biodiversity Sampler for the Millennium." In *Reproducing Reproduction: Kinship, Power, and Technological Innovation*, edited by Sarah Franklin and Helene Ragoné, 173–203. Philadelphia: Univ. of Pennsylvania Press, 1998.

Helmreich, Stefan. "Kinship, Nation, and Paul Gilroy's Concept of Diaspora." *Diaspora* 2, no. 2 (1993): 243–49.

Hickman, Mary. "The Irish in Britain: Racism, Incorporation, and Identity." *Irish Studies Review* 10 (1995): 16–20.

―――. "'Locating' the Irish Diaspora." *Irish Journal of Sociology* 11, no. 2 (2002): 8–26.

―――. "Reconstructing Deconstructing 'Race': British Political Discourses about the Irish in Britain." *Ethnic and Racial Studies* 21, no. 2 (1998): 288–307.

Hickman, Mary, and Bronwen Walter. "Deconstructing Whiteness: Irish Women in Britain." *Feminist Review* 50 (1995): 5–19.

Hill, Emmeline. "More about Genes: The Irish Really Are a Race Apart." *Inside Ireland: Your Guide to All Things Irish* 90 (Autumn 2000): 6.

―――. "Who Are WE? It's in the Genes." *Inside Ireland: Your Guide to All Things Irish* 88 (Spring 2000): 22.

Hill, Emmeline, Mark A. Jobling, and Daniel G. Bradley. "Y Chromosome Variation and Irish Origins: A Pre-neolithic Gene Gradient Starts in the Near East
and Culminates in Western Ireland." *Nature* 204 (23 March 2000): 351–52.

Home. Capuchin Annual. Dublin: Capuchin Annual, 1940.

Hood, Susan. "Chief Herald." *Irish Times.* 10 Oct. 1995.

———. *Royal Roots, Republican Inheritance: The Survival of the Office of Arms.* Dublin:
Wolfhound Press, 2002.

Hooton, E. A. "Stature, Head Form, and Pigmentation of Adult Male Irish." *American Journal of Physical Anthropology* 26 (1940): 229–49.

Hooton, E. A., and C. W. Dupertuis. *The Physical Anthropology of Ireland.* Papers of
the Peabody Museum of Archaeology and Ethnology, Harvard Univ., 30, no.
1 and 2, Cambridge, Mass.: Peabody Museum of Archaeology and Ethnology, Harvard Univ., 1955.

Houston, Cecil J., and William J. Smyth. *Irish Emigration and Canadian Settlement: Patterns, Links, and Letters.* Toronto: Univ. of Toronto Press, 1990.

Hout, Michael, and Joshua Goldstein. "How 4.5 Million Irish Immigrants became 40 Million Irish Americans: Demographic and Subjective Aspects of
the Ethnic Composition of White Americans." *American Sociological Review* 59
(1994): 64–82.

Howe, Stephen. *Ireland and Empire: Colonial Legacies in Irish History and Culture.* Oxford: Oxford Univ. Press, 2000.

The Human Journey, National Geographic television documentary, 2004.

Huxley, Julian, A. C. Haddon, and A. M. Carr-Saunders. *We Europeans: A Survey of
"Racial" Problems.* London: Jonathan Cape, 1935.

Ignatiev, Noel. *How the Irish Became White.* London: Routledge, 1995.

Ingold, Tim. "Ancestry, Generation, Substance, Memory, Land." In *The Perception of the Environment: Essays on Livelihood, Dwelling, and Skill,* 132–51. London:
Routledge, 2000.

"An Irish King Rules Gene Pool." *Los Angeles Times.* 21 Jan. 2006.

Jacobson, Matthew Frye. *Special Sorrows: The Diasporic Imagination of Irish, Polish, and
Jewish Immigrants in the United States.* Berkeley: Univ. of California Press, 2002.

Jeffery, Keith. "The Great War in Modern Irish Memory." In *Men, Women, and
War,* edited by T. G. Fraser and Keith Jeffery, 136–57. Dublin: Lilliput Press,
1993.

———. "Irish Culture and the Great War." *Bullán* 1, no. 2 (1994): 87–96.

Jobling, Mark A. "In the Name of the Father: Surnames and Genetics." *Trends in
Genetics* 17, no. 6 (2001): 353–57.

Jobling, Mark A., and Chris Tyler-Smith. "Fathers and Sons: The Y Chromosome and Human Evolution." *Trends in Genetics* 11 (1995): 449–56.

———. "The Human Y Chromosome: An Evolutionary Marker Comes of Age." *Nature* 4 (2003): 598–612.

Johnson, Nuala C. "The Spectacle of Memory: Ireland's Remembrance of the Great War, 1919." *Journal of Historical Geography* 25, no. 1 (1999): 36–56.

Jones, Greta. "Contested Territories: Alfred Cort Haddon, Progressive Evolutionism, and Ireland." *History of European Ideas* 24, no. 3 (1998): 195–211.

Kaplan, Caren. "Deterritorializations: The Rewriting of Home and Exile in Western Feminist Discourse." *Cultural Critique* 6 (1987): 187–98.

———. *Questions of Travel: Postmodern Discourses of Displacement.* Durham, N.C.: Duke Univ. Press, 1996.

Karnbach, William Francis Marmion, Lord of Duhallow. *Gaelic Titles and Forms of Address: A Guide in the English Language.* Kansas City: Irish Genealogical Foundation, 1997.

Kearney, Richard. *Postnationalist Ireland: Politics, Culture, Philosophy.* London: Routledge, 1997.

———. "Thinking Otherwise." In *Across the Frontiers: Cultural, Political, Economic Ireland in the 1990s,* edited by Richard Kearney, 7–28. Dublin: Wolfhound Press, 1988.

Kennedy, Billy. *Faith and Freedom: The Scots-Irish in America.* Belfast: Ambassador Productions, 1999.

———. *Heroes of the Scots-Irish in America.* Belfast: Ambassador Productions, 2000.

———. *The Making of America: How the Scots-Irish Shaped a Nation.* Belfast: Ambassador Productions, 2001.

———. *Our Most Priceless Heritage: The Lasting Legacy of the Scots-Irish in America.* Belfast: Ambassador Productions, 2005.

Kennedy, Siobhan. "Irish King Left a Wide Genetic Trail: Scientists Say 3 Million Men Are Descended from Niall of the Nine Hostages." 2006. Available at http://msnbc.msn.com/id/10892117/.

Kenny, Kevin. "Diaspora and Comparison: The Global Irish as a Case Study." *Journal of American History* 90, no. 1 (2003): 134–62. Available at http://www.historycooperative.org/journals/jah/90.1/kenny.html.

———. "Race, Violence, and Anti-Irish Sentiment in the Nineteenth Century." In *Making the Irish American: History and Heritage of the Irish in the United States,* edited by J. J. Lee and Marion R. Casey, 364–78. New York: New York Univ. Press, 2006.

Kiberd, Declan. "Strangers in Their Own Country: Multi-Culturalism in Ireland." In *Multi-Culturalism: The View from the Two Irelands*, by Edna Longley and Declan Kiberd, 45–74. Cork: Cork Univ. Press, 2001.

King, Desmond. *Making Americans: Immigration, Race, and the Origins of the Diverse Democracy.* Cambridge, Mass.: Harvard Univ. Press, 2000.

Kirby, Peadar, Luke Gibbons, and Michael Cronin, eds. *Reinventing Ireland: Culture, Society, and the Global Economy.* London and Sterling, Va.: Pluto Press, 2002.

Koch, Christopher. *The Many-Coloured Land: A Return to Ireland.* London: Picador, 2002.

Lacey, Brian. "The Northern Ui Neill, Ancestors of the O'Neills." Paper presented at the O'Neill Summer School, 16 June 2005.

Lee, J. J., and Marion R. Casey, eds. *Making the Irish American: History and Heritage of the Irish in the United States.* New York: New York Univ. Press, 2006.

Leerson, Joep. "Celticism." In *Celticism*, edited by Terence Brown, 1–20. Amsterdam: Rodopi, 1996.

Lentin, Ronit. "Responding to the Racialisation of Irishness: Disavowed Multiculturalism and Its Discontents." *Sociological Research Online* 5, no. 4 (2001). Available at http://www.socresonline.org.uk/5/4/lentin.html.

Lentin, Ronit, ed. *Emerging Irish Identities.* Dublin: National Consultative Committee on Racism and Interculturalism, 2000.

———. *The Expanding Nation: Towards a Multi-Ethnic Ireland.* Dublin: Trinity College, 1999.

Lentin, Ronit, and Robbie McVeigh, eds. *Racism and Anti-Racism in Ireland.* Belfast: Beyond the Pale, 2002.

Leonard, Jane. "The Twinge of Memory: Armistice Day and Remembrance Sunday in Dublin since 1919." In *Unionism and Modern Ireland: New Perspectives on Politics and Culture*, edited by Richard English and Graham Walker, 99–114. Dublin: Gill and Macmillan, 1996.

Lloyd, David. "Epilogue, 'Living in America': Politics and Emigrations." In *Ireland after History*, by David Lloyd, 101–8. Cork: Cork Univ. Press, 1999.

Local Identities: An Exploration of Cultural Identity. Belfast: Northern Ireland Museums Council, Northern Ireland Regional Curators Group, 2000.

Longley, Edna. "Multi-Culturalism and Northern Ireland: Making Differences Fruitful." In *Multi-Culturalism: The View from the Two Irelands*, by Edna Longley and Declan Kiberd, 1–44. Cork: Cork Univ. Press, 2001.

———. "Pulling Down the Cultural (De)fences." *Fortnight* 279 (1989): 26–30.

Longley, Michael. "Memory and Acknowledgement." *Irish Review* 17/18 (1995): 153–59.

Loughrey, Patrick. *The People of Ireland.* Belfast: Appletree Press, 1988.

Lowenthal, David. *The Heritage Crusade and the Spoils of History.* Cambridge: Cambridge Univ. Press, 1998.

Luibhéid, Eithne. "Childbearing against the State? Asylum Seeker Women in the Irish Republic." *Women's Studies International Forum* 27 (2004): 335–49.

———. "Irish Immigrants in the United States' Racial System." In *Location and Dislocation in Contemporary Irish Society: Emigration and Irish Identities,* edited by Jim Mac Laughlin, 253–73. Cork: Cork Univ. Press, 1997.

Lynch, Thomas. *Booking Passage: We Irish and Americans.* London: Jonathan Cape, 2005.

Lysaght, Charles. Foreword to *Vanishing Kingdoms: The Irish Chiefs and Their Families.* Walter J. P. Curley, 16. Dublin: Lilliput Press, 2004.

———. "The Irish Peers and the House of Lords: The Final Chapter." In *Burke's Peerage and Baronetage,* 106th ed., edited by Charles Mosley, xli–xlii. London: Fitzroy Dearborn, 1996.

Mac an Ghaill, Mairtin. "Beyond a Black-White Dualism: Racialisation and Racism in the Republic of Ireland and the Irish Diaspora Experience." *Irish Journal of Sociology* 11, no. 2 (2002): 99–112.

Mac an Ghaill, Mairtin, and Chris Haywood. "Young (Male) Irelanders: Postcolonial Ethnicities—Expanding the Nation and Irishness." *European Journal of Cultural Studies* 6, no. 3 (2003): 386–403.

Mac Laughlin, Jim. "The Devaluation of 'Nation' as 'Home' and the De-politicisation of Recent Irish Emigration." In *Location and Dislocation in Contemporary Irish Society: Emigration and Irish Identities,* edited by Jim Mac Laughlin, 179–208. Cork: Cork Univ. Press, 1997.

———. "Emigration and the Construction of Nationalist Hegemony in Ireland: The Historical Background to 'New Wave' Irish Emigration." In *Location and Dislocation in Contemporary Irish Society: Emigration and Irish Identities,* edited by Jim Mac Laughlin, 5–35. Cork: Cork Univ. Press, 1997.

———. "'Pestilence on Their Backs, Famine in Their Stomachs': The Racial Construction of Irishness and the Irish in Victorian Britain." In *Ireland and Cultural Theory: The Mechanics of Authenticity,* edited by Colin Graham and Richard Kirkland, 50–76. London: Macmillan, 1999.

Mac Póilin, Aodán. "'Spiritual Beyond the Ways of Men': Images of the Gael." *Irish Review* 10 (1994): 1–21.

MacCarthy, Terence, MacCarthy Mór, Prince of Desmond. *The Niadh Nask, History, and International Roll, 1996.* Clonmel: Niadh Nask, 1996.

———. *Ulster's Office 1552–1800: A History of the Irish Office of Arms from the Tudor Plantations to the Act of Union.* Little Rock, Ark.: Gryfons, 1996.

MacCurtain, Margaret, and Donncha O Corráin, eds. *Women in Irish Society: The Historical Dimension.* Dublin: Arlen House, 1978.

MacLysaght, Edward. *Changing Times: Ireland since 1898.* Gerrards Cross: Colin Smythe, 1978.

———. "The Irish Chieftainries." In *Burke's Introduction to Irish Ancestry,* 45–46. London: Burke's Peerage, 1976.

———. *The Surnames of Ireland.* 1957; Dublin: Irish Academic Press, 1997.

Magee, Jack. Untitled contribution to *Cultural Traditions in Northern Ireland: Varieties of Irishness,* edited by Maurna Crozier, 37. Belfast: Institute of Irish Studies, 1989.

Malkki, Liisa. "National Geographic: The Rooting of Peoples and the Territorialisation of National Identity among Scholars and Refugees." *Cultural Anthropology* 7, no. 1 (1992): 24–44.

Mallory, J. P. "The Origins of the Irish." *Journal of Irish Archaeology* 2 (1984): 65–69.

———. "Two Perspectives on the Problem of Irish Origins." *Emania* 9 (1991): 53–58.

Mallory, J. P., and Barra Ó Donnagháin. "The Origins of the Population of Ireland: A Survey of Putative Immigrations in Irish Prehistory and History." *Emania* 17 (1998): 47–81.

Marks, Jonathan. "'We're Going to Tell These People Who They Really Are': Science and Relatedness." In *Relative Values: Reconfiguring Kinship Studies,* edited by Sarah Franklin and Susan McKinnon, 355–83. Durham, N.C.: Duke Univ. Press, 2001.

Marmion, William F. "Nobiliary Titles in the Republic." *Irish Roots* 3 (1995): 6–7.

Marston, Sallie. "Who Are 'the People'? Gender, Citizenship, and the Making of the American Nation." *Environment and Planning D: Society and Space* 20 (1990): 449–58.

Mathieu, Joan. *Zulu: An Irish-American's Quest to Discover Her Roots.* Edinburgh: Mainstream Publishing, 1998.

Matthews, Thomas. *The O'Neills of Ulster: Their History and Genealogy.* Dublin: Sealy, Bryers, and Walker, 1907.

McCarthy, Tony. "A Link with Our Ancient Past." *Irish Roots* 3 (1993): 22–23.

McEvoy, Brian Patrick. "Genetic Investigation of Irish Ancestry and Surname History." Ph.D. dissertation, Trinity College, Dublin, 2005.

McEvoy, Brian, Martin Richards, Peter Forster, and Daniel G. Bradley. "The *Longue Durée* of Genetic Ancestry: Multiple Genetic Marker Systems and Celtic Origins on the Atlantic Facade of Europe." *American Journal of Human Genetics* 75 (2004): 693–702.

McKinnon, Susan. *Neo-liberal Genetics: The Myths and Moral Tales of Evolutionary Psychology.* Chicago: Prickly Paradigm Press, 2005.

McKittrick, David. "The True Father of Ireland; Niall of the Nine Hostages: 1,500 years after His Death, He Has up to 3 Million Descendants." *Belfast Telegraph.* 21 Jan. 2006, 22–23.

McNarey, Eoghan. "'I've Got a Little List . . . ': Gaelic Chiefship and the Irish Republic." *Irish Roots* 4 (1993): 14–15.

McVeigh, Robbie. *The Racialisation of Irishness: Racism and Anti-Racism in Irish Society.* Belfast: Centre for Research and Documentation, 1996.

"Medieval Irish Warlord Boasts 3 Million Descendants." *New Scientist.* 18 Jan. 2006.

Michaels, Walter Benn. "The No-Drop Rule." *Critical Inquiry* 20 (1994): 758–69.

———. "Race into Culture: A Critical Genealogy of Cultural Identity." *Critical Inquiry* 18 (1992): 655–85.

Miller, Kerby A. *Emigrants and Exiles: Ireland and the Irish Exodus to North America.* New York: Oxford Univ. Press, 1985.

———. "Emigration, Capitalism, and Ideology in Post-Famine Ireland." In *Migrations: The Irish at Home and Abroad,* edited by Richard Kearney, 91–108. Dublin: Wolfhound Press, 1990.

———. "'Scotch-Irish,' 'Black Irish,' and 'Real Irish': Emigrants and Identities in the Old South." In *The Irish Diaspora,* edited by Andy Bielenberg, 139–57. Harlow, Essex: Longman, 2000.

———. "'Scotch-Irish' Myths and 'Irish' Identities in Eighteenth- and Nineteenth-Century America." In *New Perspectives on the Irish Diaspora,* edited by Charles Fanning, 75–92. Carbondale: Southern Illinois Univ. Press, 2000.

———. "Ulster Presbyterians and the 'Two Traditions' in Ireland and America." In *Making the Irish American: History and Heritage of the Irish in the United States,* edited by J. J. Lee and Marion R. Casey, 255–70. New York: New York Univ. Press, 2006.

Montgomery-Massingberd, Hugh, ed. *Burke's Introduction to Irish Ancestry.* London: Burke's Peerage, Ltd., 1976.

———. *Burke's Irish Family Records.* London: Burke's Peerage, Ltd., 1976.

Moore, Laoise T., Brian McEvoy, Eleanor Cape, Katharine Simms, and Daniel G. Bradley. "A Y-Chromosome Signature of Hegemony in Gaelic Ireland." *American Journal of Human Genetics* 78 (2006): 334–38.

Morash, Chris. "Celticism: Between Race and Culture." *Irish Review* 20 (1997): 29–36, 44–45.

Morgan, Hiram. "Patriot or Traitor: The Career of Hugh O'Neill, Great Earl of Tyrone." Paper presented at the O'Neill Summer School, 16 June 2005.

Morrison, Angeline D. "Irish and White-ish: Mixed 'Race' Identity and the Scopic Regime of Whiteness." *Women's Studies International Forum* 27 (2004): 385–96.

Moss, John. *Invisible among the Ruins: Field Notes of a Canadian in Ireland.* Dublin: Univ. College Dublin Press, 2000.

Motherland: A Genetic Journey. Takeaway Media Production for BBC 2, directed by Archie Baron and produced by Tabitha Jackson, 2003.

"Murder Victim's Family Plead for an End to the Killings." *Irish News.* 3 Jan. 1998, 1.

Murphy, Andrew. "Ireland and Ante/Anti-colonial Theory." *Irish Studies Review* 7, no. 2 (1999): 153–62.

Murphy, James. "Finding Home: Aughkiluberd, 1969." *New Hibernia Review/Iris Éireannach Nua*, 8, no. 3 (2004): 12–17.

Murphy, Sean. *Erin's Fake Chiefs.* Bray: Centre for Irish Genealogical and Historical Research, 2001.

Murphy, Sean J. *Twilight of the Chiefs: The MacCarthy Mór Hoax.* Dublin: Maunsel, 2004.

Nash, Catherine. "Equity, Diversity, and Interdependence: Cultural Policy in Northern Ireland." *Antipode* 37, no. 2 (2005): 272–300.

———. "Genetic Kinship." *Cultural Studies* 18, no. 1 (2004): 1–34.

———. "Local Histories in Northern Ireland." *History Workshop Journal* 60 (2005): 45–68.

"Nationalist Myth Challenged: John Tyndall Comments on Some New Evidence." *Spearhead.* Available at http://www.spearhead-uk.com/0001-jt3.html.

Negra, Diane. "The Irish in Us: Irishness, Performativity, and Popular Culture." In *The Irish in Us: Irishness, Performativity, and Popular Culture*, edited by Diane Negra, 1–19. Durham, N.C.: Duke Univ. Press, 2006.

Neill, Kathleen. *O'Neill Commemorative Journal of the First International Gathering of the Clan, 20–27 June 1982.* Belfast: Irish Genealogical Association, 1982.

Nic Craith, Máiréad. *Culture and Identity Politics in Northern Ireland.* Basingstoke: Palgrave Macmillan, 2003.

———. *Plural Identities, Singular Narratives: The Case of Northern Ireland.* New York and Oxford: Berghahn Books, 2002.

———. "Politicised Linguistic Consciousness: The Case of Ulster Scots." *Nations and Nationalism* 7, no. 1 (2001): 21–38.

Northern Ireland Office. *The Agreement: Agreement Reached in the Multi-party Negotiations.* Belfast: Northern Ireland Office, 1998.

Novas, Carlos, and Nicholas Rose. "Genetic Risk and the Birth of the Somatic Individual." *Economy and Society* 29 (2000): 485–513.

Ó Donnabháin, Barra. "aDNA and Archaeology." *Archaeology Ireland* 15, no. 2 (2001): 34–35.

Ó Gráda, Cormac. *Black '47 and Beyond: The Great Irish Famine in History, Economy, and Memory.* Princeton, N.J.: Princeton Univ. Press, 1999.

O'Day, Alan. "Revising the Diaspora." In *The Making of Modern Irish History*, edited by D. George Boyce and Alan O'Day, 188–215. London: Routledge, 1996.

O'Faolain, Sean. *The Great O'Neill: A Biography of Hugh O'Neill, Earl of Tyrone, 1550–1616.* London: Longmans, Green, 1942.

O'Halloran, Clare. *Golden Ages and Barbarous Nations: Antiquarian Debate and Cultural Politics in Ireland, c. 1750–1800.* Cork: Cork Univ. Press, 2004.

O'Hart, John. *The Irish and Anglo-Irish Landed Gentry When Cromwell Came to Ireland; or, A Supplement to Irish Pedigrees.* Dublin: M. H. Gill and Son, 1884.

———. *The Irish and Anglo-Irish Landed Gentry When Cromwell Came to Ireland; or, A Supplement to Irish Pedigrees.* 5th ed. Dublin: James Duffy, 1892.

———. *Irish Pedigrees; or, The Origin and Stem of the Irish Nation.* 1st ed. Dublin: McGlashan and Gill, 1876.

———. *Irish Pedigrees; or, The Origin and Stem of the Irish Nation.* 5th ed., London, Glasgow, and New York: James Duffy, 1892.

O'Leary, Brendan. "The Nature of the British-Irish Agreement." *New Left Review* 233 (1999): 66–96.

O'Leary, Philip. "Yank Outsiders: Irish Americans in Gaelic Fiction and Drama of the Irish Free State, 1922–1939." In *New Perspectives on the Irish Diaspora*, edited by Charles Fanning, 253–65. Carbondale: Southern Illinois Univ. Press, 2000.

O'Neill, Raymond, Lord O'Neill. "The O'Neill Family." In Lord O'Neill, *Shane's Castle and Nature Reserve: Official Guide.* Shane's Castle, Antrim: Lord O'Neill, 1987.

O'Neill, Terence Marne, Baron O'Neill of the Maine. *The Autobiography of Terence O'Neill.* London: Rupert Hart-Davies, 1972.

"O'Neills Proclaim New Chieftain." *Belfast Telegraph.* 23 June 1982.

O'Rahilly, T. F. *Early Irish History and Mythology.* Dublin: Dublin Institute for Advanced Studies, 1946.

O'Sullivan, Patrick. "The Displacement of Identity: On Being Irish." *Political Geography* 13, no. 3 (1994): 270–78.

O'Sullivan, Patrick, ed. *The Creative Migrant.* Leicester: Leicester Univ. Press, 1994.
————. *The Irish in the New Communities.* Leicester: Leicester Univ. Press, 1992.
————. *Irish Women and Irish Migration.* Leicester: Leicester Univ. Press, 1995.
————. *The Meaning of the Famine.* Leicester: Leicester Univ. Press, 1997.
Owen, James. "Millions of Men May Be Descended from Irish King, Study Says." *National Georgraphic,* 20 Jan. 2006. Available at http://news.nationalgeographic.com/news/2006/01/0120_060120_irish_men.html.
Parkhill, T., and M. Ferguson. *Conflict: The Irish at War.* Belfast: Ulster Museum, National Museums and Galleries of Northern Ireland, 2004.
Peskett, Hugh. "Scottish and Irish Chiefs." In *Burke's Peerage, Baronetage and Knightage, Clan Chiefs and Scottish Feudal Barons,* 107th ed., edited by Charles Mosley, li–lii. Stokesley: Burke's Peerage and Gentry, 2003.
Povinelli, Elizabeth A. "Notes on Gridlock: Genealogy, Intimacy, Sexuality." *Public Culture* 14, no. 1 (2002): 215–38.
Pyne, Peter. "The Teaching of History to Adults in a Culturally Divided Society: A Northern Ireland Case Study (1)." *Etudes Irelandaise* 12 (1989): 171–91.
Rains, Stephanie. "Irish Roots: Genealogy and the Performance of Irishness." In *The Irish in Us: Irishness, Performativity, and Popular Culture,* edited by Diane Negra, 130–60. Durham, N.C.: Duke Univ. Press, 2006.
Relethford, J. H. "Effects of English Admixture and Geographic Distance on Anthropometric Variation in Nineteenth-Century Ireland." *American Journal of Physical Anthropology* 76 (1988): 111–24.
————. "Genetic Drift and Anthropometric Variation in Ireland." *Human Biology* 63 (1991): 155–65.
————. "Genetic Structure and Population History of Ireland: A Comparison of Blood Group and Anthropometric Analyses." *Annals of Human Biology* 10 (1983): 321–34.
Relethford, J. H., F. C. Lees, and M. H. Crawford. "Population Structure and Anthropometric Variation in Rural Western Ireland: Isolation by Distance and Analysis of the Residuals." *American Journal of Physical Anthropology* 55 (1981): 233–45.
————. "Population Structure and Anthropometric Variation in Rural Western Ireland: Migration and Biological Differentiation." *Annals of Human Biology* 7 (1980): 411–28.
Relethford, J. H., and M. H. Crawford. "Anthropometric Variation and the Population History of Ireland." *American Journal of Physical Anthropology* 96 (1995): 25–38.

Relethford, John H. "Anthropometric Data and Population History." In *Human Biologists in the Archives: Demography, Health, Nutrition, and Genetics in Historical Populations,* edited by D. Ann Herring and Alan C. Swedlund, 32–52. Cambridge: Cambridge Univ. Press, 2003.

———. *Reflections of Our Past: How Human History Is Revealed in Our Genes.* Boulder: Westview Press, 2003.

Robinson, Mary. "Address by An tUachtarán, Mary Robinson at the Dinner of the First Irish Genealogical Congress on Tuesday 24 September 1991." In *Aspects of Irish Genealogy, Proceedings of the First Irish Genealogical Congress,* 7–8. Naas: First Irish Genealogical Congress Committee, 1993.

———. "Cherishing the Irish Diaspora." Joint sitting of Dáil Éireann and Seanad Éireann on the occasion of the address by Mrs. Mary T. W. Robinson, Uachtárán na hÉireann, 2 February 1995. Dublin: Stationery Office, 1995.

Roediger, David. "Reflections on 'Whiteness and Ethnicity in the History of "White Ethnics" in the United States.'" In *Race Critical Theories: Text and Context,* edited by Philomena Essed and David T. Goldberg, 493–95. Maldon, Mass.: Blackwell, 2002.

———. *Towards the Abolition of Whiteness: Essays on Race, Politics, and Working Class History.* London: Verso, 1994.

———. *The Wages of Whiteness: Race and the Making of the American Working Class.* London: Verso, 1991.

Rose, Nicholas. "The Politics of Life Itself." *Theory, Culture, and Society* 18 (2001): 1–30.

Ryan, Ray. "Reunion of Clans 'Uplifts Nation.'" *Examiner,* 12 Aug. 1996, 2.

Scott, James, C., John Tehranian, and Jeremy Mathias. "The Production of Legal Identities Proper to States: The Case of the Permanent Family Surname." *Comparative Studies in Society and History* 44, no. 1 (2002): 4–44.

Sharrock, D. "Irish Factions Unite to Remember the Dead: Enmity Put Aside as Republic Honours Those Who Died in British Uniform." *Guardian.* 11 Nov. 1995.

Shirlow, Peter, Brian Graham, Kieran McEvoy, Félim Ó hAhmail, and Dawn Purvis. *Politically Motivated Former Prisoner Groups: Community Activism and Conflict Transformation, a Research Report Submitted to the Northern Ireland Community Relations Council.* Belfast, 2006.

Shirlow, Peter, and Mark McGovern. "Introduction: Who Are 'the People'? Unionism, Protestantism, and Loyalism in Northern Ireland." In *Who Are 'the*

People'? Unionism, Protestantism, and Loyalism in Northern Ireland, edited by Peter Shirlow and Mark McGovern, 1–15. London: Pluto Press, 1997.

Shirlow, Peter, and Brendan Murtagh. *Belfast: Segregation, Violence, and the City*. London: Pluto, 2006.

Simpson, Bob. "Imagined Genetic Communities: Ethnicity and Essentialism in the Twenty-first Century." *Anthropology Today* 16 (2000): 3–6.

Sloan, Barry. "'The Overall Thing': Brian Friel's *Making History*." *Irish Studies Review* 8 (1994): 12–16.

Smith, Anthony D. *The Ethnic Origin of Nations*. Oxford: Basil Blackwell, 1986.

———. *Myths and Memories of the Nation*. Oxford: Oxford Univ. Press, 1999.

Smyth, Ailbhe. "'A Great Day for the Women of Ireland': The Meaning of Mary Robinson's Presidency for Irish Women." *Canadian Journal of Irish Studies* 18, no. 1 (1992): 61–75.

Smyth, William J. "Excavating, Mapping, and Interrogating Ancestral Terrains: Towards a Cultural Geography of First and Second Names in Ireland." In *Surveying Ireland's Past: Multidiscipilinary Essays in Honour of Anngret Simms*, edited by Howard B. Clarke, Jacinta Prunty, and Mark Hennessy, 243–80. Dublin: Geography Publications, 2004.

Solnit, Rebecca. *A Book of Migrations: Some Passages in Ireland*. London: Verso, 1997.

Stepan, Nancy. *The Idea of Race in Science: Great Britain 1800–1960*. London: Macmillan, 1982.

Strathern, Marilyn. *After Nature: English Kinship in the Late Twentieth Century*. Cambridge: Cambridge Univ. Press, 1998.

———. "Cutting the Network." *Journal of the Royal Anthropological Institute* (n.s.) 2 (1996): 517–35.

Sunderland, E., D. Tills, C. Bouloux, and J. Doyle. "Genetic Studies in Ireland." In *Genetic Variation in Britain*, edited by D. F. Roberts and E. Sunderland, 141–59. London: Taylor and Francis, 1973.

Sykes, Bryan. *The Seven Daughters of Eve*. London: Bantam Press, 2001.

Tóibín, Colm. *The Irish Famine*. London: Profile Books, 1999.

"Trace Your Border Reiver Roots by DNA!" *Ulster Scot*. July 2004, 6.

Tunney, John. "The IGP: A Tourist Agenda for Genealogy." *Irish Family History* 6 (1990): 61–65.

Turner, Brian, and Aodán Mac Póilin. "What's in a Name." BBC Radio Ulster, 2001 and 2002.

Turner, Brian S. "Distributional Aspects of Family Name Study Illustrated in the Glens of Antrim." Ph.D. dissertation, Queen's Univ., Belfast, 1974.

———. "Distributional Study of Family Names." *Ulster Local Studies* 8, no. 3 (1983): 5–9.

———. "Family Names: Notes and Queries on Derry's Top Ten." *Templemore: Journal of the North West Archaeological and Historical Society* 3 (1990): 46–48.

———. "An Observation on Settler Names in Fermanagh." *Clougher Record* 8, no. 3 (1974): 285–89.

———. Review of Robert Bell, *The Book of Ulster Surnames* (Blackstaff Press, 1988). *Ulster Folklife* 35 (1989): 137–39.

———. "Scottish Borderers on an Irish Frontier: The Transformation of Lancie Armstrang." In *The Debateable Land: Ireland's Border Counties,* edited by Brian S. Turner, 45–50. Belfast: Ulster Local History Trust in Association with the Heritage Council, 2002.

———. *Surname Landscape in the Country of Fermanagh.* Downpatrick: Turner Circle, 2003.

Tutton, Richard. "'They Want to Know Where They Came From': Population Genetics, Identity, and Family Genealogy." *New Genetics and Society* 23 (2004): 105–20.

Valiulis, Maryann Gialanella. "Power, Gender, and Identity in the Irish Free State." *Journal of Women's History* 6 (1995): 117–36.

"Victim's Mother Pleads for Peace." *Irish News.* 3 June 1999, 5.

Wade, Nicolas. "If New York's Irish Claim Nobility, Science May Back Up the Blarney." *New York Times.* 18 Jan. 2006.

Walter, Bronwen. "Irishness, Gender, and Place." *Environment and Planning D: Society and Space* 13 (1995):35–50.

———. *Outsiders Inside: Whiteness, Place, and Irish Women.* London: Routledge, 2001.

War and Conflict in Twentieth-Century Ireland: A Travelling Exhibition from the Ulster Museum. Belfast: Ulster Museum, 2000.

Warner, Richard. "De Bello Hibernico: A Less Than Edifying Debate." *Archaeology Ireland* 10 (1996): 38–40.

———. "Who Are the O'Neills." Paper presented at the O'Neill Summer School, 16 June 2005.

Warner, Richard B. "Cultural Intrusions in the Early Iron Age: Some Notes." *Emania* 9 (1991): 44–52.

Waters, Mary C. *Ethnic Options: Choosing Identities in America.* Berkeley: Univ. of California Press, 1990.

Watson, Julia. "Ordering the Family: Genealogy as Autobiographical Pedigree." In *Getting a Life: Everyday Uses of Autobiography,* edited by Sidonie Smith and Julia Watson, 297–323. Minneapolis: Univ. of Minnesota Press, 1996.

Who Do You Think You Are? BBC television series, series 1, 2005; series 2, 2006.

The Wings of the Seraphim, Today and Yesterday in Northern Ireland Series, BBC Radio Ulster, Northern Ireland Community Archive, Ulster Folk and Transport Museum, 1986.

Winters, John. "Irish Genealogical Project: Genealogy in Ulster." *Irish Family History* 9 (1993): 25–26.

Wolff, Janet. "On the Road Again: Metaphors of Travel in Cultural Criticism." *Cultural Studies* 7, no. 3 (1993): 224–39.

Woodman, Peter C. "Who Possesses Tara? Politics in Archaeology in Ireland." In *Theory in Archaeology: A World Perspective*, edited by Peter J. Ucko, 278–97. London: Routledge, 1995.

Wright, Frank. "Reconciling the Histories of Protestant and Catholic in Northern Ireland." In *Reconciling Memories*, edited by Alan D. Falconcer and Joseph Liechty, 128–48. Dublin: Columba Press, 1998.

Zerjal T., T. Xue, G. Bertolle, R. S. Well, W. Bao, S. Zhu, R. Qamar, Q. Ayub, A. Mohyuddin, S. Fu, P. Li, N. Yuldasheva, R. Ruzibakiev, J. Xu, Q. Shu, R. Du, H. Yang, M. E. Hurles, E. Robinson, T. Gerelsaikhan, B. Dashnyam, S. Q. Mehdi, and C. Tyler-Smith. "The Genetic Legacy of the Mongols." *American Journal of Human Genetics* 72 (2003): 717–21.

Index

Note: Italic page numbers denote illustrations.